DEBATING SHARIA:
ISLAM, GENDER POLITICS, AND FAMILY LAW ARBITRATION

Edited by Anna C. Korteweg and Jennifer A. Selby

In response to the Islamic Institute of Civil Justice's announcement in 2003 that it would begin offering Sharia-based services in Ontario, a provincial government review gave qualified support for religious arbitration. The controversial decision attracted widespread attention and ultimately led to a ban on religiously based family law arbitration in the province. This collection of essays sheds light on how the debates surrounding these events in Ontario exemplified public concern over the role of religion in the political and judicial sphere and the place of Islam in Western nation states.

Focusing on the legal ramifications of Sharia law in the context of rapidly changing Western liberal democracies, *Debating Sharia* approaches the issues from a variety of methodological perspectives. Among the topics explored are the divorce and mediation practices of Ontario Muslims; the legal implications of religiously based arbitration; the jurisprudential and historical accounts of Sharia; and the portrayals of race, gender, agency, multiculturalism, and secularism in the public debate.

ANNA C. KORTEWEG is an associate professor in the Department of Sociology with a cross-appointment to the Centre for European, Russian, and Eurasian Studies at the Munk School for Global Affairs at the University of Toronto.

JENNIFER A. SELBY is an assistant professor in the Department of Religious Studies at Memorial University of Newfoundland.

EDITED BY ANNA C. KORTEWEG
AND JENNIFER A. SELBY

Debating Sharia

Islam, Gender Politics, and Family Law Arbitration

UNIVERSITY OF TORONTO PRESS
Toronto Buffalo London

©University of Toronto Press Incorporated 2012
Toronto Buffalo London
www.utppublishing.com
Printed in Canada

ISBN 978-1-4426-4262-1 (cloth)
ISBN 978-1-4426-1145-0 (paper)

Printed on acid-free, 100% post-consumer recycled paper with vegetable-based inks.

Library and Archives Canada Cataloguing in Publication

Debating Sharia : Islam, gender politics, and family law arbitration / edited by Anna Korteweg and Jennifer Selby.

Includes bibliographical references.
ISBN 978-1-4426-4262-1 (bound).   ISBN 978-1-4426-1145-0 (pbk.)

1. Islamic law – Canada.   I. Korteweg, Anna   II. Selby, Jennifer A.

KBP67.D42 2012   340.5'90971   C2012-900024-8

This book has been published with the help of a grant from the Canadian Federation for the Humanities and Social Sciences, through the Aid to Scholarly Publications Program, using funds provided by the Social Sciences and Humanities Research Council of Canada

University of Toronto Press acknowledges the financial assistance to its publishing program of the Canada Council for the Arts and the Ontario Arts Council.

 Canada Council Conseil des Arts
for the Arts du Canada

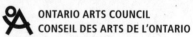 ONTARIO ARTS COUNCIL
CONSEIL DES ARTS DE L'ONTARIO

University of Toronto Press acknowledges the financial support of the Government of Canada through the Canada Book Fund for its publishing activities.

For our children, Michal and Ruben (AK), and Alanna (JS).

Contents

Part Six: Managing Religion in the Canadian State

Concluding Thoughts

Acknowledgments

This volume is the product of a number of conversations and collaborations. In the spring 2009, Anna presented on a panel organized by Kathy Bullock for the Association of Muslim Social Scientists of North America's Canadian Regional Conference. Jennifer organized a similar panel for the American Academy of Religion meetings in the fall, on which Anna presented as well. Our participation in these panels led us to recognize how an edited volume could grapple with the complexity of this debate from a variety of disciplinary perspectives. A spirited dinner conversation after the second panel, comparing our different disciplinary approaches to these issues, led us to collaborate on this book. Starting with the panellists on the two panels, we invited a number of other scholars working in this area and were fortunate that many we approached were able to contribute.

While individual contributors have included acknowledgments in their chapters, there are a number of individuals whose support buttressed the book as a whole. We learned a great deal working on the book and are tremendously grateful to the contributors for their insights, integrity, and enthusiasm (and their timely responses to seemingly never-ending queries!). We thank University of Toronto Press editor Virgil Duff who initially supported the volume, and Doug Hildebrand who ably took over following Virgil's retirement. Thank you both for providing prompt and sound advice with good humour. The thoughtful suggestions of three anonymous reviewers improved the volume. We also thank Linn Clark for her editorial support, UTP's Harold Otto for attentive copy-editing, and Anne Laughlin and Shoshana Wasser at UTP for moving the volume through production.

We acknowledge our respective colleagues and departments for their encouragement, as well as able research assistance from Salina Abji and Meagan White. The Aid to Scholarly Publications Program with the Canadian Federation for the Humanities and Social Sciences is also acknowledged here for its support.

Lastly, we thank our partners, Jim Davis and Oscar Moro Abadía, for their patience, encouragement, and cooking.

DEBATING SHARIA:
ISLAM, GENDER POLITICS, AND FAMILY LAW ARBITRATION

INTRODUCTION

Situating the Sharia Debate

Foreword: Sharia and the Future of Western Secularism

JOCELYNE CESARI

The recognition of Muslim minorities in European and North American societies, thrown into the media spotlight after 9/11 and attacks in Europe, has introduced debate over the compatibility of Islam with Western norms. Sharia law, perhaps more than any other aspect of Islam, is perceived as a threat to Western culture and evokes an emotional response in conjuring images of amputation and stoning. As the authors in this volume make clear, however, there is a significant gap between legal reality and political discourse central to current debates about Sharia in Europe and North America. *Debating Sharia* grapples with this topical question by turning to a public debate that unfolded when, in late 2003, a small Muslim organization announced it would offer Sharia-based arbitration of private (family) affairs in line with the laws then governing arbitration in Ontario, Canada. The contributors to this volume rightly differentiate between the reality of Islamic law within the legal systems of Canada and the politicization of post-9/11 debate on Sharia. Many of the findings of this volume are congruent with processes unfolding across Europe and in the United States.

Malleability of Sharia

Muslims believe that Islamic law originates from divine revelation and serves as a guide to divine will, from which the term Sharia (meaning 'path' or 'road') is derived. Islamic law has developed through the centuries beyond the original revealed text of the Qur'an, covering numerous topics for which revelation did not provide explicit prescriptions. For this reason, there is a distinction in classical Islamic theory between *Sharia* and *fiqh* (positive law). The principal techniques for fiqh develop rules in the absence of divine edicts in the Qur'an or *hadīth*; these techniques include, among others, *qiyās*, or analogical reasoning (applying a rule provided in revelation to a new situation), and *ijmā*, or consensus of the scholars. In other words, the transformation of the divine principles into positive legislation is the consequence of human work, that is, of lawyers and scholars of Islam. As the authors in this volume make clear, it is significant that Sharia is not codified. Instead, it is the result of a process involving knowledge, judgment, techniques of interpretation, and the study of legal doctrines and principles. In these ways, Sharia depends on the efforts of scholars. Traditionally, interpreting Sharia has been a continuous process of implementing this positive law controlled by *imams*. Therefore, positive law has taken different forms according to its historical context and the influence of various political communities.

In most contemporary Muslim states, Sharia is confined to family law, despite recent controversy about the expansion of Sharia to areas of criminal law (*u'dud*). Examples of criminal sentences include stoning to death, as has happened in Mauritania, and harsh corporal punishments such as those inflicted by the Taliban in Afghanistan. The introduction of Islamic legal principles to constitutional laws has sparked debate from Iran to Iraq, and Afghanistan is a recent development. In most cases, the implementation of Sharia is discussed in the framework of human rights and suggests that Sharia and human rights are incompatible (Tibi 2008). It is worth mentioning the claim that divine law is comprehensive and therefore a source of constitutional law diverges from the traditional perception of political entities in Islamic history, which is based on the distinction of Sharia from *siyasah* (politics) (Carney 2003).

Usually, these debates on Islam are transferred to Europe without taking into account its completely different context. In the Western world, where there is democratic constitutionalism, the debate does not stem from constitutional issues. Contrary to the widespread belief that Muslims in the West seek the inclusion of Sharia in the constitutions of European countries, most surveys show that Muslims are quite satisfied with the secular nature of European political regimes. When Muslims agitate for change, they engage in politics and the democratic process, utilizing mainstream parties and institutions (see Nyiri 2007). At the same time, it does not mean that they renounce Islamic principles and legal rules to guide or structure their daily lives. This conclusion also came through several surveys led in Europe and the United

States from 2007 to 2008 (see Cesari 2010), and is echoed in the Ontario context. Julie Macfarlane's subjects described in this volume expressed similar attachments to religious marriage and religious divorce regardless of the level of their religious practice or belief.

Religiosity and use of law is therefore a complex negotiation. Research suggests different and sometimes contradictory attitudes among Muslims towards European and North American secular laws: both complete rejection and complete acceptance of secular civil law are rare. This nuance is further complicated in a context of heightened securitization in both continents following the 9/11 and 7/7 attacks. Nevertheless, the general trend across Europe is of an accommodation of Islamic requirements within national laws. This reconciliation has often been conducted in an indirect way through European legal decisions rather than by Islamic legal experts or Muslim theologians (Boumidienne 1995). Consequently, a slow and 'invisible' form of personal Islamic law is being constructed and adapted to Western secular laws. Of course, European judges do not claim Islamic authority, but the fact that most clerics do not contest their decisions, or sometimes even endorse them illustrates the law's adaptation. It is also reflective of the malleability of Sharia itself, something highlighted in many of the contributions to this volume.

Also confirmed by the authors of this volume is that in most cases related with family life negotiation is still the strategy of choice. The recognition of individual freedoms and the consideration of each party's best interests lead to compromises that change not only the letter but also the spirit of the Islamic laws, stripping them of the official meanings they have in Islamic societies. A number of examples can illustrate a transformation in which Islamic regulations are 'acclimatized' to Western legal norms. The first concerns the acceptable period of time one's widowhood should last. Traditional Islamic law specifying the amount of time that must elapse before one is allowed to remarry cannot be strictly enforced in European societies. Laws governing inheritance offer another example of the flexibility involved in translating old practices into new contexts. Once again, the Islamic laws on inheritance, a holistic system elaborated in a context where men had the exclusive obligation of providing for the women, specify that for every part given to the daughter, two parts must be given to the son. This ruling cannot always be strictly adhered to in practice (especially in legal systems influenced by Roman law, which ensure that each descendant be provided for equally). In 1975, Zaki Badawi established a ready-made Islamic will to solve the contradiction between European and Islamic norms. For years, according to his own admission, no one used it (see Nielsen 1993), perhaps indicating that Muslims in Europe are generally quite comfortable with Western norms of inheritance.

As we can see in the Sharia debate in the Canadian context, it is in matters of divorce that changes in Islamic law have been the most significant, but also the most difficult to identify. Even though a divorce can still be officially carried out within religious law, unofficially it may have been already initiated by the wife in the civil court system. In addition, divorce is increasingly a topic of discussion for both members of the married couple. That husband and wife both abide by traditional Islamic law does not necessarily determine the degree of oppression or inequality within a marriage. Negotiation in divorce proceedings is one of the two main categories in which Islamic laws find themselves transformed within the context of Western democratic societies; polygamy is the other.

Sharia Debates

Negotiation between Western and Islamic law is a fact of legal life in a number of Western immigrant-receiving countries, including Canada. These debates, however, are far less accommodating and nuanced than the legal practices they purport to discuss. In February 2008, when Archbishop of Canterbury Rowan Williams suggested that 'there is a place for finding what would be a constructive accommodation with some aspects of Muslim law' (Williams 2008) much of the British public was outraged. Critics in this case, as in the Canadian context, viewed Archbishop Wlliams' proposal as the imposition of religious law and the end of their traditional separation of Church and State. Williams, however, observed the need to deconstruct the Western perception of Islamic law, and he pointed out that some aspects of Sharia, including Islamic banking, have already been incorporated in European culture. Indeed, Pearl and Menski call the hybrid legal system now evolving in England *Angrezi Shari'a* (1998, 74) and go on to explain: 'While English Law is clearly the official law, Muslim Law in Britain today has become part of the sphere of unofficial law. This analytical paradigm indicates that Muslims continue to feel bound by the framework of the *Shari'a*. Thus, rather than adjusting to English law by abandoning certain facets of their Shari'a, South Asian Muslims in Britain appear to have built the requirements of English Law into their own traditional legal structures.' (75)

This emergent hybrid product is stamped with the seal of Western individualist culture. In other words, Europeans view it as compatible with the principle of individual freedom. The recognition (even implicitly) of such a principle is currently redefining Islamic regulations on the status of the individual and the family, the two main areas in which discord arises between Western legal norms on the rights of individuals and the legal norms of Muslim countries.

That there is no clear desire among Western Muslims to change the secular nature of their states of residence does not preclude tensions between Islamic prescriptions and the provisions of secular law. Islamic traditions of marriage, divorce, and child custody most often cause friction between devout Muslims and European civil law. In legal practice, the question of whether to take Muslim family law into account in the regulation of daily life is bound to the condition that these laws meet the criteria prescribed by human rights and fundamental liberties. For this reason personal status appears problematic in the process of integrating Muslims, to the point that some compare the situation to a conflict of civilizations (Mercier 1972; Deprez 1988). However, even though the silent majority of Western Muslims already accept Islam's compatibility with human rights, fringes of the Muslim population exist that reject this paradigm and act in violent manners that strongly influence perceptions of Islam and Muslims.

The important question raised by the Muslim presence in the West is how the protection of specific subcultures can favour, rather than stifle, individual emancipation. Sometimes, Islamic groups collectively request rights that limit individual freedom. The Rushdie affair was an illustration of such a dilemma, as Muslims in England claimed the right of Islam to be protected by the Blasphemy Law (that before its repeal in 2008 applied only to Christianity as held by the Church of England). Within all of these Western Sharia debates, individual freedom and respect for difference are under intense scrutiny. Individual freedom is perceived as threatened by forced marriage, polygamy, and inequality between husband and wife in the divorce procedure. Tensions may occur between the dominant civil laws and the prescriptions of Islamic religion concerning family. It is clear, however, that there is a great deal of adaptation when it comes to issues of potential conflict between Sharia and civil laws. Respect for difference is also problematic, because Islam as a religion and culture is still perceived as alien and external to Europe. Promoting equality between cultures involves redefining public culture and the status of Islam within public space. In the post-9/11 context, some Muslim claims champion the European conception of human rights, by arguing, for example, that laws banning religious symbols from French public schools are contradictory to ideas of fundamental rights. Sharia and its threat to secular principles has also gained political visibility in the United States where in the fall of 2010, the citizens of Oklahoma decided to vote in favour of banning Sharia references from the court system.

Conclusion

The major areas of conflict between Islam and secularism in the West are within civil law and culture, rather than politics. As demonstrated in debates in the West over the headscarf and sexual orientation, morality and sexuality constitute the greatest divergence between Muslims and non-Muslims. Furthermore, *hijab* controversies, the Rushdie affair, and the Danish cartoon crisis reveal tensions between the status of religion in European public space, as well as questioning the goals of multiculturalism.

These heated debates on Islam and secularism in Europe, Canada, and the United States reveal that the real challenge is for each country to redefine its specific public culture. Islam makes it necessary to rethink and contextualize the principle of equality between cultures, thus incorporating ideals of tolerance and pluralism in the debate. The multicultural policies that predominate in European societies do not promote flexibility of these Western liberal ideas, thereby disregarding the values of Europe's minority cultures. The test is similar for Canada. The challenge is now to include Islam within its dominant narrative. In such conditions, we might wonder whether agreement on shared cultural and social values is still possible. The paradox is that for Muslims, the answers tend to be in the affirmative, whereas non-Muslims tend to answer negatively, especially in the post-9/11 context. The question then is how majoritarian groups can learn and adapt following debates like that examined in this volume.

REFERENCES

Boumidienne, Halima. 1995. 'African Muslim Women in France.' In Michael King, ed., *God's Law versus State Law*, 49–61. London: Grey Seal.
Carney, Abdel al-Hakeem. 2003. 'The Desacralization of Power in Islam.' *Religion, State, and Society* 31: 203–19.

Cesari, Jocelyne, ed. 2010. *Muslims in the West after 9/11: Religion, Law and Politics*. New York: Routledge.

Deprez, Jean. 1988. 'Droit international privé et conflit de civilisations. Aspects méthodologiques. Les relations entre systèmes d'Europe Occidentale et systèmes islamiques en matière de statut personnel.' *Recueil des Cours de l'Académie de la Haye* 211(4): 9–372.

Mercier, Paul. 1972. *Conflits de civilisation et droit international privé: polygamie et répudiation*. Geneva: Droz.

Nielsen, Jørgen S. 1993. *Emerging Claims of Muslim Populations in Matters of Family Law in Europe*. CSIC Papers No. 10. Birmingham: Centre for the Study of Islam and Christian-Muslim Relations.

Nyiri, Zsolt. 2007. 'Muslims in Europe: Basis for Greater Understanding Already Exists.' Gallup Polling. Accessed 12 Jan. 2011. http://www.gallup.com/corporate/115/About-Gallup.aspx.

Pearl, David, and Werner Menski. 1998. *Muslim Family Law*. London: Sweet and Maxwell.

Tibi, Bassam. 2008. 'The Return of the Sacred to Politics as a Constitutional Law: The Case of the Shari'atization of Politics in Islamic Civilization.' *Theoria* 55: 92–119.

Williams, Rowan, Archbishop of Canterbury. 2008. BBC Interview by Christopher Landau, 7 Feb. Accessed 12 Jan. 2011. http://www.archbishopofcanterbury.org/1573.

Introduction: Situating the Sharia Debate in Ontario

JENNIFER A. SELBY AND ANNA C. KORTEWEG

In late 2003, the Canadian media reported that the Islamic Institute of Civil Justice (IICJ) would begin offering arbitration services in family disputes in accordance with established Islamic law and the province of Ontario's 1991 Arbitration Act. A vociferous two-year international debate followed this announcement. Ostensibly this discussion centred on the province's use, legislation, and determination of the limits of alternative dispute resolution (ADR). At its starkest, however, the debate portrayed the issue as one in which Canadian Muslims, guided by international Islamic fundamentalists, sought to create a parallel legal justice system, which, opponents feared, would weaken the rights of Muslim women and the functioning of the liberal democratic state. The resulting public debate did little to address the complex issues at stake.

Contributors to this volume show that the debate could have informed discussion on a number of issues important to Muslim communities in Canada and to non-Muslim Canadians, like the limits of multiculturalism, the full membership of those who actively practise non-Christian religious traditions, the place of religion in the public sphere and discourses that connected Sharia-based arbitration with the systematic oppression of Muslim women. While multiculturalism came up in public debate, few participants thoughtfully addressed the question of whether religious minority groups should have rights based on distinct group practices. Participants in the controversy largely failed to give insight into questions regarding the limits on full membership of people who actively practise non-Christian religious traditions in countries, like Canada, that are secular while remaining shaped by various forms of Christianity. In addition, while public debate on Sharia-based arbitration could have addressed the meanings of secularism as well as the place of religion in the public sphere more generally, it did not do so.

A different but related issue that emerged concerns the rights of women. This issue had more prominence than multiculturalism, but produced less insight. In particular, in public debates, Islam was often assumed to be a patriarchal religious tradition. Private contracts, such as those generated in arbitration procedures, can shield parties from judicial scrutiny and may appear to enable Muslim men to oppress Muslim women (but see the chapters by Macfarlane and Cutting). In the public debate in Ontario, a specific understanding of multiculturalism combined with ideas regarding women's rights to ostensibly link Sharia-based arbitration and the systematic oppression of Muslim women. For strong supporters of gender equality, questions about multiculturalism, group rights, and religion in the public sphere had an easy answer: keep religion out of the public sphere and enforce an expansive definition of secularism. However, this answer had little relationship to what was actually happening outside the gaze of public debate.

This volume reflects widespread scholarly and activist agreement that the public debate regarding Sharia-based arbitration largely failed to generate a productive discussion of these issues. The contributors to this book lay the groundwork for such a conversation by outlining the ways in which faith-based principles inform privately negotiated contracts among North-American Muslims. From there, a number of contributors analyse the myriad possibilities for gender unequal arbitration in family matters and address existing unequal gender practices within Muslim communities and beyond. By analysing the ethnographic realities, legal possibilities, religious practices, political opportunities, and discursive parameters of the accommodation of Islam in the Western context exemplified in Ontario, Canada, the authors in this volume examine the disjuncture between the fears expressed in the Ontario Sharia debate and the realities of on-the-ground practices from a variety of academic and activist perspectives.

The debate inspired Julie Macfarlane and Christopher Cutting to conduct ethnographic research into the divorce practices of Canadian and North American Muslims. Their respective chapters demonstrate that the debate's premise was erroneous: religiously based family law arbitration was not something that Canadian Muslims engaged in or that Muslim Arbitration Boards conducted. Cutting shows that religiously based family law arbitration has never been formally practised by Ontario Muslim communities. Instead, Muslims needing guidance in conducting family matters associated with divorce in accordance with their faith typically turn to imams and Islamic legal counsel for mediation, a practice that is not governed (even following the province's 2006 amendment) by the Arbitration Act. Insofar as these religious leaders grant divorces, they are religious divorces (or a religious sanction of the separation) with the vast majority of couples seeking a religious divorce in conjunction with civil law procedures. In short, Muslim women and men seek guidance from religious leaders in moments of family breakdown, with almost all requests for a religious divorce coming from women whose ex-husbands do not cooperate in granting them a religious divorce, which is a male prerogative under many interpretations of Muslim law.

Second, legal scholarship by Audrey Macklin and Faisal Kutty in this volume shows that the very idea of 'one law for all' used to justify abolishing all faith-based arbitration at the close of the debate in 2006 is false. Couples habitually contract out of the default provisions of the Family Law Act, privatizing contracts regarding family matters and placing them outside of state oversight. Faith-based arbitration thus continues to be possible within this privatized system in the wake of the debate: religion can inform an arbitrator's rulings, so long as the texts of final rulings use the language of Canadian law. This suggests that analyses of the ways that women's equality and women's rights are threatened by the practice of privately ordering legal arrangements regarding family matters should extend beyond assessing Islamic legal principles.

Third, religiously informed interpretation of law also enters the debate. The common interpretation of Islam as informed by rigid doctrine is belied by the distinction between *fiqh*, or Islamic jurisprudence, and Sharia which was often misunderstood in the debate (including by some Muslim interlocutors). Sharia refers to the God-given ethical principles that guide conduct, while fiqh covers interpretation of various religious texts, which for Muslims (as for Jews) take on the imperative of law, although not in the way someone solely subjected to Western law would understand it. A number of contributors to this volume, most prominently L. Clarke, Anver Emon, and Nevin Reda, underline the complications of arbitrating within the context of Islamic jurisprudential practices or fiqh while maintaining the underlying principles of Sharia. At the same time, several chapters outline the ways in which Canadian and Islamic legal principles can be compatible.

The 'Sharia debate' offered an opportunity to discuss the place of Muslims in contemporary Canadian society beyond these legal questions. Yet, an overarching theme of this volume is that public discourse unfolded in ways that were detrimental both to fostering the participation of Muslim communities in broader Canadian society and to the ongoing development of Islamic jurisprudence in the context of family law. Moreover, public debate failed to deeply engage the gender issues at stake – including those related to privatizing the legal ordering of family matters in general, and those related to particular issues within Muslim communities, whether they stem from the application of Islamic legal principles or not.

Social scientists contributing to this volume, including Katherine Bullock, Jasmin Zine, Anna Korteweg, Alexandra Brown, and Jennifer Selby, suggest that the tenor of the debate needs to be analysed against the backdrop of two broader historical processes unfolding in the contemporary encounter between Islam and the West. First, the timing of the debate is notable. It parallels other post-9/11 tensions, with Ontario Premier Dalton McGuinty making the final pronouncement ostensibly removing the possibility of conducting faith-based arbitration from the law on 11 September 2005, a Sunday afternoon, which normally is not the time politicians choose to hold press conferences. Second, friction surrounding the integration of immigrants in Western Europe and, to a lesser degree, in Canada, centres on the long-standing presumed incompatibility between majority Christian and Muslim religious values. Often at stake in the recent articulations of these value differences are perceived gender inequality and the treatment of women within Islam (see Gaspard and Khosrokhavar 1995; Abu-Lughod 2002; Keaton 2006; Bowen 2007; Scott 2007; Mahmood 2008; Razack 2008; Joppke 2009; Cesari 2010). The Sharia debate in Ontario was no different.

As an introduction to this volume, the remainder of this chapter has three goals: (1) to introduce the legal context of the debate, (2) to outline a chronology of the debate, and (3) to discuss the key issues at stake in the 'Sharia debate' through a preview of the chapters that make up this book. Our introduction of the legal context begins with a historical-analytical approach to situate the debate in changes to the provincial Arbitration Act made in 1991 and contemporary understandings of Islamic law. While often excluded in chronologies of the dispute, this legislative shift set the stage for the Sharia debate twelve years later. This overview provides legal background for the book chapters. In addition, we introduce the major Islamic legal concepts at play in these contemporary discussions of religious legal practice.

Next, we provide a chronology of the public debate, culminating with the changes to the Arbitration Act in 2006. We focus on the wide variety of actors involved in the debates, both from Muslim and non-Muslim communities, and the key claims they staked out. In our discussions of the legal context and the chronology of the debate, we draw from the book's chapters to outline not only what was discussed in media representations but also what subsequent scholarly and activist enquiry has taught us about the practices associated with Muslim life in the Canadian context. We hone in on the following areas of contestation: religious law, multiculturalism, and women's rights.

Our overview is organized according to the six major parts of this volume, which address: first, ethnographic evidence of Islamic legal mediation in family affairs in North America; second, the Western legal context; third, the meanings and practices of Islamic law in Western contexts; fourth, Muslim scholar-activists' engagement with the debate; fifth, Islam, gender politics, and racialization in media representations of Sharia; and last, the politics of Canadian multiculturalism and its intersections with secularism. By way of conclusion, we suggest that, taken together, these chapters illustrate how the debate reflects a shifting religio-cultural Ontario at the beginning of the twenty-first century. We posit that the debate became so impassioned because it touched on a number of changes in contemporary Canadian society since the 1960s including the rise, and perhaps signs of decline, of multiculturalism as ethos and as policy; a significant increase in religious diversity in the country's urban centres; growing rights accorded to women; and most recently, securitization and Islamophobia following 11 September 2001.

The Legal Landscape: Secular and Islamic Law

The debate surrounding faith-based arbitration in Ontario was sparked by media coverage of the announcement by Syed Mumtaz Ali, a retired lawyer and spokesperson for the Institute for Islamic Civil Justice, that the IICJ was registered as a business and would begin offering religiously based arbitration to Muslims in accordance with the provincial Arbitration Act and the Canadian Charter of Rights and Freedoms. Often exluded in chronologies of the debate, the roots of the issue stemmed from changes to the Ontario Arbitration Act made more than a decade earlier. The Ontario Arbitration Act of 1991 was established in

part to diminish a backlog in the courts and reflected a broader movement towards privatization, the transfer of the government-controlled,
court-based application of family law to more expedient individual
agreements by arbitrators and mediators. This shift allowed for religious as well as non-religious arbitration in private matters, including
family and business disputes. The act governed only private affairs and
arbitrators, but not mediators because arbitration and mediation are
distinctly different practices. In arbitration, participating parties must
agree beforehand whether the arbitrator's ruling will be advisory or
binding. If it is binding, the parties submit their cases to the arbitrator
(as they would in court) and are obliged to abide by the arbitrator's
decision. Under mediation, however, the parties negotiate until they
arrive at a contract that is acceptable to all parties involved. Because the
Arbitration Act governed only arbitration, parties were free to mediate
and draw up private contracts outside of the parameters of the act.

Family law in Ontario is a complicated mix of federal law (the Divorce
Act) and provincial law (the Family Law Act). Agreements or 'domestic
contracts' resulting from private negotiations (arbitrated or mediated)
fall under the Ontario Family Law Act, with the exception of divorce,
which is a federal matter. From 1992 to 2006, parties were permitted to
bargain matters falling under the provincial statute according to their
own values and priorities, so they could request mediation, or arbitration, based on a legal regime other than Ontario or Canadian family
law – such as religious law. Proponents of the 1991 Arbitration Act
highlighted the efficiency, low cost, privacy, less adversarial, and less
intimidating nature of private arbitration. As Audrey Macklin discusses in her chapter on the privatization of law, critics of arbitration typically point to the misuse of power and replication of inequities in the
private system, particularly the financial, emotional, and social dependence of some women on men. For instance, while the default divisions
of assets under family law now take into account that a spouse who
earns no income still contributes to the family assets, individual couples can generate prenuptial agreements or divorce settlements that
differ dramatically from these default provisions. Under the act, a party
who feels wronged by a particular arbitration decision is required to
petition the court to review the arbitrator's award. In other words, with
the exception of contracts governing custody and child support arrangements (which are automatically reviewed by a judge), alternative
dispute resolution contracts are not vetted by the judiciary unless a
party requests it. This procedure puts the onus of ensuring fairness on

the individual, rather than on a more systematic, institutionalized legal review process.

After the Arbitration Act became law in 1992, some Jewish and Christian groups set up alternate dispute resolution boards that arbitrated in accordance with their religious principles. Their legal agreements did not raise public concern. In contrast, media coverage of the 2003 IICJ announcement that it would begin conducting faith-based arbitration based on Islamic legal principles was extensive. The coverage misconstrued the Muslim Arbitration Board (Dar al-Qada)[1] as a proposal to *extend* the law to include arbitration based on Islamic religious principles, which attracted a great deal of public attention. In reality, the Arbitration Act already allowed this arbitration, offering an alternative to litigation in ordinary courts for issues governed by provincial law. The IICJ's Muslim Arbitration Board, in which civil disputes surrounding divorce and inheritance could be settled invoking fiqh or an Islamic system of jurisprudence, paralleled Jewish arbitration practices governed by Beit Din.

Although ADR had been practised without fanfare in Ontario since its legislation in 1991, elements in the IICJ's announcement set off alarms among the general public and some factions of Canadian Muslim communities. When Syed Mumtaz Ali said that the IICJ would operate as a tribunal to arbitrate in family and inheritance matters based on its interpretations of Islamic family law, these services were dubbed 'Sharia courts,' and evoked images of oppressive, patriarchal practices associated with interpretations of Islamic law in other countries. As Nevin Reda demonstrates in Chapter 7, Ali did little to dispel public anxiety as he publicly distinguished between 'good' and 'bad' Muslims; the former would be obliged to use tribunals like those offered by the IICJ. This kind of coercive language, which left Muslims no real choice if they perceived themselves as religiously observant and in line with Ali's notions of piety, was troublesome both within and outside Muslim communities. Ali's announcement created the impression that he was working towards replacing Canadian law with ill-defined Sharia law for Ontario's Muslim populations.

Sharia, however, is not a single codified written text or a set of texts to which one can easily refer or from which one can draw judgment, nor is it the totality of Muslim duties or a summation of the traditions of Islam. Etymologically, the word 'Sharia' (also Shariah, Shari'a)[2] can be translated as 'a path leading to the water.' Many interpret the metaphor to refer to a journey towards spiritual knowledge, and more broadly to the development of a way of living according to that knowledge. The more precise term for the Islamic system of jurisprudence is fiqh, which refers to human attempts to understand God-given ethical mandates. For both Sunnis and Shi'ites, fiqh has emerged through various constantly evolving interpretations of four primary sources: the Qur'an, the *hadīth* (sets of practices and sayings related to the Prophet Muhammad), *qiyas* (reasoning by analogy), and *ijma* (consensus) by learned Muslims or Islamic scholars known as the *ulama* (see An-Na'im 2008, 10–12). Sharia gradually evolved over two centuries after the death of Muhammad in 632 CE and is still central to everyday Muslim life.

The media portrayed Islamic law as patriarchal and authoritarian, as punishment rather than rehabilitation-oriented, and (perhaps most importantly) as unchanging. Advocates of contemporary legal reform in Islam concur that that Orientalist fears continue to frame how Sharia was framed in the West as the 'repression of women, physical punishment, stoning and all other such things' (Ramadan 2004, 66), generating distrust and suspicion of Islamic scholars and intellectuals. In his analysis of the debate, Anver Emon (Chapter 6 in this volume) notes that neither the mediatized public debate nor public policy debates provided a substantive description of Sharia to counteract these presuppositions. He charts this colonial-infused Orientalist perspective from the nineteenth century through to the popular uses of the term in the contemporary Ontario context.

In Chapter 9, Jasmin Zine similarly suggests that throughout the debate, reductive, binary formulations of Sharia were presented as static containers for cultural preservation and cultural destruction. She argues that these formulations do not support the broad and complex terrain on which Islamic epistemology continues to grow, in defiance of either set of static norms and assumptions that seek to contain it. Emon and Lynda Clarke (Chapter 5) demonstrate that the contemporary Muslim world is not uniform in its interpretation of fiqh (see also Ahmed 1992, 89). This unevenness underlies some of the key contentions with respect to implementing this system of law for the purposes of binding arbitration in Canada. The lack of uniformity generated concerns among Muslim communities about which interpretations of Islamic jurisprudence would be invoked – and whether these would be in the best interests of women, who, as Zine also argues, have not fared well in the area of family law (including divorce, alimony, and child custody) under many traditional interpretations (see also Esposito and DeLong Bas 2001; Bakht 2006; Fournier 2010; Nielsen 2010). Chapters by Julie Macfarlane, Christopher Cutting and Lynda Clarke also note concerns regarding the patriarchal nature of Islamic divorce or *talaq*, which under traditional Islamic juristic traditions accords unilateral extra-judicial divorce rights solely to men, grants women limited alimony ranging from three months to one year, depending on the legal school of thought, and typically favours men in child custody and inheritance rights. In addition, their ethnographic evidence suggests that some imams are ill-equipped to respond to domestic abuse. Yet, a depiction of 'Sharia law' as introducing the cutting off of hands and the stoning of women prevented an in-depth public discussion of the attributes of Sharia-based arbitration and mediation.

Chronology of the Debate

Following Syed Mumtaz Ali's announcement on behalf of the IICJ and the international public outcry at the notion of 'Sharia courts,' Ontario Premier Dalton McGuinty sought advice from Attorney General Michael Bryant and Sandra Pupatello, the Minister Responsible for Women's Issues. In June 2004, Bryant and Pupatello appointed former Attorney General Marion Boyd to conduct a formal review of the use of arbitration in family and inheritance law in the province. Boyd had strong credentials, given her career in politics in the left-wing New Democratic Party, her feminist advocacy, and her work with battered women. For six months, Boyd accepted submissions in person, by phone, and in writing from private individuals and more than fifty groups. She met with women's organizations, religious bodies, immigrant settlement organizations, family lawyers, arbitrators, mediators, and concerned citizens. As shown in the chapters by Katherine Bullock and Faisal Kutty, during this process Muslim organizations in favour of allowing faith-based arbitration began to mobilize – partly to have a voice in Boyd's review and partly to counter the media's frequent negative stereotyping of Muslims and Islam.

Other activists targeted the so-called Sharia courts. For prominent women's organizations such as the pro-faith Canadian Council of Muslim Women (CCMW) and the secular International Campaign against Shariah Courts, led by Iranian refugee-turned-Canadian citizen Homa Arjomand, the idea of religion-based arbitration raised serious concerns. These organizations expressed apprehension that Sharia law would be invoked in ways counter to women's interests, making two broad claims: (1) Muslim women's rights would be better protected under the Canadian legal system, and (2) the rights accorded to women by the Canadian Charter were by and large already consistent with the

Islamic principles of social justice (CCMW Position Paper 2004). On their website, the CCMW highlights how marriage contracts can include both Islamic and Canadian law. However, in their concern for the wide-ranging interpretive nature of Sharia and the historical dominance of patriarchal pronouncements in that interpretation, they lobbied against faith-based arbitration. Kutty, who acted as lead counsel for a coalition of Muslim organizations in favour of continuing to allow faith-based tribunals, argues in Chapter 6 that because mechanisms for resolving disputes in local mosques already exist, the institution of tribunals based on Islamic law could formalize them and make the processes more transparent. Kutty suggests that the 'indigenization' of certain aspects of Islamic law could foster a robust multiculturalism and further the integration of Canadian Muslims into the Canadian legal system, until now based largely on Christian influences.

In the midst of these debates, in December 2004, Boyd published forty-six recommendations in a 191-page report entitled 'Dispute Resolution in Family Law: Protecting Choice, Promoting Inclusion.' She concluded that binding religious arbitration of family law issues based on 'Islamic legal principles' was permissible according to the Arbitration Act. Furthermore, she wrote: 'The Review did not find any evidence to suggest that women are being systematically discriminated against as a result of arbitration of family law issues. Therefore the Review supports the continued use of arbitration to resolve family law matters' (2004, 133). She noted that the IICJ 'was simply using the 'Arbitration Act' in the manner in which it was intended, as a framework for the provision of private arbitration services' (2004, 6). While supporting binding religious arbitration, Boyd did express concern for the protection of individual rights, and proposed amendments to the Arbitration Act to address concerns about gender inequality. A significant portion of her report set out pertinent elements of family law and the arbitration regime to readers.

Boyd carefully outlined how she considered the jurisdiction of public arbitration courts, the limits of the Family Law Act, and how arbitration intersects (and does not) with both the 1982 Charter of Rights and Freedoms and the 1988 Multiculturalism Act. She emphasized the voluntary nature of family law arbitration (both parties, and in the case of divorce both partners, must agree to the process). She stressed that secular Canadian courts were available should one party disagree. Once individuals agreed to the process, the decisions rendered by an arbitrator were legally binding; parties were to agree on the process, not on the results (Boyd 2004, 10). Alexandra Brown, in Chapter 11, argues that the report ultimately supported a multicultural ideology in tone and form, working to maintain the Canadian state more than emphasizing the complexities of religion and family law in Ontario. Indeed, in her executive summary, Boyd characterized the primary tension within the debate as that between respect for minority groups and protection of individual rights, or the limits of multiculturalism. Macklin notes in her chapter that through the report's subtitle of 'Protecting Choice, Promoting Inclusion,' Boyd sought to accomplish twin goals: protecting women's entitlement to choose appropriate tribunal arrangements, and simultaneously promoting the inclusion of minority groups within broader Canadian society. The public debate, however, did not move in this direction. As exemplified by the CCMW, the International Campaign against Shariah Courts, and other groups that mobilized against religiously based ADR, a great deal of the public debate about Islamic family law in Ontario centred on women's rights and possible abuses, placing these against the rights of groups to practise their religion in the public sphere.

The summer of 2005 saw a great deal of activist activity against the institutionalization of Islamic faith-based arbitration, with a number of women's groups staging international protests against the adoption of 'Sharia law' in Ontario. The resulting public debate did not reflect how ordinary Sharia is in the everyday lives of many Canadian Muslims, but instead portrayed it as alien within a liberal democratic context. Nor did the debate reflect the complexity or malleability of Sharia. Rather, it created two positions: one for the institutionalization of Sharia-based arbitration boards and one against. Within the Muslim community, Ali's announcement ignited concern for some and the possibility of religious affirmation for others (see Sharify-Funk 2009). As both Bullock (Chapter 8) and Kutty (Chapter 4) recount as proponents of such arbitration, communications from the premier's office during this summer led them to believe erroneously that McGuinty would adopt Boyd's recommendations. Most secular organizations (including Muslim ones) opposed the IICJ's Arbitration Board, with a total of eighty-seven human rights groups opposed to its institutionalization (Weinrib 2008, 257). The seventeen-member Liberal Party women's caucus also influenced the debate; one unnamed member later recounted, 'We needed to go with a clearer separation of religion and state. We were a loud voice in ... the final decision [to formally end faith-based arbitration]' (Brennan 2005).

Jennifer Selby notes in Chapter 12 that the debate moved towards linking shared civic secularism and women's rights against accommodation of religions in the public sphere. On 8 September 2005, Attorney General Michael Bryant stressed the importance of protecting gender equality:

> We have heard loud and clear from those who are seeking greater protections for women. We must constantly move forward to eradicate discrimination, protect the vulnerable, and promote equality. As the Premier reiterated this week, we will ensure that women's rights are fully protected. We are guided by the values and the rights enshrined in our Charter of Rights and Freedoms. We will ensure that the law of the land in Ontario is not compromised, that there will be no binding family arbitration in Ontario that uses a set of rules or laws that discriminate against women. (Attorney General 2005)

Despite the impressions held by Bullock and Kutty, McGuinty reneged on his office's verbal assurances on 11 September 2005, when he announced his intention to recommend amendments to the Arbitration Act to ban religious arbitration. In other words, the Ontario government was not going to adopt the recommendations set out in the Boyd Report. Seeking to end months of debate, McGuinty said he would not allow his province to become the first Western government to allow the use of Islamic law to settle family disputes, and that the boundaries between church and state would be clearer if religious arbitration was banned completely: 'There will be no Shariah law in Ontario. There will be no religious arbitration in Ontario. There will be one law for all Ontarians' (Simmons 2010). Of note, the Premier mentions Islam alone even though Jews and Christians were also utilizing the system.

In February 2006, the Ontario government enacted the Family Statute Law Amendment Act (FSLAA), which restricted binding family arbitration for everyone in the province, in keeping with a number of Boyd's recommendations but without following her general, positive conclusions about the advisability of faith-based arbitration.

Contestations in the Debate and Chapter Contributions

The chapters in this volume are organized into six main sections. The first half of the book, Parts I to III, focuses on the lived and jurisprudential meanings of Sharia, and questions the conceptualizations of Sharia that dominated public debate. Part I examines the practices of imams and the people who turn to them to mediate divorces and other family matters. Part II assesses the Canadian legal context, focusing on the questions and opportunities that arise when discussing the accommodation of faith-based arbitration. Part III analyses Islamic legal history and jurisprudence as fluid and historically contingent phenomena.

In Part I, law professor Julie Macfarlane and religious studies scholar Christopher Cutting illustrate through social scientific analyses of legal practices within Ontario and North American Muslim communities how religion-based family law arbitration has never been formally practised. Instead, Muslims requiring guidance about family matters associated with divorce typically turn to imams and Islamic legal counsels for mediation, not arbitration, in accordance with their faith, whether or not they are active in their mosques. As Cutting notes, this engagement ensures they are 'considered legitimately divorced within their religious community and before their God.' Imams typically encourage couples to obtain a civil divorce, but go to various lengths in making suggestions regarding how the civil divorce should deal with the division of assets, custody arrangements, etc. In so doing, religious leaders often reinterpret earlier Islamic rulings, and may come much closer to default provisions of the law than was suggested during the public debate of gender inequality in Sharia-based arbitration. This kind of mediation continues today, as these practices are not governed (even following the province's 2006 amendment) by the Arbitration Act.

In Part II, Audrey Macklin, a professor of law and a legal scholar of citizenship, and Faisal Kutty, a practising lawyer with a long-standing commitment to integrating Islamic principles in Western legal practice, demonstrate that the very notion of 'one law for all' (as pronounced by Premier Dalton McGuinty to end the debate) is false. Couples of all faiths often contract out of the default provisions of the Family Law Act, by privatizing contracts regarding family matters and placing them outside of state oversight. In their respective chapters, Macklin and Kutty also show how faith-based arbitration continues to be possible within the privatized system: religion can inform an arbitrator's rulings, as long as the texts of final rulings use the language of Canadian law and make no reference to religious principles. Given that there is much leeway in how people divide assets and arrange their private affairs, this creates the possibility of inequality. In other words, religious leaders can still act as arbitrators so long as they do not explicitly use religiously understood language or references. Macklin draws on the precedent-setting 2003 Hartshorne case to show that in light of privatization, arguments against faith-based arbitration only hold if we consider non-Muslim women to be fully capable of consent, regardless of social and cultural pressures, while considering Muslim women to be fully 'encultured subjects' who cannot be understood as persons outside of their cultural contexts. Kutty, who acted as lead counsel for a coalition of Muslim organizations in favour of continuing to allow faith-based tribunals, argues that because mechanisms for resolving disputes in local mosques already existed, the institutionalization of tribunals based on Islamic law would have simply formalized these and made the processes more transparent. Kutty turns to his interpretation of fiqh, or Islamic jurisprudence, to demonstrate that such arbitration is not only allowed by most Islamic law, but that it fits well with Islamic jurisprudential practice (showing how fiqh is continuously debated among scholars of Islam; Nevin Reda in Chapter 7 rejects this position).

In Part III, L. Clarke and Anver Emon highlight the complications of arbitration within the context of Islamic jurisprudential practices (which are themselves disputed and politicized) while maintaining the underlying commonly understood principles of Sharia. Clarke, a scholar of religion, examines how Sharia is an important focal point for discussions of identity and integration of Muslims in Western nation states. She takes a constructionist perspective related to Islamic law and examines how certain versions become legitimized in Western contexts. She notes how the interpretation of Sharia is a key component to determining authority and who can interpret the tradition in the diaspora. Emon, a legal scholar and professor of law whose expertise is in the history of Islamic law, similarly highlights the historical diversity of approaches within Islamic jurisprudence. He uses the history of family courts in India to demonstrate how colonial encounters between Islam and practices of governance and jurisprudence based in Christian liberal democratic traditions created a far more rigid set of 'Muslim laws' than had been the case under Muslim rule. Both Clarke and Emon argue that narrow conceptions of Islamic law – whether as codifying, limited, and dogmatic systems of law that support patriarchal privilege with a divine seal of authority or as the institutionalization of premodern barbaric rites such as stoning – limit the ability of Muslim intellectuals, scholars, and jurists interested in reform.

Parts IV to VI focus on questions of multiculturalism, the racialization of Muslim communities, and women's rights. Contributors discuss how conceptualizations of Sharia, Muslim communities, and gender equality were promulgated by the media and acted on by policymakers. Part IV includes chapters written by Islamic scholar Nevin Reda and Katherine Bullock, a political scientist and founder of the Tesselate Institute. Both relied on scholarly analysis to inform their activism during the debate and their contributions illustrate how the debate engaged people not only on a scholarly, but also on a personal and political level. Reda and Bullock held different positions in the debate's theological and political issues. Reda carefully disentangles the meanings of the word 'Islam' to highlight the complications inherent in relying on Islamic law to address family law. She suggests that given these constraints, mediation, rather than arbitration, is preferable for resolving contracts and disagreements. Bullock recounts her difficulties in joining the media debate as a religiously observant woman who, unlike Reda, supported Sharia-based arbitration. Bullock uses her political science toolkit to analyse her experience of being silenced by journalists who only had one box to slot her into: that of a woman unaware of the fundamentalist patriarchal gender relations supported by Sharia arbitration.

Part V sets out the various discursive strategies engaged in by participants in the debates. Jasmin Zine, a sociologist and Islamic studies scholar, highlights (in Chapter 9) the nuanced tensions between Muslim women's feminist and religious desires, stressing the need for constructive debate that incorporates the complexities of Islamic jurisprudence and practice while critiquing the various ways in which those complexities were simplified. While Zine clearly delineates how the tone of the debate impeded discussions of gender issues in Muslim communities, Anna Korteweg, a sociologist and scholar of gender relations, analyses (in Chapter 10) how media representations depicted observant Muslim women as lacking in agency and in need of rescue by the state. Both Zine and Korteweg point to the ways in which public debate informed the racialization of Canadian Muslims.

Part VI situates the debate within the context of Canadian multiculturalism and secularity. Alexandra Brown, an anthropologist, analyses (in Chapter 11) how the Boyd Report sustained multiculturalism as a government-approved ideology that governs difference. Although McGuinty eventually rejected the report's principal proposal, the government maintained its institutionalization of a multicultural ethic, which, Brown argues, masks state complicity in social inequalities and racism. Religious studies scholar Jennifer Selby recasts the debate in Chapter 12, by investigating what it said about how religion emerged in the public sphere. In particular, she questions the seeming neutrality in Premier McGuinty's 2005 concluding call for 'one law for all Ontarians' as a way to secularize legal proceedings in the province. By examining a separate 2007 debate on religious school funding, she highlights the continuing Christian biases within so-called neutral secularism, the blurred distinctions of private and public spheres, and a privileging of anti-religious feminist politics.

The volume's conclusion uses the commonalities across the chapters to explore the implications of the Ontario Sharia debate for similar deliberations in Western Europe and elsewhere in North America. Friction surrounding the integration of immigrants in Western Europe, and to a lesser degree in Canada and the United States, centres on the longstanding presumed incompatibility between Western liberal democratic and Muslim religious values. Debates about Sharia in Britain and other countries, as well as debates about the partial hijab and now the burqa and niqab across Europe, have recently served as venues to articulate perceived value differences in gender inequality and the treatment of women within Islam. The Sharia debate in Ontario was no different, as broader concerns around religious pluralism, diversity, and women's rights were debated through the lens of the public acceptability of Islam.

Conclusions

This introduction has shown that even if there were no empirical data suggesting that Islamic faith-based family law arbitration ever took place in Ontario, Syed Mumtaz Ali's announcement raised a number of significant questions for politicians, policy makers, women's organizations, Muslim organizations, and the public at large. The chapters in this volume depict how the Sharia debate came to reflect a number of contested social processes unfolding in contemporary Ontario: increasing religio-cultural diversity, declining support for multiculturalism and religion in the public sphere, and continuing negotiations regarding the rights of women. The religious demography in Canada's urban centres has changed over the last decades. The year 1967, when the country formally changed its immigration policy to a 'points system,' signals the beginning of this shift. In the twenty-first century, most new immigrants are settling in Canada's largest cities: Montreal, Vancouver, and Toronto. According to 2001 Census data, most Canadian Muslims live in the Greater Toronto Area and their population has grown at a considerable rate (Jedwab 2005). The most recent reliable data predict that by 2017, the Canadian Muslim population will be approximately 1.6 times the 2001 population of 579,645 (about 2% of the total Canadian population; see Statistics Canada 2001a; Jedwab 2005). According to the same 2001 data, 29 per cent of the Muslim population in Toronto is under 15 years of age (Statistics Canada 2001b). Also, compared with other growing non-Christian groups in the GTA (Sikhs, Hindus, and Buddhists) Muslims are among the most ethnically diverse (Bramadat 2005). As many as sixty ethnically differing mosques and community spaces, along with a number of Muslim community groups, formed a diverse spectrum in the Sharia debate. Several authors in this volume demonstrate how this caused internal tensions within the very diverse Ontarian Muslim community.

The debate also reflects how changing religious demography in contemporary Ontario has affected discussions about the 'limits' of multiculturalism. Canadians are often proud of their multicultural tradition. Young Muslim adults, who may feel threatened in the public sphere as Muslims, turn to multiculturalism as something that grants them the right to call themselves Canadian, with all the protections that entails, while being religiously, ethnically, and culturally different from the majority (Nagra 2010). Multiculturalism is thus attached to the right of religious freedom, not only as a guide to Canadian policy making but also as a publicly shared culture. Unlike other Western nations, Canada does not have a legal separation of church and state; much of how religious freedom is articulated nationally and provincially relates to interpretations of the Charter of Rights and Freedoms and the Multiculturalism Act. At the same time, multiculturalism, as the grounds for lawmaking, has a built-in tension between group rights (such as those of religious communities) and individual rights (such as those of women). As exemplified by the Sharia debate, this tension can become an avenue to attack multiculturalism by those who fear the heterogeneity of values under a multicultural deliberative ethos.

Finally, the Sharia debate involved the agency of women within private arbitration agreements. Muslim women received the greatest scrutiny and concern. The debates exemplified political philosopher Susan Moller Okin's (1999) adage that multiculturalism is 'bad for women,' insofar as it can pose a threat for women in the private sphere. Okin conceded that all cultures are suffused with patriarchal practices and ideologies concerning gender, but she posited that non-Western cultural minorities in particular typically allow women little power. The debates thus called into question the purported dangers of multicultural relativism, and its presumed disregard for how women's rights may be compromised by certain cultural practices. The chapters in this volume suggest that discussions will be more fruitful if they focus on practices that actually exist, and if they incorporate the perspectives of a wide variety of stakeholders.

NOTES

1 Dar al-Qada is translated as 'Muslim Arbitration Board' but literally means 'the house of law.' *Da:r* (in Arabic) means 'house' or 'hall' and *qaDa:* (in Arabic), 'judgment.'
2 Sharia is sometimes spelled Shariah, Shari'ah, Shari'a. The use of an apostrophe corresponds to the letter hamza (a glottal stop) in the Arabic alphabet. It is not always capitalized – those who do capitalize it, as we have opted here, do so out of respect for the religious origin of the word. For consistency, we asked the authors in the volume to standardize the spelling as Sharia. Although some used other (capitalized) variants in their original submissions, the change was not considered problematic.

REFERENCES

Abu-Lughod, Lila. 2002. 'Do Muslim Women Really Need Saving? Anthropological Reflections on Cultural Relativism and Its Others.' *American Anthropologist* 104 (Sept.): 783–90.
Ahmed, Leila. 1992. *Women and Gender in Islam: Historical Roots of a Modern Debate*. New Haven: Yale University Press.
An-na'im, Abdullahi Ahmed. 2008. *Islam and the Secular State: Negotiating the Future of Shari'a*. Cambridge, MA: Harvard University Press.
Attorney General. 2005. 'Statement by Attorney General On the Arbitration Act, 1991.' 8 Sept. Accessed 2 Sept. 2010. http://www.attorneygeneral.jus.gov.on.ca/english/news/2005/20050908-arb1991-st.asp
Bakht, Natasha. 2006. 'Were Muslim Barbarians Really Knocking on the Gates of Ontario? The Religious Arbitration Controversy – Another Perspective.' *Ottawa Law Review, 40th Anniversary Edition* 35 (Summer): 67–82.
Bowen, John R. 2007. *Why the French Don't like Headscarves: Islam, the State, and Public Space*. Princeton: Princeton University Press.
Boyd, Marion. 2004. 'Dispute Resolution in Family Law: Protecting Choice, Promoting Inclusion.' Ministry of the Attorney General. Accessed 30 Aug.

2010. http://www.attorneygeneral.jus.gov.on.ca/english/about/pubs/boyd/fullreport.pdf.

Bramadat, Paul. 2005. 'Beyond Christian Canada: Religion and Ethnicity in a Multicultural Society.' In Paul Bramadat and David Seljak, eds., *Religion and Ethnicity in Canada*, 1–19. Toronto: Pearson Longman.

Brennan, Richard. 2005. 'Liberal Women "Loud Voice" on Shariah.' *Toronto Star*, 13 Sept., A15.

CCMW (Canadian Council of Muslim Women). 2004. 'Position Statement on the Proposed Implementation of Sections of Muslim Law [Sharia] in Canada.' Accessed 23 Jan. 2011. http://www.ccmw.com/activities/act_arb_muslimlaw_sharia.html.

Cesari, Jocelyne, ed. 2010. *Muslims in the West after 9/11: Religion, Law and Politics*. New York: Routledge.

Esposito, John L. and Natana J. DeLong-Bas. 2001. *Women in Muslim Family Law*. 2nd ed. Syracuse: Syracuse University Press.

Fournier, Pascale. 2010. *Islamic Marriage in Western Courts: Lost in Transplantation*. Farnham: Ashgate.

Gaspard, Françoise, and Fahrad Khosrokhavar. 1995. *Le foulard et la République*. Paris: La Découverte.

Jedwab, Jack. 2005. 'Canada's Demo-Religious Revolution: 2017 Will Bring Considerable Change to the Profile of the Mosaic.' *Association for Canadian Studies/Association d'études canadiennes*. Accessed August 15, 2011. http://www.acs-aec.ca/oldsite/Polls/30-03-2005.pdf.

Joppke, Christian. 2009. *Veil: Mirror of Identity*. Cambridge, MA: Polity Press.

Keaton, Trica Danielle. 2006. *Muslim Girls and the Other France: Race, Identity Politics and Social Exclusion*. Bloomington: Indiana University Press.

Mahmood, Saba. 2008. 'Feminism, Democracy, and Empire: Islam and the War of Terror.' In Joan Wallach Scott, ed.,*Women's Studies on the Edge*, 81–114. Durham: Duke University Press.

Moller Okin, Susan. 1999. 'Is Multiculturalism Bad for Women?' In Joshua Cohen, Matthew Howard, and Martha C. Nussbaum, eds., *Is Multiculturalism Bad for Women?*, 7-26. Princeton, NJ: Princeton University Press.

Nagra, Baljit. 2010. *Unequal Citizenship*. Doctoral dissertation, University of Toronto.

Nielsen, Jørgen S. 2010. 'Shari'a between Renewal and Tradition.' In J.S. Nielsen and L. Christoffersen, eds., *Shari'a as Discourse: Legal Traditions and the Encounter with Europe*, 1–16. Farnham: Ashgate.

Ramadan, Tariq. 2004. *Western Muslims and the Future of Islam*. London: Oxford University Press.

Razack, Sherene. 2008. 'Modern Women as Imperialists: Geopolitics, Culture Clash, and Gender after 9/11.' In *Casting Out: The Eviction of Muslims from Western Law and Politics*, 83–106. Toronto: University of Toronto Press.

Scott, Joan Wallach. 2007. *The Politics of the Veil*. Princeton: Princeton University Press.

Sharify-Funk, Meena. 2009. 'Representing Canadian Muslims: Media, Muslim Advocacy Organizations, and Gender in the Ontario Shari'ah Debate.' *Global Media Journal* 2(2): 73–89.

Simmons, Harvey. 2010. 'One Law for all Ontarians.' 14 Sept. Accessed 22 Jan. 2011. http://www.thestar.com/opinion/editorialopinion/article/860513--one-law-for-all-ontarians.

Statistics Canada. 2001a. 'Population by Religion, by Province and Territory: 2001 Census: Quebec, Ontario, Manitoba, Saskatchewan.' Accessed 21 Jan. 2011. http://www40.statcan.ca/l01/cst01/demo30b-eng.htm.

Statistics Canada. 2001b. 'Religion and Age Groups for Population, for Canada, Provinces, Territories, Census Metropolitan Areas and Census Agglomerations.' Accessed 15 August 2011. http://www12.statcan.ca/english/census01/products/standard/themes/RetrieveProductTable.cfm?Temporal=2001&PID=68339&APATH=3&METH=1&PTYPE=55430&THEME=56&FOCUS=0&AID=0&PLACENAME=0&PROVINCE=0&SEARCH=0&GC=0&GK=0&VID=0&VNAMEE=&VNAMEF=&FL=0&RL=0&FREE=0&GID=431591

Weinrib, Lorraine. 2008. 'Ontario's Sharia Law Debate: Law and Politics under the *Charter*.' In Richard Moon, ed., *Law and Religious Pluralism in Canada*, 239–63. Vancouver: UBC Press.

PART ONE

Practising Religious Divorce among North American Muslims

1 Practising an 'Islamic Imagination': Islamic Divorce in North America

JULIE MACFARLANE

Divorce is an unpleasant and commonplace reality in North America (Canada 2006). Now Muslim communities in North America are facing rising rates of marriage breakdown. Although divorce was relatively unusual among the parents of the present generation of North American Muslim, and almost unheard of a generation before, divorce is now increasingly common among younger people and as a result, more openly discussed and debated. Despite the impulse in Islam – in common with other major religious traditions – to emphasize marriage and minimize divorce, one imam admitted to me frankly that he had conducted more divorces in the last year than marriages.

Behind the Headlines: An Empirical Study

The study described in this chapter was first conceived following the 2003–05 'Sharia debate' in Ontario. Frustrated by the absence of empirical data in media reporting, I wanted to find out what was actually happening in mosques across North America which offered marital counseling and Islamic divorce to community members. Interviews were conducted with 214 imams, religious scholars, community leaders, social workers, and divorced men and women (this latter group are described here as the 'participants'), between 2006 and 2010. Face-to-face data were being gathered principally in Detroit/ Dearborn, Los Angeles, Toronto, Windsor/London, Ottawa, and London, England. In addition, many telephone interviews were conducted with individuals in cities all over the United States and Canada.

The primary objective of the study was to document, using a qualitative, interview-based approach, how North American Muslim communities

manage divorce, and to explore what types of Islamic family processes – marriage, reconciliation efforts, and divorce – remain important and vibrant in twenty-first century North America. I wanted to
better understand the motivations of both the users and the facilitators
of processes for marital counselling and divorce, the role of the extended family, and to chart the wide range of variations in procedure and
practice. The result is a picture of private dispute resolution – or 'private ordering' – that occurs frequently, informally, and with little consistency and wide variations in procedure and outcome. To date there
has been virtually no data collection or formal monitoring of the practice of Islamic divorce either inside or outside Muslim communities in
North America.

I also anticipated – although the depth of the data surpassed my
expectations – that gathering such a large volume of data on the topic
of divorce from North American Muslim would illuminate some of the
critical social and cultural forces at play in these communities. Extensive
and frank interviews with men and women who had faced marital
problems, most of whom ultimately divorced, illuminated the broader
changes taking place within diverse Muslim communities in North
America as they adjust not only to life in the West, but also to more
systemic changes in societal norms. This data is described and analysed
in my book (Macfarlane 2012). The experiences of men and especially
women with the related systems of Islamic marriage (*nikah*) and divorce, as well as the perspectives and attitudes of religious leaders, social workers, and other professionals working with Muslim families,
offer insights into a community in transition. A North American Islamic
identity is being shaped not only by religious but also by cultural factors – for example, attitudes towards the equal participation of women
in work and education, gender roles and expectations within marriage
(e.g., how to structure a contemporary marriage partnership where
both spouses work outside the home), the role of the extended family in
choices over a marriage partner, and attitudes towards divorce itself.
The meaning of these choices extends beyond traditional religious observance. Instead, they reflect the development of an 'Islamic imagination' among Muslim families whose children are born and raised in
North America – what Tariq Ramadan calls 'the building of the Muslim
personality in the West and … in the modern era' (Ramadan 2004, 7).

After a four-month immersion course in Islamic family law, I began
by talking to the imams, who are almost always the facilitators of
Islamic divorce. The data set includes in-depth interviews with more

than forty imams or religious leaders, who are commonly charged with responsibility for both reconciliation and divorce processes and widely regarded as the 'gatekeepers' of religious divorce by their community. The imams represent both Sunni and Shia communities, and all five schools of Islamic jurisprudence (the majority describe themselves as Hanafi; the other four schools are Maliki, Shafi, Hanbali and Jaafari). However, virtually every one of the imams made the point that in practice, they adopt whichever school's rule is the most appropriate, in their view, to the individual circumstances. The following comments are typical: 'I use the school that can solve the problem before me'; 'As a Muslim living in the West I cannot afford to follow just one school. I must construct a modern approach that responds to the reality of the contemporary West and in particular ... the diversity of (Muslim) communities'; and 'We are not here to be Hanafi, Maliki and so on – but to be a human being.' This means that the (relatively small) differences between the schools do not impact significantly on the ways that the imams approach questions of, for example, permission to divorce, support, property division, and child custody. Neither was there any correlation between the overall approach taken to divorce and whether the imam was Sunni or Shia; far more significant were his values (traditional/progressive) regarding family life, a woman's role in the family, and sometimes the degree of conservatism of his community (which may cause him to refuse divorce when the law would technically allow it).

The data set also includes interviews with Muslim social workers and community workers, marriage counsellors, therapists and other mental health professionals, religious scholars and academics, and Muslim family lawyers. These professionals provided me with valuable insights into the ways in which their communities were evolving, the continued desire for religious sanction for divorce, and the work of the imams (of whom they were often critical) and with whom they sometimes worked directly, either by screening cases or taking referrals.

After the first eighteen months, the study focused on the personal stories of men and women who had experienced divorce (the 'participants'). Interviewees were solicited via imams and other professionals, presentations in mosques and community centres, the project website (www.islamicdivorce.org), and a Facebook page, using a snowballing approach, especially effective among women participants. The study eventually collected 104 extremely detailed personal accounts of marital conflict, efforts at reconciliation, and steps to obtain both religious and civil divorce. The majority of participant stories come from women (approximately 80%; 20% were from men), probably because they are required to be more proactive than men (unlike men, women need permission for divorce and must be divorced before they can be remarried in Islam). Although not asked directly to explain the causes of conflict in their marriage, almost all participants offered that information in the course of telling their story, allowing for further analysis of the causes of conflict.

By no means do all North American Muslims seek a religious sanction for divorce, and just how many do is unknown. The small proportion – less than 10 per cent – of the participants who rejected the idea of consultation with an imam and were clear that they did not want an Islamic divorce are probably not representative of the general population, because the study solicited respondents who would talk about their experience of religious divorce. However, what the study does clearly show is that the desire for religious divorce among North American Muslims is both widespread and common. I was able to identify many individuals for whom a religious sanction was very important, each of whom knew of others who had also sought religious divorce. The demographics of the sample also show that those who seek religious divorce are an extremely diverse group. They include many highly qualified professionals (e.g., with graduate degrees) as well as those with lower levels of education (e.g., a high school diploma and no post-secondary education); and both first- and second-generation Muslim North Americans as well as recent immigrants. Approximately half the participants came to North America as adults (often to study), a quarter as young children, with the other 25 per cent born in the United States or Canada. Participants also came from all ethnic groups. Almost half the sample identified as South Asian (predominantly Indo-Pakistani), nearly 30 per cent said that their families came originally from the Middle East, 10 per cent identified as African (originating from North Africa – e.g., Egypt – and other parts of Africa, primarily Somalia), and 6 per cent were African-American. Three per cent were Caucasian converts to Islam. Almost 20 per cent of the marriages were cross-cultural. This breakdown is close to the estimated ethnic breakdown in the North American Muslim population; the one group that may be under-represented is African-American/Canadian Muslims (U.S. Department of State and Bureau of International Programs 2009). In short, there is no 'typical' profile for those who want a religious sanction for divorce.

Different interview formats were used for the different respondent groups: imams and other facilitators of divorce processes; participants (divorced men and women); and community specialists (social and community workers, therapists and mental health professionals, lawyers). Semi-structured interviews could last anywhere between thirty and ninety minutes. All interviews were noted contemporaneously, including transcribing many direct quotations. Audio recording was avoided because it seemed to alienate some early respondents and generally reduced respondent comfort with sharing sensitive and/or personal data The data were analysed using the NVivo 7 software (www. qsr.org) and a variety of other manual processes including story synopses, a model for distinguishing different divorce process narratives (referred to later in this chapter), outcome narratives, participant motivations, and typologies for mapping the imams' approaches and interventions.

In this chapter, I begin with a short overview of the practice of Islamic marriage and divorce among North American Muslims. I offer a brief primer on the legal principles that govern Islamic divorce and then compare Islamic divorce – as a system of 'private ordering' – with 'official' state-sanctioned legal procedures in Canada.

In the remainder of the chapter I shall focus on some of the most significant findings from my study, beginning with motivations for seeking religious divorce. I then describe four different narratives of seeking (and sometimes obtaining) Islamic divorce, based on the stories told to me by participants and the information gathered from interviews with imams and other professionals. The picture that emerges is far more ad hoc – there is wide regional diversity and little consistency – and much less sinister – for example, I found no evidence of compulsion or coercion, and few cases differed dramatically in outcome from a legal divorce, which most participants also obtained – than the notorious (but undefined) 'Sharia divorce' often presented by news outlets.

There are nonetheless legitimate and important concerns about the barriers presented to women seeking divorce, a lack of recognition in many quarters of the dangers of domestic abuse, and a disproportionate impact of community disapprobation on women seeking divorce. These and other challenges facing the continuing practice of Islamic divorce are discussed further below.

Marriage and Divorce among North America Muslims

Many North American Muslims continue to exercise an 'Islamic imagination' in approaching life's critical transitions – birth, marriage, divorce, and death. For those who describe themselves as observant, it is self-evident that they would seek counselling from a religious leader for marital conflicts, especially since Islam (in common with other faiths) regards marriage as a for-life commitment. If they need to divorce, they seek a religious sanction. But the desire for an Islamic approach to marriage and divorce is not limited to observant Muslims. In common with many other ethnic, religious, and cultural groups, moments of crisis and transition often lead to reaffirmation of emotional and behavioural touchstones – for example, within Christianity, we know that many more people get married in church, baptize their babies, or hold religious ceremonies for burial than attend church on a regular basis. When it comes to dealing with life's crises, it is commonplace for individuals to feel that they must 'get it right' by resorting to traditional practices that they and their families believe will ensure that they have met their religious and moral obligations. This is a critical point because it shifts our understanding of what 'religion' means in contemporary North American life, imbuing it with cultural and social norms. There are signs here of the development of a wide spectrum of individual orientations towards faith and belief, which includes cultural as well as religious commitment, which are played out both publicly (as observance) and privately (as personal spirituality and conscience).

Following this pattern, the number of Muslim North Americans who marry using a nikah or marriage contract is far higher than those who regularly attend prayers (Canadian Institute of Policy Studies 2008) or even consider themselves to be observant. The proliferation of 'boilerplate' nikahs on the World Wide Web is evidence of the continuing vibrancy of this practice. Using a nikah or marriage contract (along with a legal marriage ceremony) is widely expected and practised, whether one's family is conventionally 'religious' or not. Whatever their ostensible level of religiosity, and despite the fact that the nikah is not considered to be a sacrament but a legal contract, many Muslims regard the nikah as a contract among three parties – 'myself, my husband, and God.' All but six of the more than a hundred marriages in this study had a nikah. For each individual this had some significance – sometimes fleeting, sometimes deeper – as a faith-based commitment. Similarly, many of the participants who sought an Islamic divorce were not traditionally observant and some described themselves as adopting a secular lifestyle (see below, 'Motivations'). The continued commitment to using a nikah serves to reinforce the use of Islamic divorce since many participants described the need to 'square the circle' – as one male participant put it, 'If you come in by the Islamic door, you should leave by the Islamic door.'

Peacemaking, accommodation, and compromise in family disputes are central Islamic values – the Qur'an contains many verses which exhort Muslims to rely on the advice and judgment of family members in resolving disputes (*Qur'an Translated*, verses 40:12, 5:95, 40:47–8, 2:13, 3:55). The family has historically played a primary role in both the creation and the dissolution of marriage partnerships in Muslim communities. Islamic marriage is often described as a 'marriage of two families' rather than just two people. Similarly, there is a long tradition of trying to resolve marital discord by discussion involving the wider family and not just the couple. These ideas animate a continuing tradition of family and community-based dispute resolution in which everyone is assumed to share these values and work towards a resolution.

There is, evidence of significant generational change in the norms surrounding the role of the extended family in the private life and decision making of their adult children, in both wider society and Muslim communities. Some participants resented the intrusion of one or other's extended family into their marital conflict, and in some cases this became another source of conflict with their spouse. Others described feeling family pressure or even coercion to remain in a marriage, often in order to avoid family shame. Family intervention, however well-intentioned, may also reflect traditional and patriarchal assumptions about gender roles in marriage which are no longer assumed by their adult children. Where the two families held quite different views on gender roles in marriage – which was not uncommon – the intervention of the extended family may polarize the positions being taken by husband and wife and make the conflict worse, not better.

Nonetheless, the experience of both participants and imams attests to the continuity of traditional norms regarding family-based problem solving. In some cases the imams themselves are acting as a substitute for the extended family, because first-generation immigrants may have left their extended families in their country of origin and turn instead to their imam. Another factor is the long shadow of 9/11 and Islamophobia; some Muslim counsellors and mental health professionals told me that many Muslim families avoid going to public agencies because of fears about discrimination or at least, ignorance of Muslim culture and beliefs. This observation is borne out by other research (Abu-Ras, Geith & Cournos 2008, Abu-Ras & Abu-Bader 2008).

There is a natural progression in marital discord from speaking with family members, to some type of family conference, to consultation with an imam or other third party. There is no given or universal procedure for obtaining an Islamic divorce in North America, nor any universally recognized outcomes. Each imam follows his own process, usually interviewing each spouse (where both are willing to participate) and perhaps convening a joint meeting, which will sometimes include members of the extended family. If a divorce is approved, some imams will write this out, but the form of documentation varies and sometimes there is none at all. Some imams will advise parties that if they have a civil decree from a North America court, this will be deemed to be the equivalent of a religious divorce (according to a widely cited *fatwa*; see European Council for Fatwa and Research 2008). In some instances they will prepare a paper to this effect, in others this advice is simply given orally. In other words, Islamic divorce in North America manifests no consistent formal process, but lives instead in the beliefs and imaginations of those Muslim men and women for whom it is psychologically and spiritually important.

Every imam, religious scholar, lawyer, community leader, and social worker whom I interviewed in the Muslim community believes that divorce is rising rapidly among North American Muslims (Ba-Yunus 1999, 2001). Almost unheard of and certainly unspoken of two generations earlier, Muslim communities all over North America are now confronting how they might manage the reality of divorce as a relatively common phenomenon. The imams receive little if any training to prepare them for dealing with serious conflicts, especially where there is violence or abuse in the marriage. The rising levels of divorce are spurring a vigorous debate in the community over how North American Muslims approach marriage, including the role of pre-marital education and counseling for young Muslim couples, individual versus family choice of spouse, the extent and nature of contact between a couple before marriage, and the continuing practice of matching North American-born Muslims with partners coming from a Muslim country.

Attitudes towards divorce are still dominated by the assumption – especially among the older generation – that divorce means that the spouses (but in particular, the wife) have failed. Some Muslims regard divorce as a mark of shame on the family, despite the fact that provisions for divorce within Islam have existed since the seventh century, with the Prophet Muhammad described as sanctioning divorce in a number of hadīth (Syed 2004, 67). At the same time, the Qur'an places great importance on marriage and family, and divorce is described in hadīth as the 'most hated permitted thing' (Hadīth of Abu-Dawud 2001). More conservative and sometimes extremely intolerant attitudes towards divorce and divorced women appear to be especially strong in some communities (most noticeably South Asian Muslim communities) and less so in others (e.g., among Muslims originating from Africa). Almost every participant described their fear at the reactive judgment of their families and communities, a fear that is particularly strong among women, who are often seen as 'at fault.' The wide range of tolerance among different communities, and the contrast (pointed out by many respondents, including imams) with Qur'anic teaching, suggests that this may be a cultural attachment rather than a religious orientation. One woman told me, 'This is not an articulated thing, but an unconscious burden on women. This is not Islam, this is the culture.' While most younger women appear to have been accepted, over time, as divorcees by their families and communities – and many have remarried – the fear of an exclusionary social stigma remains strong. In some cases, there is a lingering sense of negative difference: 'You are known as not just as a girl, but as a divorced girl.'

Islamic Law and Divorce

There are some important differences between the development of Islamic law, its rules regarding divorce, and the common law that operates in Canada and the United States. While these differences cannot be described in detail here, it is useful to understand how Islamic law has developed over time from Qu'ranic sources, and the recourse it provides for divorce.

The imams who oversee religious divorce in North America ground their advice in Islamic family law, often somewhat loosely applied. There is a range of knowledge about Islamic law among the imams in this study; some are highly educated, while others have minimal knowledge. Their focus is on adapting the legal rules to the particular problem, a well-established principle of Islamic legal theory (Emon 2004, 379–81). Their primary source is the Qur'an, which contains between eighty and two hundred verses that relate to potential legal principles or rules. Since Muhammad was illiterate, the Qur'an was written down by the Companions of the Prophet, who also created other textual sources for Islam and the earliest development of Islamic law. Principal among these are the Sayings of the Prophet or *hadīth*, which are believed to be narratives of 'what the Prophet had said, done or tacitly approved' (Hallaq 2006, 42) and the Sunna of the Companions of the Prophet which comprise examples of exemplary conduct taken from the Prophet's life.

These sources were crucial in the construction of a moral and legal code from the seventh century on. Islamic law was developed by *alim* and *qadi* (scholars and judges). Rules and legislation based on the textual sources described above emerged as *fiqh* or laws, in an effort to draw practical, everyday principles from the Qur'an. In developing fiqh, Muslim jurists also placed varying degrees of emphasis on the consensus of the community (*ijmā*), independent reasoning (*ijtihad*), and reasoning by analogy (*qiyās*). Different schools of Muslim law emerged which adopted somewhat different methodologies and slight variation in laws. These schools of jurisprudence continue to hold sway in different parts of the Muslim world today.

Islamic family law is what remains of a more comprehensive legal system including commercial and land laws which existed prior to nineteenth-century colonization. Post-colonization, legal systems in many Muslim countries were codified and adopted the commercial and land codes of the colonizing power. The family law system – the laws relating to marriage, divorce, and inheritance – was left relatively untouched. As 'private' law, family law was regarded as relatively politically unimportant; and maintaining Islamic family law avoided possible confrontation between modern Islamic governments and their respective *ulama* (influential theologians) (Mir-Hossein 1993; An-Naim 2002, 17–18). This means that in Muslim countries, divorce continues to be regulated according to modified versions of classical Islamic law, with some late twentieth and twenty-first century reforms designed to enhance the rights of women (e.g., their ability to release themselves from marriage, protection against unreasonable divorce by their husband, and restrictions on polygamous marriages) (An-Naim 2002).

The two primary routes to divorce in Islam do not necessarily require the intervention of a third party, although there are a number of stories in hadīth of the Prophet Muhammad being consulted on such divorces, and in contemporary North America the imams are often asked to give permission for divorce. The first route is *talaq*. Talaq is unilateral divorce by the husband, and does not require the consent of the wife in order to be valid. To ameliorate the effects of talaq effected without consultation, judicial registration (and notice to the wife) is now required in most Muslim legal systems (An-Naim 2002, 229–37). Talaq is also subject to a number of rules developed by the classical schools of Islamic law to discourage hasty divorce; for example, most schools require that talaq should be pronounced three times before divorce is irrevocable to allow for a 'cooling off period' and disqualify any pronouncement made in anger.

The second classical form of divorce is *khula*, which is divorce by agreement between husband and wife. While widely understood as divorce at the initiative of the wife, khula nonetheless requires the consent of her husband (although some jurisprudence suggests that he cannot withhold such consent 'unreasonably'). Where a wife asks for khula, she will generally forfeit her deferred *mahr*, which is a sum provided for in her marriage contract payable in the event of divorce or the death of her husband (some or all of the mahr may also be payable on marriage). Where a husband will not give consent to khula, permission may be substituted by a judicial authority on a variety of grounds including failure to maintain, abandonment, ill-treatment or cruelty, or in some schools and jurisdictions, basic incompatibility (Eposito and Delong-Bas 2001, 33–4). This is often described as *faskh*, or judicial annulment. In North America, in the absence of Islamic courts (Fournier 2010), imams may make this assessment. This is one of the most controversial (and inconsistent) areas of their practice.

The major substantive differences between the Islamic and the common law system in Canada and the United States in relation to the consequences of divorce concern spousal support, matrimonial property, and child custody. Classical Islamic law does not provide for spousal support in the same way as the common law system, although every nikah must include a mahr which if deferred until death or divorce, functions as a lump sum payment (although there is no stipulation as to amount, and this can vary widely). There is no concept of shared property in Islamic law, and each spouse keeps their own property, including what they brought into the marriage and any income the wife has earned during the marriage. In practice, however, many divorcing Muslim couples agree (and occasionally have stipulated in their nikah) to divide property equally, adopting common law principles. As well, some imams (although by no means all) will encourage payment of spousal support on a voluntary basis. Child support is always required, but is only payable by the father. In classical Islamic law, children are considered to be in the legal custody of their father after they reach a certain age (around puberty for both boys and girls) but in practice the imams refer to the 'best interests of the child' principle applied by U.S. and Canadian courts. In the more than a hundred stories I documented I did not come across a single case in which an imam gave custody to a father against the wishes of a mother (although I did interview two women whose young children were removed from them by an overseas court). In all the cases that were resolved in North America, children either stayed with their mother or in just a few cases, custody was shared. Ironically, the single exception was a case in which a six-month-old baby was removed from the mother and given to the husband's family by a Canadian court, not by an imam. Many imams told me that they referred any custody dispute to the courts. Of course, this does not mean that custody disputes never arise between couples in North America in which imams adjudicate in favor of the father, but this study suggests that this is uncommon. However, I did come across a number of cases in which husbands used their presumption of custody as leverage in their negotiations.

The interpretation and implementation of classical Islamic law principles by North American imams and religious scholars, in the absence of reformist legislation or Islamic courts, is the beginning of the development of a North American Sharia. Tariq Ramadan describes this evolution as 'the Islamic principle of integrating all that does not contradict the prohibitions and making it our own' (Ramadan 2004, 224). Examining the individual practice of more than imams, this study shows that in some cases, a North American Sharia is indeed developing in ways that recognize the changing conditions of family life and the expectations and role of women. In others, it appears to be locked into a classical image of seventh-century family life.

The Relationship between Islamic Divorce and the Formal Legal System

Islamic divorce in North America is a system of private ordering, running parallel to, but outside of, the formal system of laws and courts. Systems of private ordering are common in every country, community, and organization. They may in fact have as great an impact, or even greater, on the lives of those who choose to use them than the state-sanctioned system, especially if they represent meaningful principles and process not available in the state system. In common with other systems of private ordering, Islamic divorce depends on the commitment of those who use it – rather than the state – for its authority and legitimacy (Macfarlane 2007, 489–94).

The Legal Status of Islamic Divorce

As a system of private ordering, Islamic divorce in North America - just as religious marriage, or nikah – is neither recognized nor sanctioned by the state. This means that a couple using a nikah must also register their marriage with the civil authorities if they wish to be regarded as legally married; likewise an Islamic divorce obtained in North America via an imam or other religious authority is not a legal divorce without a civil court order (*Hosain* v. *Malik* 1995). Because there are no Islamic courts in Canada or the United States, an agreement to divorce applying the principles of Islamic law is no more enforceable than an agreement to divorce made between any two separating spouses across their kitchen table – it requires the authorization of a court before it has any legal effect. This means that a legally married woman who has been divorced by her husband under Islamic law – with or without her consent – is not legally divorced in either the Canada or the United States until she obtains a civil divorce. Any subsequent remarriage by either husband or wife without a civil divorce would be bigamy.

All the imams I interviewed understood that North American courts do not recognize Islamic divorce and most explicitly encourage the parties to seek a civil, legal divorce as well as an Islamic divorce. Some imams require this before they will approve a religious divorce. All the Muslim men and women interviewed for this study who were legally married also obtained a civil divorce. However, those who also sought an Islamic divorce experienced this process as more psychologically meaningful, giving them closure and allowing them to 'feel' divorced. In contrast, the legal divorce was 'just the filing of the paperwork.' These individuals did not see themselves as having chosen Islamic divorce 'over' state divorce, but rather as utilizing the state system to formalize their arrangement (and secure access to formal enforcement mechanisms). As one participant put it, 'The common law allowed me to feel practically and cognitively divorced – the Islamic process allowed me to feel spiritually divorced.'

Many participants described a strong attachment to their right to access formal legal institutions, but a parallel commitment to identify as Muslim by doing what is expected – securing religious sanction for divorce – by their family and community. They do not see this choice as diminishing their identification as Canadian (or American) citizens. This finding attacks the assumption – made by some media at the time of the 2003–05 Ontario Sharia debate, and again in the firestorm ignited by a speech given by the Archbishop of Canterbury in 2007, arguing that British Muslims should be free to use their private ordering systems (Williams 2008) – that by using Islamic divorce North American Muslims are somehow being 'disloyal' citizens (Harkipal Singh 2003; Harris 2003; British Broadcasting Corporation 2008).

The Legal Effect of Islamically Based Agreements
about Divorce Consequences

Many imams restrict their role in marital dissolution to simply agreeing to (or refusing) divorce. Some continue to work with the parties regarding the further consequences of divorce, for example financial arrangements, child custody, and the division of property and other assets. In many instances, the parties want these agreements to reflect Islamic principles; for example the payment of the mahr but no further alimony (or perhaps set-off of the mahr against any other financial agreement), child support payable by the father, and property division reflecting prior ownership rather than blended property. Sometimes the agreement will be a blend of Islamic and common law principles, for example, where support is paid by either spouse to the other on a voluntary basis, or where property is treated as blended, and then divided.

There is some potential for these agreements to have legal effect. The first – given great play in the Ontario Sharia debate but no longer available since the 2006 amendments – was under the 1991 Ontario Arbitration Act. Before 2006, this statute recognized and enforced the outcomes of any arbitration according to any form of law, including religious law. It is noteworthy, however, that no applications had ever been brought under the act to either enforce or appeal the decisions of Muslim arbitrators, in contrast, for example, with applications to appeal decisions of the Jewish Beth Din (Colman 2010). This difference may be explained by the fact that participants in my study told me consistently that they saw no reason to ask a Canadian court to review an outcome which they considered to be the word of God (Gaudreault-DesBiens 2005, 19).

At the time of the Ontario Sharia debate, there was a widespread misapprehension – probably based on the claims of one Muslim advocacy group (the Darul Qada) which described itself as offering 'Muslim arbitration tribunals' – that the imams were conducting formal 'court-like' arbitrations, including, for example, an oral hearing process, the presentation of evidence, and a written decision. In the vast majority of cases, the process followed bears little or no resemblance to a formal arbitration. The imam talks with one or sometimes both spouses in either his office or their home, and sometimes their family members. There is no formal hearing or evidence presented, no legal representation of the parties, only rarely a written agreement to arbitrate, and no record of the proceedings (aside from the outcome, in a few cases).

Ultimately the imam either approves, or refuses to grant, a divorce. The closest that Islamic divorce as it is presently conducted in North America comes to a formalized arbitration model is where a panel of imams will consult with one another over whether to approve a divorce. The vast majority of Islamic divorces continue to be handled by individual imams. It is possible, but unknown, whether these processes could have been deemed 'family arbitrations' under the act before the 2006 amendments, since no application was ever brought regarding a Muslim arbitration.

The second means of giving legal effect to the consequences of Islamic divorce would be if a written contract were made following a voluntary agreement between the parties, and signed by both. This agreement could be enforced as a private contract in the same way as any other mediation agreement. It would be unenforceable if there were any evidence of pressure or coercion, in common with other mediation agreements (Coben and Thompson 2006, 81–3). In other words, an agreement for, for example, child support or property distribution determined by an imam and committed to writing without the consent of both spouses would be clearly unenforceable as a private contract.

The possibility that an agreement regarding the consequences of Islamic divorce might be recognizable under the Ontario Arbitration Act was closed by amendments that removed the provision recognizing religious arbitration (Ontario 2006). Other North American jurisdictions continue to allow for religious arbitration under their arbitration statues (e.g., Revised Statutes of British Columbia, Commercial Arbitration Act 1996 c. 55 s23; New York Civil Practice Law and Rules Law s.7501; Statutes of Nova Scotia Commercial Arbitration Act, 1999, c. 5). The Ontario amendments ended the relationship between the courts and the Beit Din (Jimenez 2005) and made no difference at all to Muslim 'arbitrations' which had never used the Act for either appeals or enforcement and continue to operate as private, informal processes. It is still possible that an agreement made regarding the consequences of Islamic divorce with an imam could be enforced as a private contract (if it is written up), but any such application would be subject to the strict requirement of voluntariness that is imposed on all mediated agreements.

Instead, I came across a number of instances where agreements over the consequences of divorce – worked out with an imam or sometimes, a Muslim lawyer – reflected Islamic principles, or some combination of Islamic and common law principles. Such agreements are then submitted to the court in a divorce application to be formalized as consent orders. This practice is entirely unaffected by the amendments to the Arbitration Act (these are not 'arbitrations' under the act but 'agreements' by consent). The court will generally approve such an application, provided that it is not framed as a religious contract (*Marriage of Dajani* 1988; *Kaddoura* v. *Hammoud* 1998) (most imams are aware of this and take care to draft these agreements without religious language) and does not contradict or substantially diminish common law principles (e.g., the requirement of child support). On the face of it, this practice is no different from the approval of consent orders negotiated without reference to faith-based principles. The most significant differences between Islamic law and common law relate to spousal support and how property is divided between the spouses, and the family courts frequently approve consent orders (particularly for short marriages) that depart from strict legal principles in these respects.

Who Chooses Islamic Divorce?

There is a wide range of motivations for seeking an Islamic divorce as well as a civil divorce. Most of the participants understand it to be a Sharia compliant divorce, which releases them from the marriage contract or nikah they made with their spouse but also with God. Muslims understand Sharia as the 'path' of righteous living for each individual, and believe that this is revealed in the Qur'an, the Sunnah, and hadīth. The participants express many different understandings and interests in the application of Sharia to their own divorce. Few distinguish between Sharia (the immutable word of God revealed to the Prophet Muhammad) and principles of Islamic law (a constantly evolving system developed by jurists from the scared texts). Participants have a range of knowledge about the rules of Islamic family law, and many hold beliefs that have no basis in the law but rather reflect cultural beliefs. A prime example of this is the sense among some communities that divorce is intolerable, which is clearly at odds with the teaching of the Qur'an and other texts, as well as the Islamic jurisprudence (see above).

Those participants who are more traditionally religious want to follow what they understand as Sharia in as many aspects of their life as possible. These individuals are often concerned with the detail of following what they believe to be the correct procedure – for example, the correct pronouncement of talaq, or conforming with the *iddath* (the requirement that a divorced wife remain for three months in her husband's house to ensure that she is not pregnant). Those whose lifestyle is relatively secular (e.g., they do not attend prayers, and would celebrate Islamic festivals as a cultural tradition, rather than as a religious obligation) are drawn to the rules and traditions of their faith only when they find themselves facing a personal crisis, such as divorce. Their needs are often met by a more perfunctory procedure, for example, simply stating talaq at the end of a civil court hearing, or obtaining a paper from the imam stating that they are divorced that they can show to their family.

Four different types of motivation emerge from the data. For many participants, more than one of these is relevant to their desire to obtain a religious divorce. The resulting picture is complex and multilayered.

Religious Obligation

As one might expect, some participants described their reason for seeking an Islamic divorce in terms of religious duty. This motivation is expressed as a clear and unavoidable obligation, rather than as a weighing of alternatives. As one participant expressed it, 'It is not a matter of choice.' For a Muslim who understands Sharia to determine every choice they must make, the application of Islamic principles to the ending of their marriage is 'obvious': 'Everything I do is according to what God tells us in the Qur'an. It was common sense for me to go to the imam and I could not imagine any other way.'

Female participants who are motivated by a strong religious faith often go to great lengths to obtain a religious sanction for divorce, spending many months seeking religious opinions, returning over and over to the same imam, or going between different imams (the phenomenon of 'imam shopping') in order to obtain a 'blessing' for their decision. One female participant expressed this need as follows:

It [Islamic divorce] settles them that they closed all the gaps in their faith, they have done everything that they could do, and they have something from an imam or religious scholar that says that they have done everything they could have done and they are free and clear.

There is a focus on meeting one's obligations, rather than seeking and obtaining one's entitlements. These narratives understand 'rights' as something more than access to legally protected entitlements in the style of the common law model (e.g., support, asset distribution, child support) – but rather the conscious taking and execution of one's responsibilities as a Muslim and as a good human being. Many women who have encountered multiple obstacles to obtaining religious divorce nonetheless continue to describe Islamic divorce as their 'right' because it enables them to fulfil their responsibilities fairly and with dignity and fairly. The fulfillment of obligations in accordance with Sharia is considered more important and worthwhile than accepting the entitlements offered by the common law system, regardless of the practical or material consequences of that choice. These participants frequently equate fairness (understood as following through on commitments to Islamic principles in marriage made at the time of the nikah) with obligation, and elevate obligation above entitlement. For example:

> [Muslims] accept God's standard of fairness as above any biased human standard of fairness.

> Even if the law in Canada gives me more – like rights of women – I prefer always to go to the Sharia … I do not want to sacrifice my afterlife, for something small in this life … I will sacrifice things in this world, in order to be rewarded afterwards.

This perspective sees law as not simply about entitlement and enforcement of rights, but focused on personal responsibility for the moral order of one's life. This is not a matter of legal compulsion, but a personal matter between the individual and God (Quaraishi 2008, 63).

An Islamic Identity

For many other participants, Islam represents a tradition of social and community living rather than a more conventionally organized religious duty. One imam evocatively described this group as:

> The 'in-between people,' who are proud of their identity as Muslims and [want] to do this appropriately and Islamically.

A religious scholar expressed this as follows:

> To retain that [Islamic] identity, it is often necessary to … accept the traditions, because of the need to be part of that identity space … many Muslims reject the religious commitment but retain the cultural commitments.

It would be misleading, however, to assume that these Muslims are 'merely' cultural in their commitment or entirely secular in their life-style. For many, it was important to describe their spirituality, a sense of a personal and private relationship with God. Islam is focused on a personal relationship with God, and even Muslims who appear rela-tively secular in their lifestyle still feel a connection to a faith tradition. One female participant described herself as 'not outwardly religious, but my spiritual side is very important to me.' Another woman partici-pant offered this eloquent explanation:

> Religion is just a set of rules and regulation and practices. It can lead to spiritual enlightenment but not necessarily – in many cases it is an inhibi-tor. Spirituality is a person's relationship to the creative force and a per-son's connection to the whole universe. I think that God is more concerned about that relationship and doesn't give two cents about how you pray and what you call him.

The imams recognize that many of those who come to them for di-vorce do not practice Islam in a traditionally observant fashion. Their understanding is that these individuals are looking for affirmation or an absolution that they have followed the 'right' course Islamically. For example:

> [When there are] life altering things people choose to do Islamically.

> [People are seeking] ... an affirmation that they don't need to feel guilty.

> Even if they are secular [Muslims], they don't want to mess with sensitive family issues ... they want to do it right.

Finding Closure

An important aspect of what motivates all Muslims – whether tradi-tionally observant or more secular – in seeking Islamic divorce is a need for closure. Closure enables the individual to accept their new, unmar-ried status and to move on with their life. One imam described this as a desire for 'spiritual peace [which] is universal ... every human being is looking to satisfy their conscience.' This comment recognizes the spiri-tual needs described by some participants above. Again, this conscience takes many different forms – for some it may be closely connected to a sense of religious duty; for others, it is a psychological need for an appropriate ritual of closure.

A critical dimension of closure for Muslim women is the possibility of remarriage. They need a religious divorce in order to be free to remarry, or even to consider other relationships. This sense of constraint also affects women who are not observant – as one woman told me, 'I had coffee with a man and it felt wrong!' Otherwise, they would still be married in the eyes of God and would feel unable able to move on to either the possibility or the reality of new relationships. The commitment not to engage in another relationship until properly released is a faith-based belief and not a legal one: this perspective was shared by women who are married by nikah only.

Closure was not only an issue for the storyteller him or herself. Some female participants expressed a concern that without a religious divorce, their spouse would continue to behave as if they were still married; sometimes this meant continuing to treat their wives as their 'property.' Otherwise, as one woman expressed it, 'In his mind, I would still be his wife.'

Some participants talked about an Islamic divorce as completing the circle where they had begun with an Islamic contract of marriage. This contract could only be undone if her conscience and her community was satisfied that she was released from her commitment in the eyes of God. As one woman put it:

> If you want to be married you have to use the nikah. If you want to be divorced you have to get your talaq from your husband or the imam, or else you are still married – or else if you were to remarry that would be *haram* because you would still be married ... [Y]ou cannot be married without a nikah – you cannot be unmarried without having a talaq.

In approximately one in five cases in the sample, a participant was unable to obtain an Islamic divorce for a variety of reasons (see the discussion below), and instead had to be content with a civil decree of divorce only. Some of these individuals continued to feel and express a lack of closure, because they did not secure religious permission for ending their marriage. Others were satisfied by the advice given by some imams that a civil divorce with the consent of the husband was the equivalent of a religious divorce (European Council on Fatwa and Research 2008).

Practical Considerations

A final group of reasons offered by participants (also suggested by imams) to explain the desire for Islamic divorce are wholly practical in nature. While these factors are given less play by participants than those already described, they are raised quite consistently. Those mentioned most often are timing and costs. In Islam there is no waiting period before an application can be made for divorce, compared with the common law, where most jurisdictions require a period of physical separation, usually six months to one year, before a petition for divorce can be brought. There are lower costs associated with obtaining a religious divorce (the services of the imam are free in virtually all cases) followed (or preceded) by filing for uncontested civil divorce, which can be managed without the assistance of a lawyer. Some participants said that a primary factor in seeking an Islamic divorce facilitated by an imam or other third party was to reduce the costs of hiring separate lawyers and fighting a protracted legal battle.

Islamic Divorce in Practice

The Participants

Because the structure of Islamic family law affords the husband a unilateral right to divorce, but requires the wife to obtain permission from her husband, or a third party, the majority of the personal narratives in my study describe the efforts made by women to obtain Islamic divorce. The imams are in agreement that most commonly they are contacted first by the wife alone seeking their advice and assistance. The sample also includes cases where husband and wife approach the imam together, and some cases where the husband tried to obtain approval from an imam but his wife was not interested in participating.

Not everyone who seeks a religious divorce obtains one, which points to the inconsistency of the practice of the imams and explains the phenomenon of 'imam shopping.' In approximately one in eight cases, the participant was unable to obtain a religious divorce despite their efforts. The most common reason for this was that the other spouse – either the husband or wife – would not cooperate in the process of talking with the imam and instead chose an exclusively legal route to divorce. For women, this usually meant that in the absence of their husbands no imam would agree to give permission for divorce. Approximately one in ten marriages were ended by divorce in a Muslim country in an Islamic court. In less than 10 per cent of cases, individuals were not interested in an Islamic divorce at all, either because this was unimportant to them or because they felt that an Islamic divorce would disadvantage them (note that this number is probably artificially low because the study solicited participation in relation to religious divorce). Finally, in a few cases – approximately 10 per cent of the sample – the spouses were reconciled (this percentage is also artificially low for the same reason).

In approximately 15 per cent of cases in which religious divorce was sought, no third party was involved at all and instead the participants (sometimes with the assistance of their families) completed their divorce themselves by agreement. In these instances the husband simply stated 'talaq' ('I divorce you') to his wife, thereby satisfying the requirements of Islamic law. This approach requires cooperation between husband and wife, and a sound knowledge of Islamic law. In all other cases in which religious divorce was obtained and /or sought, a facilitator was used.

The Facilitators

The facilitators of Islamic divorce in North America are almost always imams, or occasionally, a religious scholar or self-styled arbitrator. Even more infrequently, participants apply to a panel of imams and follow a more formal paper process. Typically, the imam offers formal advice, but also establishes a place for the spouses to speak with one another, facilitates the dialogue, and helps the parties to agree on an outcome. The imam's role falls somewhere between an arbitrator – who gives an opinion (oral only in most cases) on whether divorce is permissible, Islamically – and a mediator – who tries to find an outcomes that both parties can accept.

The extent of the imams' involvement varies. Some who encounter resistance on the part of one or other spouse will advise them to go to a family lawyer and terminate their part in the process. Others clearly spend more time and energy trying to work through conflicts with the couple and trying to achieve either reconciliation, or an agreement to accept divorce. At this stage there are further differences in procedure. Some imams will 'sign off' once permission for religious divorce has been agreed on, without attempting to fashion any agreement regarding child support, payment of the mahr, and so on. Others go much further and attempt to draw up a detailed understanding regarding support, children, property, and other issues consequent on divorce. This agreement can then be submitted to a court in an application for uncontested divorce.

Narratives of Divorce

Four distinctive narratives are representative of the principal storylines and experiences I have heard from both men and women who have sought religious divorce.

1 The 'Dialogue Model'

Closest to the spirit of the Qur'anic text, some divorces take place as a result of the husband and wife working together – perhaps with a counsellor, more often with an imam, and occasionally simply with each other – to come up with an outcome that is consistent with their Islamic values and practical for their family (*Qur'an Translated*, verses 2:226–32, 65:1–7). Approximately a quarter of the narratives in my database describe such an approach.

Where divorce is agreed mutually via dialogue, the most common presentation is as talaq. Despite the fact that this is formally the unilateral right of the husband, in these cases the wife agrees and accepts the divorce, and talaq is used as the simplest method of ending the marriage. In contrast, khula ushers in potential disputes over the circumstances in which the wife may still keep her mahr (Spectorsky 1993, 51–2), avoided if talaq is used. It appears to be less shameful for the divorce to take place using talaq than by khula, because khula represents the rejection of the husband by the wife. A number of imams commented that they might persuade a husband reluctant to agree to divorce that it would look better if he accepted that the marriage was over and use talaq, rather than force his wife to ask for khula.

2 The Wife as the Subject of Talaq

Some of the most painful stories in the sample are of an entirely unexpected talaq. The wife is taken by surprise to be pronounced as 'divorced' by her husband, with or without the legitimation of an imam. These cases represent just 7 percent of the database (and half of them are descriptions of a unilateral talaq processed in an overseas court). Based on what I have been told by imams, social and community workers, and women participants, this is almost certainly a significant under-estimation of how often Muslim women in North America are dispatched by their husbands in this way, and with the muted or sometimes active support of an imam. One would not expect many men who had acted in this way to come forward voluntarily for an interview. Their wives may also feel that their story of rejection is too personal to share.

Many North American imams told me that they feel very uncomfortable with talaq as a unilateral approach. Many speak of trying to slow the process down, to persuade the husband to take some more time to consider this decision and its consequences. One went so far as to say 'Islam hates the talaq. We try to prevent the talaq.' A small number told me that talaq was no longer available to Muslim men in North America because they had abused this privilege. Most imams would not go this far – a more typical comment is 'If he is insisting on it, we have no choice' – but the majority of those interviewed told me that they try to discourage unilateral talaq.

3 The Wife Seeking Khula/Faskh

Approximately 35 per cent of the stories in the database describe attempts – both successful and unsuccessful – to obtain a divorce initiated by the wife. Common causes of conflict are second wives or adulterous relationships; differing orientations to religious practice; mismatched expectations about gender roles, especially in relation to outside work and education; and domestic violence. There are a variety of practices among the imams in relation to requiring husbands to pay the mahr in these circumstances.

The line between khula (where the wife's request for divorce is accepted by her husband, and she usually forfeits the mahr in exchange for her release) and faskh (where a judicial authority – a role played by the imams in North America, not all of whom have extensive knowledge of Islamic law – substitutes its own permission for that of a recalcitrant husband) is unclear. Some imams describe their granting of permission to a woman in the absence of her husband's permission as khula, where it may be more accurately described as faskh. As well, the practice regarding whether or not a woman retains her right to mahr seems to be dependent on how egregious the imam considers the husband's behaviour to be, and since this is a subjective judgment there is little consistency. Because in practice there is little to distinguish them, I include cases described as both khula and faskh in this section.

Some imams are more comfortable than others substituting their own judgment for that of an errant or even violent husband. Some imams will not give divorce under any circumstances without the permission of the husband. These imams are often very concerned about backlash from men in their community if they appear to be overly 'liberal' in granting divorce against the wishes of the husband. This fear is most apparent in communities with more conservative attitudes towards divorce.

Those imams who will give women divorce in the absence of their husbands – the majority of those I interviewed – regard this as an important means of addressing what would otherwise be an unjust situation, contrary to the values of Islam. One told me, '[Our purpose] is to prevent the suffering of women'; and another said, 'Sharia would not allow this type of suffering.' Some imams are extremely flexible in relation to the circumstances under which they will allow divorce for women who come without their husbands. One told me, 'In practice, the concept of khula is wide enough to accommodate all kinds of reasons.' Others are more constrained in their granting of a sanction without the participation of both spouses.

In practice, the application of the Islamic law on this matter is highly susceptible to the third party's views on women's rights. There is the potential for some pressure to be placed on the husband to grant permission for divorce where conditions appear appropriate, and in practice the claim of the wife will likely have greater force where, in practical terms, the marriage is already over (e.g., the husband has left and/or stopped supporting the family). Most imams who are approached by women alone adopt a routine approach to attempting to contact the women's husband before agreeing to divorce; for example, three attempts, attempts over a stipulated period such as six months to one year. If there is no response from the husband, they will proceed with the divorce.

The significance attached by an imam to allegations of domestic violence is also extremely inconsistent and raises many concerns about safety and fairness. Many do insist that divorce is always permissible where a man has been physically violent towards his wife, although they apply many different standards of what 'acceptable' abuse might be – for example, relatively few appear to recognize emotional abuse. Other imams clearly minimize domestic abuse and in addition sometimes discourage women from seeking help from outside authorities (who may be presented as destroying marriage with un-Islamic notions, rather than offering safety and security). One imam told me,

> Domestic violence depends on [its] severity. If the husband is threatening her life, they must be separated ...The Qur'an teaches a system of discipline but not to leave any mark on a woman.

Another imam commenting on a particular case told me, 'He raised his hand – she opened her mouth – maybe she deserved it.' Some women describe imams who are unsympathetic towards their descriptions of domestic violence as telling them to go home and 'try again,' or respond with expressions such as 'I've heard worse.' The phenomenon of 'imam shopping' described by a number of female participants illustrates the reality of this dilemma for abused women seeking religious divorce. There is usually at least one imam in each community who is widely known to be more sympathetic towards women in such desperate situations, and the women have generally identified who is the 'go-to' imam in such situations (Magid 2007, 187).

4 Failure to Obtain a Religious Divorce

Not everyone who seeks a religious divorce will obtain one. Approximately 20 per cent of those who sought a religious sanction did not receive one to their satisfaction. The most common reason given by the participants to explain this was a lack of cooperation by the other spouse who was unwilling to go to an imam or to resolve the issues Islamically. For some female participants, their husband had already left and was uncontactable (e.g., he had abandoned the family or remarried Islamically). Most frequently the other spouse simply refused to participate in a process with the imam, instead going directly to court (this choice most frequently exercised by women), or simply avoided discussion altogether (the avoider was most commonly the man, for whom permission is of lesser practical consequence because he can remarry Islamically without a religious divorce).

For female participants who cannot obtain cooperation from their husbands, failure to obtain a religious divorce is often manifest as their failure to find an imam who will agree to grant them a divorce without the permission of their husband. From the perspective of women – especially those who have engaged in extensive 'imam shopping,' without success – this is due to the unwillingness of the imams to afford them their rights to divorce where their husband unreasonably withholds his consent. Some imams agree with this analysis and are critical of their colleagues who refuse to sanction religious divorce. One arbitrator expressed this feeling as follows:

> Imams hide under the mask that it is not right to destroy the family – but really the man is already destroying the family – the imam does not want to deal with it, and he makes the woman continue to live in these situations.

Conclusions

Islamic divorce is a system of private ordering with a secure place in the hearts and minds of a significant number of North American Muslims. Simply rejecting the practice of Islamic marriage and divorce is not an option – the challenge is how to establish proper standards of fairness, consistency, and responsiveness to the reality of marital conflict and the rising rate of divorce. Many imams' offices feel like crisis centres, and often feel chaotic, with many more people looking for support and advice than available resources can handle. If mosques and Muslim community centres are to continue, as seems inevitable, to play a critical role in marriage and divorce processes, they need both more, and more professional, resources.

Deepening concern in the North American Muslim communities over the rising level of divorce is reflected in a number of recent initiatives including the expansion of pre-marital counseling programs, programs such as the Healthy Marriage Initiative (Muslim Matters 2008), and projects addressing domestic violence such as the Michigan Peaceful Families Proclamation (Siblani 2007). However, attention also needs to be paid to the enhancement of religious divorce processes to address current deficiencies. These include a striking inconsistency in the practice of the imams in facilitating divorce, especially for women; a tendency for imams to reflect the cultural values of their particular communities, which in some instances are extremely intolerant of divorce and stigmatize divorced women; and evidence of the minimizing of the complexity, dangers, and impact of domestic violence by some imams and communities, including discouraging accessing outside authorities. Efforts to systematize the process of awarding divorce are seen in the nascent development of regional panels of imams following stated procedural rules, although questions of qualification and legitimacy remain (Bano 2007). In Toronto, two colleges have recently established training for imams that includes not only religious instruction but also counselling, managing marriage and divorce processes, and family therapy.

An emergent Sharia for Islam in North America, reflected in religious divorce processes and outcomes, must take account of the conditions and the complexities of a multicultural, predominantly non-Muslim society. Muslim diasporas – a constant feature of Islamic history, beginning with the journey from Mecca to Medina in 622 CE – mean that the practice of Sharia has needed to adapt continuously in response to new contexts and conditions. A distinctive and vibrant North American Muslim identity is starting to develop. This is no single identity but a series of interconnected identities, reflecting the extraordinary diversity of the Muslim community in North America, and inclusive of both religious and secular Muslims. The community faces the challenge of both broader societal and generational change which raises questions about, for example, the role of the extended family in marriage and divorce; the role of women within a marriage partnership, including rights to education and work; the adequacy of pre-marital education and a boilerplate nikah which may reflect outdated values (for example the asymmetry in the right to divorce between husband and wife); and the lack of training for imams, who are still predominantly from overseas and often poorly acquainted with North American culture.

The response of policy makers to the practice of Islamic divorce will influence public opinion and set a benchmark for state accommodation and tolerance of religious practices. Internal reforms and responsive policy making are inextricably related – many participants told me that their sense of growing hostility and fear towards Muslims since 9/11 on the part of both the general public and the state has affected them deeply and pulled them towards their Muslim identity, which they now feel they need to protect and assert. This response appears to be true for both 'religious' and 'secular' Muslims, and the result – a more isolated and alienated community – is the opposite of what multiculturalism intends. The way in which North American policy makers chose to handle the relationship between private Islamic dispute resolution and public systems of justice will be very significant in setting a tone for future relations between Muslims and non-Muslims in North America.

REFERENCES

Abu-Ras, W. 2003. 'Barriers to Services for Battered Arab Immigrant Women in a Detroit Suburb.' *Social Work Research and Evaluation* 3(4): 49–66.

An-Naim, Abdullah A., ed. 2002. *Islamic Family Law·in a Changing World: A Global Resource Book*. London: Zed Books.

Bano, Samia. 2007. 'Islamic Family Arbitration Justice and Human Rights in Britain.' *Journal of Law, Social Justice and Global Development*, Special Issue 1 (Dec.). Accessed 22 Jan. 2011. http://www.go.warwick.ac.uk/elj/lgd/2007_1/bano.

Ba-Yunus, Ilyas. 1999. 'Divorce.' *Pakistan Link* (Sept.): 42.

– 2007. 'How do Muslims in North America Divorce?' In M. Akhtar, ed., *Muslim Family in a Dilemma*. Lanham, Maryland: University Press of America.

British Broadcasting Corporation. 2008. 'Archbishop Sparks Sharia Law Row.' Feb. Accessed 30 Oct. 2010. http://news.bbc.co.uk/1/hi/uk_politics/723335.stm.

British Columbia. 1996. Revised Statutes of British Colombia, Commercial Arbitration Act c.55 s.23.

Canada, Government of. National Vital Statistics Reports. 2006. 'Marriages and Divorces.' *National Vital Statistics Reports* 54(20). Accessed 22 Jan. 2011. http://www.cdc.gov/nchs/data/nvsr/nvsr54/nvsr54_20.pdf.

Canadian Institute of Policy Studies. 2008. *The Canadian Muslim Profile Survey*. Accessed 24 Dec. 2010. http://www.c-ips.ca/Projects.html.

Coben, J., and P. Thompson. 2006. 'Disputing Irony: A Systematic Look at Litigation about Mediation.' *Harvard Negotiation Law Review* 11(43): 51–5.

Colman, Yechiel. 2010. 'Ensuring Enforceability of Beis Din's Judgments.' Accessed 30 Oct. 2010. http://www.jlaw.com/Articles/beisdin3.html.

Emon, Anver M. 2004. 'Natural Law and Natural Rights in Islamic Law.' *Journal of Law and Religion* 20(2): 351–95.

Eposito John L., and Natana J. DeLong-Bas. 2001. *Women in Muslim Family Law*. Syracuse: Syracuse University Press.

European Council for Fatwa and Research. 2008. Fatwa (17) Resolution 3/5, 'Ruling on a Divorce Issued by a Non-Muslim Judge.' In *Resolutions and Fatwas*, Second Collection. Translated by Shakir Nasif al-Ubaydi and Anas Osama Altikriti. Ed. by Osama Altikriti and Mohammed Adam Howard. Accessed 30 Oct. 2010. http://www.e-cfr.org/en/index.php?ArticleID=285.

Fournier, Pascale. 2010. *Islamic Marriage in Western Courts: Lost in Transplantation*. Farnham: Ashgate.

Gaudreault-DesBiens, Jean-Francois. 2005. 'The Limits of Private Justice? The Problem of State Recognition of Arbitral Awards in Family and Personal Status Disputes in Ontario.' *Perspectives* 16(1): 18–31.

Hadith of Abu-Dawud. 2001. *A Manual of Hadith*. Verse 13:3. Translated by M. Muhammad Ali. Dublin, OH: Ahmadiyya Anjuman Ishat Islam Lahore USA.

Hallaq, W. 2006. *The Origins and Evolution of Islamic Law*. Cambridge: Cambridge University Press.

Harkipal Singh, Sara. 2003. 'Religious Law Undermines Loyalty to Canada.' *Vancouver Sun*, 10 Dec., A23

Harris, Ghammin. 2003. 'Sharia Is Not a Law by Canadian Standards.' *Vancouver Sun*, 15 Dec., A15.

Hosain v. Malik. 1995. 108 Md. App. 284; 671 A.2d 988.

Jimenez, M. 2005. "Decision on Shari'a Sparks Jewish Protest." *The Globe and Mail, 13 Sept.*

Kaddoura v. Hammoud. 1998. 168 D.L.R. (4th) 503.

Macfarlane, Julie. 2007. 'Working towards Restorative Justice in Ethiopia: Integrating Traditional Conflict Resolution Systems with the Formal Legal System.' *Cardoza Journal of Conflict Resolution* 8(2): 487–500.

– 2012. *Islamic Divorce in North America: A Shari'a Path in a Secular Society*. Oxford: Oxford University Press.

Magid, Mohammed. 2007. 'Affecting Change as an Imam.' In Salma Elkahdi Abugidieri and Maha Alkhateeb, eds., *Change from Within: Diverse Perspectives on Domestic Violence in Muslim Communities*, pp. 187–202. Great Falls, VA: Peaceful Families Project.

Marriage of Dajani. 1988. 204 Cal. App. 3d 1387; 251 Cal. Rptr. 871.

Mir-Hossein, Z. 1993. *Marriage on Trial: Study of Islamic Family Law*. London: Tauris.

Muslim Matters. 2008. 'MANA Conference: The Healthy Marriage Community.' Accessed 30 Oct. 2010. http://muslimmatters.org/2008/12/02/mana-conference-the-healthy-marriage-community-covenant.

New York State. n.d. New York Civil Practice Law and Rules, Law s.7501.

Nova Scotia. 1999. Statutes of Nova Scotia, Commercial Arbitration Act, c.5.

Ontario. 1991. Ontario Statutes, Arbitration Act 1991. c.17, s.32(1).

– 2006. Ontario Statutes Bill 27, Family Statute Law Amendment Act.

Quaraishi, Asifa. 2008. 'Who Says Sharia Demands the Stoning of Women? A Description of Islamic Law and Constitutionalism.' *Berkeley Journal of Middle Eastern and Islamic Law* 1(1): 163–77.

Qur'an Translated: Message for Humanity. 2005. Translated by Marmaduke Pickthall. Washington, DC: International Committee for the Support of the Final Prophet.

Ramadan, Tariq. 2004. *Western Muslims and the Future of Islam.* Oxford: Oxford University Press.

Siblani, M. Kay. 2007. 'Religious Leaders Join Battle against Domestic Violence.' Arab-American News, 1 Dec. Accessed 30 Oct. 2010. http://www.arabamericannews.com/news/index.php?mod=article&cat=Community&article=387.

Spectorsky, S., trans. 1993. *Marriage and Divorce: Responses of Ibn Hanbal and Ibn Rahwayh* Austin: University of Texas Press.

Syed M. 2004. *The Position of Women in Islam: A Progressive View.* Albany: State University of New York Press.

U.S. Department of State and Bureau of International Programs. 2009. *Being Muslim in America.* Accessed 30 Oct. 2010. http://www.america.gov/publications/books/being-muslim-in-america.html.

Williams, Rowan, Archbishop of Canterbury. 2008. 'Civil and Religious Law in England: A Religious Perspective.' Accessed 30 Oct. 2010. www.archbishopofcanterbury.org/1581.

2 Faith-Based Arbitration or Religious Divorce: What Was the Issue?

CHRISTOPHER CUTTING

Based on my empirical research with faith-based groups in southern Ontario from 2007 to 2009, I argue that in practice the most pressing issue of the 'Sharia debate' for Muslim leaders and adherents in Ontario was not faith-based arbitration, but rather religious divorce.[1] Much of the so-called Sharia debate focused on the plight of vulnerable peoples in the context of faith-based arbitration. The media generally, and Muslim and non-Muslim feminists specifically, expressed concern that Muslim women and children might not receive fair and equitable treatment in the event of a civil dispute (such as a contested will) or of a marriage breakdown (involving disputes over spousal support, child support, custody, or division of family resources) (see Boyd 2004). Much of the public 'Sharia debate' assumed that Muslim community leaders were fully aware of the Arbitration Act and intended to use it to make third-party decisions on behalf of, for example, divorcing Muslim couples in ways that would be detrimental to Muslim women. However, my fieldwork findings suggest two unanticipated results. First, Muslim couples in the process of divorce did not seek out full arbitration agreements on the matter of divorce itself. Rather, the majority of Muslims approaching Muslim leaders for assistance with civil disputes were looking for a religious divorce in addition to a legal divorce.[2] Second, Muslim women constituted the vast majority of those approaching Muslim leaders and other Muslim organizations for assistance in securing a religious divorce. I argue that for these reasons the 2006 policy change enacted by the McGuinty government has made little difference on the ground, and that the most pressing issue impacting Ontarian Muslim women's rights and wellbeing – the granting or withholding of religious divorce – has been ignored.

To consider the disparity between the prevalent discourse and Muslim religious arbitration on the ground, the first part of this chapter reports my findings regarding the practices of Muslims with regard to private ordering of civil disputes within three organizations: the Islamic Institute for Civil Justice, the Darul Iftaa (literally, House of Advisory Counsel or Opinion) of the Canadian Council of Muslim Theologians, and the Islamic Social Services and Resources Association. I briefly mention research on other similar Muslim dispute resolution service providers in Ontario. Based on my fieldwork research findings, I demonstrate that by far the most prevalent practices taking place among Muslim communities in Ontario are Muslim divorce and Muslim mediation. Arbitration is not a common practice.[3] Muslim women are the overwhelming majority of clients seeking these services. These findings challenge the negative representations of Muslim dispute resolution proliferated during the public debate. The second part of the chapter discusses the relevance and impact of this reality for public policy and practice.

My fieldwork research is based on informal semi-structured interviews with thirty Muslims in leadership, lay, and Muslim social work positions in the communities. Two Muslim organizations were kind enough to share brief anonymous case summaries of Muslim divorce/dispute resolution cases. I have received twenty-one such case summaries in total to date. I examined these fieldwork results for common themes and issues that cut across the majority of the interviewees and I construct my argument around representative examples from my fieldwork.

The Limited Demands for Islamic Arbitration vs the Widespread Demands for Religious Divorce

Many Muslims in the Canadian context, and particularly Muslim women, will seek out a religious divorce in addition to a civil divorce. Not all Muslims will do so, either because they may not be observant to that degree or they (or their community) might consider a civil divorce to be Islamic. However, my research suggests that numbers of Muslims do seek out religious divorce and that their communities and religious leaders reinforce the importance of acquiring an Islamic divorce in addition to the civil divorce in order to be considered legitimately divorced within their religious community and before their God. I have found that religious divorces do not typically involve negotiating terms addressed in a civil divorce such as the division of property, support payments, or custody, issues that might be subject to arbitration. However, without a religious divorce many women suggest they will experience social barriers to remarriage within their community, and they may fear that they are committing adultery if they remarry under Canadian law. In extreme cases, ex-husbands will behave as if they are still married, leaving some women feeling oppressed and helpless to fully dissolve a relationship. Therefore, acquiring a religious divorce is of great importance to many Muslim women in the Canadian context (see also Macfarlane, this volume). I conducted research at three organizations that are confronted with Muslim women's requests for aid and guidance in obtaining a religious divorce: The Islamic Institute of Civil Justice, the Darul Iftaa, and the Islamic Social Services and Resources Association.

The Islamic Institute for Civil Justice

Perhaps the most instructive examples of the prevalence of religious divorce over faith-based arbitration are within the practices of the Islamic Institute for Civil Justice (IICJ). It is surprising that although the IICJ is the organization responsible for making the 2003 public announcement of faith-based arbitration as available to Muslim communities, they have never performed, or apparently even intended to ever practise formal religious arbitration. This continues to be the case, even though they understand that it is still available under certain new guidelines outlined in the revised 2006 Ontario Arbitration Act.[4] Fear in the debate likely stemmed from the initial statements of the late Syed Mumtaz Ali, the founder and head of the institute, who pronounced that 'good' Muslims would be obliged to utilize faith-based arbitration (see Van Rhijn 2003; see also Reda in this volume). I was unable to interview him, as he was quite aged at the time of my fieldwork and had withdrawn from public activities. However, a small number of arbitrators and mediators associated with the IICJ now work for an organization called Muslim Mediation Services (MMS). It is from the IICJ/MMS that I received my information through their kind provision of anonymous case summaries and a lengthy in-person interview.

The MMS is the only Ontarian Islamic organization I found to be both aware of the new regulations under the amended Arbitration Act and in a position to adhere to them in order to perform court-enforceable arbitration. The 2006 amendments to the Arbitration Act require several protective measures be taken in the context of a formal arbitration if the resulting arbitral award is to be enforceable.[5] MMS members have the appropriate training the new regulations demand: they keep written records, they are aware of the requirement to provide independent legal advice (ILA), they work within the bounds of Canadian law, and are familiar with the Family Law Act.[6] In addition, this organization is aware of the ambiguity of the new regulations. Although the act now states one must arbitrate exclusively according to Canadian law, the MMS claims that in a sense this sanction only means that they do not 'mention God' in the final report (two IICJ/MMS interview respondents). Therefore, the IICJ/MMS operates on the understanding not only that Islamic law may be practised in the context of mediation and the result be made enforceable in a private contract, but also that Islamic law may be practised in formal arbitration and the arbitral award made enforceable as long as the amendments to the Arbitration Act are followed. One of the central reasons they are able to proceed accordingly in good conscience is because Canadian family law explicitly allows a great deal of flexibility for disputants to come to their own resolution. For example, any separating couple can come to any arrangement of custody, maintenance, or division of resources that they agree on (see Macklin, this volume). There are certain default norms in the event of a disagreement, but these can be contracted out within the context of the Family Law Act.[7] However, although the MMS is in a position to understand and effectively use the revised Arbitration Act in this way, they have never done so.

As part of my research with the IICJ, I was provided anonymous case summaries of all formal cases handled by the IICJ and MMS that they completed from their inception in 1999 up to and including 2008. There have only been sixteen completed cases, with an additional six cases initiated in 2008 that were not complete at the time of my research. The vast majority of cases concern the granting of religious divorces. There is also one business dispute, one customer dispute with a car repair shop, and one employer's dispute with an ex-employee regarding final wages. None of the divorce cases address significant issues that can typically be enforced or appealed by a secular court such as custody, support payments, or division of family property. The divorce case summaries only state that a religious divorce was granted to the applicants, all of whom are women, and they either order the husband to pay the *mahr* (Islamic dowry) or the wife to repay her mahr. In some cases the husband is ordered to share the costs of the religious court and incidental expenses. The issues of custody, maintenance, and division of assets are not matters addressed in these decisions, either because they have been decided already by the parties themselves or by the courts. In all cases a civil divorce was already obtained, or was in the process of being obtained. Only one case addressed financial issues regarding marriage breakdown, and it consisted of mediation leading to the drawing up of a separation agreement. In this case the wife received custody of the children, and the husband agreed to support the children as he was able; the amount was not specified, presumably because he did not have regular work at the time of the agreement. Perhaps, given this context, the wife retained the right to amend the contract to include a specific amount in the future.

The IICJ/MMS's comprehensive record of cases reflects no cause for alarm, in contrast to the moral panic expressed in the media during the 'Sharia debate.' In fact, while this organization calls what it does 'arbitration,' most of what it does, especially regarding divorce, has nothing to do with agreements enforceable in Ontario courts. Specifically, the Ontario courts do not enforce or appeal religious divorce. It is conceivable the courts might enforce the payment of the mahr under contract law, but in most cases this amount was a few hundred dollars, with no case of more than a lump sum payment of $2,000.[8] The separation agreement is the only contract in the MMS file enforceable by an Ontario court, but is enforceable as a contract, not as arbitration. And the contents of the agreement were not decided by a third party, but as the result of mutual agreement facilitated by mediation.

Given their lack of engagement with formal arbitration services, it is ironic that the IICJ was the organization that brought the issue into the media in the first place. Although the IICJ/MMS is the only Muslim organization that was fully aware of the new Arbitration Act regulations and was equipped to perform arbitration that could be enforced by Ontario courts, the organization does not in fact appear to have ever undertaken formal arbitration. Despite the fears expressed following Mumtaz Ali's announcement, neither the MMA nor the IICJ has made a binding third-party decision on any substantial family matter that can be enforced in Ontario courts beyond a few small claims. In addition, they have addressed far fewer cases than many of the other Muslim organizations I document below.

Darul Iftaa of the CCMT

The granting of religious divorces within Muslim communities in Toronto is *the* major civil dispute issue, and the 'freeing' of Muslim women from the oppression of so-called limping marriages has been a central aim of Muslim leaders and organizations generally, and the Darul Iftaa in particular. Islamic law is understood by the majority of Sunni scholars and imams to accord husbands a unilateral right to divorce. This legal understanding is why men seldom approach imams for a religious divorce. A man may pronounce the *talaq* (Islamic term, deriving from Arabic, meaning divorce) three times and the couple may be considered religiously divorced without witnesses or imams involved. However, although most schools of Islamic law allow for wife-initiated divorce, even in these circumstances if the husband does not ultimately grant the talaq because of recalcitrance or simply because he cannot be found or contacted, the couple may not be considered religiously divorced. It is for this reason that the vast majority of Muslims approaching religious leaders for a religious divorce are women, as Islamic law allows for a Muslim judge to grant a religious divorce on the husband's behalf (see Macfarlane, this volume). This unequal access to religious divorce is the result of a patriarchal system of law. However, I argue that Muslim communities generally, and the Darul Iftaa in particular, are attempting to resolve the problems this patriarchal system causes women in a pro-women manner.

The Darul Iftaa has dealt with a far greater number of cases involving civil disputes among Muslims than the IICJ/MMS. The Darul Iftaa is a division of the Toronto-based Canadian Council of Muslim Theologians (http://iftaa.jucanada.org). Even though this division of the CCMT has only been in operation since early 2007, by the summer of 2008 they had received between 100 and 150 cases dealing mainly with granting religious divorces (two Darul Iftaa interview respondents). When I spoke with the Darul Iftaa in the late spring of 2008, they had already received forty-seven cases that year. Although the Darul Iftaa has a well-designed, organized, and maintained website, they are otherwise wary of explicitly advertising their services for fear they would be overwhelmed with new cases. Currently, clients are referred to the Darul Iftaa through imams who are aware of the organization or are dues-paying members. (The CCMT has a membership of more than 100 religious leaders mostly in the Toronto area.) The rationale for creating the Darul Iftaa was overwhelmingly centred on granting religious divorces to women in 'limping marriages.'[9]

Most of the members of the CCMT and the majority of Darul Iftaa's clients are of South Asian background. South Asians make up one-third of the more than 300,000 Toronto-area Muslims, comprising its largest single ethnic group (Beyer 2005). The *muftis* (certified Muslim judges) most active in the Darul Iftaa were trained in the Islamic Family Law system of India for several months. The training consisted of attending to the practices of daily Indian Islamic Family Law court proceedings.[10] These muftis continue to consult their mentors in India on jurispruden- tial questions regarding issues not dealt with previously in the Canadian context.[11] The Darul Iftaa by their own designation claims to adhere to a very orthodox school of Islam (two Darul Iftaa interview respon- dents). However, the support for women in limping marriages has led imams associated with the Darul Iftaa to turn away from its general adherence to an orthodox interpretation of the Hanafi School. Because the allowances for granting a *faskh* or annulment of an Islamic marriage in the Hanafi School are limited, the Darul Iftaa has borrowed heavily from the Maliki School in order gain much increased latitude for free- ing women oppressed by limping religious marriages where the Darul Iftaa regard the Maliki School to be more liberal in a number of ways.

All of the cases brought to the Darul Iftaa to date have been brought by women. They are all marriage annulment cases.[12] There is a wide- spread belief among many Muslims in Toronto that only a qualified Islamic judge can pronounce a religious divorce on behalf of a husband unable, or more often unwilling, to grant a talaq or accept *khula* (a wife- initiated divorce, normally requiring her to return her dowry), and people with this qualification are apparently hard to come by.[13]

The Darul Iftaa generously provided me with five anonymous sam- ple case summaries of the types of cases they have dealt with in the previous eighteen months. They all deal with wives who have been abandoned or legally divorced by their husbands but have not been granted a religiously valid divorce.[14] In four of the five cases the men never appeared before the Darul Iftaa even after being repeatedly sum- moned to defend their case for keeping the religious marriage intact. The wife is asked to bring at least two male witnesses to support her claims that her husband is not fulfilling his religious duties or her reli- gious rights. In cases where a wife was not able to bring the requisite number of witnesses, that the husband does not appear counts against him and the divorce is granted. The religious reasons for granting the divorce recorded are fairly extensive including quotations from the Qur'an and hadīth and a number of jurists, often filling four pages of single-spaced text. The reasons for granting the divorce range from husbands not providing financially for wives because of abandonment, to verbal abuse by husbands, to husbands cheating on their wives, and 'irreconcilable differences' (their translation of *Shiqaaq*).[15]

In some cases the husband appears at initial divorce hearings, often getting into abusive arguments with the Darul Iftaa, and alleging that their wives were coerced by her parents to get the divorce. These are the only cases the Darul Iftaa has had where coercion was suspected as a factor in a woman's approaching the organization. However, in these cases the husbands turned out to be making the accusation in an effort to frustrate the attempts of their wives to get a religious divorce. The Darul Iftaa in each case called the wife suing for divorce numerous times and asked repeatedly, while she was alone and away from her parents, whether she was being coerced to obtain a religious divorce. All wives consistently held that they were not and wanted genuinely to be free to move on with their lives. The husbands very often ultimately cut off all relations with the Darul Iftaa and refuse to appear at any future hearings. All of these women were granted the divorce.

It appears that very few women are refused a faskh from the Darul Iftaa on the ground they could not justify it religiously because the wives had left their marriage partners to have an affair, and often were currently living with their boyfriends, whom they wanted to marry after procuring the religious divorce. The Darul Iftaa muftis expressed shock that these women would openly and without shame come to a known orthodox Islamic organization making such a request while in many cases living with a non-marital partner. It is indeed puzzling why these women came to this particular organization rather than another more liberal imam or Muslim organization. Nevertheless, these refusals again illustrate the unequal treatment of women in Muslim divorce, as men have a unilateral right to divorce independent of any religious authority (see Macfarlane, this volume).

The religious divorce documents clearly state on every page that they are strictly the rulings of a religious authority and not a legal document.[16] The Darul Iftaa informed me that they do not attempt to deal in a formal way with any monetary issues regarding division of assets or support. These elements are simply too contentious, they state, and they have enough contentiousness to deal with from recalcitrant husbands who want to keep their wives within limping marriages. If clients request the judge's opinion about religious norms for custody, support, or division of assets they will give it informally (orally), but they are clear that these do not constitute any formal religious or legal ruling.

The implications of the Darul Iftaa's services for the public concerns raised about faith-based arbitration are striking. Religious divorces have nothing to do with faith-based arbitrations that may be enforced by the state. A religious divorce cannot be appealed or enforced by a secular Canadian court. This distinction means that the most pervasive form of religious oppression within Muslim communities in Ontario pertains to something that secular courts can do nothing about. Although not perfect, however, contrary to stereotypes which depict Islam as patriarchal, numerous Muslim organizations and leaders have spent enormous energy and resources attempting to correct the injustice of 'limping marriages,' and routinely face the abusive treatment of recalcitrant husbands in the process. The granting of religious divorces in Muslim communities of Toronto is the major issue, and the 'freeing' of Muslim women from this oppression has been a central aim of Muslim leaders and organizations generally, and the Darul Iftaa in particular.

Islamic Social Services and Resources Association

The Islamic Social Services and Resources Association (ISSRA) was established in Toronto in 1990.[17] ISSRA sees approximately two new cases regarding family issues per week, and therefore addresses approximately one hundred new cases every year. *Masjids* (mosques) all over Toronto refer their adherents to ISSRA if they feel their needs cannot be met at the local level.[18] ISSRA estimates that approximately 70 per cent of these cases have to do with marriage and divorce issues, and 30 per cent have to do with mediating parent-child relationships. ISSRA also estimates that about 60 per cent of marital issues are reconciled through counselling, while roughly 40 per cent end in divorce (ISSRA interview respondent). Of the people who initially approach ISSRA for assistance, approximately 80 per cent are women. As a result of its advocacy of Muslim women's rights against the sometimes unfair demands of husbands, ISSRA reports that it has gained the reputation of being 'pro women' (two ISSRA interview respondents).

ISSRA has not done and does not do formal arbitration of civil disputes. However, they have mediated between family members on a wide variety of issues, which in many cases has influenced how families have settled divorces in the civil courts regarding issues of maintenance, division of resources, and custody. Once again the most significant issue by far is that of securing religious divorce for women. ISSRA also reports that many men believe it is their right to keep their wives tied to limping marriages, and a number of husbands apparently use this situation against their ex-wives out of bitterness and as a tool of revenge. ISSRA always counsels women that they have the right of religious divorce and has granted a number of these despite husbands' refusals to pronounce talaq or agree to khula.

Before an Islamic divorce is granted, ISSRA requires a civil divorce be procured, and the organization provides a referral list of Muslim lawyers for independent legal advice for the purposes of civil divorce. However, ISSRA often suggests mediating financial issues rather than going to court because the court process is much more expensive, adversarial, and takes a greater emotional toll on couples. Furthermore, according to ISSRA, the mediated arrangements are often very similar to what is awarded in civil courts. ISSRA's preferred approach is for the mediator to ask the wife what she feels she needs with regards to support, and then attempt to negotiate this request with the husband, rather than for the mediator to try to come up with a number on behalf of the couple. ISSRA reports that many women are not interested in an equal division of family assets because either they have not been married for long, the family does not have many resources, or they are only interested in enough support to get on with their lives.

A number of husbands agree to support their wives and children and honour that agreement. A number of other husbands agree to support, but then default on the payments. ISSRA tries to contact these men to encourage them to restart the payments, which is effective in some cases. On many occasions, however, ISSRA's calls are simply not returned. Sadly, in most situations the husband has disappeared either to another country or to an unknown address. ISSRA has noted a general reluctance of women to pursue ex-husbands for support either through ISSRA or the civil courts because they do not want to undergo the emotional difficulty and time-consuming work for what they expect will be very little payoff. ISSRA further notes reluctance among Muslim women to approach the secular system, as many feel it is not Islamic. ISSRA always counsels clients that Canada's justice system shares with Islam its struggle to effect justice, and further advises that the Canadian justice system is in many ways itself Islamic. ISSRA laments that they do not have more power to enforce support payments on women's behalf.

ISSRA's experiences with religious divorce lead to a number of observations. First, even this very organized Muslim body has never practised formal arbitration, or even intended to. Second, outside of arbitration there remains great leeway for faith-based principles to be drawn up in contracts that are then enforceable by Canadian law, such as prenuptial agreements, separation agreements, or wills. ISSRA has mediated many separations and counselled a number of people on wills that are then drawn up in legally enforceable documents. The changes to the Arbitration Act do not change the nature or enforceability of these private contracts. The power of the state may be used to enforce the private religious decisions of citizens who draw up those decisions in legal contracts. Third, there is apparently very little difference between what people agree on in divorce through mediation with ISSRA and the arrangements arrived at in court. ISSRA reports one husband who sought to dispute a separation agreement in court because he felt he could pay less than what ISSRA was asking him to agree to. And finally, religious divorce for women in limping marriages is by far the most prevalent of all the issues ISSRA addresses.

Imams and Muslim Leaders in the Greater Toronto Area Generally

In all of my research to date I have not found a single instance of a formal signed arbitration (faith-based or otherwise) taking place in Muslim communities. However, although no one appears to be arbitrating formally in Muslim communities of Ontario, a number of imams are assisting Muslims through faith-based mediation in the formation of separation agreements, wills, and prenuptial agreements. All of these contracts are enforceable by provincial law. This practice is noted above with ISSRA and in one instance with the IICJ. It is also practised among a number of other leaders and mediators with whom I spoke. For example, one self-described 'moderate' Muslim scholar encourages the forming, through mediation, of separation agreements that appear very equitable in comparison with Canadian default norms of family law. In view of Ontario's Family Law default norms, equitable divisions of family assets are sought and reasonable amounts of child support are recommended. This scholar reasons, based on Sharia, that the Canadian context must be taken into account when sorting these issues out between couples, and he also suggests that the intent of Sharia – which he believes to be equitable, fair, and just – must be translated into the modern Canadian context. In his opinion, older rulings would no longer be just in current Canadian society, where women are not cared for in the same extended-family contexts as they were centuries ago. This scholar highly encourages couples to get a mediated agreement drawn up in a formal separation agreement, precisely because it is then a contract that can be enforced by the state. This agreement is mainly to benefit women, who are most often in need of the enforcing power of the state, usually to make men pay the promised child support.

Another imam from the Toronto area who could be read as more conservative-leaning also appeared to take measures to ensure equity and fairness with regards to women in mediating separation agreements. His calculation of support took into account the lifestyle the wife was accustomed to during marriage. The value of the mahr had to take into account the value of the currency at the time the contract was made relative to its value in Canadian dollars at the time, and then inflation had to be taken into account, so that the true value of the original mahr was preserved. This imam also strongly encouraged the couple to enter the results of the mediation in a separation agreement. Here he sought to make evident his mediation so that its results would not be lost in a later secular court decision. This request raises some concern of coercion. However, in one of the cases the imam shared with me the couple did end up taking the matter to civil court after all, and ironically, after the couple paid the lawyers tens of thousands of dollars, the wife ended up with half the amount of support that she would have received if the couple had agreed to the imam's recommendations.[19]

The majority of leaders I spoke with agreed that a woman is Islamically entitled to child support for as long as she takes care of the children, and that she is at least entitled to the assets she brought to the marriage, any earnings she has made, and any inheritance that she has received. A wife is entitled to support from her husband throughout the marriage, and many also stated if that support is not fully rendered during the marriage it is payable in some form on divorce. Not all agreed that a fifty-fifty division of the family assets was Islamic, but some did, and the vast majority made recommendations for support and division of assets that would likely be interpreted as reasonable and fair in Canadian courts. However, there is no way to know if all imams are as equitable in their mediation of civil matters as those with whom I spoke. What is clear however is that the new protections of the Arbitration Act do not apply to mediations of private contracts, or to the most prevalent issue: religious divorce. For these reasons, I argue the amendments to the Arbitration Act have had little practical impact on the ground, and there remains a great deal of potential for further public policy to address the untouched issues discussed above. I conclude below with such public policy recommendations.

Mediation and Religious Divorce: Discussion and Conclusion

One of the main points I have sought to emphasize in this chapter is the contrast between the issues that were thought to be important in the public 'Sharia debate' regarding faith-based arbitration and the issues that are actually important to Ontario Muslims. Not unreasonably, the public debate imagined that the most important issue had to do with formal arbitration.[20] This assumption meant that much of the debate focused on issues that could be legally decided by a third party in the context of arbitration, such as amounts of spousal support and child support, and division of resources on marital breakdown. But arbitration proper occurs only when two parties in dispute choose a third party to make a binding decision on behalf of both parties. Very few in the Muslim community, leaders or adherents, were or are interested in formal faith-based arbitration as such. The majority of clients seeking Muslim civil dispute resolution services are women in need of a religious divorce. Furthermore, the majority of Muslims who are seeking advice from religious leaders on how to divide resources, establish amounts for child and spousal support, or informally decide custody Islamically in the event of divorce are not interested in subjecting these decisions to formal arbitration. And I found no Muslim leaders or organizations that were anxious to encourage couples to have these issues formally arbitrated, religiously or otherwise. This is not the case because Muslims now imagine faith-based arbitration to be legally forbidden. The demand or desire is simply not there. The most dramatic case in point is that of the IICJ. As I mentioned, the IICJ is the only organization I found that fully understood the nature and requirements of the Arbitration Act. Further, they understand that limited forms of 'faith-based arbitration' are *still allowable and legally enforceable* even under the new amendments to the act as long as certain requirements and guidelines are followed. However, the IICJ has never performed a formal arbitration process, nor have their clients requested or inquired about it. And the IICJ has not attempted to use its knowledge of the Arbitration Act to either market or pressure formal arbitration onto their clients. Rather, the majority of the small number of clients of the IICJ, as is the experience of *all* other Muslim organizations and leaders I have interviewed, are looking for assistance with some form of religious divorce, whether it be talaq, khula, or faskh.

I do not want to suggest here that the amendments to the Arbitration Act were not important. Clearly, there are many positive benefits from the amendments. Because the previous version of the Arbitration Act was intended more for resolving business disputes, the relationship between the Arbitration Act and the Family Law Act had never been clearly established. The amendments define this relationship much more carefully and explicitly. Also, the previous Arbitration Act had far too few protections for vulnerable people built into the arbitration process. The amendments now include several of the recommendations made by the Boyd Commission, as well as a few that were not recommended, such as requiring independent legal advice.[21] The only arguably contentious issue regarding the amendments was the decision to ban the use of any legal system other than Canadian law in arbitrations.[22] If a law other than Canadian law is used in formal arbitration the award will not be enforceable under the Arbitration Act. This amendment has effectively ended the use of 'religious laws' in formal arbitration. However, as the website for the Attorney General's Office points out, religious figures can still act as arbitrators and may still give mediatory advice based on religious laws that may then be entered into enforceable civil contracts (www.attorneygeneral.jus.gov.on.ca/english/family/arbitration/faith-based.asp). Importantly, arbitrators cannot 'force' a decision based on religious law as an arbitrator in the context of a 'formal' arbitration, although they may perform 'advisory' arbitrations that are not binding. In my view the amendments that have been made to the Arbitration Act are valuable and important, and I do not want to detract from this reality. My point here is that *in practice* although this policy change has made potential uses of the Arbitration Act much more just for possible future use, the vast majority of private ordering of civil matters in Muslim communities remains untouched.

Was Moral Panic Really Justified?

Having established the importance of the issue of religious divorce over the issue of formal faith-based arbitration for Ontario Muslims, I turn to the possible importance and impact of these findings. First, the empirical inaccuracies of much of the negative media discourse and portrayals of Muslim civil dispute resolution are noteworthy. Contrary to these representations, I found several Muslim organizations and leaders attempting to accomplish Muslim divorce in a way that was intended, and perceived by clients, to be highly supportive of Muslim women's rights and interests. The vast majority of clients approaching Muslim leaders and organizations regarding civil matters are Muslim women looking for assistance relating to some aspect of Islamic divorce. In the majority of cases I found leaders and organizations undertaking efforts to free women from their religious marriages. That is not to say that there are not issues of inequity and patriarchy to be addressed. Unequal access to religious divorce is the practice of a patriarchal system of law. Therefore, I do not mean to paint an overly positive picture that suggests there are no problems with private ordering of civil disputes in Ontario's Muslim communities. Rather, I seek to challenge and complicate the much starker and overwhelmingly negative portrayals of Muslim dispute resolution that proliferated in the media during the 'Sharia debate.'

Missing the Policy Boat

This leads me to my second point. I am persuaded by my findings that policy-wise the Ontario provincial government has 'missed the boat' for a number of reasons. The positive elements of the amendments to the Arbitration Act notwithstanding, little policy has arisen as a result of the 'Sharia debate' that has helped the vast majority of Muslims currently seeking private dispute resolution in civil matters. Most Muslims engaging with these resolution services are seeking some form of religious divorce. And there are issues of inequity and patriarchy that the amendments to the Arbitration Act do not touch. There are at least two issues to consider here. First, one of the main sources of oppression from which Muslim women suffer is being stuck in a 'limping marriage.' This situation arises because men have a unilateral right to divorce independent of any religious authority, while women do not. Many imams and Muslim organizations are attempting to remedy this by freeing Muslim women from limping marriages.

Second, completely outside of 'formal arbitration' some imams may not be equitable in a number of areas having to do with informal civil dispute resolution. I will give three types of examples. Some imams are not willing to grant a religious divorce where clearly the state would grant a legal divorce.[23] In addition, although my findings suggest that this may be rare, some imams may give informal religious advice to divorcing couples regarding support payments, division of resources, and custody which may not be in accordance with the default norms of Ontario's Family Law Act. Such decisions are not being made in the context of the Arbitration Act, but they are fully enforceable by the state if they are entered into a civil contract such as a separation agreement.

Finally, some imams clearly do not recognize or know how to address domestic abuse. I interviewed several who did take it seriously and immediately advised Muslim women to call the police, but both Julie Macfarlane (in this volume) and I found some Muslim leaders who did not act effectively or appropriately on this issue. Once again, the amendments to the Arbitration Act make virtually no difference on any of these issues.[24]

What Is to Be Done?

What, if anything, can be done policy-wise that might help Muslim women and men seeking assistance from their community regarding religious divorce and other civil disputes? I suggest three proposals. First, I turn to the issue of the granting of the religious divorce. Is there anything the state can do to improve this process? To consider this query I turn to communities of Canadian Jewish women who have recently lobbied the government to change state legislation to require Jewish men to grant a religious divorce once a legal divorce has been granted (Joseph 1994; Kayfetz 1986; Leung 2008). Something similar might be considered for Muslim communities where husbands refuse to give the talaq and imams refuse to grant a religious divorce on behalf of the husband. Also, a formal or informal commission might be set up that could consult with Muslim communities regarding a larger Ontario Muslim consensus on the status of the legal divorce as equivalent to a religious divorce. A number of imams and organizations in Ontario already state that legal divorce in the Canadian context is equivalent to an Islamic divorce religiously. There are international examples for this as well. An umbrella organization of Muslim leaders in New York has declared that legal divorces are valid as Islamic divorces (personal communication, 7–10 November 2009). If this kind of endeavour were successful in Canada, it could resolve the majority of the issues that arise in the context of religious divorce that I have raised in this paper. Finally, the government could assist in community building in the sense of helping Muslim communities to educate their adherents about their rights under Islamic law, including specifically the possibility of recognizing a Canadian civil divorce as equivalent to a religious divorce, which several imams in Ontario do already.[25]

Second is the issue of potentially inequitable recommendations made by Muslim leaders and organizations for resolving civil disputes. The matter of potentially inequitable advice based on particular Muslim interpretations of Islamic law regarding the terms of divorce remains an issue for some Muslim women who might approach Muslim leaders who hold to patriarchal interpretations of Islamic law. Once again, with the assistance of community members willing to participate, the government could facilitate community education regarding the rights of Muslim men and women, and the options for divorce. Although some may think the state should not involve itself in such things, there is precedent. The Liberal McGuinty government has already quietly funded a number of such projects in the Muslim community. For instance, the McGuinty government has given funds to the Canadian Council of Muslim Women to enable the CCMW to commission three such projects. The first project concerns the domestic contract. The CCMW is aware that many practising Muslim women want their marriages to reflect their religion meaningfully, and to that end the CCMW has drawn up a sample Muslim marriage contract that clearly lays out women's Muslim and Canadian rights. The second project will develop educational materials concerning marriage and divorce more generally, especially issues related to foreign marriages and divorces. And the third project aims to create better awareness of arbitration and mediation. The CCMW is also lobbying the government to provide legal aid to people looking for faith-based arbitration. Currently it is not the usual practice of the government to provide legal aid in this context. This amendment appears to be a major shortcoming, for even though the Arbitration Act now requires independent legal advice for arbitrations, the people who will likely need it most – vulnerable peoples with few financial resources – are precisely those who would not be able to afford the lawyers in order to benefit from the protections the new legislation provides. Furthermore, the CCMW has lobbied the government to train 'cultural interpreters' (CCMW interview respondent) who understand better the diverse cultures and religions of peoples accessing the justice system so that they may be more accommodating and understanding of differences, making the secular legal system potentially more accessible and welcoming to wary Muslims. These kinds of projects are excellent precedents, and public policy could distribute them more widely, and market them more effectively in Muslim communities.

Third is the issue of domestic abuse. It is encouraging to find that a modest number of mosques and Muslim organizations are holding their own community education workshops on domestic violence.[26] These gatherings are certainly in the minority, but it is important to note that they are already taking place. Government and Muslim and non-Muslim community organizations and NGOs might be able to assist in organizing and carrying out educational workshops designed to educate Imams and other religious leaders in particular regarding how to deal appropriately with domestic violence in Ontario.

Several voices raised legitimate concerns about the potential for state enforcement of inequitable religious arbitrations in the so-called Sharia debate. The McGuinty government's decision takes important steps in protecting vulnerable peoples in the context of formal arbitration. However, anyone seriously concerned with protecting the rights of vulnerable peoples in private disputes must further address ongoing linkages between private and public domains. The CCMW is attempting to do just that, through continued lobbying of the government and publicly funded awareness-building projects. Meanwhile the vast majority of instant advocates for Muslim women who spoke out during the dramatic media debate have all but forgotten the issue. Understanding and developing the ongoing linkages between the modern Canadian state and the private practice of religion is key to ensuring the protection of the rights of vulnerable peoples. My study of faith-based religious groups in southern Ontario highlights how what is at stake for such people – religious divorce – has been largely ignored by government and public policy.

NOTES

1 This chapter is based on research for my doctoral dissertation at the University of Waterloo between 2007 and 2009. This project was funded by a Canada Graduate Scholarship from the Social Sciences and Humanities Research Council of Canada (SSHRC).
2 For a discussion of the different types of religious divorce relevant to Muslims please see Julie Macfarlane's chapter in this volume.
3 As I document below, this is not simply because faith based arbitration was not available or allowed before or now. My research suggests that it is because there is simply no demand for it among Muslims or Muslim service providers, and most surprisingly, even by those organizations reported in the media to have been pursuing the practice of faith-based arbitration
4 This is not to say they may not pursue this in future. However, currently I base my conclusion on the actual practices of the IICJ combined with what I gathered from my interview with the IICJ all of which is documented in this chapter

5 For example, disputants must have independent legal advice, arbitrators must keep written records of proceedings and must be trained as outlined by the Attorney General's Office of Ontario, and the arbitration must adhere to 'Canadian law' alone (Attorney General 1991).

6 The mediator/arbitrator I spoke to was not a trained lawyer but claimed to possess the appropriate background training required by the revised Ontario Arbitration Act such as acceptable formal course training as an arbitrator/mediator, and training in how to screen for domestic abuse.

7 Although an arbitrator must sign a document stating that he or she did not use any other legal system than Canadian law it may be possible, for example, for an arbitrator to decide a father should have custody because it is judged to be in the best interests of the child, or, for example, to decide a certain division of resources and support is fair and in the best interests of the children based entirely on the arbitrator's judgment of the situation in the context of Canadian law. It is not clear how such a situation would be dealt with as there are few if any relevant test cases that have been brought to the courts to be enforced or overturned. Natasha Bakht notes that 'religious arbitrators can simply conform to the regulations regarding training and record keeping and then perform religious arbitrations that are consistent with Canadian Family Law ... the *Family Law Amendment Act* permits religious arbitrations that conform to Canadian Family Law' (Bakht 2007, 141–2).

8 Although Ontario courts have been reluctant to enforce mahr awards, British Columbia courts have been more open to enforcing them (Bunting and Mokhtari 2009, 241).

9 The phrase 'limping marriages' appears to have become widely used in Europe. It refers to couples who have been granted a civil divorce but have not been granted a religious divorce. Many women feel that they are unable to remarry within their religious community without being granted a religious divorce in addition to a secular civil divorce (Kramer 2005).

10 For a discussion of the issues relating to British colonial influence on the formation of Anglo-Muhammedan law, please see Anver Emon's chapter, this volume.

11 For example, finding religious legal reasons for granting a *faskh* (an Islamic marriage annulment) to a woman requesting a divorce because her husband was not ultimately granted immigrant status to come to Canada, and she does not want to move to South Asia because she is from Canada (two Darul Iftaa interview respondents).

12 Julie Macfarlane has made the important point that many so-called khulas are in fact faskhs, or marriage annulments. I have found that many imams have worked hard to encourage Muslim men to grant the talaq as well.

13 Although I have found a number of organizations and individual imams who do grant religious divorces, the Darul Iftaa is by far the most organized and thorough, and handles the greatest number of cases specifically to do with granting faskh. The charge for the Darul Iftaa's services is $200 for administrative costs. However, if the applicant cannot afford the fee she is not required to pay, although most are able to.

14 To the best of my knowledge these cases were randomly selected, although one case appears to have been selected intentionally because of its exceptional nature.

15 According to the representatives of the Darul Iftaa I spoke to, *Shiqaaq* is a term refering to a marriage that has broken down to the point that divorce has become a reasonable option. These representatives translate the term *Shiqaaq* as 'irreconcilable differences' – the closest legal equivalent in Canadian secular divorce law.

16 Darul Iftaa Documents nos. 1 through 5 on file with the author. See also http://iftaa.jucanada.org/uploads/ MCo9V4LBmItlEqMLo58MLQ/ksao_VsL0kFYGrkibMbOrQ/Darul-Iftaa-Application.pdf.

17 ISSRA provides many social services and coordinates numerous social programs and hundreds of volunteer staff. (http://www.issra.ca/).

18 ISSRA serves people from very diverse ethnic backgrounds, and thus applies the school of Islamic law appropriate to a client's place of origin upon request.

19 I am aware that my evidence comes from imams who might want to create the impression of gender fairness given the tenor of the 'Sharia debate.' However, my research access to several diverse imams who provide dispute resolution services, together with my access to several case files and personal interviews with Muslim women in the communities, including some women who have had a Muslim divorce themselves, suggest that although there are likely inequitable and patriarchal religious leaders and dispute resolution service providers in Ontario, there are also several that are quite equitable by Ontario's family law standards.

20 'Formal' arbitration is redundant, but I include it to emphasize the difference between that and 'informal' mediation.

21 For a more detailed account of the amendments to the Arbitration Act please see the introduction to this volume.

22 Natasha Bakht, for example, argues that banning religious arbitration was a mistake (Bakht 2005).

23 For example, more than one of my interview respondents informed me that a woman approached them for a religious divorce after she had been refused a religious divorce from another imam.

24 I do not want to mention these issues in a way that simply confirms the stereotypes proliferated in the press during the 'Sharia debate.' Just like non-Muslim communities in Ontario, there are several people living and acting justly, and there are a number of people and institutions that continue to struggle with patriarchy and other forms of inequity.

25 Although this recommendation might raise concerns regarding assumptions about secularism being a clear separation between church (religious institutions) and the state, my recommendations build on several already existing connections between religious institutions and the state in Canada, in a country that has never, in fact, fully embraced the American model of a 'wall of separation' (Biles and Humera 2005).

26 I found three institutions that undertook such workshops recently between 2006 and 2009.

REFERENCES

Attorney General. 1991. Arbitration Act. S.O. c.17. Accessed 22 Jan. 2011. http://www.e-laws.gov.on.ca/html/statutes/english/elaws_ statutes_91a17_e.htm. http://www.attorneygeneral.jus.gov.on.ca/english/ family/arbitration

Bakht, Natasha. 2006. 'Were Muslim Barbarians Really Knocking on the Gates of Ontario? The Religious Arbitration Controversy – Another Perspective.' Ottawa Law Review, 40th Anniversary Edition 35 (Summer): 67–82.

– 2007. 'Religious Arbitration in Canada: Protecting Women by Protecting Them from Religion.' Canadian Journal of Women and the Law 19(1): 119–44.

Beyer, Peter. 2005. 'Appendix: Demographics of Religious Participation in Canada.' In Paul Bramadat and David Seljak, eds., Religion and Ethnicity in Canada, pp. 235–40 . Toronto: Pearson Longman.

Biles, John, and Ibrahim Humera. 2005. 'Religion and Public Policy: Immigration, Citizenship, and Multiculturalism – Guess Who's Coming to Dinner?' In Paul Bramadat and David Seljak, eds., Religion and Ethnicity in Canada, pp. 154–77. Toronto: Pearson Longman.

Boyd, Marion. 2004. Dispute Resolution in Family Law: Protecting Choice, Promoting Inclusion. Accessed 22 Jan. 2011. http://www.attorneygeneral.jus. gov.on.ca/english/about/pubs/boyd.

Bunting, Annie, and Shaki Mokhtari. 2007. 'Migrant Muslim Women's Interests and the   Case of "Sharia Tribunals" in Ontario.' In Vijay Agnew, ed., Racialized Migrant Women in Canada: Essays on Health, Violence, and Equity. Toronto: Toronto University Press.

Joseph, Norma Baumel. 1994. 'Freeing the *Agunot* by Amending the Law.' *Ecumenism* 115 (Sept.).

Kayfetz, Ben. 1986. 'Canadian Law Eases Halachic Divorce Get for Jewish Women.' *Patterns of Prejudice* 20(2): 37–9.

Kramer, Julian Y. 2005. 'Stumbling Legislation and Limping Marriages: A Case Study from Norway.' Paper presented at the Metropolis International Conference, 21 Oct., Toronto.

Leung, Wendy. 2008. 'Canada: Ex-Husband Appeals Jewish-Divorce Landmark Ruling.'*Women Living under Muslim Laws Online.* 15 Feb. Accessed 22 Jan. 2011. http://www.wluml.org/english/newsfulltxt.shtml?cmd% 5B157%5D=x-157-560515.

Van Rhijn, Judy. 2003. 'First Steps Taken for Islamic Arbitration Board.' *Law Times,* 24 Nov.

PART TWO

Regulating Faith-Based Arbitration

3 Multiculturalism Meets Privatization: The Case of Faith-Based Arbitration

AUDREY MACKLIN

The ties that bind individuals to religious and cultural communities may be experienced by members as simultaneously enriching, oppressive, formative, and constraining of the self. The multiculturalist state, committed to the liberty and equality of all members within its sphere of governance, is alternately directed to protect the encultured subject's liberty by respecting certain practices of her sub-state community, and enlisted to protect her equality rights by refusing to accommodate other practices of those same communities.

Who is this 'encultured subject'? I borrow the formulation from the popular term 'racialized subject.' The latter term reminds us that race is not a feature intrinsic to a person or group, but rather an identity projected on some, but not others, through the social process of racialization. The 'encultured subject' captures an analogous ascription of a fixed identity on one who is regarded as distinctively constituted by, and indivisible from, a particular culture or religion. She is thus differentiated from the liberal subject who simply holds spiritual beliefs or engages in particular religious or cultural practices. These descriptors are no more descriptively or normatively valid in the context of culture than race. After all, all individuals exist within a cultural matrix that shapes them, and few are so devoid of the capacity for autonomy that they utterly lack agency. Yet, much like race, these artificial constructs of the encultured and the liberal subjects produce real political and legal effects. Some critics of the Sharia arbitration controversy have critiqued the work that the encultured subject performed onstage during that debate (Bakht 2006; see also chapters by Bullock, Korteweg, and Zine, this volume). My chapter supplements this analysis by exploring the work that the liberal subject performed offstage in structuring the legal framework within which private dispute resolution remains situated.

I contend that casting the dangers and problematic dimensions of faith-based arbitration as a prototypical multicultural dilemma has the effect of obscuring and depoliticizing the secular and public legal apparatuses that enabled it. It hides the fact that, as Wendy Brown observes, 'liberalism *is* cultural': 'This is not simply to say that liberalism promotes a certain culture – say, of individualism or entrepreneurship – though certainly these are truisms ... Rather, the theoretical claim here is that both the constructive and repressive powers we call those of culture – the powers that produce and reproduce subjects' relations and practices, beliefs and rationalities, and that do so without their express choice or consent – are neither conquered by liberalism or absent from liberalism' (2006, 22–3).

In so stating, I do not deny the importance of the specific multicultural dimensions of the issue, which others analyse in this volume and elsewhere. My goal is not to defend legally enforceable faith-based arbitration against a secular, public alternative, but rather to shed critical light on the character of that secular, public alternative. I do so in two ways. First, I demonstrate how the proposal for faith-based dispute resolution was mischaracterized as a demand for a separate and parallel regime; in reality, it represented only a variant of private ordering already authorized within the existing architecture of family law.[1] I foreground this privatization of justice (especially family law), not multiculturalism, as a terrain of normative conflict. On this view, the specifically cultural and religious dimensions of the Sharia arbitration debate exposed and accentuated – but did not create – tensions already embedded in the privatization of family law.

Second, I argue that even in its secular, public rendition, the existing regime permits outcomes that might discomfit opponents of faith-based arbitration who were animated by concerns of gender equity in family law. This irony matters in the context of the debate, because the demise of judicially enforceable faith-based arbitration in Ontario in 2006 left the judicial enforceability of other mechanisms of faith-based family dispute resolution untouched.

To bring the politics of the existing legal framework into clearer view, I review a leading case from the Supreme Court of Canada concerning a marriage agreement (also known as a prenuptial agreement) between a secular professional couple. I use the judgment in *Hartshorne* v. *Hartshorne* (2004) to illustrate now existing standards applicable to judicial assessment of private contracts that permit divergence from the default standards in Canadian family law. Just as the spectre of the encultured subject (in the form of the oppressed Muslim woman) haunted the arbitration debate, so too does a particular vision of the unencumbered liberal subject operate in the background of the decision in *Hartshorne*. In light of the Court's reasoning in *Hartshorne*, I ask how the principles it espouses would apply today to negotiated or mediated agreements whose terms are governed by religious norms, and which remain legally enforceable under Ontario law.

My conclusion gestures towards a possible institutional response to the challenges posed by the Sharia arbitration controversy. It is modest and merely suggestive of future directions, for two reasons: First, I resist the scholarly impulse to devise generalized theoretical schemata that will pre-emptively classify and resolve the normative puzzles generated by the complex and shifting geometry of multicultural interaction between state, individual and community[2]. Such generalized frameworks fail, in my view, to take account of the diversity of law as a mode of regulation and the particularity of the contexts in which it is deployed. Second, I argue that the deficiencies attributed to faith-based arbitration are actually instantiations of larger tensions between private ordering and public justice in the specific context of family-law dispute resolution. A policy response directed only at faith-based dispute arbitration will necessarily be incomplete. My conclusion thus returns me to where I begin: the problematic dichotomy between the encultured and the liberal subject, and its unsustainability as a matter of legal principle and institutional design.

Surveying the Legal Terrain

The secular legal system is not generally regarded as implicated in the form or substance of whatever multicultural 'problem' between individual and community that it is called on to resolve. Legal enactments are represented as the instruments through which the state manifests its public reason in regulating how actors ought to and shall behave. But the norms and processes of the legal order often shape the emergence of multicultural dilemmas; as such, the legal regime is as much a part of the problem as the solution. At a minimum, it should be apparent that the state and its legal system simultaneously configure and reflect the social meaning and political implications of culture, liberty, and equality. Although this should caution against any attempt to assign an unreflexively prescriptive role to law as a neutral arbiter of competing claims, assumptions about the putative neutrality of law prove difficult to dislodge, especially when positioned against the avowed partiality of culture.

Ayelet Shachar's thorough analysis of the Sharia arbitration debate describes the proposal as an attempt to 'privatize diversity,' insofar as it would 'permit parties to move their disputes from public courthouses into the domain of religious or customary sources of law and authority' (Shachar 2008, 575). My approach differs, insofar as I foreground the acknowledged fact that proponents of faith-based arbitration were not actually rejecting or withdrawing from the state's family law regime. Rather, they simply availed themselves of the opportunity embedded in the state's existing regulatory regime of family law (Bakht 2006; Farrow 2006; Shachar 2008). That regime authorizes parties to resolve aspects of their family disputes through private mechanisms as a matter of principle and encourages them to do so as a pragmatic matter. The process of contracting out of the statutory regime is so pervasive that the under-resourced, overburdened family court apparatus depends on parties avoiding recourse to the courts by opting for private ordering.

A review of the family law context as it existed when the controversy erupted assists in situating the debate. The family law regime governing couples in Ontario is a complicated admixture of federal law (the Divorce Act) and provincial law (the Family Law Act). For our present purposes, it suffices to note that the statutes set out default rules for distribution of property, support (spousal and child), and custody following relationship breakdown. Reformist projects over the past thirty years or so have made considerable progress in addressing the gendered consequences of marriage breakdown. Judicial decisions and legislative changes altered traditional rules of property division to recognize the role that the unpaid labour of wives plays in enabling husbands to maximize their career development and accumulate wealth. Legislative principles guiding provision of spousal support acknowledge that many women forfeit their own careers in the paid labour force to stay home with children, and some may simply never attain full financial independence, much less the financial position they would have attained had they not married (Family Law Act 1990).

Although these default rules leave considerable room for judicial discretion in recognition of the infinite real-life variation in circumstances, the default point of departure is equal division of family property, plus spousal support obligations that recognize the price that a primary caregiver of children (usually a mother) pays in terms of financial independence and earning capacity.

At the same time, parties can, to a significant degree, contract out of the process and substance of the statutory family law regime. Rather than litigating property division, custody, and child and spousal support in the ordinary courts, parties can resolve these issues by negotiating an agreement on their own (with or without the involvement of lawyers) or with the intercession of a neutral mediator. The resultant agreements are labelled 'domestic contracts' under the Ontario Family Law Act. They include prenuptial agreements concluded before a couple gets married, which in some cases amount to anticipatory separation agreements (McLeod 2004; see *MacLeod* v. *MacLeod* 2008; *Hartshorne* v. *Hartshorne* 2004), as well as actual separation agreements that are devised on relationship breakdown. In Ontario, judges can intervene and vary domestic contracts if the terms are, in the idiom of contract law, 'unconscionable.'

Parties who are separating and who do not arrive at a negotiated or mediated settlement may still avoid litigation by engaging an arbitrator of their choosing to adjudicate the dispute in a less formal manner than a courtroom trial before a judge. Prior to 2006, the Arbitration Act dealt with family arbitration in the same way as commercial disputes. However, Canadian law always prohibited parties from arbitrating status, including marriage, divorce, or paternity.[3] Negotiated and mediated domestic contracts, along with arbitration, constitute the instruments of private ordering in family law.

Having embarked on negotiation, mediation, or (less often) arbitration, the parties may adopt the statutory scheme regarding division of property, support, and custody as the normative framework for resolving their dispute. Alternatively, they may operate according to their own preferences, values, and priorities. Section 35 of the 1996 Ontario Arbitration Act expressly stated that an arbitral tribunal 'shall apply the rules of law designated by the parties.' The drafters of the legislation probably contemplated that parties who did not elect to be governed by Ontario law would choose the law of another Canadian jurisdiction, an option sometimes exercised in commercial disputes. Nevertheless, nothing in the legislation precluded the choice of religious law over secular law, or the law of Saudi Arabia over the law of Canada for that matter.

Where parties avoid litigation and resolve their matters privately, a court would likely never see the contract, settlement, or award in advance of its implementation. The notable exception involves child support. If a couple wishes to divorce, a judge will require evidence that appropriate child support arrangements have been made prior to issuing a divorce decree.

Parties to a domestic contract or arbitration may choose to file the contract, settlement, or award with the ordinary courts and convert the private agreement into an enforceable court order. This means that if one party defaults on the agreement, the other party can seek judicial enforcement. In practice, private agreements tend not to be filed unless and until an aggrieved party believes the other has defaulted. Once again, no judge will review the domestic contract, settlement, or award prior to converting it into an enforceable court order. This means, in effect, that the state lends its coercive power to enforcement of agreements with little or no advance scrutiny of their content.

Prior to the legislative reforms precipitated by the Sharia arbitration debate, parties to arbitration could determine in advance how binding the arbitral award would be. An award could be advisory, meaning that it must be submitted to a judge for review and approval. At the other end of the spectrum, the parties could agree to preclude any appeal of the arbitral award to the courts. This was an important difference between arbitral awards and domestic contracts. Courts always retained authority to set aside domestic contracts if a dissatisfied party persuaded a court that the terms were 'unconscionable,' but if the parties to an arbitration agreed in advance to preclude appeal to the courts, the arbitral award would be immunized from judicial oversight. Of course, as a practical matter, the courts were and remain relatively inaccessible to those parties (often women), who bear the financial and emotional burden of instigating litigation.

Muslim Family Law Arbitration

As other contributors to this volume explain, Marion Boyd's review of Islamic family law arbitration in Ontario catalyzed what could – with only slight exaggeration – be characterized as two opposing answers to Susan Moller Okin's provocative question 'Is Multiculturalism Bad for Women?' (Okin 1999). At the risk of homogenizing internal variations on either side, the following stylized propositions capture the essence of the opposing positions:

Freedom of religion (as guaranteed by s. 2 of the Canadian Charter of Rights and Freedoms) and our commitment to multiculturalism (as endorsed by s. 27 of the Charter) encourages us to respect different faith communities, and the constitutive role that these play in the lives of individual citizen. Islam is not monolithic, static, or intrinsically misogynistic. If people within a given identity group consensually agree to be guided in their private lives by their religious beliefs and do so within the confines of the existing law (in this case, the Arbitration Act), we should not interfere simply because we may disagree with individual outcomes.

versus

Delegating state power to faith-based arbitrators sacrifices Muslim women on the altar of multiculturalism. Given the patriarchal orientation of Islam (or at least the elite who exercise leadership within Muslim communities), arbitration according to Muslim law will systematically disadvantage women and leave them unprotected by the state from the social, physical, financial and emotional harm inflicted in the name of religion. Many Muslim women are newcomers to Canada, unfamiliar with their rights, and especially vulnerable to forms of physical, psychological and material abuse from kin and community. A commitment to the equality of women (as required by s. 15 of the Canadian Charter of Rights and Freedoms) requires that Islamic tribunals not be permitted to operate under the Arbitration Act.

Indeed, Boyd asserts in her executive summary that the 'fundamental tension that must be addressed is between respect for the minority group and protection of a person's individual rights within that minority' (Boyd 2004a: 3). Presumably, it is the protection of women's entitlement to choose and the promotion of minority group inclusion within broader society that the report's sub-title 'Protecting Choice, Promoting Inclusion,' tacitly endorses.

I have elsewhere analysed the participation of the Muslim women's organizations through the lens of citizenship (Macklin 2009). Other contributors to this volume have described the positions adopted by various individuals and groups who made submissions to Marion Boyd, as well as the recommendations contained in Boyd's final report.

For present purposes, I highlight three of Boyd's conclusions. First, Boyd recommended subjecting family law arbitral awards to the same rules as domestic contracts under the Ontario Family Law Act. The main consequence would be that if and when an arbitral award was challenged in court, a judge could set aside the award on the same grounds as domestic contracts, including 'unconscionability' (Boyd 2004b, 4). Next, she advocated supporting civil society efforts to 'explain rights under Ontario and Canadian law in a way that is likely to be comprehensible to people of diverse backgrounds and culture' (Boyd 2004b, 10).

Finally, while she was mindful of the pressure a woman might experience to engage in faith-based arbitration, Boyd's recommendations rejected the idea that explicit or implicit threats of social, religious, financial, or immigration penalties – essentially, non-violent coercion predicated on structural inequality – would or should vitiate consent to arbitrate: 'The law of contracts and Part IV of the *Family Law Act* offer the option to set aside an agreement where there has not been true consent because the person was pressured or coerced into entering into an agreement. More subtle community pressure may not qualify as coercion for this purpose, whereas threats of violence from a partner or family member almost certainly would' (Boyd 2004b, 136).

In September 2005, the Ontario government announced that it would not adopt the main recommendations of the Boyd Report. Instead, it would amend the law to deny legal recognition to faith-based arbitration of family law disputes under the Arbitration Act, and to bring arbitration of family law disputes under the purview of the Family Law Act. This amendment would mean that parties would no longer have the option of insulating arbitral awards from appeal to the courts by a dissatisfied party. In announcing his decision, Attorney General Michael Bryant explicitly invoked gender equality and anti-discrimination as the motive for the rejection of the Boyd Report's main recommendation in favour of faith-based arbitration:

> We have heard loud and clear from those who are seeking greater protections for women. We must constantly move forward to eradicate discrimination, protect the vulnerable, and promote equality. As the Premier re-iterated this week, we will ensure that women's rights are fully protected. We are guided by the values and the rights enshrined in our *Charter of Rights and Freedoms*.
>
> We will ensure that the law of the land in Ontario is not compromised, that there will be no binding family arbitration in Ontario that uses a set of rules or laws that discriminate against women. (Bryant 2005)

A few months later, the government enacted the Family Law Statute Amendment Act, which restricted judicially enforceable family law arbitrations exclusively to those applying the default rules contained in Ontario family law legislation, or the law of another Canadian jurisdiction. Section 3(5) of the Family Law Act of 2006 stated that 'in a family arbitration, the arbitral tribunal shall apply the substantive law of Ontario, unless the parties expressly designate the substantive law of another Canadian jurisdiction, in which case that substantive law shall be applied.' This means that family law arbitration in Ontario privatizes the process of dispute resolution, but the substance of the law applied by the arbitrator remains public. In addition, parties to arbitration can no longer shield awards from appeal to the courts.

To the extent that the issue was presented as a staging of Okin's question 'Is multiculturalism bad for women?' Boyd gave a qualified 'no,' while the Ontario government said 'yes.' Yet, in the end, the decision by the Ontario government to deny legal recognition to faith-based arbitration does not prevent parties' from engaging mediators (as opposed to arbitrators) who can guide them towards an agreement using faith-based principles. Nor does it prevent parties from negotiating agreements according to advice from religious authorities about the requirements of religious law. Section 59.2(2) of the amended Family Law Act leaves open the enforceability of domestic contracts negotiated or mediated in accordance with religious norms, including some version of Islamic law:

> 59.2 When a decision about a matter described in clause (a) of the definition of 'family arbitration' in section 51 is made by a third person in a process that is not conducted exclusively in accordance with the law of Ontario or of another Canadian jurisdiction,
>   (a) the process is not a family arbitration; and
>   (b) the decision is not a family arbitration award and has no legal effect
>   (2006, c. 1, s. 5 (10))
> (2) *Nothing in this section restricts a person's right to obtain advice from another person.* (2006, c.1, s.5 (10); emphasis added).

To reiterate an earlier point, most private dispute resolution in family law occurs by negotiation or mediation, not arbitration. Therefore, the legislated end to the debate about faith-based arbitration will not actually terminate legal enforcement of mediated or negotiated agreements that are based on religious law.

Another Look at the Legal Landscape

A casual observer of the controversy within and beyond Ontario might plausibly have construed the Muslim arbitration initiative as heralding an unprecedented establishment of a parallel and independent system of religious law and the concomitant retreat of the secular legal system. I hope the first part of this chapter clarifies that this portrayal – one set of rules for Muslims, and another for everyone else – is misleading in respect of Ontario and many other Canadian and common law jurisdictions.[4] Had Muslim leaders actually mounted a campaign based strictly on multiculturalist arguments to exempt Muslims qua religious minority from the family law regime applicable to everyone else, they would have encountered implacable, unequivocal, and swift rejection. Despite Canada's commitment to multiculturalism, instances of autonomous legal regimes outside of federalism hardly exist. Aboriginal peoples continue to struggle to create spheres of territorial and jurisdictional autonomy. Accommodation within existing laws, rather than the delegation of legal authority as such, marks the Canadian practice of multiculturalism. The principle that equality and the rule of law require 'one law for all' retains considerable durability and resonance in public discourse. A bald demand for a separate and autonomous Muslim legal system would have had no traction.

The twist in the Sharia arbitration debate is that the 'one law for all' governing family law in Ontario was a law that lets parties make their own law: It sets out default rules to be applied by a court in relation to property division, custody, and child and spousal support, and then authorizes consenting parties to opt out of the process and substance of the public legal regime. Instead of litigating, parties can arbitrate, mediate, or negotiate. Instead of applying a set of publicly promulgated rules of general application, parties can reject the provisions in the Family Law Act and choose another set of legal rules off the pluralist legal shelf, or tailor make their own rules via contract. Finally, the Family Law Act and the Arbitration Act made the outcomes of private ordering enforceable by a court. Therefore, the 'one law for all' turned out to be a law that allows parties to contract out of the process and substance of that law. With the exception of the substantive law applicable in arbitration, this remains the case today.

My central claim, then, is that the debate about faith-based arbitration transpired on a discursive terrain already circumscribed by the logic of privatization, as promoted by the Arbitration Act and the domestic contract provisions in the Family Law Act. To put it another way, faith-based arbitration and its normative driver, multiculturalism, were already nested within the domain of privatization and neo-liberal ideals of choice, liberty, and autonomy. Public facilitation of private ordering in family law paved the way for faith-based arbitration in Ontario.

The trend towards privatization of government functions accelerated in the 1980s and 1990s as neo-liberal economic models extolled the virtues of the market and private ordering over state regulation. This disenchantment with the state extended to dispute resolution, especially in the commercial sphere, where sophisticated economic actors set up private arbitration regimes to achieve faster, cheaper, and (according to some) better results. Meanwhile, as family law regimes across Canada incorporated greater attention to gender equity in statutory provisions regarding property division and spousal support (partly to prevent divorcing women from becoming impoverished and dependent on state support), they also formalized opportunities for couples to 'opt-out' of the statutory allocations. Such opportunities came through privately negotiated domestic contracts that regulated custody, access, property division, and support according to the parties' own values, priorities, and wishes. In all these contexts, privatization was promoted as autonomy-enhancing, less adversarial, and more efficient.

In light of these converging patterns of privatization in the commercial and family law spheres, family law arbitration could best be viewed as a formal hitching of private dispute resolution to the public justice system. By allowing the parties to select their arbitrator, their law and their preferred level of judicial review, family law arbitration played squarely into discourses of individual choice, and of freedom from an interventionist state. At the time of the Arbitration Act's passage in the early 1990s, feminists criticized the characterization of arbitration in family law disputes as autonomy-enhancing when it occurred under conditions of systemic inequality. They cited the potential for abuse of power, sheltered behind the rhetoric of choice and shielded from public oversight by the privacy of the arbitration room. Feminists lost that battle.

This historical context of arbitration opened certain discursive doors for proponents and closed others for opponents of faith-based arbitration. Proponents could correctly assert that they asked for nothing more than equal benefit of the existing regime. The range of rationales – efficiency, cheapness, respect for religious beliefs, user-satisfaction, choice, discretion – operating from diverse normative premises, could each be deployed towards a common position in favour of faith-based arbitration.

The Arbitration Act already permitted arbitration of family law disputes, already permitted parties to choose alternative normative frameworks (including religious law), and already permitted parties to shield outcomes from meaningful judicial oversight. Given these conditions, one could not easily target faith-based arbitration from among alternative normative frameworks without allegedly breaching the constitutionally protected freedom of religion and/or endorsement of multiculturalism. One could not single out Islamic law for exclusion without meeting the accusation of discrimination between religions. Equality, freedom of religion, and multiculturalism could all be deployed in good faith in the service of faith-based family law arbitration. Supporters could easily accommodate proposals to strengthen procedural protections to ensure free and informed consent. After all, such modifications presupposed that genuine consent could and would result if only participants were free from the threat of physical violence and received enough accurate legal information about the likely consequences of their participation.

Opponents of Islamic arbitration were thus placed in the unenviable position of demanding retraction of some aspect of the status quo. The Canadian Council for Muslim Women, along with the National Association of Women and Law and the National Organization of Immigrant and Visible Minority Women, adopted a position that corresponded to the margin of overlap between them, namely, a shared concern about the exploitation of gendered inequality under a privatized regime of justice. In effect, they tapped into the general case against binding, enforceable arbitration of family law disputes. To the extent that certain renditions of Islamic law were particularly inequitable towards women, and devout Muslim women (especially recent immigrants) were especially vulnerable to forms of coercion not visible as such in law, Islamic family law arbitration could be viewed as an exemplar of the larger problem of private justice in the realm of family law as conceived under the Arbitration Act.

This line of argument was never fully developed by the interlocutors in the debate, but it is worth pursuing the inquiry with explicit attention to the state of Canadian law on domestic contracts that deviate from the statutory default regime. The trajectory of this analysis is not aimed at Islamic law per se. Instead, it focuses on the state's configuration of family law into a regime that permits parties to 'opt-out' of the public process and the default public rules contained in the statute. This potentially leaves all parties – secular and religious, rich and poor, Canadian-born and immigrant – with qualitatively different outcomes than would obtain under the default public regime.

The mechanism in Ontario for preventing injustice arising from these domestic contracts is the option of challenging a domestic contract before a neutral and independent judge, who is able to vary or set it aside if one party concealed his or her true financial situation, if a party did not understand the nature or consequences of the contract, or if the contract is 'unconscionable.'[5] This combination of private ordering and public oversight is the gold standard against which faith-based arbitration was measured and found wanting. It continues to govern the enforcement of domestic contracts, which, to reiterate, may represent the outcome of secular or faith-based negotiation or mediation. The lingering question, then, is how well public judicial oversight of private domestic contracts actually ensures that domestic contracts (secular or otherwise) meet a normatively acceptable standard of fairness, gender equality, respect for autonomy, and attention to exploitation.

To assess the performance of the status quo, I offer the Supreme Court of Canada judgment in *Hartshorne* v. *Hartshorne* (2004) a precedential case involving a secular, professional couple contracting-out of the default statutory rules of property distribution in British Columbia. This analysis returns me to the distinction I drew in the introduction between the encultured and the liberal subject. If the oppressed Muslim woman, psychically and socially imprisoned in her cultural context, haunted the Sharia arbitration debates, then it is her foil, the culturally unencumbered and rational, free agent, who informs the majority judgment's view of Kathleen Harthshorne. *Hartshorne* provides a cautionary tale for those who believe that the present regime – with its denial of faith-based arbitration awards but recognition of domestic contracts – eliminates the dangers or reduces the potential harms that opponents associate with faith-based arbitration. The explanation for this does not reside solely in the religious norms that inform the content of the domestic contract, but rather in the principles by which a public, secular court will review and enforce a domestic contract. These include contested conceptions of agency, law's need to hold people to their voluntarily assumed obligations, and related questions about the role of inequality of bargaining power in evaluating the fairness of an agreement.

The case of *Hartshorne* v. *Hartshorne* concerns a 'prenuptial' agreement presented by Robert to Kathleen days before their wedding, and signed by Kathleen on their wedding day. Robert and Kathleen Hartshorne were both lawyers. They met and commenced a romantic relationship in 1982 when Kathleen was working as a junior lawyer in Robert's law firm. They began cohabiting in 1985. Kathleen bore their son in 1987, after which she left legal practice and remained at home. From this point onwards, Robert 'gave her a monthly allowance, as well as access to some credit cards for the purpose of charging expenditures for the household' (Court of Appeal 2002, 10). The couple married in 1989, after she had been out of the paid work force for two years. She was also (unknown to both at the time) pregnant with their daughter.

This was a second marriage for both parties. Kathleen entered the marriage with significant debt from her first marriage. Robert entered into the marriage with significant assets, including his law practice, pension, and vacation properties. In the course of Robert's first divorce, the default regime of property division applied, meaning that he and his first wife (also a practising lawyer) divided their assets equally. Robert Hartshorne testified that 'he had worked hard to get where he was, he had to divide up his assets following his first marriage break-down and, in his view, he made it clear to [Kathleen] that he was never going to let that happen again, as he did not intend to share his assets' (*Hartshorne* v. *Hartshorne* 2002, 13).

The marriage agreement stipulated that 'during their marriage each of them shall be completely independent of the other as regards enjoy-ment, control, administration and disposal of all property, both real and personal, whether owned at the commencement of the said marriage or acquired thereafter.' The agreement further stated that Robert was the purchaser of the matrimonial home, 'for every year they cohabit, Kathleen, after the marriage, will be entitled to Three (3 percent) per cent of the market value ... up to a maximum of Forty-nine (49 percent) per cent of the market value.'

Robert presented Kathleen with the draft agreement a few weeks before the wedding. Kathleen sought independent legal advice nine days prior to the wedding. The next day, her lawyer advised her that the agreement was grossly unfair compared with her entitlements under the statutory family law regime in British Columbia:

> In our opinion, a Court would easily find such provision to be unfair and would intervene to redistribute the property on a more equitable basis.
>
> We would strongly recommend against your executing the Agreement in its present form. We do not agree ... that the Agreement would be signed voluntarily or that it would not be unconscionable or unfair to you.
>
> ... as the date of the marriage is rapidly approaching, we suggest that you deal with this matter as quickly as possible. The pressure on you to negotiate such an important matter with the wedding in only a few days is extreme. (quoted in *Hartshorne* v. *Hartshorne* 2002, 15)

On the day of the wedding, Kathleen Hartshorne made minor amendments to the marriage agreement and signed it. She inserted the following terms at the bottom of the contract:

9. The parties acknowledge that:
   a. Each has had independent legal advice;
   b. Each understands his or her respective rights and obligations under this Agreement;
   c. Kathleen is not signing this Agreement voluntarily, but at the insistence of Robert.

A majority of the Supreme Court of Canada, reversing two lower court judgments, upheld the terms of the marriage agreement (*Hartshorne* v. *Hartshrone* 2004).

The normative framework governing the marriage agreement might be best described as the abstract principle of formal equality: the property allocation on divorce should leave each party with whatever property or assets that person brought into the marriage *and* acquired thereafter in his or own name, including the matrimonial home. In jurisprudential terms, this case represents a reversion to the pre-reform era. The case that mobilized activists and catalysed reform was a notorious 1973 Supreme Court of Canada judgment in *Murdoch* v. *Murdoch* (1975), in which a ranch wife was denied a share of the ranch property held in the husband's name, even though she contributed both labour and (arguably) money to its acquisition and development. Within this patriarchal normative framework, property division on dissolution of marriage tracked the titleholder, typically the husband. The contribution of the stay-at-home wife's labour was not understood as giving rise to an entitlement to assets acquired or improved during the relationship as long as title was held in the husband's name.

The terms of the marriage agreement between Robert and Kathleen Hartshorne roughly instantiate these values, and they predictably operated to the detriment of Kathleen Hartshorne insofar as their marriage conformed to the stereotype of breadwinner husband and stay-at-home wife with no independent income. Kathleen was in no position to acquire property or accrue income of her own.

When the couple separated after nine years of marriage (over 12 years of cohabitation) and two children, Mrs Hartshorne's entitlement under the prenuptial agreement consisted of approximately 20 per cent of the family assets. Mr Hartshorne walked away from the marriage with a net worth of $1.2 million dollars and Mrs Hartshorne walked away with a net worth $280,000. In other terms, the assets available on dissolution of the marriage were split 80/20 in favour of Mr Hartshorne.[6]

In comparison with Ontario, British Columbia's default regime is more generous to the economically weaker spouse. In addition, where parties opt out and enter into a domestic contract, a reviewing court in British Columbia may intervene if the outcome of the agreement is 'unfair' at the time of distribution, which is less strict than the standard of 'unconscionability' in Ontario (*Hartshorne* v. *Hartshorne* 2002, 14).

Kathleen Hartshorne successfully argued at trial that the marriage agreement was unfair, and the British Columbia Court of Appeal upheld the trial judge's reapportionment of assets from 80/20 to a 60/40 split. The Supreme Court of Canada allowed Mr Hartshorne's appeal and rejected the argument that the marriage agreement was unfair. The Supreme Court employed a test developed in an earlier case for assessing whether a domestic contract was fair at the time it was made and, if so, whether it remained fair at the time of implementation. The test can be framed as three questions:

1. Did one party exploit the other's vulnerability at the time of contract formation such that the latter's consent was not voluntary?
2. Did the terms of the agreement 'fail [...] to comply substantially' with the objectives of the default statutory regime? (*Hartshorne* v. *Hartshorne* 2004, 41)
3. Did the actual circumstances of the parties diverge so significantly from their expectations of the future at the time of contract formation as to conclude that implementation of the contract would no longer be fair? (*Hartshorne* v. *Hartshorne* 2004, 44)

In answer to question 3, the majority of the Supreme Court of Canada found no significant disparity between the expectations of the parties and what transpired. Life unfolded roughly the way the parties expected: Mr Hartshorne continued his law practice and Ms. Hartshorne stayed home and raised their two children, the first of whom had special needs.

Was Kathleen's consent to the agreement voluntary? All judges, at all levels, agreed on the point that Kathleen Hartshorne was not coerced or under duress when she signed the prenuptial agreement on her wedding day. Kathleen's self-serving declaration in the agreement that she was not signing 'voluntarily' but rather 'on Robert's insistence' was given no weight. The dissent does acknowledge the imbalance of power between husband and wife before and after the wedding, but concludes that Kathleen's vulnerability, dependence, and evident distress about the terms of the prenuptial agreement did not vitiate Kathleen's consent (*Hartshorne* v. *Hartshorne* 2004, 90).

Importantly, the inequality of bargaining power did signal to the dissent that a court 'should be alive to the possibility that the agreement was unfair' in substance (*Hartshorne* v. *Hartshorne* 2004, 90). Conversely, the majority describes the agreement as reflective of the 'intention of the parties,' and admonishes that 'if the Respondent truly believed that the Agreement was unacceptable at that time, she should not have signed it' (*Hartshorne* v. *Hartshorne* 2004, 65). In the result, the majority endorses a zero-sum approach to autonomy and consent: If the circumstances do not amount to 'duress, coercion or undue influence' in law then the irrebuttable presumption is that both parties acted autonomously, and the imbalance in power is not relevant to any subsequent assessment of the fairness of the content of the agreement.

The requirement that a private agreement substantially comply with the statutory objectives of the default regime provides a constraint on the range of private arrangements that will be deemed fair. Section 65 of the British Columbia Family Relations Act states as follows:

> 65c(1) If the provisions for division of property between spouses under ... their marriage agreement ... would be *unfair* having regard to
>
> (a) the duration of the marriage,
> (b) the duration of the period during which the spouses have lived separate and apart,
> (c) the date when property was acquired or disposed of,
> (d) the extent to which property was acquired by one spouse through inheritance or gift,
> (e) the needs of each spouse to become or remain economically independent and self-sufficient, or
> (f) any other circumstances relating to the acquisition, preservation, maintenance, improvement or use of property or the capacity or liabilities of a spouse,
>
> the Supreme Court, on application, may order that the property covered by ... the marriage agreement, as the case may be, be divided into shares fixed by the court. (emphasis added)

In *Hartshorne*, the majority of the Supreme Court of Canada weighed two factors heavily in arriving at the conclusion that the 80/20 property split was not unfair when viewed against the objectives of the Family Relations Act. First, under s. 65(1)(c), Robert Hartshorne acquired most of his property before the marriage. Second, the needs of Katherine Hartshorne to regain her capacity to become economically self-sufficient (s. 65(1)(e) and the career impediment imposed by her continued responsibilities as custodial parent (s. 65(1)(f)) could be addressed by appropriate provision of spousal and child support, which were not affected by the marriage agreement, but had also not yet been resolved.

Dissenting Justice Deschamps insisted that 'fairness is a concept that is independent of any agreement.' The fairness of a marriage agreement should be measured by the deviation from the outcome a judge could reasonably have ordered under the statutory regime. A 'great disparity' should not merit deference by a court.[7]

For present purposes, I am willing to concede that *Hartshorne* is a difficult case about which reasonable people can disagree. On the one hand, Kathleen Hartshorne was in a precarious position at the time of the wedding. She had been at home with their child and financially dependent on Robert for two years when they married (Shaffer 2004). Regardless of Robert's intention and desire that the couple share their lives but not their property and assets, the social reality of cohabiting in a conjugal relationship over time casts doubt on the possibility and legitimacy of fixing and sustaining this permanent financial bifurcation in advance. The imposition of the agreement by Robert on Kathleen so soon before the wedding doubtless exacerbated the pressure on Kathleen to sign.[8] On the other hand, Kathleen Hartshorne was an educated person, had the benefit of independent legal advice, and understood the nature and consequences of the agreement when she signed it. The embarrassment of cancelling a wedding, and the alternative of returning to the paid workforce as a lawyer and single parent (assuming the couple did not simply continue cohabiting) did not amount to coercion that vitiated her consent.[9] She might have made a bad choice in signing the prenuptial agreement, but respect for autonomy requires the law to enforce bad choices as well as good ones. Rescuing people from their own poor judgment may seem attractive in the short run, but ultimately patronizes and infantilizes them (Leckey 2008). For a variety of reasons, legal doctrine (in family law and elsewhere) cannot easily discard or dilute liberalism's commitment to individual agency and autonomy that 'contributes to the personalization of politically contoured conflicts and inequalities' (Brown, 2006: 17).

Hartshorne is a thoroughly secular product of the privatization authorized by the current family law regime. My excursion into this case of a middle-class professional, secular couple is intended to clarify the normative benchmark against which faith-based domestic contracts will be judged. What can it tell us about private resolution of family law issues in the context of religious couples using faith-based principles to determine property, custody, and support?

Hartshorne teaches that respect for the autonomy of parties 'to apply their own values and pursue their own objectives in reaching a settlement' (*Miglin* v. *Miglin* 2003, 55) means that domestic contracts can instantiate norms that might otherwise appear retrograde or inegalitarian – like the idea that a stay-at-home wife's domestic, social, and emotional labour do not contribute to the acquisition or value of assets held in the husband's name. Much of the debate over Sharia arbitration concerned the alleged rules of Islamic family law, and their unfairness to women judged by contemporary North American standards. Assume for present purposes that a devout Muslim couple wish to be guided by their imam's understanding of what religious law requires on divorce, and that the imam's interpretation would, in fact, result in the wife of twelve years obtaining 20 per cent of the family assets and a 27 per cent share of the family home. Even if this happens, the fact that the wife agreed to be guided by patriarchal inegalitarian norms cannot warrant intervention solely on the basis that the norms find their origin in religious beliefs.

Hartshorne also teaches that the test for coercion is stringent, is not satisfied by proof of unequal bargaining power, and that it will be difficult for a party resisting enforcement to demonstrate lack of consent at the time of contract formation. One can easily imagine that a Muslim woman might, like Kathleen Hartshorne, obtain independent legal advice that fully informs her of the nature and relatively detrimental consequences of a proposed agreement. Yet, she signs it anyway. Independent legal advice only ensures that the party is informed, not empowered.

Unfairness (much less unconscionability) will be difficult to prove if events unfold more or less as anticipated at the time of the agreement. Similarly, an imbalance of bargaining power between the parties that falls short of vitiating consent will not influence the assessment of whether the terms 'substantially comply' with the objectives of the state's default regime from which the parties have contracted out.

Opponents of faith-based arbitration emphasized the many potential sources of pressure imposed on a Muslim wife to induce her to acquiesce to arbitration by a religious authority. Indeed, it is conceivable that lack of education and/or job skills, linguistic abilities, financial desperation, precarious immigration status, and, of course, any real or apprehended risk of violence could lead a court to conclude that a particular Muslim woman did not genuinely consent to the terms of the domestic contract. But these factors do not depend on religiosity and are not unique to devout Muslims.[10]

This leaves the social pressure that a Muslim woman might experience from within her community to resolve family matters internally and according to religious norms. Recall here that the Boyd Report states that 'more subtle community pressure may not qualify as coercion ... whereas threats of violence from a partner or family member almost certainly would' (Boyd 2004b, 136). This acknowledgement seems to correctly state the law. *Hartshorne* implicitly disregards the pressure Kathleen Hartshorne felt at the prospect of calling off a wedding on the church steps, or the potential stigma attached to being a single working mother. The pressures on Kathleen seem typical of mainstream North American cultural values regarding women, marriage, and motherhood circa 1989. Signs that these values continue to exert considerable force are easy enough to find. But we tend not to understand these attitudes as immutable cultural commitments, but rather as political commitments that can be scrutinized, revised, and rejected. In declaring that Kathleen should not have signed the agreement if she thought it was unfair, the Court ascribes to Kathleen Hartshorne the capacity to withstand the pressure of cultural expectations (as Kathleen perceived them). If this is correct, then the same standard should apply to Muslim women, with the same result.

It is tempting to argue that *Hartshorne* was rightly decided for a domestic contract between a secular couple but would have been wrongly decided had the agreement's terms disclosed a religious pedigree. In my view, an attempt to draw a distinction along these lines is untenable. Perhaps one could insist that the social and personal cost of 'exit' from a religious community is qualitatively different and higher than the costs to Kathleen Hartshorne of rejecting marriage to Robert Hartshorne. In other words, the cultural context within which the encultured woman finds herself is more encompassing, less porous to other currents of thought, and so exerts a distinctly greater coercive force on her. Thus, Kathleen's consent might plausibly be construed as voluntary, while a Muslim woman's is not. However, can we read this conclusion from the fact of the encultured subject's membership in a faith community? A distinction of this sort risks the same pernicious patronizing stance towards the encultured woman that supporters of the majority in *Hartshorne* worry about. The encultured subject is regarded as intrinsically impaired in her capacity for consent *because of* her cultural embeddednesss (and not because of contingent vulnerabilities, like immigration status or poverty). Conversely, her secular counterpart is recognized as an autonomous subject, unencumbered by the cultural influences on her, or at least able to critically reflect on and detach from them:[11] Kathleen Hartshorne possesses her culture, but the Muslim woman is possessed by hers.[12] This stark rendering of the liberal subject on one side, and the encultured subject on the other, means that the *politics* of subordination and inequality disappear between the cracks.

Of course, the difficulty is that both the encultured and the liberal subject are stylized types that suppress and constitute the other. If one applies *Hartshorne* consistently, religious women should be held to the terms of their faith-based domestic contracts according to the same principles as secular women. This would mean that even if patriarchal religious norms underpin a domestic contract, and the resultant contract disadvantages the woman in comparison with the default regime, the contract should not be unenforceable for those reasons alone. This is the ironic outcome of liberalism's demand that culture be '"liberalized" through privatization and individualization' (Brown 2006, 21). This is not necessarily a bad outcome, but it should trouble opponents of faith-based arbitration who identified Islam as the villain of their narrative.

The only alternative for disqualifying faith-based contracts is to regard the encultured subject as intrinsically incapable of genuine consent. This might allow a court to invalidate terms of a religiously inspired domestic contract it would otherwise uphold if they appeared in a non-religious domestic contract. The problems with this approach should be obvious.

Of course, the very activism of the Canadian Council of Muslim Women (CCMW) in opposing Islamic arbitration belies the stereotype of the meek and shrouded Muslim woman. Ironically, the Boyd Report invoked the dynamism of the CCMW to refute the claims of vulnerability made by CCMW on behalf of other Muslim women. Boyd was so impressed with the CCMW and other grassroots organizations that she concluded that these organizations could undertake legal literacy programs within their communities, thereby redressing the ignorance of Muslim women about their rights under Canadian family law. Thus, insulation of arbitration from public scrutiny need not raise undue concern about the welfare of Muslim women because civil society (in the form of the CCMW) would fill the void with education 'about rights, obligations and options with respect to family law' (Boyd 2004b, 131). The fact that the CCMW 'worked hard since its inception within the various Islamic communities to enhance the role of women within the faith and to foster an understanding of the principle of equality so central to Islamic teachings' (Boyd 2004b, 130) is deployed in part to obviate public responsibility for protection of vulnerable women in favour of civil society assuming the task. In effect, the review commends privatized protection (by civil society) as the principal safeguard against the risks created by the privatization of dispute resolution in family law.

The review goes on to extol the Canadian Coalition of Jewish Women as 'a strong role model to other women's groups concerned about potential abuses of religiously based mediation and arbitration' (Boyd 2004b, 130). The coalition has indeed produced and disseminated educational materials to observant Jews on this theme. Nevertheless, promoting the Canadian Coalition of Jewish Women as a role model for Muslim women seems ironic, and not for the reasons that one might think. Apart from educating Jewish women about the Jewish divorce process, the notable achievement of the coalition was to successfully lobby for amendments to the Divorce Act and the Family Law Act to protect Jewish women from intransigent husbands who withheld the *get* from their wives.[13] In other words, the coalition sought and obtained state intervention precisely because its own educational efforts could publicize but not ameliorate the substantive gender inequity of Jewish law.

Multiculturalism Meets Privatizations: Options for Reform

A central issue for feminists in the Islamic arbitration debates concerned whether and how secular law should protect encultured women from the risk of oppressive intra-communal practices. The public spotlight shone most intensely and harshly on the putative existence of a unified Islamic law, its content, its variability, its manipulation in the service of patriarchy, and the extent to which women would be coerced into submitting to Islamic arbitration. Few proponents of Islamic arbitration actually denied the possibility that certain interpretations of Islamic personal law could be inimical to the welfare of Muslim women. However, the prevalence of those interpretations, the ability of Muslim women to assert and defend their own interests, and the competing value to participants of engaging in faith-based dispute resolution were all hotly contested. The discussion then devolved into a set of options as stark as it was false: permit Islamic law arbitration or prohibit it.

In reality, the question was never whether Muslim men and women could lawfully rely on religious authorities to negotiate domestic contracts, to mediate disputes, or to arbitrate the consequences of marital dissolution. They have done so in the past, they do so now, and they will continue to do so in the future.[14] They may participate more or less voluntarily, and abide by more or less fair outcomes. The state possesses neither the will nor the resources to police whether and how people resolve disputes outside the formal judicial system. Indeed, unless and until one party takes the initiative to engage the formal legal system to enforce the agreement, the interaction will be insulated from judicial scrutiny. The state may refuse to enforce a given agreement, but it will not prohibit willing parties from creating and abiding by it.

This complex question of the interface between the state and private dispute resolution was largely deflected in the discussions regarding Sharia arbitration. For example, Marion Boyd's Report made only one relevant recommendation: 'The Ministry of the Attorney General should conduct further policy analysis of the legality and desirability of providing a higher level of court oversight to settlements of family and inheritance cases based on religious principles than is available to non-religiously based settlements under Part IV of the *Family Law Act*' (Boyd 2004, 12).

Boyd's proposal assumes for the sake of argument what she earlier rejected as unfounded on evidence, which is the claim that settlements informed by religious principles are more likely to harm women's interests than settlements generated by secular bargaining practices. Therefore, she proposes consideration of options for calibrating judicial oversight of contracts depending on whether they are the product of religious or secular principles.

I take no position on the empirical validity of this assumption. However, I reiterate the point that domestic contracts mediated or negotiated with the guidance of a religious adviser remain legally enforceable. Judicial oversight is available to an aggrieved party if and when she has the resources to commence litigation, which may never happen, or may not happen until long after the contract has been implemented. As I noted earlier, however, there is one important exception: a judge will review a domestic contract to ensure adequate provision of child support prior to granting a divorce.[15] Presumably, the rationale for this ex ante review is that there is an overriding public interest in ensuring that the material needs of children are met, and the state does not believe that children can or should bear the burden of litigation to secure adequate support.

This practice of ex ante review of child support is suggestive of a different configuration of the private/public interface than what currently prevails. It is but one model for how a private (and possibly religious) legal order could be brought into constructive dialogue with public, secular legal institutions. As noted earlier, several proponents of faith-based arbitration who participated in the review insisted that decisions rendered by religious arbitrators could and would be consistent with the Canadian Constitution and Ontario family law (Boyd 2004b, 43–5, 63).[16] Indeed, Boyd observed that 'again and again, members of the Muslim community assured the Review that Muslims who live in countries not governed by Islamic law are required by their faith to be obedient to the law in place in their country of residence' (2004b, 124). Taking these claims at face value, subjecting faith-based domestic contracts to some form of public judicial oversight should be less threatening to the integrity of faith-based domestic contracts than it might otherwise appear. In any event, it would certainly provide an open forum for testing the hypothesis of the compatibility of religious and secular norms.

Obviously, any policy option carries implications for utilization of judicial resources, the interaction of religious and secular norms, the nature of the task performed by mediators and arbitrators, and the allocation of the burden of accessing the courts. And any scheme animated by a concern for vulnerable parties that requires them to initiate the process by commencing litigation is less likely to be effective than one that triggers scrutiny automatically on conclusion of the agreement or issuance of an arbitral award (see also Shachar 2008, 598).

The option presented above does not exhaust the range of possibilities, and, indeed, other commentators have offered creative proposals that resemble elements of my proposal and differ in other respects (Emon, this volume; Shachar 2008). To the extent that I endorse bringing the secular, public legal order and the full range of private mechanisms amenable to the application of faith-based principles – arbitration, mediation, and negotiation – into conversation with one another, my recommendation is broadly compatible with Ayelet Shachar's promotion of 'transformative accommodation' as a model for managing relations between the state and minority religious communities (Shachar 2001). However, any serious attempt to design a viable policy must delve more deeply into the precise features and operation of the existing legal architecture in the specific jurisdiction of Ontario than is possible within the scope of this chapter.

In any case, any proposal that purports to address exclusively faith-based domestic contracts evades two important questions that my analysis of the legislative scheme and the jurisprudence compels asking: First, if the concern animating judicial intervention is unfair agreements, what difference does it make whether the impugned terms were the product of religious principles or of purely secular financial self-interest – or even sheer vindictiveness – backed up by superior bargaining power? It is not obvious why ostensibly unjust private contracts based on religious principles would or should warrant greater concern than similarly unfair private contracts based on secular principles. Once we abandon the false antithesis between the encultured and the liberal subject, there can be no principled answer to this question.

Relatedly, domestic contracts do not generally set out the normative framework that guides the parties. They usually contain only the outcome of the application of those norms, namely the terms of the settlement. If the agreement does not signal its religious provenance (e.g., through the use of revealing terms such as a *get* in Jewish law, or a *mahr* in Muslim law, or the identification of the mediator as a cleric), the religious predicates of the agreement may be undetectable anyway.

Ultimately, one arrives at a second, broader inquiry that tugs at the normative basis of all domestic contracts: By what standard should one assess a settlement's fidelity to the public norms of justice and fairness contained in family law statutes? Opponents of faith-based arbitration repeatedly invoked 'one law for all' as a slogan directed against alternative normative frameworks based on religion. But if one is serious about promoting public over private norms, one must necessarily target the scope of public law's allowance of private ordering, because this is what enables the 'personalized law for each' to displace the 'one law for all.' Faith-based settlements constitute only a tiny subset of these personalized legal codes.

Competing understandings of the outer limits of private ordering is precisely what separates the majority and dissent in *Hartshorne*: The majority valorizes the ability of parties to fashion rules that reflect 'their personal vision of fairness,' above the virtues of enforcing standardized public norms (Shaffer 2004 in Leckey 2008, 34). In a sense, the majority conceives of private ordering as a process that itself expresses a public value of liberal autonomy. The dissent, however, attends to the content of the rules and the outcomes they produce. The dissent sees the default rules as embodying public standards of fairness, and would rein in the exercise of private ordering where it produces substantive outcomes that deviate too far from the range of outcomes potentially available under the default public rules.

Robert Leckey (2008) correctly observes that a thorough and critical re-engagement with the virtues and limits of private ordering in family law has yet to take place. It is beyond the scope of this chapter to pursue that issue, except to observe that the Sharia arbitration debate did not advance thoughtful deliberation about it. The interlocutors were almost entirely preoccupied with arguing about the substance of Sharia law and characterizing the Muslim woman's vulnerability. What proponents of the 'one law for all' campaign did not contemplate is the possibility that the *secular* law might have to revise its own norms regarding what constitutes a fair agreement, if judicial supervision according to public norms is to do the work that proponents imagined it already does. That opportunity was lost amid the hype, the misinformation, and the intemperate tone of participants on both sides of the issue. But unless and until that conversation about private ordering in family law is initiated in earnest, the problems that animated people of all faiths, good faith, bad faith and no faith to engage in the Sharia arbitration debate will go elsewhere, but will not go away.

ACKNOWLEDGMENT

For helpful critical comment and constructive suggestions, the author warmly thanks the editors, as well as Howard Kislowicz, Robert Leckey, Martha Shaffer, and three anonymous reviewers. The author also thanks Mai Taha for excellent research assistance and gratefully acknowledges the financial support of the Social Sciences and Humanities Research Council of Canada. This chapter updates a paper first presented in 2006 and circulated thereafter on the Internet under the title 'Post-Neoliberal Multiculturalism: The Case of Faith-Based

Arbitration,' http://www.cpsa-acsp.ca/papers-2006/Macklin.pdf. Since the circulation of that conference paper, several published articles on the topic have appeared, some of which advance similar arguments to those I initially presented. They include the following: Bader (2009); Baines (2006); Bakht (2006); Bhabha (2009); Farrow (2006); Gaudreault-DesBiens (2005); Hirschl and Shachar (2008-2009); McGill (2007); Weinrib (2008); Shachar (2008); Von Torne (2007-2008); Walker (2006). I have endeavoured to acknowledge those similarities as appropriate.

NOTES

1 Private ordering refers to processes and rules that are determined by private parties to govern their interactions, as opposed to statutes of general application enacted by the legislature in the name of the public good.

2 Will Kymlicka's (1995) distinction between impermissible external restrictions on cultural minority practices and impermissible internal restrictions is a case in point. Denise Réaume makes the important point that 'no exhaustive list of discrete cultural rights or group-differentiated rights, no comprehensive blueprint dictating where and when and how special treatment of culture minorities is appropriate, is likely to capture multiculturalism as a legal phenomenon. Efforts to produce lists and blueprints can be illuminating; ultimately, though, legal experience cannot be so confined. The only rule that could hope to capture how the law should respond to conflict arising out of cultural difference across the many contexts in which the issue may arise would be too abstract to be much help' (2001, 194–5).

3 In addition to policy reasons militating against allowing the determination of status via arbitration, Canada is a federal state, and the solemnization of marriage and its dissolution through divorce fall within federal jurisdiction. The provinces do not have jurisdiction over marriage and divorce. Similarly, arbitrators do not have jurisdiction over criminal law.

4 Jean-François Gaudreault-DesBiens (2005, 166) mounts a scholarly defence of the claim that faith-based arbitration amounts to 'what is essentially an identity-based system of parallel justice' that is qualitatively distinct from 'the use of non-state norms in the context of particular, individualized settlements arrived at by the parties to family law-related disputes.' His distinction is based on two contestable propositions. First, he asserts that the challenges of discerning consent are unique and more vexing in the

context of religious communities than in the secular setting. I dispute this proposition in my analysis of *Hartshorne,* infra. Second, Gaudreault-DesBiens' characterization of what faith-based arbitration *is* frequently shades into what he apprehends it may presage. Calling the proposal for faith-based arbitration a 'parallel system of justice' is less a description than a prediction based on a slippery slope argument in which Gaudreault-DesBiens asserts that 'the State recognition of omni-competent [sic] religious arbitral tribunals ... is a step closer to a broader recognition of these tribunals' *exclusive jurisdiction* and thus *sovereignty* over a certain community of believers' (164, emphasis added). Arbitral tribunals recognized under the Family Law Act could never claim 'omni-competence' in matters of family law, and their jurisdiction was dictated by the parties according to the terms of their agreement to arbitrate. At this point, Gaudreault-DesBiens is no longer addressing the specific impact of family arbitration on individual participants, but rather warning that the recognition of arbitrations conducted within religious communities 'may lead to the mutation of social minorities into political ones.' He offers no evidence or argument in support of this assertion. In any event, I would suggest that Gaudreault-DesBien's conception of the character of minority religious communities is overly rigid and monolithic. Moreover, if Gaudreault-DesBien's fears about the impact of faith-based arbitration are well-founded, the fears are as likely to be realized through the ongoing enforcement of faith-based domestic contracts anyway. Negotiated and mediated agreements have historically been, and will continue to be, the dominant mechanism of privatization in family law.

5 Subsection 56(4) of the Family Law Act states: 'A court may, on application, set aside a domestic contract or a provision in it, (a) if a party failed to disclose to the other significant assets, or significant debts or other liabilities, existing when the domestic contract was made'; (b) if a party did not understand the nature or consequences of the domestic contract; or (c) otherwise in accordance with the law of contract. The law of contract allows a court to refuse to enforce an unconscionable contract.

6 It should be noted that Mr Hartshorne was still obliged to pay child and spousal support to Ms. Hartshorne.

7 As it turned out, another six years of litigation after the Supreme Court of Canada judgment demonstrated that Robert Hartshorne was equally recalcitrant on the matter of spousal and child support. In June 2010, the British Columbia Court of Appeal ordered him to pay approximately $350,000 in retroactive spousal support and $250,000 in retroactive child support (*Hartshorne* v. *Hartshorne* 2010).

8 Indeed, in 1998, the U.K. Government recommended that prenuptial agreements *not* be considered legally binding 'where the agreement is made fewer than 21 days prior to the marriage (this would prevent a nuptial agreement being forced on people shortly before their wedding day, when they may not feel able to resist)' (quoted in *Radmacher* v. *Granatino* 2010, UKSC 42, para. 5). The U.K. government did not legislate, however. In the Radmacher case, the U.K. Supreme Court elevated the status of prenuptial agreements in English law to presumptively binding. An eight-to-one majority (Baroness Hale dissenting) endorsed the enforceability of prenuptial agreements on roughly the same terms as the Supreme Court of Canada majority in *Hartshorne*.

9 Kathleen would have been entitled to child support whether or not she married Robert, and possibly to a measure of spousal support as well.

10 Indeed, some Canadian courts already appear willing to regard religiously based domestic contracts as potentially valid and enforceable. See, e.g. *Khan* v. *Khan* (2005); *Nasin* v. *Nasin* (2008). In each case, a prenuptial contract contained religiously inspired terms. The courts were willing to regard the respective agreements as potentially valid domestic contracts, but ruled that the particular circumstances of contract formation in each case did not meet formal requirements denoting that the parties understood the nature and consequences of the agreement and signed voluntarily.

11 One could take the position that courts could determine on a case-by-case basis (as they do now) when the communal pressure brought to bear on a Muslim woman vitiates consent.

12 I encountered this expression several years ago but cannot locate the source. Wendy Brown (2006) recently stated something similar.

13 Section 56(5) of the Family Law Act states: 'The court may, on application, set aside all or part of a separation agreement or settlement, if the court is satisfied that the removal by one spouse of barriers that would prevent the other spouse's remarriage within that spouse's faith was a consideration in the making of the agreement or settlement' (R.S.O. 1990, c. F.3, s. 56 (5)). Section 21(1) of the federal Divorce Act authorizes a court, inter alia, to dismiss an application for a civil divorce by a husband who withholds the 'get' from his wife.

14 For an interesting and generally sympathetic account of mediation among minority ethnic, religious, and sexual communities, see Freshman (2004).

15 I rely here on informal conversations with a practising family lawyer.

16 Referencing Council on American-Islamic Relations Canada, Islamic Council of Imams – Canada, Christian Legal Fellowship, Boyd wrote, 'When pressed by the Review, even the Islamic Institute of Civil Justice has

consistently stated that arbitration under Muslim family law would still have to accord with Canadian and Ontario law' (Boyd 2004b, 124).

REFERENCES

Bader, Veit. 2009. 'Legal Pluralism and Differentiated Morality: Shari'a in Ontario.' In R.D. Grillo, ed., *Legal Practice and Cultural Diversity*, 49–72. Aldershot: Ashgate.

Baines, Beverley. 2006. 'Equality's Nemesis.' *Journal of Law and Equality* 5: 57–80.

Bakht, Natasha. 2006. 'Were Muslim Barbarians Really Knocking on the Gates of Ontario? The Religious Arbitration Controversy – Another Perspective.' *Ottawa Law Review, 40th Anniversary Edition* 35 (Summer): 67–82.

Bhabha, Faisal. 2009. 'Between Exclusion and Assimilation: Experimentalizing Multiculturalism.' *McGill Law Journal* 54: 45–90.

Boyd, Marion, 2004a. *Dispute Resolution in Family Law: Protecting Choice, Promoting Inclusion*. Executive Summary. Accessed 24 July 2010. http://www.attorneygeneral.jus.gov.on.ca/english/about/pubs/boyd/executivesummary.pdf.

Boyd, Marion. 2004b. *Dispute Resolution in Family Law: Protecting Choice, Promoting Inclusion*. Accessed 24 July 2010. http://www.attorneygeneral.jus.gov.on.ca/english/about/pubs/boyd/fullreport.pdf.

Brown, Wendy. 2006. *Regulating Aversion: Tolerance in the Age of Identity and Empire*. Princeton: Princeton University Press.

Bryant, Michael, Attorney General. 2005. Statement on Arbitration Act. Accessed 16 May 2006. http://www.attorneygeneral.jus.gov.on.ca/english/news/2005/20050908-arb1991.asp.

Farrow, Trevor C.W. 2006. 'Re-framing the Sharia Arbitration Debate.' *Constitutional Forum* 15(2): 79.

Freshman, Clark. 2004. 'The Promise and Perils of "Our" Justice: Psychological, Critical and Economic Perspectives on Communities and Prejudice in Mediation.' *Cardozo Journal of Conflict Resolution* 6: 1–18.

Gaudreault-DesBiens, Jean-François. 2005. 'Constitutional Values, Faith-Based Arbitration, and the Limits of Private Justice in a Multicultural Society.' *National Journal of Constitutional Law*: 155–91.

Hirschl, Ran, and Ayelet Shachar. 2008–09. 'The New Wall of Separation: Permitting Diversity, Restricting Competition.' *Cardozo Law Review* 30: 25–35.

Kymlicka, Will. 1995. *Multicultural Citizenship*. Oxford: Oxford University Press.

Leckey, Robert. 2008. *Contextual Subjects: Family, State, and Relational Theory.* Toronto: University of Toronto Press.

Macklin, Audrey. 2009. 'Particularized Citizenship.' In in Seyla Benhabib and Judith Resnik, eds., *Migrations and Mobilities: Gender, Citizenship, and Borders,* 276–303. New York: NYU Press.

McGill, Shelley. 2007. 'Family Arbitration: One Step Forward, Two Steps Back.' *Journal of Law and Social Policy* 21: 49.

McLeod, James. 2004. 'Annotation: *Hartshorne* v. *Hartshorne.*' *Reports on Family Law* 47:10–18.

Okin, Susan Moller. 1999. 'Is Multiculturalism Bad for Women?' In Joshua Cohen et al., eds., *Is Multiculturalism Bad for Women?*, 7–26, 115–32. Princeton: Princeton University Press.

Réaume, Denise 2001. 'Legal Multiculturalism from the Ground Up.' In Ronald Beiner and Wayne Norman, eds., *Canadian Political Philosophy: Contemporary Reflections,* 194–206. Oxford: Oxford University Press.

Shachar, Ayelet. 2001. *Multicultural Jurisdictions: Cultural Differences and Women's Rights.* Cambridge: Cambridge University Press.

– 2008. 'Privatizing Diversity: A Cautionary Tale from Religious Arbitration in Family Law.' *Theoretical Inquiries in Law* 9: 573–607.

Shaffer, Martha. 2004. 'Developments in family law: The 2003–2004 Term.' *Supreme Court Law Review* 26: 407–39.

Von Torne, Lars. 2007-2008. 'Multicultural Misunderstandings: Impressions from the Canadian Debate and a Few Lessons for Germany.' *International Journal* 63: 553.

Walker, Eli. 2006. ''Don't Throw Out My Baby!' Why Dalton McGuinty Was Wrong to Reject Religious Arbitration.' *Appeal Review Current Law and Legal Reform* 11: 94.

Weinrib, Lorraine. 2008. 'Ontario's Sharia Law Debate: Law and Politics under the *Charter.*' In Richard J. Moon, ed., *Law and Religious Pluralism in Canada,* 239–63. Vancouver: UBC Press.

LEGAL INSTRUMENTS AND JUDGMENTS

Arbitration Act, S.O. c. 17. 1991.
British Columbia Family Relations Act, RSBC. 1996.
Family Law Act, RSO. 1990. c. F-3, as am. SO 2006.
Hartshorne v. *Hartshorne.* 2002. 6 B.C.L.R. (4th) 250, 31 R.F.L. (5th) 312, 220 D.L.R. (4th) 655 (BCCA).
Hartshorne v. *Hartshorne.* 2004. 1 SCR 550, 2004 SCC 22. (SCC).

Hartshorne v. *Hartshorne*. 2010. BCCA 327 (28 June 2010) (BCCA).
Khan v. *Khan*. 2005. 15 RFL (6th) 308.
MacLeod v. *MacLeod*. 2008. UKPC 64.
Miglin v. *Miglin*. 2003. 1 S.C.R. 303.
Murdoch v. *Murdoch*. 1975. 1 SCR 423.
Nasin v. *Nasin*. 2008. 291 DLR (4th) 432
Radmacher (formerly Granatino) v. *Granatino*. 2010. UKSC 42

4 'Sharia' Courts in Canada: A Delayed Opportunity for the Indigenization of Islamic Legal Rulings

FAISAL KUTTY

The date of 11 September 2005 is etched in the minds of several Ontario Muslims. On that fateful Sunday, Premier Dalton McGuinty announced his decision to preclude the use of religious laws in resolving family disputes under the Arbitration Act, 1991.[1] I concur with many observers that this announcement was a political exercise in 'smoke and mirrors' and does not effectively prevent people from resolving disputes using religious principles. It merely contributed to the negative perception of Islam and Muslims and served as a hindrance to the acceptance of Islam and Muslims on an equal footing in Canadian society. The passage of the Family Statute Law Amendment Act, 2005[2] formalizing Premier McGuinty's decision served to fuel debates that have been raging in liberal democracies for some time. Those opposed to arbitrating family disputes using religious principles under the Arbitration Act raised legitimate concerns about gender equality and minority rights within religious communities (Shachar 2005, 64; Boyd 2004). They questioned the role of religion in secular society and opposed what they saw as a privatization of the legal system (Bakht 2004). Proponents, however, contended that religious groups should be able to govern their lives according to their consciences within the parameters of law if the constitutional right to freedom of religion and association are to have any real value. Consenting and informed adults must be able to make religious choices even if these are not seen as 'correct' by a majority of the population, they argued. The issues, of course, transcend dispute resolution and tug at fundamental tensions surrounding multiculturalism and national identity, the separation of church and state, the limits of accommodation, and legal pluralism within a liberal democracy.

In this chapter I limit myself to arguing that the government of Ontario delayed an opportunity to contribute to the evolution of Islamic law by indigenizing Islamic legal rulings. Such a process would enable integration of Muslim citizens into broader Canada society by allowing them to maintain their identity and develop their practices in an 'organic' manner.[3] In the first section, I provide a brief overview of the Muslim communities' response to the proposal put forth by the Islamic Institute of Civil Justice (IICJ) and my role as counsel to various community groups in this matter. In the second section, I situate the debate within the context of the existing legal framework for family law in the province. In the third section, I explore the indigenization potential provided by this opportunity. More specifically, I argue that this controversy provided an opportunity for the *ummah* (Muslim community)[4] to struggle internally with its customs, practices, and principles. This community-led, bottom-up model of Islamic reform, which Mashood Baderin has accurately labelled 'the socio-cultural and harmonistic approach,' is the most sustainable, peaceful, and legitimate route to develop new rulings and laws (although addressing a different context; see Baderin 2007). I suggest that this organic bottom-up consensus-building approach to Islamic reform would be in line with the long established Islamic traditions of *tajdid* (renewal) and *islah* (reform) (Voll 1983). Such a community-led process is also necessary to ensure that integration is a two-way process of accommodation between the majority and minority communities. By way of conclusion, I argue that rather than ameliorating the potential issues within the community, as this process of indigenization could have done, the premier's decision actually did nothing to address them and perpetuates the existence of unregulated and unsupervised mediations and arbitrations using religious principles.

Muslim Communities' Reaction and Response

Among the province's growing, diverse Muslim population, opinions ranged from apathy regarding the debate, to fear that tribunal decisions may be biased against women, to wholehearted endorsement of Islamic jurisprudence. Some thought of it as a panacea that would solve their alleged inability to live as 'good' Muslims, while others saw wholesale government-sanctioned discrimination against Muslim women. The majority of Ontario Muslims, however, did not see arbitration as a critical issue for the community and only gave it passing interest (see also the chapter by Bullock). A combination of misunderstanding, ignorance, and the careless pronouncements from all sides of the issue, as well as inaccurate and biased media coverage helped fuel a firestorm (Morris 2006; Thornback 2005, 12). Many uncritically accepted the misunderstanding first promoted, most likely inadvertently, by the IICJ and later by the media that the government had approved new 'Sharia Courts' with coercive powers to force all Muslims to arbitrate using Islamic laws. Opponents from both within and outside the community, some who saw the initiative as 'Muslim barbarians knocking on the gates of Ontario' (Bakht 2007, 123), mobilized their resources and reacted swiftly on a global level. They launched a 'no-Sharia' campaign, which confirmed the Islamophobic fears of some.[5] These fears were exacerbated by well-intentioned but misguided feminists who were coming to the aid of 'imperiled Muslim Women' (Razack 2007, 10, 12; Bakht 2006).

In response to the mounting pressure from women's groups[6] and two secular[7] Muslim groups, in September 2004 the government formally asked former attorney general and women's rights advocate, Marion Boyd, to study the issue. At this time, I was engaged by five of the largest national Muslim groups to advocate for choice with some additional checks to ensure that the vulnerable were not coerced, exploited, or abused in the process.

I can appreciate that many were concerned about the exploitation of Muslim women. However, at times public discourse crossed into Islamophobia. For instance, in November 2004, I sat on a panel at the University of Toronto where some lawyers suggested that Muslim lawyers should not be able to participate in such arbitrations or in providing independent legal advice to Muslim women because they may be biased and may participate in the abuse of women (see University of Toronto Student Affairs Office and the Faculty of Law Diversity Committee St George Campus 2004). In another instance, a non-Muslim Toronto lawyer who was a partner at a prominent Bay Street law firm was singled out by his firm because he had made representations in favour of allowing faith-based arbitration and because he had encouraged a female Muslim law student intern to write in support of the initiative in a major daily newspaper. The firm was concerned about the public relations harm of being associated with the 'wrong' side of this controversial issue. This response motivated the lawyer to leave the firm.[8] In sum, the debate was highly emotional, and those who spoke in favour of faith-based arbitration were often seen as contributing to the exploitation and abuse of women (see also the chapter by Bullock).

Many in the community did not appreciate the widespread belief evident during the debate that Muslim women would necessárily be abused and exploited if the choice were available. As Mihad Fahmy, a Muslim woman lawyer who advocated faith-based arbitration, wrote: 'You may also have bought into the argument that Canadian-Muslim women will somehow be coerced into the proposed faith-based arbitration process. This, even though the same concern is not expressed with respect to Jewish and Christian women, some of whom already choose to settle family law and inheritance disputes according to the laws of their respective faiths. It is frustrating that such biases and stereotypes about Islam, and Muslim women in particular, have been driving the debate regarding religious-based arbitration' (Fahmy 2004).

The hysteria reached a fevered pitch when Quebec Member of the National Assembly Fatima Houda-Peppin (a self-proclaimed secular Muslim) initiated and tabled a motion to ban Islamic tribunals (Seguin 2005). The minor detail that makes this motion Islamophobic is that the province of Quebec's Civil Code specifically precludes the use of arbitration in the context of family law disputes.[9] As if to ensure that this was not lost on Muslims, the Quebec International Relations Minister, Monique Gagnon-Tremblay, reinforced hate and fear by stating: 'Muslims who want to come to Quebec and who do not respect women's rights, or rights, whatever they may be, in our civil code ... [should] stay in their country and not come to Quebec, because it's unacceptable' (De Souza 2005).

These Islamophobic announcements contributed to the involvement of many Muslims who were initially complacent or apathetic. In fact, the five national Muslim organizations – the Islamic Society of North America (ISNA), the Islamic Circle of North America (ICNA), the Muslim Association of Canada (MAC), the Canadian Muslim Civil Liberties Association (CMCLA) and the Canadian Council on American-Islamic Relations (CAIR-CAN) – only actively became involved in the issue when the discourse shifted to attacking Islam and singling out Muslims. CAIR-CAN was given a lead role in this initiative by the collective and I acted as lead counsel. In this capacity I met with various parties and spoke on numerous panels, including one organized by a leading opponent of the initiative, the CCMW (together with the Status of Women Canada, Rights and Democracy, Canadian Women's Foundation, and Change Canada Foundation), in April 2005, entitled 'Is There Room for Women's Equality Rights in Religious Arbitration?' Some of the organizers were upset with me because I urged the attendees to read their own report prepared by University of Ottawa law professor Natasha Bakht and the Boyd Report so they could make an informed decision on this issue. Bakht's report set out the existing family law regime and the protections and appeal/judicial review available in the traditional as well as alternative dispute resolution routes. Boyd's in-depth investigation led her to conclude that dispute arbitration in accordance with religious laws should continue, but that the arbitration law needed to build on more safeguards to address some of the issues with arbitration in general (see also the chapters by Macklin and Macfarlane). The emotions were high; at one point, I was booed and heckled on stage during my presentation in front of between three or four hundred attendees.[10]

As the debate raged, a more formal meeting attended by representatives of each of the groups I acted for, a number of local mosques, as well as another national coalition group, the Coalition of Muslim Organizations (COMO), took place at the sixth annual MAC-ICNA joint convention held in Mississauga in September 2005.[11] Collectively, these groups were particularly concerned about the paternalism and Islamophobia inherent in much of the discussion. I was invited to brief this larger group and a decision was made to become more active in the debate. One of the major suggestions was to have Muslim women take the lead. Unfortunately, it was too late into the game to make any real inroads (Jiminez 2005a, 2005b).[12]

In the months leading up to the 11 September 2005 decision to dismantle all religiously based family law arbitration, it appeared as though the government had no choice but to continue to allow religious arbitrations with the additional checks proposed by the Boyd Report (telephone call with counsel from the attorney general's office, summer 2005). The coalition of the five Muslim organizations I worked for argued that faith-based arbitrations should continue as a protected and viable option provided that they were voluntary, that all of Boyd's recommendations were adopted, and that the courts would only enforce decisions consistent with Canadian laws. In essence, arbitrations using religious principles should not be rejected outright, but should be evaluated in light of Ontario laws and common law principles.

Late in the summer of 2005 I received a call from the attorney general's office during which the counsel canvassed with me whether, in my opinion, my clients and the segment of the community they represented would be satisfied if the government decided that arbitral awards and decisions would be treated in the same manner as domestic contracts (separation agreements, marriage contracts, etc.). My un-equivocal response was, yes, such a proposal would be acceptable, as Muslims are asked to respect the laws of the land where they live pro-vided there is no positive obligation to breach a religious obligation. This exchange left me under the erroneous impression that the premier was simply going to adopt the Boyd Report's recommendations and treat such decisions in the same manner as domestic contracts.[13] I even informed some of my clients of this imminent possibility.

This phone call took place just weeks before opponents descended on Queen's Park (see CTV News 2011) accompanied by a number of prom-inent women's' activists, including June Callwood and Sally Armstrong, and urged the premier to ban faith-based arbitration (Jiminez 2005a, 2005b), which he did within the next few days.

Democracy does pose the threat of unbridled majoritarianism. In my experience, mass fears, hysteria, and prejudices contributed to the gov-ernment's response as they tried to appease the majority. It is at such times that one would expect to rely on constitutionalism, human rights, the principles of liberal democracy, and opposition parties to stand up in defence of minority rights or the rights of the unpopular. So it was surprising when both the New Democratic Party (NDP) and the Conser-vative Party (Tories) did not speak out in support of minority rights. In my meetings with Howard Hampton of the NDP[14] and John Tory of the Conservative Party,[15] on behalf of my clients, it became clear that both were reacting to widespread domestic and international opposition. In fact, both party leaders indicated that they never received so much op-position from an international audience on any issue. It became evident to me that explaining the progressive possibilities of Islamic law and the nuances of family law and the Arbitration Act would be drowned out by the anti-religion activists and well-intentioned but misinformed (or under-informed) women's' rights groups ostensibly trying to protect Muslim women from religion.[16] Both opposition parties in Ontario thus enabled taking away a right available to Ontarians since 1992 without any concrete evidence of harm. These members of the provincial parliament (MPPs) acted on speculation and against the recommendations of the government's own report, perhaps a first in Ontario legislative history.

Since the pronouncement, 'back room' arbitrations continue through-out the province, unregulated and unsupervised (see also Cutting and McFarlane, in this volume; Canadian Society of Muslims 2011). For instance, I have had clients approach me to complain about the Muslim Court of Arbitration (Darul Qada) because the institution has purportedly granted divorces and issued decisions without any authority (correspondence and email on file with author). It should be pointed out that divorce cannot be arbitrated. Nevertheless, in at least one such case brought to my attention, the person was Islamically divorced (against his will) from his wife after a brief conversation and some email exchanges with the Darul Qada. The person had never consented or submitted the matter to the tribunal. The wife assumed she was divorced, while the husband struggled with the legal system. Such decisions not only impact the issue of religious divorces which fall outside the scope of the existing legal regime, but a religious decision may in turn have an impact on negotiations over, inter alia, such issues as custody of children and the *mahr*.[17] I have also been approached by men and women who have had their matters settled or decided by individual imams and religious leaders. In my judgment, in most cases, the resolutions were fair and took into consideration the needs and interests of the parties and the contemporary context. However, in a small minority of cases, one party or the other was forced to accept and live with decisions that were unjust because the decision was seen as divinely ordained or inspired. A lack of knowledge about the legal system, Islamic law, and their rights under both systems makes it very easy for people to be duped, coerced, and short-changed. The lack of transparency, accountability, and regulation, and the interaction and complex interplay between the two systems allow people to pick and choose aspects of the two systems that best suit their immediate objectives. Ultimately, this situation makes it relatively easy to leverage, manipulate, and abuse a party into extracting concessions and result in potentially more exploitive settlements.

Such decisions might continue even if faith-based arbitrations were legally permitted. Nevertheless, there would be alternatives and options available, and they would be regulated and supervised. Moreover, I argue that a regulated system could more efficiently and effectively interact with the state law system. As noted by Miranda Forsyth (2007), such a planned legal pluralism can 'ensure that the various legal systems in a particular jurisdiction operate in ways that support and enrich one another, rather than undermine and compete with one another.'

The Existing Legal Framework for Family Law

Part of the confusion and hysteria over the course of the debate arose from a lack of understanding of the regime governing family law in

Ontario.[18] Family law issues in the province are governed by the Family Law Act[19] and the Divorce Act.[20] Consistent with the constitutional division of powers between the federal government and the provinces, as the name suggests, the federal Divorce Act governs divorces while the provincial Family Law Act addresses issues of property division, spousal support, and child support as well as child custody and access.[21] The legislative framework envisaged by the Family Law Act provides a default scheme in the case of a breakdown in the relationship. These default rules have evolved over time to reflect the changing mores of society and recognize the value of unpaid work provided by either spouse in enabling the other spouse to advance in his or her career. These rules also take into account that a partner may have forfeited or prejudiced his or her career growth by staying at home to care for children (see also Macklin's chapter in this volume).

Moreover, Part IV of the Family Law Act provides for parties to organize their affairs at various stages of the relationships through domestic contracts.[22] There are three types of domestic contracts: marriage contracts, cohabitation agreements, and separation agreements.[23] Common law contractual rules apply to the interpretation and enforceability of such contracts. Application may be made to a court for the setting aside of a domestic contract in one of the following three instances: (1) a party has failed to disclose to the other significant assets or debts that existed at the time the contract was entered into; (2) a party did not understand the nature or consequences of the contract; or (3) for general reasons at contract law such as undue influence, mistake, etc.[24] Courts, therefore, reserve the power to set aside agreements for a broad range of issues, in addition to its inherent *parens patriae* jurisdiction to act in the best interest of protected persons.[25]

Those opposed to family matters being arbitrated were under the false perception that the default provisions automatically and mandatorily governed all relationship breakdowns that proceeded to be resolved by means other than arbitration. As desirable as this may be, the reality is that even when matters proceed through lawyers or the legal system, parties usually do not pursue their maximum entitlements as set out in the legislation. Indeed, the system allows parties to opt out of much of the process and substance of the statutory regime to a considerable degree. Parties can negotiate and settle issues of property, support (spousal and child), as well as custody and access using any of the numerous options available to resolve disputes or simply not deal with it at all and walk away.[26] Nobody, including the state, can force anyone to pursue the default provisions or legal entitlements under the family law regime or otherwise.[27] The only mandatory dispute resolution option is the court system in the sense that a party filing a claim or bringing an action or application through the courts can compel the other party to respond. Nevertheless, even in such situations, the initiating party must take the first step in filing the matter in court and serving the other party. Generally, an affected party is under no obligation to enforce its rights whether it be through the courts or otherwise. Therefore, contrary to common perception, in theory it is impossible to force someone to arbitrate against their will. In practice, people could be coerced and pressured to submit to alternative dispute resolution (ADR) processes. This was the concern with unregulated and unsupervised ADR. From my perspective, this reality strengthens the argument for government oversight and regulation of faith-based ADR.

With the exception of the no-settlement option, in any of the resolution options the parties will negotiate and may compromise for less than their full legal entitlements or minimums as set out in legislation. They can also hold out and negotiate for more if they wish. The resulting settlements or agreements may or may not be formalized and may or may not be filed in court. Even when such agreements are filed in court as part of an uncontested divorce, for instance, the courts simply rubber stamp them; courts do not generally inquire into whether they are unfair, unconscionable, or violate public policy. There is no judicial oversight except when a party (or a public guardian if a minor is involved) decides to challenge the decision or bring it to the attention of the courts in an active manner. Such agreements and settlements are treated as legally binding, and the parties move on without any state oversight or intrusion to protect the vulnerable or weaker party. In essence, within certain constraints, the parties are free to use the default provisions or they can bargain according to their own values, priorities, and preferences in ordering their affairs during their relationship or in resolving issues at the end of the relationship.

It was therefore surprising to hear opponents of faith-based arbitration and the premier of Ontario use the expression 'one law for all' in denying orthodox Muslims just this benefit.[28] In a position paper on the tribunal by the Canadian Council of Muslim Women (CCMW 2004), posted on its website, CCMW president Alia Hogben wrote: 'We see no compelling reason to live under any other form of law in Canada, and we want the same laws to apply to us as to other Canadian women. We prefer to live under Canadian laws, governed by the Charter of Rights and Freedoms, which safeguard and protect our equality rights. Although the judicial system is not perfect, we know that there are mechanisms for change.' This statement leaves the inaccurate impression that Ontario Muslims would be forced to refer matters to the tribunal and that this arrangement was being carved out exclusively for Muslims.

As Natasha Bakht, who wrote a report that was used by various women's groups in opposing faith-based arbitration, points out in a reconsidered article published after the controversy: 'In fact, it is disingenuous to speak of "one law for all" when Ontario's family law permits parties to opt out of the default statutory regime such as the equal division of matrimonial property. Parties can, through negotiation, mediation or arbitration, based on the right to contract freely, agree to almost any resolution of their marital affairs ... couples' decisions to settle their family law affairs are generally left un-reviewed by the courts' (Bakht 2006).[29] If the right existed for people to opt out of the existing family law regime, why should religious Canadians be prevented from structuring settlements consistent with their values and beliefs, again subject to the usual contractual and common law protections and mechanisms for review?

Notably, where parties do not proceed through the courts and resolve matters privately (which is the case in a significant number of disputes), a court may never see the contract, settlement, or award. These very important and critical details were either ignored or downplayed by opponents of faith-based arbitration as they left the impression that all family matters that were settled other than by arbitration would be fully compliant with the province's family law regime.

Opportunity for the Indigenization of Islamic Legal Rulings

Both sides of the debate realized the significance of this battle over the place of Islamic law and its relationship to state law. Opponents speculated that a victory by the 'fundamentalists' in Canada would have given credence to those who stand behind Sharia in Muslim countries to the detriment of women. This ignored the fact that only very limited aspects of Islamic laws would have been engaged in the proposed initiative with respect to matters that were already subject to private contractual negotiations or where legislation provided for the right to opt out. Moreover, it also betrayed the evolutionary and context specific nature of Islamic law.

Sharia is a comprehensive guide of conduct to achieve submission to the will of God. Every believing Muslim tries to abide by his or her understanding of Sharia (see also the chapter by Clarke in this volume for an elaboration of this point). Sharia encompasses the spiritual, social, political, economic, and legal realms. Islamic laws are derived and/or formulated from five sources. These five sources, according to a broad consensus, are the Qur'an, the *Sunnah* (precedent set by Prophet Muhammad), *ijma* (consensus), *qiyās* (analogical reasoning) and *ijtihad* (independent reasoning). The Qur'an and Sunnah are primary sources, and the others are secondary sources. The act of interpretation itself, but also custom/consensus of ijma and the use of reasoning, ensure that Islamic law is not static. Indeed, Islamic scholar Mohamed Iqbal called ijtihad 'the principle of movement in the structure of Islam' (Iqbal 1977, 165).

The discovery of Islamic rules of conduct is attained through *fiqh* or jurisprudence. Fiqh is composed of the *usul al fiqh* and the *furu al fiqh*. Usul al fiqh is the methodology of jurisprudence, including the philosophy of law, sources of rules, and the principles of legislation, interpretation, and application of the Qur'an and traditions of the prophet Muhammad. Furu al fiqh are the derivates or the legal rules, which are subject to interpretation and evolution. While agreeing on major points of usul, for the most part, Muslims have historically tolerated a wide variety of opinions with regards to furu. Islamic law (furu al fiqh) has always been shaped by context and provided that the usul and the *maqasid al sharia* (higher objectives) are taken into consideration, is open to reinterpretation. Islamic laws, for the most part, are therefore shifting and contested (of course consistent with the higher objectives) rather than fixed and static.

A distinction must be made between Sharia and many of the technical legal rules derived from and through the primary and secondary sources. A *faqih*, or jurist, derived these rules or made these decisions, and thus they are not eternal. Such rules and decisions, being the result of human agency, are open to re-interpretation in light of, inter alia, new social, economic, educational, and political circumstances. There is general consensus that the body of rulings and interpretations are not binding on all peoples and all times, because essentially they are interpretations by fallible humans (mostly if not almost exclusively by men) within certain contexts.

Sharia differs from the Western legal tradition in many respects including the derivation of its legitimacy, sources, and methodology for evolution or reform. But there are also some similarities. Like most Western legal systems, Sharia is a positive system of law and not merely religious law. Additionally, both systems apply judge-made law using the case law method in their own particular ways. Moreover, both systems allow the governing authority to make legislation. Islamic law is characterized by a strong tradition of internal legal pluralism. This variety is evident from the numerous of schools of jurisprudence (with varying degrees of flexibility) which have existed throughout history (Kamali 1991). Five prominent schools (whose fiqh rulings continue to change) emerged, including the Hanafi, Shafi, Hanbali, and Maliki schools in the Sunni tradition and the Jaafari School in the Shia tradition (al-Faruqi and Faruqi 1986). This pluralism is also evident in legal adaptation to practices and customs. Islamic legal interpretations in the Middle East differ from those in South Asia, Indonesia, or Bosnia. Diversity is the norm.

Despite this nuance, complexity, and changeability in Islamic jurisprudence, and despite the fact that faith-based arbitration in Ontario would only apply to a very small area of jurisprudence, the term 'sharia courts' was used to characterize what was being sought in Ontario. In popular usage, this term raised the spectre of stoning women, capital punishment, and other such fears.[30] A significant contributing factor to this fear is the sharia-based laws and practices in certain Muslim countries. Arguments for faith-based arbitration became unwinnable no matter how nuanced or qualified once the term Sharia was associated with the issue. As Tariq Modood accurately noted in the British context: 'Part of the problem is language. The mere fact of saying something positive about "*shari'a*" leads to knee-jerk hostility amongst many people, just as the term "secularism" regrettably is understood by some Muslims as a policy of atheism, colonialism or postcolonial despotism. The use of either of these terms can lead to the closing of minds, however reasonable and qualified what is being said' (Modood 2008).

During one panel discussion in April 2004, for instance, all my nuanced legal arguments were shoved aside the moment the other panellist brought up the image of women being stoned in the streets and hands of thieves being cut off.[31] Neither would be the subject of arbitration under Islamic law or pursuant to Canadian law (Boyd 2004; al-Qurashi 2004). In fact, a tribunal would have no jurisdiction to entertain such matters. Moreover, even if such decisions were ever made by an arbitral tribunal they would not only be unenforceable but would attract criminal and civil sanctions against members of the tribunal and those who carry out such rulings. These fine details fall on deaf ears when hysteria, fear, and emotions take over.

It was also inaccurate to characterize these tribunals as full-fledged Islamic law courts, because such a characterization would include public law issues as well as the full spectrum of private law issues, the bulk of which cannot be the subject of arbitration or private resolution. The tribunals would have simply used Islamic legal principles to resolve a very specific and limited set of civil disputes which might be the subject of arbitration under the limited jurisdiction of the Arbitration Act. What would have evolved out of the proposals by the IICJ or the institution-alization of the application of Islamic legal principles in arbitration should be more accurately characterized as a form of Muslim dispute resolution consistent with Canadian laws and within the flexibility of Islamic normative practices.

Some argued that the core Islamic teachings of equality, compassion, justice, freedom, and generosity could have been brought to the fore again by using interpretations that are consistent with the spirit of Islam and the present realities (Mir-Hosseini 2003, 11). If Islamic dispute resolution is a simple exercise of grafting the Western paradigm onto the existing Islamic rules then it will not be fair or just.[32] Some of the classical and imported rules, practices and customs would not advance the cause of justice. The status quo in terms of fiqh rules and rulings characterized far too often with abuse of women and minorities is partly the product of rigid interpretations shaped by tribal and cultural norms. The purported blanket prohibition of religious arbitration undermines the work of Islamic feminists and other reformers who argue for the progressive possibilities inherent in renewed interpretations of Islamic law. Ironically, by being so vocal and adamant in opposing Islamic law, many of these activists have reinforced the idea that religion is necessarily dangerous to women, bound to patriarchy, and ultimately unchangeable. This formal arbitration initiative provided an opportunity to shed cultural baggage and revisit some of the patriarchally misinterpreted and/or context-specific rulings by refocusing on the Qur'an's emphasis on gender equality. Moreover, this was also an opportunity to take into consideration, inter alia, the modern context, new customs and practices, and the accumulated wisdom of human knowledge since the days of the classical Islamic rulings.

This 'indigenization' would be consistent with the long-established Islamic tradition of tajdid and islah, which reflect 'a continuing tradition of revitalization of Islamic faith and practice within the historic

communities of Muslims' (Voll 1983, 32). These concepts imply, among
other things, a return to the authentic sources of Islamic law, the Qur'an
and the Sunnah, for guidance in present practice; 'the assertion of the
right of independent analysis (ijtihad) of the Qur'an and the Sunnah in
this application,' rather than reliance on and application of the opinions
of past jurists (*taqlid*); and finally, a reassertion of the 'authenticity and
uniqueness' of the Qur'anic message, a universal experience applicable
to all times and places (Voll 1983, 35). Through these methods, renewers
(*mujaddidun*) and reformers (*muslihun*) revisit the sources anew in light
of present circumstances and reinterpret the universal and timeless
Islamic ideals in light of present realities and prevailing ideas (Ramadan
2009). Through tajdid (renewal), scholars embark on a 'renewal of the
reading, understanding, and consequently, the implementations of
texts in light of the various historiocultural contexts in which Muslim
communities or societies exist,' while islah encourages 'reforming the
human, spiritual, social, or political context' in light of these readings
(Ramadan 2009).

These transformative and evolutionary concepts would be instrumental to Islamic scholars attempting to formulate 'indigenous' Islamic
legal approaches to issues in the Canadian context, according to a renewed reading of the sources in light of contemporary contexts (see
Emon this volume).[33] This interpretation would entail rethinking many
of the prevailing notions and customs. Indeed, many academics, including Islamic feminists such as Ziba Mir-Hosseini, have already proposed such reforms in the Islamic legal context (Mir-Hosseini 2003, 11;
Stowasser 1996).

Tariq Ramadan (1999), a leading European Islamic reformist thinker,
proposes a model for renewal-reform that could be applicable in the
Canadian context (97). Ramadan conceives of a new approach that has
the scholars of the Islamic texts (*ulama an-nusus*), who specialize in the
'text sciences' (Qur'anic sciences, hadīth sciences, usul al-fiqh, and the
like), work together with 'scholars of the context' (*ulama al-waqi*) who
are versed in the 'context sciences' (the human, social, scientific, and
other sciences), in order to create informed Islamic legal rulings through
collaboration (129). *Fatwa* (legal opinions) issued in this manner would
have the benefit of the wisdom of textual scholars as well as relevant
experts (130–1). While his is not necessarily a novel approach, Ramadan
has reconceptualized the relationship from a hierarchical one to one of
equality (129, 134–44). He argues that both sets of scholars are equally
important in the creation of 'an applied Islamic ethics in the various

fields of knowledge' in furtherance of his expanded list of maqasid (higher objectives). Ramadan argues: 'If Islam is a universal Message, appropriate to all places over all times, then this should be shown, proved and expressed through a permanent reflection going and coming from the sources to reality and from reality to the sources. This process should be witnessed in every time, everywhere so that the application of the Islamic law remains faithful to the maqasid al-shari'a' (93). Thus, by acknowledging what is immutable and what is open to change in both the texts and the context, scholars can embark on tajdid and islah by engaging in 'critical reading, interpretations, and strategies,' and come together to create a 'common (collaborative, specialized) *ijtihad* of applied ethics' (144). The result, of course, will be a new set of normative rules, practices and principles to guide human action and relationships (144).

In the context of the Ontario faith-based arbitration debate, Ramadan's model would have been quite useful. He calls for a complete rethinking of Islamic laws from within, by recasting the existing conceptual tools and formalizing a more comprehensive dialectic between religious scholars and scholars of context. Indeed, a collaborative effort by Islamic legal scholars, Canadian legal scholars, and other experts in the development of Canadian Islamic jurisprudence may have alleviated many of the fears by identifying dangers both real and perceived elicited by the ambiguous concept of Sharia. Interestingly, as part of their recommendations to Marion Boyd (2004), the Islamic Councils of Imams Canada called for the establishment of such an integrated board of Islamic and Canadian legal scholars for the purposes of reviewing decisions made in the context of faith-based arbitration. There were few calls, however, in the way of establishing a cooperative model through which Canadian-Islamic jurisprudence could begin developing with the input of both textual and contextual scholars.

Moreover, as the Canadian Muslim community continues to establish itself in Canada, it is likely that an 'indigenized' body of Islamic law will develop.[34] The Canadian Muslim community as a whole is relatively young, and many in the wider group are relative newcomers to Canada (Statistics Canada Online 2001). There is at present, however, to use the words of Marion Boyd, a 'wealth of talent, knowledge and leadership available within the Muslim community' that must be called on. A constructive and creative Canadian Muslim identity is already in the process of evolving. Encouraging this same creative approach in the application of Islamic law in the private sphere, integrating both

Muslim and Canadian ideals, would contribute greatly to the development of an 'indigenized' Islamic jurisprudence. Consistent with the tradition of internal Islamic legal pluralism, this body of jurisprudence would reflect a broad array of views and approaches in a Canadian context. In other words, the multiplicity of interpretations and schools of thought as they exist on the ground today would continue to evolve and be formalized and tempered in accommodation.

This proposal may sound purely theoretical. Yet, over the course of my legal practice over the past fifteen years, I have been fortunate to be involved in this evolution. I have worked with clients and their Islamic scholar of choice to craft legal solutions that are consistent with both systems of law. In the process, existing Islamic rules have been changed or transformed. In the area of inheritance, for instance, scholars have rendered fatwas equalizing the shares to be given to daughters and sons.[35] The rationale provided was that the unequal distribution was ostensibly based on a son being held responsible to care for his mother and sisters. Such rights would be enforceable in an Islamic jurisdiction, but since this arrangement would not be enforceable in the Canadian context, the scholars have provided this dispensation to reflect contextual realities. Such creative reforms are being repeated throughout North America, thanks in part to institutions such as the International Institute of Islamic Thought,[36] the Fiqh Council of North America, and local mosques.[37] The Fiqh Council, for instance, is a group of Islamic scholars developing contemporary fiqh that is culturally, politically, and socially relevant to the North American or Western contexts.[38] The evolutionary and context-specific nature of Islamic law is also evident, for instance, in two rulings issued by the Fiqh Council, one endorsing Muslim participation in the U.S. military (see Islamic Center of Greater Toledo 2001)[39] and the other permitting the recreation of the bust of the Prophet Muhammad in the United States Supreme Court (al-Alwani 2000–01). In both cases, adherence to the classical rulings would not have resulted in such fatwa.

The faith-based arbitration controversy provided Ontario with a timely opportunity to develop and experiment with models of legal pluralism that could have balanced the competing rights in a manner that attempted to respect all parties and protect the vulnerable. It was also occasion to explore how Islamic law and liberal democracy can coexist and complement each other within a liberal constitutional framework.

Conclusion

The family law arbitration controversy brought to the fore a highly charged emotional debate that has been raging for some time in multicultural democracies like Canada. The tension transcends the issue of dispute resolution and tugs at two fundamental questions. The first is how to balance the collective rights of a group with the individual rights of group members – particularly the vulnerable, women, and children. The second question is how to reconcile religious rights with the separation of church and state.

Proponents of faith-based arbitrations argue that religious values can be a major part of a person's identity and can therefore influence one's attitude and approach to conflict resolution. The proponents contend that they should be able to govern their lives according to their consciences within the parameters of law if the constitutional right to freedom of religion is to have any real value. As CAIR-CAN argued: 'Supporting the creation of Islamic family law tribunals, along with those of other faith groups, is a form of accommodating the needs of religious minorities within a multicultural society. Moreover, giving members of religious minority groups the option of resolving civil disputes according to their own religious doctrine within a framework that is respectful of both Canadian law and the Charter of Rights and Freedoms is consistent with the Charter's own guarantee of freedom of religion contained in section 2(a)' (Council on American-Islamic Relations Canada Online 2004). Consenting and informed adults must be able to make religious choices even if others do not believe these are 'correct' choices. As Ronald Dworkin says about faith (albeit not in the context of this controversy), 'We can't ask people to set aside their most profound convictions about the truth of deep moral and ethical issues when we are also asking them to make decisions ... that are for most people the most basic and fundamental moral and ethical decisions they will in their lifetime be called upon to make' (Katz 2006).

In this chapter I have sought to demonstrate that Islamic legal doctrine is replete with creative methodologies of reinterpretation that can serve as rich sources for more gender-friendly practices. This interpretation lends support to the idea that a tolerable liberalism or a quasi-sovereignty route may be better models if we are to foster respectful coexistence (Swaine 2006; Williams 2005). The clear advantages are: building more constructive forms of engagement between majority and minority cultures; that by giving deliberative priority to accommodation we avoid the double standards highlighted in the faith-based controversy; and contributing to peace and coexistence by making space for rather than suppressing people's core beliefs and values. As Lucas Swaine argues, the belief among religious minorities that the liberal state aims to undermine them leads to unnecessary distrust and potentially even clashes (Swaine 2006; Williams 2005).

The prevailing approach of imposing secular values in the name of human rights fails to understand and appreciate the fundamental role accorded to religious beliefs and practices by many. I would concur with Charles Taylor and other Communitarians, at least on this point, that social and communal arrangements and institutions are crucial to the development of self-meaning and identity. In fact, those who were in favour of making this option available counter that if people of faith, Muslims included, are not allowed to exercise their religious rights within the confines of Canadian law and they are not treated or seen to be treated the same as others, this disparity will fuel the growing distrust, alienation, and marginalization felt by some in the community.

At the same time, the legitimate concerns raised by secular feminist groups, and contrary to perception, also by mainstream Muslim groups, should not be trivialized or minimized. The fear that women may feel pressured into submitting their disputes to an Islamic arbitration tribunal that may be less protective of their rights is a legitimate one. However, this understanding ignores the fact that social pressure is a reality in both the religious and secular contexts (see also the chapter by Macklin). It is not necessarily the case that religion must restrict women's rights. Moreover, this fear fails to recognize that for some women the desire to decide their dispute in accordance with their core values and principles may take precedence over any secular understanding of the right choice. Indeed, it even precludes the empowerment of religious women who seek to push the boundaries and explore the progressive possibilities of Islamic law.

Given an ostensible commitment to equality and religious freedom in the Canadian Charter of Rights and Freedoms, it would be hypocritical to prioritize secular ways as the only means of protecting the vulnerable. In this Ontario family law arbitration debate, the hypocrisy was glaring, given that the legal system itself allows and encourages the private resolution of disputes and the opting out of the statutory family law regime without any oversight or court sanction.

I concur with many observers who have concluded that the real losers in the Ontario decision are women, particularly those women who wish to live a faith-based life, as they interpret it.[40] A paternalistic attitude towards Muslims did not and will not solve the issue of social pressure and in fact will alienate many. As Boyd points out, denying Muslims the option of using religious-based ADR would not only limit their options, but it may also 'push the practice of religious arbitration outside the legal system altogether, thus limiting the court's ability to intervene to correct problems' (Boyd 2004). Alternative dispute resolution already exists within the Muslim community as it does in the broader community. People are abiding by decisions as if they were the word of God and therefore binding.[41] Formalizing the process would have opened the door towards greater transparency and accountability. As long as there are proper procedures and rules of conduct in place there is nothing preventing the community from instituting a dynamic and less disruptive alternative to the adversarial court system.

As the *Globe and Mail* (2004) editorialized at the time, 'the Islamic tribunal may send a message that Muslims can be who they are and still be as Canadian as anyone else.' I argue that a sober ex post facto rational review of the issue will reveal that exploring ways to accommodate Islamic laws within a more inclusive model of legal pluralism would provide a great opportunity to contribute to the evolution of Islamic law by pushing its progressive possibilities, indigenize Islam in Canada, and thereby help in the integration of Muslims.

ACKNOWLEDGMENT

I would like to acknowledge research assistance from Sarah Mohamed, Honours B.A. (History) from York University, and J.D. Candidate (2011), Osgoode Hall, and from Aimee Gong, J.D. Candidate (2012), Valparaiso School of Law. I would also like to thank Akbar Mohamed for his comments and Shaikh Ahmad Kutty for his comments, suggestions, and encouragement.

NOTES

1 *Arbitration Act* S.O. 1991 c.17.
2 Family Statute Law Amendment Act, S.O. 2006, c.1.

3 There is often confusion between the term *Sharia* and Islamic law or Islamic jurisprudence. I will be using Islamic law throughout this chapter. The two terms were used interchangeably and inaccurately in much of the discussion and debate around this issue. This chapter limits the discussion of Islamic law to the private realm of personal relations and contractual matters in the area of family law.

4 The *ummah* in this context would be the local Canadian or more specifically the Ontario *ummah*. This specification will be consistent with the Islamic tradition of geographically and contextually specific schools of jurisprudence. See a discussion of the differences arising from geography and other external influences (Nafi 2004, 2–60).

5 Many in the community saw some of the opponents as singling out Muslims and Islam. Interestingly, one of the main opponents, Homa Arjomand (2011), has given some credence to this by now focusing her energy on opposing Islamic education of children.

6 These include the National Organization of Immigrant and Visible Minority Women of Canada, the National Association of Women and the Law (NAWL), the YWCA Canada, and the Women's Legal Education and Action Fund (LEAF).

7 Not all secular Muslim groups were opposed. The Canadian Council of Muslim Women and the Muslim Canadian Congress were the most vocal and media savvy, and they were the main Muslim groups opposing the initiative fully. The vast majority of the groups were either silent or endorsed the idea of choice to varying degrees.

8 Although engaged actively on this issue he has never really publicized this story. He spoke about it at an event that addressed the controversy.

9 Civil Code of Quebec, S.Q. 1991, c. 64, art. 2639: 'Disputes over the status and capacity of persons, family matters or other matters of public order may not be submitted to arbitration.'

10 Revealing the lack of knowledge about the issues involved, during the question and answer session one lawyer even asked me what was wrong with Ontario law. My answer was, of course, nothing. The initiative was simply attempting to use existing Ontario law. Interestingly, a number of women also came up after my presentation and said that they had totally misunderstood the issue and although they were CCMW members they did not agree with the position of the CCMW.

11 See http://melayucanada.multiply.com/journal/item/32. Marion Boyd spoke about her report at this conference.

12 A press conference was organized to express some of the concerns (Jimenez 2005a, 2005b).

13 See discussion below in the section titled 'Existing Legal Framework for Family Law.'

14 This meeting was also attended by the executive director of the Canadian Muslim Civil Liberties Association (CMCLA), Anwaar Syed, and the Toronto head of the Canadian Council on American-Islamic Relations (CAIR-CAN), Maryam Dadabhoy.

15 This meeting was also attended by the chairman of the Islamic Council of Imams Canada, Imam Abdul Hai Patel, and Asma Warsi, a prominent woman activist in the community and editor-in-chief of *The Ambition*, a community newspaper.

16 I acknowledge there were some legitimate concerns, but all of them could have been dealt with in the legal context. I feel as though most of the feminist groups were misinformed (by anti-religion activists and radical secularists) into calling for the prohibition of all religious arbitration through fear-mongering based on the decontextualized albeit legitimate experiences of women who came from oppressive regimes. They were decontextualized because they were speaking of oppression in dictatorships that did not operate within a liberal multicultural and constitutional framework and because the full spectrum of Sharia-based laws were being applied in those jurisdictions. The discussion in our context was restricted to private law issues.

17 *Mahr* is the gift given by the groom to the bride in consideration of the marriage. In many instances a deferred mahr is used to ensure that a wife is financially protected in the event of divorce. This can often serve as a bargaining tool in the interaction and interplay between family law and Islamic family law rules in the in Western jurisdictions, including Canada (Fournier 2010).

18 Of course, the controversy was broader than family law and encompassed other personal areas of law as well. The main objections were raised in the family law context and this is the focus of this chapter.

19 R.S.O. 1990, c. F.3.

20 R.S.C., 1985, c. 3 (2nd Supp.). Divorce is not an issue that can be arbitrated.

21 There are also federal guidelines when it comes to support payments.

22 Family Statute Law Amendment Act, S.O. 2006, c.1, ss.51–60.

23 Ibid., s. 51.

24 Ibid,. s. 56(4).

25 See Bakht (2004) for a detailed discussion of when and under what circumstances courts can intervene. The courts zealously guard their right to intervene for various reasons, particularly their *parens patriae* ('parent of the nation') jurisdiction to ensure that the best interests of any children or

others under guardianship are taken into account: 'The *parens patriae* juris-diction is … founded on necessity, namely the need to act for the protection of those who cannot care for themselves. The courts have frequently stated that it is to be exercised in the "best interest" of the protected person, or again, for his or her "benefit" or "welfare." While the Superior Court retains a residual jurisdiction to use the *parens patriae* power, it will not do so lightly. This jurisdiction is to be exercised to protect children and other vulnerable individuals, not their parents. The courts have determined that *parens patriae* is available in two situations: to fill a legislative gap or on judicial review' (*M.D.R. v. Ontario (Deputy Registrar General)*, 270 D.L.R. (4th) 90). It should also be noted that a court may set aside support provisions or a waiver of support in a contract, under the authority granted it in accordance with s. 33 of the act. A court may exercise its authority under this section if: the waiver or the provision results in unconscionable circumstances; the waiver or provision means that the prospective recipient must instead depend on public assistance; or if there is a default in the support payment.

26　They could do it themselves with or without self-help kits available on the Internet and in stationery stores; use the services of a paralegal (who may or may not act for both parties) and settle it as an uncontested matter; settle the issues with the help of family, peers, or religious/community leaders; use the same lawyer to resolve these issues again as an uncontested matter; go to separate lawyers, and even in this case most of the matters are settled through negotiation and compromise; use one of the ADR options; and lastly, decide not to resolve the matter at all and simply walk away.

27　A court can intervene for a number of reasons if requested to do so by way of an action, application for judicial review, or appeal. Suffice it to note that these same avenues and interventions would be available in the context of arbitral awards (Bakht 2004).

28　The premier declared: 'There will be no Shariah law in Ontario. There will be no religious arbitration in Ontario. There will be one law for all Ontarians' (Leslie 2005).

29　See also Macklin in this volume. Bakht's first article essentially reviewed the problems with allowing faith-based arbitration. The article did acknowledge that these problems existed in the family law area irrespective of whether it was religious or otherwise. The piece concluded against allowing faith-based arbitrations based on the secular nature of society (Bakht 2004).

30 'Imagery is everything. Especially when coupled with the power of fear' (Fahmy 2004). The use of the term *Sharia* brought with it all the negative baggage associated with it.

31 Entitled 'Islamic Law and Faith-Based Arbitration: An Overview,' Noor Cultural Centre, Toronto, 16 April 2004. At this event, a group of secular 'fundamentalists' (Muslims and non-Muslims) heckled me and asked me to go 'back home' if I wanted Sharia. They only calmed down when the organizers intervened and I retorted to their heckling by suggesting that they were acting like a 'Secular Taliban.'

32 'Islamic law is being exploited in many countries to oppress women and minorities,' says Anwaar Syed of the Canadian Muslim Civil Liberties Association. 'If the tribunal wishes to institute that kind of interpretation then they will be hard pressed to find support within the community' (Kutty 2004). While cautious about the initiative put forward by the Institute, Syed's group is in favour of formalizing ADR within the community to resolve disputes amicably.

33 Emon envisages a 'marketplace' of Islamic law with new rules developing. This is not something totally new (except, of course, in terms of the setting being in the Canadian context) as it is the revival of the Islamic tradition as evident from the existence of numerous classical schools of Islamic jurisprudence.

34 There is evidence it is already developing but there is no structure, organization, or formality to the process.

35 Classical and even more contemporary Islamic inheritance rules insisted on a daughter receiving half the shares of a son.

36 http://www.iiit.org/. Accessed 20 Jan. 2011.

37 http://www.fiqhcouncil.org/. Accessed 20 Jan. 2011.

38 There is much work being done in this area by Tariq Ramadan and Hamza Yousuf. See http://www.zaytunacollege.org/academics/, accessed 20 Jan. 2011. Muzzamil Siddiqui and Taha Jabir Al Alwani are some of the leading voices. See also Imam Feisal and Abdul Rauf. http://www.cordobainitiative.org/?q=content/shariah-index-project, accessed 20 Jan. 2011.

39 This is a big shift from classical Islamic views.

40 Those Muslims who wish to use the option would simply be following a long-established practice within the Muslim tradition of arbitration (known as *tahkim*). Indeed, the Qur'an specifically refers to arbitration in the context of matrimonial disputes: 'If you fear a breach between them (man and wife), then appoint an arbitrator from his people and an

arbitrator from her people. If they desire reconciliation, God will make them of one mind. God is all knowing, all aware' (Qur'an 4:35).

41 Back alley mediations and arbitrations continue, and women are abiding by decisions that may be unfair and even exploitative because they are packaged as being from God.

REFERENCES

Alwani, Taha Jaber al-. 2000–01. '"Fatwa" Concerning the United States Supreme Courtroom Frieze.' *Journal of Law and Religion* 15: 1–28.

Arjomand, Homa. 'International Declaration, Islamic Schools Should be Banned, Children Have No Religion.' Petition Online. Accessed 20 Jan. 2011. http://new.petitiononline.com/nofaith/petition.html.

Baderin, Mashood A. 2007. 'Islam and the Realization of Human Rights in the Muslim

World: Approaches and Two Divergent Perspectives.' *Muslim World Journal of Human Rights* 4: 1–25.

Bakht, Natasha. 2004. 'Family Arbitration Using Sharia Law: Examining Ontario's Arbitration Act and its Impact on Women.' *Muslim World Journal of Human Rights* 1(1): 26–9.

– 2005. 'Arbitration, Religion and Family Law: Private Justice on the Backs of Women.' Accessed 20 Jan. 2011. http://www.nawl.ca/en/newlibrarypage/researchpapersmenu/117-arbitration-religion-and-family-law-private-justice-on-the-backs-of-women-.

– 2006. 'Were Muslim Barbarians Really Knocking on the Gates of Ontario? The Religious Arbitration Controversy – Another Perspective.' *Ottawa Law Review, 40th Anniversary Edition* 35 (Summer): 67–82.

– 2007. 'Religious Arbitration in Canada: Protecting Women by Protecting Them from Religion.' *Canadian Journal of Women and the Law* 19: 119–23.

Boyd, Marion. 2004. *Dispute Resolution in Family Law: Protecting Choice, Promoting Inclusion.* Ministry of the Attorney General Online. Accessed 13 Jan. 2011. http://www.attorneygeneral.jus.gov.on.ca/english/about/pubs/boyd/.

Canadian Council of Muslim Women. 2004. 'Position Statement on the Proposed Implementation of Sections of Muslim Law [Sharia] in Canada.' Accessed 17 Jan. 2011. http://www.ccmw.com/activities/act_arb_muslimlaw_sharia.html.

Canadian Council of Muslim Women, Status of Women Canada, Rights and Democracy, Canadian Women's Foundation, Change Canada Foundation.

2005. 'Is there Room for Women's Equality Rights in Religious Arbitration?' Symposium, 9 April, Toronto. Accessed 20 Jan. 2011. http://www.ccmw .com/documents/CCMWSymposiumReport2005.pdf.

Canadian Society of Muslims. 2003. 'Muslim Court of Arbitration.' Accessed 20 Jan. 2011. http://muslim-canada.org/DARLQADAMSHAH3 .html.

Council on American-Islamic Relations Canada Online (CAIR-CAN). 2004. 'Review of Ontario's Arbitration Process and *Arbitration Act*.' Accessed 20 Jan. 2011. http://www.caircan.ca/downloads/sst-10082004.pdf.

CTV News. 'Protesters March against Sharia Law in Canada.' 9 Sept. Accessed 20 Jan. 2011. http://www.ctv.ca/CTVNews/TopStories/20050909/sharia_ law_ontario_050908/.

De Souza, Mike. 2005. 'Quebec Leaders Warn Ontario: Reject Sharia: Minister wants Immigrants Who Support It Barred.' *National Post*, March 11.

Fahmy, Mihad. 2004. 'Shariah Law Requires Tough, Open Debate.' *London Free Press*. 14 Sept. Accessed 5 Sept. 2010. http://www.caircan.ca/oped_more. php?id=1161_0_10_0_C.

Faruqi, Ismail R. al-, and Lois Lamya Faruqi. 1986. *The Cultural Atlas of Islam*. New York: Macmillan.

Forsyth, Miranda. 2007. 'How to "Do" Legal Pluralism.' Accessed 17 Jan. 2011. http://papers.ssrn.com/sol3/papers.cfm?abstract_id=993617.

Fournier, Pascale. 2010. 'Flirting with God in Western Secular Courts: *Mahr* in the West.' *International Journal of Law, Policy and the Family* 24(1): 67–94.

Globe and Mail. 2004. 'An Islamic Court? Here? Why Not?' 28 Aug.

Iqbal, Muhammad. 1977. *The Reconstruction of Religious Thought in Islam*. Lahore: Sheikh Muhammad Ashraf.

Islamic Center of Greater Toledo. 2001. 'American Muslim Participation in the War.' Accessed 22 Jan. 2011. http://www.icgt.org/SpecialArticles/ MuslimsInMilitary.htm.

Jiminez, Marina. 2005a. 'Ontario Sharia Plan Protested.' *Globe and Mail*, 9 Sept.

– 2005b. 'Debate Stirs Hatred, Sharia Activists Say; Controversy over Faith-Based Tribunals Feeds Negative Stereotypes, Group Warns.' *Globe and Mail*, 15 Sept.

Kamali, Mohammad Hashim. 1991. *The Principles of Islamic Jurisprudence*. Cambridge: Islamic Texts Society.

Katz, Elizabeth. 2006. 'Dworkin Explores Secular, Religious Models for Society.' *Virginia Law Online*. Accessed 20 Jan. 2011. http://www.law .virginia.edu/html/news/2006_spr/dworkin.htm.

Kutty, Faisal. 2004. 'Canada's Islamic Dispute Resolution Initiative Faces Strong Opposition.' *Washington Report on Middle East Affairs*, May: 70–1.

Leslie, Keith. 2005. 'McGuinty Rejects Ontario's Use of Shariah and All Religious Arbitrations.' *Canadian Press*, 11 Sept. http://www .eligionnewsblog.com/12192/ontario-rejects-shariah-law-and-all-religious-arbitrations

Mir-Hosseini, Ziba. 2003. 'The Construction of Gender in Islamic Legal Thought and Strategies for Reform.' *Hawwa: Journal of Women in the Middle East and the Islamic World* 1: 11–31.

Modood, Tariq. 2008. 'Multicultural Citizenship and the Anti-Sharia Storm.' Open Democracy. Accessed 20 Jan. 2011. http://www.opendemocracy.net/article/faith_ideas/europe_islam/anti_sharia_storm#.

Morris, Catherine. 2006. 'Media's Mediation and Other Matters: Faith-Based Dispute Resolution in Canada.' Speaking Notes for a Panel Presentation ADR Subsection, BC Branch, Canadian Bar Association, 25 Jan., Vancouver, BC. Accessed 20 Jan. 2011. http://www.cba.org/CBA/newsletters/pdf/ADR-Morris_presentation.pdf.

Nafi, Basheer M. 2004. 'The Rise of Islamic Reformist Thought and Its Challenge to Traditional Islam.' In Suha Taji-Farouki and Basheer M. Nafi, eds., *Islamic Thought in the Twentieth Century*, 2–60. New York: St Martin's Press.

Qurashi, Zeyad al-. 2004. 'Arbitration under the Islamic *Sharia*.' *Transnational Dispute Management* 1: 2.

Ramadan, Tariq. 1999. *To Be a European Muslim: A Study of Islamic Sources in The European Context*. Leicester: Islamic Foundation.

– 2009. *Radical Reform: Islamic Ethics and Liberation*. New York: Oxford University Press.

Razack, Sherene H. 2007. 'The "Sharia Law Debate" in Ontario: The Modernity/Premodernity Distinction in Legal Efforts to Protect Women from Culture.' *Feminist Legal Studies* 15: 3–12.

Seguin, Rheal. 1991. 'Quebec Squashed Idea of Islamic Tribunals.' *Globe and Mail*, 27 May.

Shachar, Ayelet. 2005. 'Religion, State, and the Problem of Gender: New Modes of Citizenship and Governance in Diverse Societies.' *McGill Law Journal* 50: 49–64.

Statistics Canada Online. 'Religion and Immigrant Status and Period of Immigration.' Accessed 20 Jan. 2011. http://www12.statcan.ca/english/census01/products/standard/themes/RetrieveProductTable.cfm?Temporal=2001&PID=55824&APATH=3&GID=431515&METH=1&PTYPE=55440&THEME=56&FOCUS=0&AID=0&PLACENAME=0&PROVINCE=0&SEARCH=0&GC=0&GK=0&VID=0&VNAMEE=&VNAMEF=&FL=0&RL=0&FREE=0.

Stowasser, Barbara Freyer. 1996. *Women in the Qur'an: Traditions, and Interpretation*. Oxford: Oxford University Press.

Swaine, Lucas. 2006. *The Liberal Conscience: Politics and Principle in a World of Religious Pluralism*. New York: Cambridge University Press.

Thornback, James. 2005. 'The Portrayal of Sharia in Ontario.' *Appeal*: 1–12. Accessed 5 Sept. 2010. http://heinonline.org/HOL/Page?handle=hein. journals/appeal10&div=3&g_sent=1&collection=journals.

University of Toronto Student Affairs Office and the Faculty of Law Diversity Committee St George Campus. 2004. 'Keeping the Faith: Alternative Dispute Resolution in Ontario's Faith Communities.' 18 Nov., Toronto. In author's possession.

Voll, John O. 1983. 'Renewal and Reform in Islamic History: *Tajdid* and *Islah*.' In John L. Esposito, ed., *Voices of Resurgent Islam*, 32–47. New York: Oxford University Press.

Williams, Melissa. 2005. 'Tolerable Liberalism.' In Avigail Eisenberg and Jeff Spinner-Halev, eds., *Minorities within Minorities*, 19–40. Cambridge: Cambridge University Press.

PART THREE

Defining Islamic Law in the West

5 Asking Questions about Sharia: Lessons from Ontario

L. CLARKE

Readers of this volume will sense that the Ontario Sharia controversy remains very much alive long after it was brought to an official close by Ontario Premier Dalton McGuinty's announcement on 11 September 2005 that there would be 'no Shariah law' and 'no religious arbitration in Ontario.' The debate was and continues to be divisive. The events of 2003 to 2005 exposed not only a dismal view of Islam and Muslims held by some Canadians, but divisions and rifts within Muslim communities themselves. The debate over arbitration and Sharia resulted in real acrimony, which continues to this day.

If the Ontario episode had the unhappy consequences of highlighting divisions within the Muslim community and stirring up anti-Muslim prejudice, it was also a catalyst for re-examination of important legal and cultural issues in Canada. Debate at this level was relatively sophisticated and productive, since it was informed by a long record of discussion about and experience with alternative dispute resolution, legal pluralism, and multiculturalism. At the time the Ontario controversy erupted, however, there was no such long-standing discussion of or experience with Sharia. Participants on all sides of the debate were really dealing with and talking about something that was unknown. As a result, Sharia became a symbolic and emotional rather than substantive issue.

The present chapter draws on the Ontario debate to suggest questions that might help to clear away some of the murkiness and vagueness surrounding Sharia in the West. This wide focus bears explanation. The initial issue in the Ontario episode was a rather limited one, that is, whether or not to continue to allow arbitration in family law using religious (including Muslim) law, as permitted at that time by Section 32(1)

of the 1991 Ontario Arbitration Act. It was, moreover, soon evident that
not much arbitration had ever taken place. The December 2004 report
on 'Dispute Resolution in Family Law' submitted by the former attorney general of Ontario, Marion Boyd, to the Ontario government was
able to identify arbitration efforts by only two organizations.[1] Research
carried out in the wake of the controversy, including the chapters in this
volume by Macfarlane and Cutting, also suggests that most of the activity of Muslims acting as religious authorities in institutional settings in
Ontario and Canada was, in fact, not legal, but pastoral in nature.[2]
There was talk by pro-arbitrationists of a shadowy world of 'back-room
arbitrations,' that is, hidden interventions based on Muslim norms that
were disadvantageous to women, the argument being that allowing arbitration would gather informal mediation processes into a fold where
women could be protected through the application of legal principles
or judicial review.[3] It may indeed be that some kind of back-room mediation was taking place; but I am not aware that any evidence of it
emerged. Thus, it appears that, from the point of formal law, there was
a limited reality behind the Ontario arbitration debate.

Why then go on – as the various participants in the debate certainly
did – to talk about the influence of Sharia in the West? Is that not blow-
ing the issue out of proportion and perhaps also resurrecting the image
of 'Muslim barbarians knocking at the gates'?[4] The answer is that Sharia
is more than a matter of arbitration and law, even if it was a legal tech-
nicality that touched off the storm in Ontario. From a Canadian perspective, the Ontario episode was a moment in the settling in of Muslim
communities. Muslims and their aspiring spokespersons were compelled to examine the nature of their religious commitment and its relation to society in a way few had done before. As a result of the Ontario
debate, Sharia became part of the Canadian Muslim consciousness.
And this development has parallels in other Western countries. In the
West in general, consciousness of Islam and Muslim identity has come
to include a focus on Sharia, partly as a reaction to the fact that for
many non-Muslims, Sharia, with a very different image and meaning,
is seen as emblematic of Islam. Sharia, in other words, has become a
cultural and civilizational issue, and this chapter treats it in that light.

In the first section of the chapter, I ask the basic but very important
question, What is Sharia? Sharia is evidently a source of controversy
and friction between 'Westomuslims'[5] and non-Muslims, as well as between factions in the Muslim communities. But there are very different
understandings of Sharia, including images that are entirely positive or

negative. How are these understandings and images produced, and what do they express? The appropriate way to approach these questions is through discourse analysis, since meanings of Sharia in the West have been produced through language in interaction with other discourses about Islam, Western values, and women. These constructed meanings continue to dominate popular and media debate about Sharia.

If we peel away discourse about Sharia, we come to the topic of the second section of the chapter, the actual rules and norms of Muslim law and the equally controversial question, What is Muslim law? There are very different understandings and interpretations of Muslim law. Muslim law is not something fixed or easily defined, even if the Sharia debate gave that impression. The question is further complicated because Muslim law, like the more general and idealized concept of Sharia, has become part of the *imaginaire* of Muslims in the West. Talking about law and the rules of law is a way for Westomuslims of evaluating the tradition in a new environment – of debating how they should relate to their tradition, what social and gender norms they should adopt, and how they should deal with the question of integration. Conversation about Muslim life in the West through speaking about law has, in fact, become a movement, resulting in fresh translations of traditional legal works, sites that offer legal advice (fatwas) aimed at a Western audience,[6] and development of a special '*fiqh* for minorities,' that is, law for Muslim minorities in the West.[7]

It is important, at the same time, to realise that the law is not merely a debate or ideal. Norms and rules of Muslim law or ideas about them can influence and affect people's lives, not only in relatively formal contexts such as mediation but as part of the rhetoric of interpersonal relations, that is as a frame or reference used in evaluating behaviour and negotiating relationships. Norms derived from or attributed to law may, for example, be in the minds of couples or families contemplating marriage. Parents may have ideas about the authority of the wife or husband in raising children that they believe to be religiously sanctioned through law, and husbands and wives considering divorce may turn their minds to religious law if the husband wants to signal a rupture with his wife or the wife believes that she needs a religious divorce. In short, Muslim family law or the perceived standards of the law are a reference point for at least some Muslims and can have a real impact on the way people live.

How, in that case, does one go about finding out what different persons mean when they invoke Muslim law? The second section of the chapter explains why there is no fixed Muslim law and goes on to suggest a practical way of finding out what different people might mean by it by asking specific questions about family law, the law that is the focus of pro-Sharia activism in the West. My impression is that participants in the Ontario controversy did not often ask these kinds of questions.

In the third section of the chapter, I raise the question of authority. Following the thread of authority in a religious tradition can tell us much about how a tradition is formed and organized; and following the same thread in a religious conflict will lead to insight into the competing interests behind it. The Sharia controversy, I find, was less about the merits of Muslim law than about who could authentically represent the Muslim community.

What Is Sharia?

The original issue in the Ontario debate was the role of Muslim family law in arbitration. Muslim efforts at family law arbitration were, moreover, focused on one issue, that of divorce, and particularly the ability of women to obtain a divorce and divorce payments. The Sharia controversy was not, however, chiefly about present realities. The focus very quickly shifted to Muslim law altogether and 'Sharia.'

This could be seen as a reasonable step in the enquiry and a legitimate concern. After all, assessment of an unfamiliar legal practice requires information about the system of law or other background. It is also known that some Muslims profess allegiance to Muslim law as a whole or to something they call Sharia, and some pro-Sharia activists connected with the recently founded Islamic Institute of Civil Justice (IICJ) led by lawyer and community activist Syed Mumtaz Ali had indicated that they planned to expand arbitration services to other areas of family law.

In order to proceed with the enquiry, however, it would have been necessary to establish the meaning of Sharia – or, as I shall argue, to understand that Sharia is not a thing but an Idea with very different meanings for different persons. The basic question 'What is Sharia' was missed, I believe, partly because of essentialist ideas about religion and partly because the controversy expanded so quickly to acquire civilizational and even existential dimensions that it was overshadowed and left behind. Issues such as integration of Muslims into Western society, images of Islam in the media, Muslim women's agency, fulfilment of religious life, and so forth very soon took the front stage, leaving questions of actual laws and practice in the background. The Sharia controversy altogether was like a rapidly developing storm that caught the participants unprepared and then outpaced efforts to understand and deal with it.

I have spoken of essentialism in regard to religion. It seems that the error of essentialism is readily recognized in discourse about matters such as social groups and culture, but not religion. There is a widespread tendency to think of religion as possessing an essence or *an essence in the final analysis* (after supposedly non-essential aspects or 'errors' have been subtracted). This idea, of course, is held by all believers, whose faith must be directed towards something essential and cannot be hung on a mere construct.

Tendencies towards religious essentialism may also come into play as outsiders try to formulate understanding of another religion. In this case, along with prior essentialist notions about one's own religion or religion in general, the testimony of believers seems to be effective in persuading outsiders to imagine a religion as being something other than a construct. Thus, to take the example at hand, because Muslims of various persuasions speak and dispute about 'Islam,' others are even more likely to imagine that something called Islam, some essence or unconstructed Ideal, actually exists apart from the Muslims who produce it. When faced with the fact that there are different kinds of practices, beliefs, and actions in the community and many disagreements – in short, that there is no such thing as 'Islam' but merely Muslims continually producing a variegated and changing Islamic tradition – the tendency is to explain these by grouping some together and discounting others as exceptions or errors in order to create a picture of an Islam that can be understood in some manageable way – to take the most basic example, as 'bad' or 'good.'[8]

I have taken some space to characterize essentialism because this, I believe, was a fundamental problem bedevilling debates about Sharia in Ontario. I will now describe a few aspects of the problem on both sides.

The first concerns the word Sharia itself. Sharia, like Islam, is not a descriptive term, but a reference to law as an idea. The complete ideation of the word may be a modern development, since Sharia was often used in the past in the singular or plural to refer to a law or set of laws, but is not commonly used in this way nowadays. One can, in any case, see the perfection of ideation produced, in a typical development, by polemic. For the purposes of polemics, Sharia must be not a construct, but a Thing with an essence that is either good or bad.

Thus – apart from routine prejudice against Islam – it is essentialism that accounts for much of the popular and media reaction to news that 'Sharia' might find favour in Ontario. One cannot do better than cite the words of Tariq Ramadan: 'In the West, the *idea of Sharia* calls up all the darkest images of Islam: repression of women, physical punishments, stoning, and all other such things' (Ramadan 2004, 31; emphasis added).[9] Here Ramadan points to another perfection of essentialism by polemic: the timeless essence is confirmed by paradigmatic examples, non-essential aspects having been subtracted.

Nevertheless, one has to acknowledge that the tactics and statements of some pro-Sharia activists in Ontario along with the undeniable fact of Sharia agitation worldwide also contributed very substantially to public anxiety. The dystopic vision of those who fear the influence of Sharia Law in the West is fed by and mirrors the utopianism and over-reaching aspirations of international and local Sharia revivalists. The ban on Sharia voted by the Quebec's National Assembly provides an example. The ban was useless, since Quebec civil law actually does not allow private or religious arbitration in family law,[10] but the sponsor of the motion and other discussants were able to invoke a sense of crisis by referring to alleged past activities of the Saudi-based Muslim World League aimed at lobbying for Sharia tribunals in North America[11] and instances of Sharia revival in the Muslim world such as stoning (Houda-Pepin 2002; Roy 2005). It is very difficult for Muslims to communicate their own ideas about Sharia or Muslim law with things such as these happening. Muslims in Ontario were particularly unlucky in having to account for Sharia in public at an early point in the communities' development, when they had hardly begun to sort out the issues themselves. This brings us to the next effect produced by Sharia: essentialism.

Sharia was treated during the Ontario controversy as an Idea with an essence not only by those who opposed it, but also by many Muslims. For Ontaro Muslims, Sharia did not function as a descriptive term but, as is typical of Ideals, as a reference point for larger issues and emotions. Under the effect of polemic, the Idea of Sharia was then perfected in the opposite direction: it was something 'good.' It is very difficult for Muslims to communicate their ideas about Sharia or Muslim law in the face of events such as these.

One factor in the ideation of Sharia and making it essentially good is the word Sharia itself, which when rendered as 'path,' 'way,' or as was often reported in the media, 'path leading to water,'[12] has a meaning that is both positive and very general or wide. With this meaning and these characteristics, Sharia becomes a metonym for Islam and, like Islam, an umbrella concept. By umbrella concept, I mean an idea that is commodious and universally regarded as good, to which each person or party then assigns meanings they deem to be good.

The understanding of Sharia as an umbrella concept and metonym for Islam, as an ideal wider than or somehow transcending a mere body of legal rules, is to some extent in tune with traditional senses of Muslim law. In Islam as in Judaism, following law has traditionally been seen as obedience to God and a way to realize a good life. Muslim law also goes beyond legal rules enforceable by a sovereign or nation state (the narrow focus of Western realist and positivist definitions of law) to include devotions such as prayer and fasting, ethics, and moral exhortation. The Muslim theory of jurisprudence asserts that the law is derived, however imperfectly, from sacred sources, that is, from the Qur'an and the sayings and practice of the Prophet and early community known as *Sunnah* ('way of life'). Any of these characteristics might have encouraged believers to idealize and essentialize Sharia and to identify it with Islam.

As a result, Sharia, like Islam, comes to mean many different things to different believers. Each person attributes to this umbrella concept what they believe to be important, right and good. Most significantly for this study, the degree to which believers associate Sharia with actual law varies considerably. For the late Syed Mumtaz Ali, spiritus movens of the Islamic Institute of Civil Justice, which ignited the Ontario debate by proposing a grand plan to institutionalize Muslim law, Sharia is 'the Divine Law' which the Qur'an has 'explicitly emphasized that a Muslim must follow' to the exclusion of any other. In the view of Syed Ali, 'every action of mankind must be governed' by Sharia, so that 'those who choose to become or continue to remain Muslim must accept the whole code of law [without the] option to pick and choose' (Ali 2004). Here Sharia is a definite set of rules. On the other hand, many pro-arbitration respondents to the review that resulted in the Boyd Report emphasized that Sharia was an ideal that could not be entirely equated with law and should not be used to describe proposed arbitration activities (Boyd 2004, 44–5). Here Sharia is distanced from actual law or legal activity the better to function as an Ideal that might legitimate it, a common rhetorical move by advocates of the use of Muslim law.

Sharia may also be understood as a set of ethics, general rightness, or simply good behaviour. In my current field research being conducted in Canada, Britain, and the United States, lay (ordinary) Muslims who were asked the open-ended question 'What is Sharia?' were most likely to associate the word with ethical norms, for instance, behaving courteously towards others, including non-Muslims. Maintaining correct gender relations, including the wearing of hijab, was often spoken of in connection with Sharia. One respondent associated Sharia with cleanliness and orderliness, linking these to the purity and regular times required for prayer, while another thought of recognition of Sharia in the West (specifically, Britain) in terms of days off on Muslim holidays so that her children could celebrate at home. Sharia is also often characterized as a way of life or 'complete way of life,' this apparently being meant as a contrast to Western secularism.

Lay Muslims who do not speak of Sharia in legal terms are nevertheless aware that it implies some kind of law. But they are unlikely to have much idea of what that law might be, apart from rules relating to prayer, fasting, and pilgrimage. On the basis of my current research into popular perceptions of Sharia and interaction with Muslim-heritage students and other Muslim acquaintances over the years, I would say that a fair number of Muslims have some idea (though often mistaken) about the rules of divorce and that the majority are at least able to recognize features of divorce such as the dower due to the wife on marriage (*mahr*) and period (*iddah*) a woman must wait after divorce is pronounced for it to become fully effective. But knowledge of the law seldom extends beyond that.

One could not, of course, reasonably expect more. Believers in all religious traditions, including those who are very passionate and convinced, cannot necessarily recite all the dogmas of their religion, let alone complicated laws. Learned styles of religiosity are typically limited to a few, for example, religious experts or others who have made a special study or have determined to lead a special kind of life. In fact, few laypersons living under any kind of law (e.g., Canadian law) have much idea of that law, except if it happens to intersect with their affairs.

I draw attention to this obvious fact because it seemed to be widely assumed during the Ontario debates that Muslims were familiar with family law as part of their religion and would naturally want to conform to it. This notion, which may have been gathered from the statements of pro-Sharia activists, is reflected in the Canadian Broadcasting Corporation piece 'Sharia Law: FAQs,' according to which Sharia is 'a code of living that most Muslims adopt as part of their faith' that 'some countries formally institute as the law of the land' (CBC 2005). In fact, the vast majority of Muslims had not adopted any 'code of living' that was the law of any land, but were simply rallying to a symbol of Islam under attack, each investing it with her or his own meaning. Pro-Sharia activists who wished to establish actual Muslim law in the community were really engaged in a missionary-style activity, as I point out in the third section of the essay, 'The Question of Authority.'

Western Muslims are, on the other hand, usually aware of aspects of Muslim law that have become the focus of Western critiques or are used in anti-Islam diatribes found in different media, today including the internet. They are likely to have reflected on these and received or formulated explanations for them. Controversial laws mentioned spontaneously by respondents in the field research referred to above included punishments laid down in criminal law, polygamy, and the rules of war and jihad. The greatest concern, however, is the perception that particular laws or the Sharia overall disadvantages or somehow 'oppresses' women.

The history and psychology of the idea that Sharia or Islam is more unfriendly to women than other religious traditions are interesting subjects in themselves; but my focus here is on the situation of Western Muslims faced with widespread negative perceptions about gender and other well-known controversial Sharia laws. The situation involves a kind of compulsory consciousness, since an atmosphere of polemics (which reached a pitch during the Ontario controversy) encourages a feeling that one must have an answer and justified position, at least to settle one's own mind.

Western Muslims in this front-line situation may take a defiant or literalist stance, for instance by defending or at least not excluding polygamy. This was the approach of Syed Mumtaz Ali.[13] Others deal with 'bad Sharia' by subtracting or otherwise dissociating it from their own idea of Sharia or Islam. For example, most Canadian Muslims would contend, using various well-known arguments,[14] that Islam does not recommend polygamy, and I have a few times heard it remarked directly that the corporal punishments prescribed in traditional criminal law (e.g., stoning) are 'not really part' of Islam or Islamic law. To give another example, Muslims may deal with the perception that Sharia oppresses women by asserting that it actually exemplifies gender justice.

Thus, Mr Mobin Sheikh, a well-known figure in the Ontario pro-arbitration movement, cites the provision of Muslim law that allows a woman to keep all her property on divorce (his paradigmatic example of good Sharia) and asserts that 'Sharia favours women eighty per cent of the time' (Song 2004).

A more global way of arriving at an essentially good Sharia is to assert that the Sharia that exists is being improperly applied or that the practicality and justice of different parts of it will only become apparent at some time in the future when it can be instituted in its entirety. An active and accomplished young Canadian Muslim woman featured in Katherine Bullock's rich set of narratives, *Muslim Women Activists in North America* (2005), takes this approach as she asserts that 'one of the chief problems in the Islamic world today is the lack of Muslim women assisting in the interpretation of the *shari'ah* [with the result that] at times the rulings given in the Islamic court of law, in areas of personal opinion, are frequently imbalanced or misapplied' (127). The problem, in other words, is not and in fact cannot be the law itself, but mistaken interpretation. An article appearing on the site of the secular and anti-arbitration Canadian Muslim Congress says of Dr Katherine Bullock herself (who has also contributed a chapter to this volume) that she had 'publicly admitted that no country has ever implemented [Sharia] correctly'; but such a statement, of course, is not an 'admission,' but rather an assertion that Sharia, when it is finally applied correctly, will be entirely good (Dale 2010). This visionary or utopian outlook is facilitated by the modern ideation of Sharia, which allows apologists to focus on a transcendent essence rather than the actual details and problems of the law.

What Is Muslim Law?

One might assume that Muslim law is invariable and fixed. This is not the case. Muslim law, often referred to as *fiqh* or 'interpretive knowledge,' is expressed in different schools of law, differences of opinion exist between and within the schools, and interpretations evolve and change through time. Modern states also continue to introduce reforms to their fiqh-based codes. Thus, various submissions to the Boyd review quoted in the Report pointed out that Muslim law is 'not monolithic' but rather 'eclectic' (Boyd 2004, 43). It was also pointed out that Muslim law is liable to different application by judges (42) and that ideas of the law in Canada were likely to include 'elements of diversity' coming from the law and customs of different countries of origin (43). The respondents here refer to the fact that, as is the case for any law, application of Muslim law involves different practices and outcomes in different contexts. They suggest that this diversity is likely to be reflected in the Canadian scene, so that the parties might agree to arbitration with understandings of Muslim law different from each other or from what the arbitrator had in mind.

This is a valid point, which Faisal Kutty also makes in his chapter and to which I shall return in this section. The situation, however, goes far beyond it. *Muslim family law in the West is a construct, or something under construction.*

Thinking about the construction and legitimation of family law in Muslim-majority states will help to clarify this statement. Beginning as early as the nineteenth century, traditional Muslim law, by which I mean law interpreted and applied by legal scholars drawing on the traditional legal literature, was forced to retreat in the face of the power of newly formed nation states. Centralized governments put aside the Muslim jurists' law in favour of more easily administered codes, while edging them out of formal roles. Nevertheless, the reformed or modernized family law now in place in most Muslim-majority countries is widely accepted as religiously legitimate. This is partly because in most places, the new laws still bear some resemblance to traditional law. To give two examples, the divorce laws of Muslim-majority states generally preserve elements, although much altered and reformed, of the traditional procedures of divorce; and inheritance laws usually adhere to the principle, although applied less strictly than in the old doctrine, of compulsory distribution of fixed inheritance shares among members of the extended family.

Mere similarity through descent cannot, of course, alone legitimate law. One key task facing nation states claiming to apply a religiously valid law is maintenance of a conceptual link to the tradition. As states construct and reconstruct laws, they may attempt to create legitimacy by referring to the old law through devices such as bringing forward relatively progressive opinions from the rich and diverse fund of traditional fiqh, enlarging traditional principles of equity, or appealing directly to the Qur'an. Governments may introduce constitutional provisions supposedly guaranteeing that state law does not violate Sharia or seek a stamp of approval from traditional religious authorities.

These are only a few examples of legitimating measures. The process of legitimation considered in its full breadth includes social, historical, and political factors special to each jurisdiction, which need not detain us here. What is important for our discussion is the extent to which Muslim law is a construction and the degree to which its success depends on legitimation. The key thing is not that law or family law actually be derived from or consistent with traditional Muslim law, but that it be regarded as such. The systems and rules of law now operating in various Muslim-majority states are actually very different from the old law and from each other; but as long as they are regarded by the population as religiously legitimate – as 'Islamic,' or Islamic to a degree that makes them acceptable or at least tolerable – they effectively function (in conjunction, of course, with the various norms and processes of the informal sphere) as Muslim law. This explains why Muslims in the West with ties to Muslim-majority countries often believe that the rules familiar to them from home are the 'correct' ones. What has happened is that the state has succeeded in legitimating those laws in some sufficient degree.

This is not to say that legitimation of state law as acceptably 'Islamic' has been stable or sure. The authority of family and certain other (e.g., criminal) laws imposed by nation states has been challenged through the twentieth to the twenty-first centuries. Some challenges have been aimed at engaging the government in debate and influencing legal institutions. To take a leading example, reform in divorce laws continues in most countries; but it is challenged both by conservative forces who cite the Sharia to show that women should not be given much power to divorce, and women's advocates who argue, also partly on the basis of Islamic texts, that women are entitled to dissolve bad marriages.[15] Another level of challenge is aimed at pushing states in the direction of Islamization of law, that is, conformity with what is perceived to be the authentic letter of the law and the moral and gender values it is believed to express. Pakistan is one of many examples; the constitution, legislature, and courts of Pakistan have had to absorb pressures to Islamize law since at least the late 1970s (Kennedy 1992, 769–87). At a higher level still, Islamists reject the legitimacy of state law and the regimes that apply it and imagine a kind of ideal Sharia that would replace the working state model. The utopian nature of these Sharia movements is confirmed whenever a breakdown of order, such as has happened in Afghanistan and parts of Pakistan under the influence of the Taliban, allows them to gain power. There is finally no functioning legal system, but only a disorderly appeal to traditional values and symbolic measures related to dress and punishment.

The spectacular actions of the militant wing of Sharia idealizers makes them the best known; but one should also include in the category of idealizing movements the legal reform schemes of figures such as Muhammad Said Ashmawi of Egypt, Muhammad Shahrur of Syria, Fazlur Rahman of Pakistan, and indeed, Tariq Ramadan of Europe, already mentioned above.[16] Like the visions of the militant wing, the frameworks proposed by these thinkers are not legislative schemes, but calls to action in the face of an insufficiently realized Sharia; although the insufficiency in this case is not said to be lack of fidelity to the ideal tradition of the past, but failure to renew the tradition and carry it forward.

Each of these critiques, groups, or reform schemes proposes a very different construction of law and a different set of relations to traditional law (the conceptual link) that would legitimate that construction. One sees that Muslim law and ideas of Sharia are everywhere in the making in the face of new social and political realities. And this is also, of course, the situation of Muslim law in the West, where circumstances are radically new and there is no actual, working Muslim law, that is, Islamically legitimated state law, to refer to. It is not a matter of Canadian Muslims or persons in Canada who have set themselves up as religious authorities importing a tradition, even though various ideas, practices, and other bits of imported material are bound to be in the mix. As far as Muslim law plays a role in the lives of Canadian Muslims, it has to be imagined and constructed.

Given that Muslim law in the West, as elsewhere, is under construction and that there are many competing ideas of that law that may have influence on the local scene, how does one determine what anyone means by family law and which rules they believe to be valid? The best course of action, I suggest, is to be aware of the background of the traditional law and ask about particular standards and rules found there. By 'traditional law,' I mean the textual tradition, that is, the material presented in the old books of the various schools of law. Using the textual tradition as a starting point is a good test, since it compels persons applying rules or presenting their ideas about Sharia to be open and clear about their assumptions and values. Asking about what is in the texts forces those being questioned to explain how they deal with the tradition in specific instances, whether by confirming it or moving in a different direction.

It may be argued that the system laid out in the texts does not truly represent law, since practice, that is, how law is applied, is different from the letter of the law. We only get a sense of what law does when we see it in context and in action, as research into Sharia court records from the past also demonstrates.[17] Muslim family law is also understood and applied in Muslim-majority countries today differently than in the past; and it is bound to be shaped differently again in Western contexts, where it is likely that much of it will not even be invoked.

All this is no doubt true. But in that case, persons being questioned are also free to explain their practice, including whether that hearkens back to traditional legal custom or looks forward to something new. Our concern, in short, is not with defining law as an object of study, but with the practical matter of getting answers and thinking about the effect those could have. A sociological or anthropological attention to context should also not cause us to overlook the real importance of rules to the extent that focus on law-in-action leads to 'discounting the importance of legal rules' and 'lack of awareness of their impact' (Watson 1983, 1124).[18] The rules of the traditional system continue to carry great weight in Islam in particular, to the extent that, as we have seen, most Muslim-majority states feel obliged to refer to them in order to legitimate their rule.

Asking about rules also allows one to deal with legal revivalism.[19] Muslim legal revivalism, that is, the idea that traditional law should be restored on the basis of the rules set down in the classical manuals of the legal schools, does have influence. One need go no further than Toronto to find an instance of revivalism in the West. The Islamic Institute of Civil Justice proposed the application of Muslim law according to the fiqh of the different schools; and although the accounts of law linked to the sites of the institute and the Canadian Society of Muslims or posted in the name of Syed Mumtaz Ali (these being generally interconnected) offer a softened version of family law which emphasizes the moral voice, items such as quick triple divorce, wifely obedience, supervision of the wife's movements, the power of guardians to give minors in marriage, and the right of families to reject 'disgraceful' marriages remain.[20]

In the West, private law or occasional revivalism – for example, a husband announcing that he has religiously divorced his wife through triple divorce or religiously justified polygamy[21] – is also facilitated by absence of the restraint or reference point of a reformed Muslim state law and social control of an integrated community. The current legal turn in Western Muslim thought also seems to promote private revivalism as persons who might not previously have thought much about

Muslim law learn or hear about aspects of it that would confer preroga-
tives which might be religiously justified. In this way, aspects of the old
law now out of use in most Muslim countries may be brought into play,
at least as part of what I have called above the 'rhetoric of interpersonal
relations.'

Finally, pro-arbitration participants in the Ontario Sharia controversy
themselves presented traditional law as a point of departure for Muslim
law in the West. In his chapter in this volume, Anver Emon avers that it
is possible to provide a 'jurisprudential treatment or systematic analysis as to how medieval Islamic legal doctrine, preserved over centuries,
could be reconsidered, restructured, and made to accommodate competing Canadian legal and cultural values' (Emon this volume, 211) and
citation of relatively progressive opinions from the traditional books
became the stuff of academic essays arguing that fiqh had this potential
(e.g., Fadel 2009a).

It is important to understand that the appeal of almost all pro-
arbitrationists to the old law was not revivalist, but rather aimed at the
idea that Muslim law or family law could be adapted to the Canadian
environment and legal system. The law was thus characterised by persons as diverse as Mobin Shaykh, arbitration activist in the Toronto
Masjid-El- Noor (in Boyd 2004, 43 and 117), and Anver Emon as 'flexible.'[22] Having argued that the 'Muslim law' functioning in any place is
the law that succeeds in gaining legitimacy and that Muslim law in the
West in particular is under construction, I certainly agree with this assertion (although, of course, from a constructionist point of view rather
than on the basis of supposed inherent characteristics). Nevertheless,
reference to the flexibility of traditional law and its potential for accommodation entails a responsibility to explain exactly what will be done
with the rules of the traditional system and what *specific rules or practices* are now proposed as the norm. This is a most serious responsibility
in that it is a duty towards persons, that is, those who might be affected,
whether in formal or informal contexts, by rules and norms.

Here I will suggest a few basic questions that might be asked about
traditional law as a way of ascertaining the views of community authorities, a potential spouse, and so on, and demonstrate how different
the responses can be. I will use as an example a matter at the heart of
the traditional legal system, wifely obedience. According to traditional
Muslim law, a wife is bound to live in the same house as her husband
and socialize with him, not leave the house without his permission, and
be available for sex whenever he wishes. The traditional law books

clearly enumerate and elaborate these duties and also allow certain exceptions, for example: failure of the husband to pay a marriage dower (*mahr*) that was immediately due entitles a wife to refuse to go to her husband's house, provided the marriage has not been consummated; a wife has a right to visit her relatives at least a certain number of times; and a wife may refuse intercourse if she is ill.

Using the same example of obedience, I will also show how traditional norms are received, that is to say how they are understood by Muslims not positioned as authorities, including women. We will see not only that understandings are, again, diverse, but that there is often a large gap between the views of leaders or aspiring leaders and lay Muslims. This gap is so striking that a few words about it are in order.

As a result of interviews exploring knowledge and beliefs about Sharia (part of the ongoing research mentioned above) and training sessions for women based on *Muslim and Canadian Family Law: A Comparative Primer* (Clarke and Cross 2006), I have come to realize that the reception of law by Muslims in the West is even more messy than I had imagined. The views of Westomuslims – like any in a context that offers a choice of lifestyles and convictions – are assembled from pieces taken from different sources, and the degree to which they are faithful to tradition varies widely. The basic fact is that the focus of Muslims in the West is not on law as such, but rather Sharia as a discourse or symbol, which each person then invests with her or his own meaning as suits the individual's already-constituted or developing life and ideals. One imagines that it would be not quite as easy to collapse Muslim law and idealized Sharia in this way in a Muslim-majority country, since the existence of an actual law and awareness of it through general consciousness, operation, and public debates makes the tradition more familiar.

The reception of Muslim law in the West is consequently both selective and idealized. For instance, women in *Primer* training sessions showed great interest – to the point that it became difficult to move on to other subjects – in the marriage dower (mahr) as a right of Muslim women and how dower might be secured through Canadian law. They were, on the other hand, unaware that mahr can be easily lost in divorce and appeared not to consider that, in a Western context, payment of a mahr due at divorce is really the husband's decision and not a very sure prospect. In general, it seems that ease of negotiation with traditional rules and norms and readiness to fit them into one's world-view depends on how close or far interlocutors are from the patriarchal norms on which Muslim law is based.[23] Negotiation may also be facilitated by unawareness of some of the standards of the law and, as we shall see, a certain caution on the part of authorities in talking about them.

Obedience is not only, as explained above, fundamental to the legal structure of marriage defined in the books of fiqh, but also continues to have legal meaning (in the context of divorce) in various Muslim states today (Mir-Hosseini 1993).[24] Nevertheless, there is disagreement in current discourse about obedience; or at least, it is spoken about in different ways. A literal or traditional view of obedience (*tá'ah* is the Arabic legal term) is evident in a good number of English- and French-language websites where fatwas are given or other 'authoritative' material posted. For example, a commentary (translated from Arabic) on 'The Ideal Muslim Woman and Her Husband' (al-Hashimi 1999) gives detailed advice about the duties of obedience, including keeping house, not going out without the husband's permission, being available for sex whenever the husband wishes, 'respecting his wishes' concerning 'social visits, food, dress, speech' – and so on. Proper obedience is said to avoid stirring up the anger of the husband, while a husband's contentment with his wife's obedience is 'a means of her admittance to Paradise' (ibid.).[25] As is typical of contemporary conservative discourse, 'Ideal Muslim Woman' elaborates and somewhat extends the basic legal standard through citing *hadīth* (the anecdotes of the Prophet that contribute to the Sunnah); and concerning obedience, there are many.

There is, on the other hand, a widespread tendency to soften the legal duties of tá'ah. A woman living in the Netherlands complains that she is far from her family and 'very lonely' and asks the European Council for Fatwa and Research: 'Can I go out without the permission of my husband'? Although the council does 'not see a good reason for going out without the agreement of [a] husband,' this is said to be 'not an issue of superiority or inferiority,' but rather something to be addressed through 'communication and common understanding.' According to the European Fatwa Council, a wife also requires only 'general consent' and not specific permission for each occasion that she goes out for 'work, study, and the running of errands,' while 'Muslim morality also requires that the husband should tell his wife if he wants to travel or stay overnight' (Islam Online 2003, 'Taking the Husband's Permission on Leaving Home,' response posted on 31 Aug. 2003). In a similar spirit, Sheik Yusuf Estes, described as 'Chaplain of WAMY [the Saudi-based World Assembly of Muslim Youth], Virginia, USA,' declares that 'women do have a responsibility to obey their men, whether their fathers, brothers, husbands or even grown-up sons,' but also emphasizes that 'this obedience is actually to the *deen* (religion) of Allah and how they follow Islam' (Estes 2009, 'Meaning of Wife's Obedience to Her Husband,' response posted on 17 Aug. 2009).

Further still along the spectrum of discourse, the emphasis is on obedience as a principle of harmony and cooperation in a natural male-female hierarchy, rather than specific duties. Abdul-Lateef Abdullah, described as 'an American convert to Islam,' replies to the question of a German convert troubled about obedience that, 'while it is true that the husband is the head of the household in Islam, that does not mean that he runs [it] like a tyrant.' Mr Abdullah adds that 'cultural practices' must be distinguished from 'Islamic teachings'; although is not clear whether it is actual legal restrictions such as needing permission to leave the house and availability for sex that he regards as 'cultural,' or harshness in applying them (Abdullah 2008, 'Do I Have to Obey My Husband?' response posted on 7 Oct. 2008). At this level of discourse, mention of sexual obedience in particular along with the many well-known *hadīths* that support it is likely to be omitted, perhaps because the speakers feel that this most delicate part of obedience would not be well received, or perhaps because it is alien to the speakers themselves.[26]

If the duties of obedience – the legal core of tá'ah – are often softened or passed over in less conservative fatwas and other discourse, they are rarely, if ever, expressly rejected. In this case, it may be useful when asking someone about their views of the law to probe with further questions: Can a wife (or a husband) refuse sex or a particular sexual practice without a specific reason? Does a wife have a free and unfettered right to move about as she likes, without the permission of her husband? What other things – the additional duties and behaviours spoken of in hadīth and conservative writings that often cite hadīth – does a wife owe a husband? These queries may be met with ready answers, or with additional advice about fostering love and mutual respect in marriage, need for the husband to consult his wife before making decisions, and so on. Such advice is part of the very important ethical dimension of the tradition; but it may also be used to avoid speaking about the legal core, especially since most religious authorities are very reluctant to directly disagree with law.

Shaikh Ahmad Kutty, who offers legal advice through the 'Ask the Scholar' forum linked to the site of the Islamic Institute of Toronto at www.islam.ca, is exceptional among Muslim authorities in openly rejecting the traditional duties of obedience – although he does not actually say that he is disagreeing with traditional law. Shaikh Kutty steadfastly maintains that sexual contact between spouses must be 'consensual' and states clearly that the freedom of wives (as well as daughters) to leave the house and move about at their own will is a 'basic right' which it is a 'heinous sin' to deny.[27] The shaikh emphasizes an approach to Islam that includes 'spiritual wisdom and ethics,' rather than the letter of the law alone, and it appears to be the space created by ethics that allows him to move away from traditional legal standards. His practical treatment of specific matters, the result, no doubt, of inter-action with people and their problems in his counselling role, stands in marked contrast to the vague, theoretical approaches of the non-clerical Sharia activists discussed in the next section.

There is similar diversity in reception of the norms of obedience. A recent study of female converts to Islam living in Sweden suggests that differences in reception stem from the difficulty women (or perhaps converts in particular?) have in reconciling tá'ah with their strong feel-ing that Islam guarantees women's rights. Some respondents dealt with obedience by declaring that women must 'simply obey,' while others asserted that the Qur'an recommends joint decision making. The re-spondents also used negative views of 'liberated' Western women to emphasize the value of the male-female hierarchy they believed to be part of Islam (Sjöqvist 2007). A striking feature of the responses in this study was failure to mention specific legal duties of obedience or con-sequences of disobedience. Obedience seems to be widely understood rather as a kind of general marital ethic or principle of relations.

These features of reception of obedience – some difficulty in negotia-tion, favourable contrast with the West as an aid to negotiation, and delegalization in favour of ethicization – seem to be common among Westomuslims. An essay by blogger Nadirah Angail[28] (the blogger and commentators appear to be African-American) criticizes an 'American culture' that 'looks down on obedience' and 'brands' it 'oppression.' Obedience, according to Ms. Angail, 'doesn't mean the woman loses her right to be heard and the man is free to behave in any way he chooses.' If a woman is not 'selfish' and married to a 'kind, caring, considerate' man, 'obedience shouldn't be a problem' (Angail 2010a). Angail's view is neatly echoed in the comment of one of my interview-ees in Toronto, an older, professional woman who had spent much of her life in Egypt: 'The wife should obey, but the husband should make it a pleasure to obey him.' An attendee at a *Primer* training session in Montreal angrily denied that sexual obedience could be any part of the

'Sharia' at all and accused me of, essentially, making things up without reference to any source. In fact, the *Primer* quotes from about two dozen of the classics of fiqh, not because this was really necessary to outline well-known material, but because I was aware of the tendency of Westomuslims to think of law in terms of idealized Sharia.

There is also a range of 'authoritative' opinion and reception among Western Muslims of the counterpart in the traditional system of Muslim law of tá'ah, disobedience (*nushúz*) of the wife and the various consequences it entails. According to the letter of the law, if a wife refuses any of the duties mentioned above, she may lose her right to support, be deprived of intimacy, or suffer physical discipline. These consequences are discussed at length in the books of fiqh, and loss of support due to nushúz has, again, some legal meaning in the context of divorce in various Muslim states today (Mir-Hosseini 1993). I will limit myself here to discussion of physical discipline, both for the sake of brevity and because the issue is well known due to the famously problematic phrase of the Qur'an (4:34) that speaks of 'hitting' a disobedient or ill-behaved wife.

There is a very widespread tendency among Muslims positioning themselves as authorities to limit physical discipline so that it does not cause bodily harm and even to minimize it to the point that it becomes a symbolic action. The formulation of Dr Jamal Badawi, a Canadian professor of management and popular campus lecturer whose resumé also lists him as a member of the Fiqh Council of North America, is widely quoted on the subject.[29] According to Badawi (2002),

> If the problem [in a family dispute] relates to the wife's behavior, her husband may exhort her and appeal for reason. In most cases, this measure is likely to be sufficient. In cases where the problem continues, the husband may express his displeasure in another peaceful manner by sleeping in a separate bed from hers. There are cases, however where a wife persists in deliberate mistreatment of her husband and disregard for her marital obligations. Instead of divorce, the husband may resort to another measure that may save the marriage, at least in some cases. Such a measure is more accurately described as a gentle tap on the body, but never on the face, making it more of a symbolic measure than a punitive one.

Badawi goes on to caution that hitting or 'tapping' is a 'rare exception,' to be used 'in the case of lewdness on the part of the wife' or 'extreme refraction and rejection of the husband's reasonable requests on a consistent basis' (2002).[30] The mention of repeated rejection of a husband's requests may reflect the controversy in traditional law over whether hitting is justified at the first instance of disobedience, or only if it persists. The minimizing opinion in general, it should be noted, is not a product of modern apologetics, but comes from the tradition itself. Limitation on hitting and the desirability of refraining from it are significant themes of hadīth, and it is common to find warnings in the traditional law books that other allowed disciplinary measures, for example, verbal rebuke or refusing sex, should also be mild or avoided altogether.

My research findings suggest, however, that many or most Westomuslims have difficulty accepting even minimal or symbolic physical discipline of a wife.[31] The idea currently gaining popularity that the Arabic verb 'd-r-b' used in Qur'an 4:34 actually means 'go away' – so that a man who is displeased with his wife does not hit, but merely leaves or distances himself from her – is one attempt to deal with the problem of physical abuse. Another approach resembles the one illustrated above in relation to sexual obedience: denial that hitting could be part of the tradition at all. The most vivid instance I came across in my field research involved a group of female students in an Islamic College in Great Britain. Having learned in a class on Islamic law about the rules for disciplining a disobedient wife (something which they did not seem at all familiar with, despite their evident commitment to Islam), the women objected vocally and laid out their own ideas about hitting: violence in any degree is wrong, a husband who hits once is likely to do so again, and a wife who is hit should immediately leave the marriage. The participants in this discussion did not refer to scriptures or law,[32] but rather seemed – as I read the situation – to attach these assertions to their vision of Islam as a woman-favourable religion and to their own sense of authority within it. Here is a good example of Sharia being invested with the individual's own ideals and repertoire.

This picture of the articulation and reception of legal norms among Westomuslims suggests not only that one may get very different answers to questions about Sharia, but that members of the community in general may be quite at cross-purposes in their ideas and ideals about Muslim law. Scholars investigating views of Sharia in the future may find that this variety stems not only from ethnic origin, but class, gender,[33] and other life experience (e.g., conversion to Islam). The transnational nature of discourses and debates is also, no doubt, a factor; readers will have noticed that some of the more conservative material cited above is connected to Saudi Arabia. I have been particularly struck in my research by the extent to which persons with liberal outlooks or who idealize Sharia are unaware of aspects of the law they would regard as unfavourable and the wide influence of conservative views. I have referred to web sites in my account of obedience and disobedience as an invitation to readers to explore this conservative discourse for themselves.

Diversity in views and reception of Muslim law dictates caution for those dealing with Muslim law or thinking of granting Sharia state sanction, but it should also be put in context. Different and even apparently naïve understandings of Sharia or Muslim law are not somehow 'in error,' but part of an evolving tradition. If, for instance, some Muslims define obedience as a kind of respectful hierarchy and do not believe that a husband has a right to reproach, let alone punish, his wife for so-called disobedience, that must be taken seriously as an authentic Muslim view, which may finally come to define Western Islam or a part of it (although such a view, if not well justified, may be vulnerable to conservatives' invocation of texts that contradict it). Action can also contribute to the legitimation of different views; the American-based Peaceful Families Project, dedicated to 'ending domestic violence in Muslim families' (Peaceful Families Organization, n.d.), denies that discipline is part of the tradition and strives to make that a reality through its work in the community.

Conservative or revivalist interpretations may also, of course, prevail; or the community may form into different institutionalized groups defined by attitudes to the law, as the Jewish community has done. Many factors contribute to the construction and legitimation of a tradition, which is always ongoing. One key factor is authority, to which I shall now turn.

The Question of Authority

Speaking of current discord in Islam, Reza Aslan remarks that there are 'universal conflicts in all religious traditions [and] chief among these is the conflict over who has the authority to define faith' (Aslan 2006, xv). The issue of authority to define faith was indeed at work in the Sharia controversy. Writing shortly before the Sharia debate in 2001, Amir Hussain does not mention law (or even Sharia) as issues in the Toronto and Canadian communities. The exception was the Canadian Society of Muslims with its call to implement, as the society called it, 'Muslim Personal Law'; but this, according to Hussain, was 'not well supported by the majority of Toronto's Muslims' (Hussain 2001, 273–4) despite being quite fully argued since at least 1992 (Ali and Whitehouse 1992). The controversy began only when it emerged that the society and its president, Syed Mumtaz Ali, intended to use arbitration to make a bid for authority by establishing an Islamic Institute of Civil Justice as 'the beginnings of a Muslim Civil Justice System in Canada' (Ali and Mills 2010).

The society's particular project appeared, as noted above, to hold little appeal for Canadians and Ms Boyd felt obliged to remind Mr Ali that creation of a full 'justice system' was far beyond the limited scope of arbitration (Boyd 2004, 55). The initiative, however, is worth examining, not only because it sparked the Ontario debate but also because it represents at least a small part of the multi-vocal conversation about Sharia in the West.

The society's call was premised on the idea that persons who do not follow Sharia cannot be Muslims. The slipperiness of this idea – the fact that few Muslims would disagree that 'Sharia' is at least part of Islam, but that there are different understandings of Sharia and its legal content – has been discussed above. In the case of Syed Mumtaz Ali and the society, the reference is to an obligation, supposedly laid down in the Qur'an, on the part of Muslims to follow actual law, 'the whole code of law, in toto,' including, of course, personal law. Thus would it be obligatory for Muslims to choose recourse to 'Muslim Courts of Arbitration (Dar-ul-Qada) rather than secular courts' (Ali 2004).

The contemporary trends in favour of Islamization of law and rule of Sharia described in the second section of the essay have some influence in this worldview. The utopian cast is there; web pages belonging to the society or Syed Mumtaz Ali speak, for instance, of the 'protected' (*dhimmî*) status of non-Muslims (Ali 1993) and need to 'wage war' against apostates (Ali 2010a),[34] as if these were possible realities. Syed Ali's insistence that one must follow all parts of the law without exception[35] and that one can only be completely a Muslim (according, of course, to his definition) or not a Muslim at all is a common theme of modern ideologized formulations of Islam, including that of the very influential Indo-Muslim Islamist Abu al-Ala Mawdudi, to whose material he or the society sometimes refers (Nasr 1996, 55, 63–4).[36] In fact, the approach seems to be very similar to Mawdudi's in its selective assimilation of modernity (ibid., 49–68), for example, Canadian multiculturalism mixed up together with assertion of a spiritual hierarchy of Muslims

and non-Muslims. To be sure, the assortment of modern with traditional notions is much less smooth in Ali's writings than in those of
Mawdudi, partly because he depends heavily on lengthy quotations
and synopses of others' material. But the combination does seem less
odd when placed in this context. Syed Ali's willingness to work within
the system and accept a limited role for Muslim law through arbitration
in anticipation of a future entire Islamic justice system also mimics the
gradualism of Mawdudi (ibid., 96ff).

Syed Ali's revivalism seems actually to be derived from that of the
All-India Personal Law Board, founded in 1973 to preserve a separate
law for Muslims in India and devoted to the '*fiqh* of the Hanafi school
as interpreted by the Deobandis' (Sikand 2007, 73). Syed Ali's belief that
Muslims living as minorities must do their utmost to adhere to the law
has a basis in classical doctrine (see Abou el-Fadl 1994); but he refers
not to those sources but the 'legal opinion of Maulana Manzoor Nomani'
that Muslim personal law 'is a part of the religious structure of Islam
and no non-Muslim government has the right to interfere with it, so
that "Muslims living under non-Muslim systems *are required to make
every possible effort for the recognition of this principle by their governments*"'
(Ali and Hosein, n.d., original emphasis). Nomani is a well-known
Deobandi and member of the Personal Law Board. The Canadian
Society of Muslims posts material from the board,[37] the board like the
society speaks of a Dar al-Qada (roughly, 'Hall of Justice,' although
translated by the society as 'Muslim Courts of Arbitration' or 'Arbitration
Boards'),[38] and the Muslim personal law for which the board uses the
acronym MPL is called by Syed Mumtaz Ali personal/family law and
PFL. In this light, the project mounted by Syed Ali looks like an importation of an Indo-Muslim minority outlook[39] and the Indian Deobandi tradition in which he himself was trained.[40]

The exhortatory language and proposed activities of the Islamic
Institute of Civil Justice show it to be also in the nature of a missionary
movement. Although the founders have no doubt that true Muslims
are bound to follow the law – indeed that those who do not follow the
law are not Muslims - they are aware that few Muslims do so or know
what the law (in the institute's terms) is. The missives of the society
constantly urge readers to make the 'choice' of being a good Muslim by
following PFL (Ali 2004), and one of the prime missions of the institute
and society is to educate Muslims who 'for some reason did not have
the opportunity to learn' about the 'essentials' of Islamic law, through
'courses, seminars, workshops, etc.' (Ali and Hosein, n.d.).

Once a bid for authority through Sharia was issued from these quarters, others quickly followed. The appeal of other Muslim advocates of arbitration was, however, quite different from that of the sponsors of the IICJ. First, the concern was not for Muslim law as such and certainly not an effort to draw Canadian Muslims to it, but for Sharia. Readers of this chapter will readily understand why Sharia has more attraction than Muslim law. Second, Muslim advocates of arbitration took care to emphasize that Sharia would be entirely compatible with and subordinate to Canadian law, an argument faintly similar to but more modest and acceptable than Syed Ali's invocation of multiculturalism as a warrant for legal isolationism. Third, arguments were made on the basis of reason rather than a religious obligation to follow Muslim law, that is, ADR as an opportunity for religio-cultural fulfilment; equality with other communities who had already enjoyed the power of arbitration; arbitration as an opportunity to reform Muslim law; and, as mentioned in the Introduction, ADR as a way to rescue women from 'back-room arbitration' and the problem of obtaining a divorce in particular.

The overall characteristic of these arguments I wish to draw attention to here is their wide appeal, that is to say their potential to broadly mobilize Canadian Muslims along with some non-Muslim opinion. This appeal also depended on, if I may say so, a very great vagueness about the details of what particular law and norms would be invoked and how those might actually be applied. The single example given above of traditional rules and current discourse about obedience demonstrates the necessity of asking and speaking about these details, which are hardly details at all. To continue the example of obedience, Jamal Badawi is reported to have argued before an audience of students at Concordia University in Montreal that 'Sharia is not inflexible but rather a broad set of norms that contains few laws per se' (Stastna 2005); but I have not found any statement by him explaining how physical discipline and other 'broad norms' (e.g., inequality in witness) he sets out in his famous 'Gender Equity in Islam' (2002) would be treated in tribunals.

Academic writings advocating Sharia ADR also stayed at the level of the general and theoretical, rather like the Sharia-idealizing reform schemes mentioned in the second section. The argument commonly made was that Muslim law, which had proved flexible and adaptable in the past, possessed the resources to adjust again to new circumstances (see also Emon, this volume). A related argument was framed in terms of legal pluralism and the ability of liberal democratic states to accommodate flexible 'Shariah values' (Fadel 2009b). The first argument

seems to reflect current Western scholarship on Sharia, which emphasizes the dynamism and responsiveness of fiqh and jurisprudential
theory (*usúl al-fiqh*),[41] and the second emerges from an ongoing discussion[42] about how to acculturate Sharia to Western contexts by drawing
on principles and methods of Muslim jurisprudence. Both are interesting projects that may bear fruit in the future, but they do not do much
to address the specific and practical questions about actual laws that
would need to be answered before proceeding to arbitration. Returning
again to obedience as an example, Anver Emon offers as evidence that
'the law can and must change' in different contexts and will therefore
do so in arbitration the fact that the ninth-century jurist al-Sháfi'í altered some of his rulings following a move from Iraq to Egypt (Emon
2005). But one of the changes reported to have been made by al-Sháfi'í
is from the view that hitting a wife is justified at the first instance of
disobedience to the view that it is justified only if disobedience persists
(Túsí 2003 [1417], vol. V, 415; al-Sháfi'í 1982 [1402], vol. V, 207–8).[43]
Clearly, it is not enough to argue that a law was capable of change in the
past or that it is 'flexible.' Constructing and legitimating a new Muslim
law for the West is a radical project which will require much thought
and work and, above all, a very long time.

Against this background, the strands of the Sharia controversy outlined in the previous sections come together to form a picture of a contest not over law as such, but over the authority to define faith, (the idea
of) Sharia having become the symbol of that faith. 'Bad Sharia' and anti-
Islam reaction were certainly key to securing this position for Sharia.
Once Sharia had become the symbol of Islam – something that was possible because few questions were asked about actual Muslim law, each
person or group having their own sufficient imagination of it – it became a great rallying cry, with the potential for whoever could capture
the issue of taking on a leadership role. To argue for arbitration became
to advocate for the viability and admissibility of Islam on par with other religions, for its honour, so to speak. Aspiring leaders of the community entered vigorously into the contest, which was further sharpened
by the prospect of gaining influence through representing the community to power. This prospect, in my view, was one reason for constant
assurance from all sides that Sharia could be made to work smoothly
and entirely in concert with Canadian law.[44]

In the meantime, more liberal Muslim groups who associated Sharia with conservatives and perceived that its 'victory' would be to the conservatives' advantage were preoccupied with denying them that prize. The protests of academic experts that Sharia was or could be something entirely different from that spoken of by the media and revivalists came with an implied offer to guide a program of arbitration-backed legal reform.[45] It is interesting that most of the prominent persons and aspiring leaders in the Sharia controversy were non-traditional authorities, for example, holders of doctorates in technical fields, rather than traditional authorities such as seminary-trained imams. This reflects a type of Muslim leadership common in the West; but one wonders what interest traditional authorities would have in a movement that would ultimately formalize their pastoral and mediatory roles and shift authority to other persons.[46]

The rush to authority sparked by the prospect of arbitration can best be understood in light of the conditions of the recently established Canadian Muslim communities and also of Islam in the West. It is becoming apparent that Western Islam as a world of thought is not being created entirely or perhaps even primarily through institutions or by recognized authorities. The limited reach of institutions has been noted, for instance, in the case of France, where despite some effort by the French government to create official representation,[47] membership of the three main umbrella organizations along with approximately 60 per cent of Muslim associations 'probably does not exceed 10 to 15 per cent' of the Muslim population (Laurence and Vaisse 2006, 99–100).

There is no current account of institutionalization and authority in Canadian Islam; but anecdotal evidence suggests both a lack of reach *and* (perhaps different from the French case) development of authority structures.[48] Amir Hussain describes an inspiring but also fractious history of institutions in Toronto – now the centre of Muslim population in Canada – from prayer groups in the 1950's to 'national' organizations in the 1970s and forward. The divisions in that time arose from varied ethnicities and different styles of Islam partly connected with ethnicity, as well as orientations towards conservative or liberal positions (Hussain 2001, 28). The result today seems to be a series of mosques and centers similarly marked off from one another by ethnicity and/or style, along with a number of aspiring all-Muslim or 'national' organizations representing different points of view. These organizations – the Canadian Society of Muslims, Muslim Canadian Congress, Canadian Islamic

Congress, and Canadian Council of Muslim Women – are not in the nature of pyramids constructed on a wide member base, but rather quite small and sometimes personality-based. The Muslim Students Association (MSA) gained its apparently broader base by depending on the already existing structures of universities; while both the MSA and ISNA (Islamic Society of North America, an outgrowth of the MSA) are not Canadian but all-North American organizations depending, like the Canadian examples above, on new media and the device of national conferences to maintain a profile and network.

These characteristics of Muslim Canadian institutions may be part of an early stage of development. The effects on authority of another phenomenon, that of Muslim *bricolage* in the Western environment, may be more lasting. Scholars of Western Islam have suggested that fragmentation of authority structures is due to a process of 'individualization' in which Muslims, especially of the second generation, leave behind the normative tradition and create their own in relation to the new environment.[49] A similar development is described by Ihsan Yilmaz in relation to Muslim law: 'post-modern fragmentation' ensues as the legal schools dissolve and individuals act as 'micro-mujtahids' (Bearman, Peters, and Vogel 2005, 192), producing countless 'neo-ijtihads' (Yilmaz 2003). Although we have again to rely on non-Canadian (chiefly European) data for individualization, the composite and sometimes auto-justified views on obedience and disobedience related above testify to the broad influence of individualization in construction of Islam and Muslim law.

Thus, we have a situation in which authority is uncertain and open; readers will have noticed that although I speak in the second section of authoritative views and the reception of those views, it is not always clear what role a speaker is playing, especially when the medium is the internet. The circumstances of Canadian Muslim communities are very different from the picture painted by the Boyd Report in which 'religious law serves to determine who is considered a full member of the religious community' and 'those who do not conform to religious law may find themselves ostracized, disentitled to practise their religion within the community or entirely disowned by the community' (Boyd 2004, 39).[50] There is no Church to deny Muslims membership in the community or participation in sacraments and no group for Canadian Muslims with authority centered on law parallel to the rabbinate or institutionalized body wielding authority over Sharia such as the Jewish Beis Din. In fact, there is no clear or necessary authority at all, while Westomuslims display a tendency to construct their own various Islams and Sharias. These circumstances both sharpen competition for authority and defeat it.

NOTES

1 Nevertheless, the report attempts to present arbitration as a well-tried option for Muslim communities. Apart from arbitration by the Masjid-el-Noor mosque in Toronto, it cites the nationwide Conciliation and Arbitration Boards of the Canadian Shia Ismaili community. Boyd discusses the Ismaili case at length as if it were a potential model for other Muslims (Boyd 2004, 57–60). The Ismaili case, however, is unique. The Ismailis are a very small, fairly homogeneous, prosperous, and somewhat Westernized minority with an unusually high degree of community organization and institutionaliza-tion, all of which had been well developed before coming to Canada. Most important, the Ismailis have a highly articulated system of authority, based on the hereditary leadership of an 'imam,' currently known as the Agha Khan, whose guidance, including in matters of law, is absolute. Thus, for the Ismailis, an arbitration system is relatively easy to define, organize, and con-trol, and their law, which is quite different from that of other Muslims, is more flexible. Boyd also takes the Ismaili case as evidence that 'Muslim fam-ily law has been and is being used now to resolve disputes successfully' not only in Sunni, but also Shi'ite contexts (61). However, Agha Khani (Nizari) Ismailism, which is, historically speaking, a Shi'ite splinter group, is also very different from majority, mainstream Shiism.

2 Apart from the instances of Masjid-el-Noor and the Ismailis, the Boyd Report cited only services offered at 'mosques and community centres' which were 'more or less formally structured, and may be organized as mediation or conciliation rather than binding arbitration' (ibid., 61). An imam I interviewed in Montreal in 2006 – a Shi'ite and, therefore, theoreti-cally charged with instructing his community in the rulings of a Grand Ayatollah – stated that only a very small proportion of his activity had anything to do with law, and all of that concerned divorce. See also Potvin and Saris (2009).

3 Boyd herself expressed fears that the end of arbitration would result in Sharia ADR going 'underground' in 'mosques and community centres [where] it will just happen' and 'people will follow it [without] the protec-tion of the law' (quoted in Sims 2005). University of Toronto Professor Ayelet Shachar also argues that disallowing arbitration results in 'relegation

of group-based dispute-resolution processes to a no-man's land of shadowy, unofficial systems' (2008, 604 and 605).

4 In the memorable phrase of Natasha Bakht: 'Were Muslim Barbarians Really Knocking on the Gates of Ontario? The Religious Arbitration Controversy – Another Perspective' (2005).

5 I have coined this term in recognition of the fact that Muslims in the West find themselves in a special position that entails particular challenges and opportunities, which are leading to new and distinctive religious cultures as Islam becomes nativized.

6 The website of the Islamic Institute of Toronto (www.islam.ca) is a good example; some of the contents are mentioned below.

7 For a recent, critical overview, see Caeiro (2010).

8 James Thornback (2005) has noticed the same binary view.

9 The original French of the word 'idea' is *la notion* (Ramadan 2003, 61).

10 So a sitting member of the Assemblée nationale had to be reminded on 13 Dec. 2004 when he expressed fears that the minister of justice was treating with a Montreal Muslim organization to make family mediation using Sharia official (http://www.assnat.qc.ca/fr/travaux-parlementaires/assemblee-nationale/37-1/journal-debats/20041213/2699.html).

11 Member of the Assemblé nationale Mme Houda-Pepin referred principally to a gathering of imams in Washington in 1991. I have not found independent information about this gathering and Houda-Pepin's office did not answer to my enquiry; but see Irshad Abdal-Haqq and Qadir Abdal-Haqq (1996), who refer to several activities, beginning in 1988 with a meeting of 'Muslim representatives' to plan a 'national network of Islamic arbitration boards in major cities across the continent that would address family law issues' (74).

12 E.g., in a CBC background piece appearing on 26 May 2005 (http://www.cbc.ca/news/background/islam/shariah-law.html). Boyd also reports that this was the characterization of 'many Islamic respondents' (Boyd 2004, 44).

13 Syed Mumtaz Ali was widely reported to have acknowledged the practice of polygamy in the Canadian Muslim community and to have looked forward to its decriminalization (e.g., *National Post* 2006).

14 E.g., citing Qur'an 4:3, which states that one should only marry one wife 'if you fear that you cannot do justice,' in conjunction with 4:129, which states that it is impossible to treat wives equally.

15 For a recent summary of divorce reform and resistance in Arab states, see Welchman (2007, 107ff).

16 In his Chapter 17, entitled 'In Search of a Legal Methodology,' Hallaq (2009) includes short accounts of Ashmawi, Rahman, and Shahrur.

Discussions of Ramadan tend to be coloured by the controversy he has aroused; chapters pertaining to law in his *Western Muslims and the Future of Islam* (2004) and *Radical Reform: Islamic Ethics and Liberation* (2009) give first-hand access to his thought.

17 It has been only a few decades since Western scholars of Shariah have turned away from logocentric study of law to consider context and practice, but we now have a very large body of literature on 'law in action' in both pre-modern and modern times. Tucker (1998) is a vivid and accessible work in the field.

18 Sally Falk Moore provides the classic statement by an anthropologist on balance between study of context and rules: 'Rules or the abstract definitions of principles ... are part of the way people think and talk about social life in general, which is quite distinct from (though related to) the way they deal with it in concrete instances. Law involves both' (2000, 147).

19 On revivalism and its prospects (based on the case of Hindu and Muslim law in India, but with useful observations for discussion of the phenomenon in general), see Galanter (1972).

20 For triple divorce, see 'My Love and My Choice,' edited by Syed Mumtaz Ali (2010). For other laws: 'Muslim Personal Law – An Exposition,' by Athar Husain (2010). Punishment for *zina* (fornication) as a necessary 'cleansing' measure is described in 'What Is behind the Veil?' by Mawdudi (2010, evidently from his famous 'Purdah and the Status of Women in Islam' but 'edited' by Syed Mumtaz Ali).

21 An instance in the Greater Toronto Area involving an imam received some publicity (Javed 2008).

22 Revivalist Syed Mumtaz Ali characterized Muslim law in the same way, but as an assertion of its superiority: 'In many ways, Islamic PFL is more flexible, accessible, simple and progressive than are its Canadian counterparts' (An Interview with Syed Mumtaz Ali 'A review of the Muslim Personal/Family Law Campaign' coordinated by Rabia Mills (first published Aug. 1995).

23 Distance from patriarchal norms, of course, varies in any society, class being one possible factor.

24 As always, context and practice should be taken into account. For instance, Amira el-Azhary Sonbol shows how the modern state formally enforced obedience by returning women to their homes, something that was not envisioned in the traditional system, or at least in Ottoman court records (1998, 285–94).

25 This is an extract from a larger work by Muhammad Ali al-Hashimi (1999).

26 See, however, the matrimonial site www.zawaj.com: 'What Every Teenager
   Needs to Know (About Sexuality),' by Alia Amer (2010)C:\Documents
   and Settings\alaughlin\Local Settings\Temporary Internet Files\Content.
   Outlook\Y1JFZKFQ\ and also 'Husband's Rights Concerning His Wife'
   (Muslim Woman 2010), a site apparently maintained by a female convert.
   Both quote several of the relevant hadīth.
27 Search the quoted words on the site.
28 See Nadir Angal (2010b).
29 For use of Badawi's words in a fatwa, see the unfortunately titled 'Wife
   Beating in an Islamic Perspective,' respondents Jamal Badawi and
   Muzammil H. Siddiqi (the exchange is dated 21 April 2004); Siddiqi is here
   identified as 'former President of the Islamic Society of North America'
   (ISNA).
30 Badawi's 'Gender Equity in Islam' (2002) is posted on many places on the
   Internet, e.g. http://www.islam101.com/women/equity.html. The site of
   the Canadian Society of Muslims also includes a link (http://muslim-
   canada.org/sitedex2.htm) to a version of 'Gender Equity.'
31 Discipline through denial of intimacy and stopping support do not seem
   to stir up much debate, despite mention of the former in the Qur'an and
   much discussion of the latter in the books of law.
32 For an exposition of this point of view that does deal with Qur'an and
   hadīth, see Trilling (2010).
33 E.g., an interviewee in Samia Bano's study of Sharia councils in Britain
   reported that her husband hit her and asserted that he was religiously
   allowed to, as long as he did not 'harm' her; the interviewee was 'shocked'
   at this claim being made in the name of Islam (2007, 22).
34 Denigration or intentional denial of books of traditional law is said to be
   one instance of blasphemy or apostasy.
35 E.g., 'You are not given [the] option to pick and choose ... A Muslim does
   not have the choice to say, for instance, that he likes to be governed by every Quranic injunction except [Qur'an 4:35]' (Ali 2004). Qur'an 4:35, which
   speaks of arbitration between a man and wife, is apparently a proof-verse
   used by the Islamic arbitration movement to establish a Qur'anic 'imperative for Muslims to settle disputes through arbitration and reconciliation'
   (see Abdal-Haqq and Abdal-Haqq 1996, 75–6).
36 Notice the similarity of Syed Mumtaz Ali's pronouncement quoted in the
   previous note to the following statement from a pamphlet of the Jamaat-i
   Islami, a party founded by Mawdudi: 'The Islamic way of life must be
   based on the Qur'and on sunnah, all of which must be accepted. One may
   not pick and choose among the precepts of the Shariah' (Binder 1963, 87).

37 'Muslim Personal Law – An Exposition,' by Athar Husain (2010), the fullest account of law posted by the society, carries the headeding, 'Published by the All-India Personal Law Board.'

38 For the board, see: http://www.aimplboard.org/ (home page, with a link to the Darul Qaza Committee); for the society, see Ali and Mills (2010).

39 Mr Ali actually points out that Muslim law in India under British rule was 'integrated into the British system' and asks why Muslim law should not be in a similar situation in the 'former British colony' of Canada 'now that Muslims constitute the largest religious minority' in Canada (Ali 2010b).

40 A short biography (see Muslim Canada Organization 2010) names Manazir Ahsan Gilani, a prominent Deobandi, as one of his teachers. One supposes that the 'Beoband' and 'Nadwa' named as 'other prominent scholars' actually refer to the famous Deobandi Darul Uloom and the Nadwat al-Ulama academies, or teachers trained in them.

41 This trend extends to a certain idealism about the law of the past and an assertion that these ideal features were damaged by colonialism and the territorial legal codes of the nation state. Wael Hallaq and Amira El-Azhary Sonbol are two prominent representatives of this school of thought.

42 Two recent examples are Kamali (2007) and March (2009).

43 In the *Umm*, in which he expresses his later opinion, al-Sháfi'í also cautions against hitting and insists that it should not result in physical harm. Such statements are common in the traditional lawbooks.

44 Another reason, I believe, is the integrationism of Canadian Muslims. A call to Muslims to follow a law entirely separate from that of the rest of Canadians would gain very little support.

45 Emon (2005) speaks of a 'vacuum of authority' created by incompetence in both Canadian and Muslim law that could be filled by 'serious education and training.'

46 Emon (2005) denigrates the imams ('not the intellectual crème de la crème') and openly calls for the installation of different kinds of authorities through arbitration who would apply his own ideas.

47 In the form of a Conseil Français du Culte Musulman (CFCM). For a short account in English of the Conseil and developments leading to it, see Fernando (2005).

48 This and the remarks below apply chiefly to the Sunni communities. The Shi'ites have a clearer and stronger structure of authority in the form of networks headed by the Grand Ayatollahs; see Takim (2009). Although more research is needed, it appears that Shi'ite authorities (apart from the Ismailis) stood aside of the Ontario Sharia debates.

186 L. Clarke

49 For an assessment of the literature, see Peter (2006).
50 Speaking not only of the Muslim but also Catholic (presumably Roman Catholic), Anglican, and Jewish communities.

REFERENCES

Abdal-Haqq, Irshad, and Qadir Abdal-Haqq. 1996. 'Community-Based Arbitration as a Vehicle for Implementing Islamic Law in the United States.' *Journal of Islamic Law* 1: 61–88.

Abdullah, Abdul-Lateef. 2008. 'Do I Have to Obey My Husband?' 7 Oct. Accessed 12 Dec. 2010. http://www.islamonline.net/servlet/Satellite?pagename=IslamOnline-English-Cyber_Counselor/CyberCounselingE/CyberCounselingE&cid=1213871662252.

Abou el-Fadl, Khaled. 1994. 'Islamic Law and Muslim Minorities: The Juristic Discourse on Muslim Minorities from the Second/Eighth to the Eleventh/Seventeenth Centuries.' *Islamic Law and Society* 1(2): 141–87.

Ali, Syed Mumtaz. 1993. 'Treatment of Minorities. The Islamic Model' Accessed 13 Dec. 2010. http://muslim-canada.org/minorities.html.

– 2004. 'The Good Muslim/Bad Muslim Puzzle.' Accessed 12 Dec. 2010. http://muslim-canada.org/goodbad.html.

– 2010a. 'Apostasy and Blasphemy in Islam. The Salman Rushdie Issue: A Synthesis of the Islamic Law of Blasphemy/Apostasy in the Context of Canadian Multiculturalism.' Accessed 12 Dec. 2010. http://muslim-canada.org/apostasy.htm.

– 2010b. 'Why Was the Institute Formed?' Accessed 13 Dec. 2010. http://muslim-canada.org/IICJ.html.

– ed. 2010. 'My Love and My Choice.' Accessed 12 Dec. 2010. http://muslim-canada.org/mylove.htm

Ali, Syed Mumtaz, and Azim Hosein. n.d. 'An Essential Service in Canada: Muslim Marriage, Mediation, and Arbitration Service.' Accessed 11 Dec. 2010. http://muslim-canada.org/brochure.htm.

Ali, Syed Mumtaz, and Rabia Mills. 2010. 'Darul Qada (The Beginnings of a Muslim Civil Justice System in Canada).' Accessed 12 Dec. 2010. http://muslim-canada.org/DARLQADAform2andhalf.html

Ali, Syed Mumtaz, and Enab Whitehouse. 1992. 'The Reconstruction of the Constitution and the Case for Muslim Personal Law in Canada.' *Journal of Muslim Minority Affairs* 13(1): 156–72. Accessed 13 Dec. 2010. http://www.informaworld.com/smpp/title~db=all~content=t713433220~tab=issueslist~branches=13 - v13; http://muslim-canada.org/caseforpfl.pdf.

Amer, Alia. 2010.'What Every Muslim Teenager and Adult Needs to Know about Sexuality.' Accessed 12 Dec. 2010. http://www.zawaj.com/articles/teenager_know.html.

Angail, Nadirah. 2010a. 'On Obedient Wives.' Accessed 11 Dec. 2010. http://muslimmedianetwork.com/mmn/?p=6737.

– 2010b. 'Nadirah Angail: Writer. Editor. Therapist. Life Lover.' Accessed 11 Dec. 2010. http://www.nadirahangail.com/

Aslan, Reza. 2006. *No God but God: The Origins, Evolution, and Future of Islam.* New York: Random House.

Badawai, Jamal. 2002. 'Gender Equity in Islam.' Accessed 12 Dec. 2010. http://www.islam101.com/women/equity.html.

Badawi, Jamal, and Muzammil H. Siddiqi. 2004. 'Wife Beating in an Islamic Perspective.' Exchange on 21 April. Accessed on 13 Dec. 2010. http://www.islamonline.net/servlet/Satellite?pagename=IslamOnline-English-Ask_Scholar/FatwaE/FatwaE&cid=1119503544256

Bakht, Natasha. 2006. 'Were Muslim Barbarians Really Knocking on the Gates of Ontario? The Religious Arbitration Controversy – Another Perspective.' *Ottawa Law Review, 40th Anniversary Edition* 35 (Summer): 67–82. Accessed 12 Dec. 2010. http://ssrn.com/abstract=1121790.

Bano, Samia. 2007. 'Muslim Family Justice and Human Rights: The Experience of British Muslim Women.' *Journal of Comparative Law* 1(4): 1–29.

Bearman, Peri, Rudolph Peters, and Frank E Vogel, eds. 2005. *The Islamic School of Law: Evolution, Devolution and Progress.* Cambridge, MA: Islamic Legal Studies Program, Harvard Law School, Distributed by Harvard University Press.

Binder, Leonard. 1963. *Religion and Politics in Pakistan.* Berkeley: University of California Press.

Boyd, Marion. 2004. *Dispute Resolution in Family Law: Protecting Choice, Promoting Inclusion.* Ministry of the Attorney General. Accessed 13 Dec. 2010. http://www.attorneygeneral.jus.gov.on.ca/english/about/pubs/boyd/fullreport.pdf.

Bullock, Katherine. 2005. *Muslim Women Activists in North America: Speaking for Ourselves.* Austin: University of Texas Press.

Caeiro, Alexandre. 2010. 'The Power of European Fatwas: The Minority *Fiqh* Project and the Making of an Islamic Counterpublic.' *International Journal of Middle East Studies* 42: 435–49.

CBC. 2005. 'CBC News Indepth: Islam.' 26 May. Accessed 12 Dec. 2010. http://www.cbc.ca/news/background/islam/shariah-law.html.

Clarke, L., and P. Cross. 2006. *Muslim and Canadian Family Law: A Comparative Primer.* Toronto: CCMW. Available in French: 2006. *Guide Comparatif: Lois*

Musulmanes et Canadiennes de la Famille. Toronto: Conseil canadien des
femmes musulmanes.

Dale, Gary. 2010. 'Sharia Myths and Facts.' Accessed 12 Dec. 2010. http://
www.muslimcanadiancongress.org/20051012.html.

Emon, Anver. 2005. 'A Mistake to Ban Sharia.' *Globe and Mail,* 13 Sept.
Accessed 13 Dec. 2010. http://www.law.utoronto.ca/faculty_content.asp?
itemPath=1/7/1/0/0&contentId=1174

Estes, Yusef. 2009. 'Meaning of Wife's Obedience to Her Husband.' 17 Aug.
Accessed 12 Dec. 2010. http://www.islamonline.net/servlet/
Satellite?pagename=IslamOnline-English-Ask_Scholar/FatwaE/
FatwaE&cid=1119503544256

Fadel, Mohamed. 2009a. *Political Liberalism, Islamic Family Law and Family Law
Pluralism: Lessons from New York on Family Law Arbitration.* University of
Toronto Legal Studies Research Series No. 09-05. Accessed 12 Dec. 2010.
http://ssrn.com/abstract=1421978. Forthcoming in *Marriage and Divorce in
a Multicultural Context: Multi-Tiered Marriage and the Boundaries of Civil Law
and Religion,* ed. Joel A. Nichols. Cambridge: Cambridge University Press.

– 2009b. 'Islamic Politics and Secular Politics: Can They Co-Exist?' *Journal of
Law and Religion* 25: 101–18.

Fernando, Mayanthi. 2005.'The Republic's "Second Religion": Recognizing
Islam in France.' *Middle East Report: Europe and Islam – The Challenge of
Inclusion* 35(2): 12–17.

Galanter, Marc. 1972. 'The Aborted Restoration of "Indigenous" Law in India.'
Comparative Studies in Society and History 14(1): 53–70.

Hallaq, W. 2009. *Sharī'a. Theory, Practice, Transformations.* Cambridge:
Cambridge University Press.

Hashimi, Muhammad Ali al-. 1999 (repr. 2005). *The Ideal Muslimah: The True
Islamic Personality of the Muslim Woman as Defined in the Quran and Sunnah.*
Translated by Nasiruddin al-Khattab. Riyad, Saudi Arabia: International
Islamic Publishing House. Accessed 13 Dec. 2010. http://www.wefound
.org/texts/Ideal_Muslims_files/herhusband.htm.

Houda-Pepin, Fatima, 2002. 'Journal des débats de l'Assemblée nationale.'
Accessed 13 Dec. 2010. http://www.assnat.qc.ca/fr/travaux-parlementaires/
assemblee-nationale/37-1/journal-debats/20051125/2839.html.

Husain, Athar. 2010. 'Muslim Personal Law – An Exposition.' Accessed
12 Dec. 2010. http://muslim-canada.org/muspersonallawpt2_1.
html#guardianship.

Hussain, Amir. 2001. 'The Canadian Face of Islam: Muslim Communities in
Toronto.' Doctoral dissertation, University of Toronto. Accessed 12 Dec. 2010.
http://www.collectionscanada.gc.ca/obj/s4/f2/dsk3/ftp05/NQ63783.pdf.

Islam Online. 2003. 'Taking the Husband's Permission on Leaving Home.'
 Exchange on 31 Aug. 2003. Accessed 12 Dec. 2010. http://www.islamonline
 .net/servlet/Satellite?pagename=IslamOnline-English-Ask_Scholar%
 2FFatwaE%2FFatwaEAskTheScholar&cid=1119503543306.

Javed, Noor. 2008. 'GTA's Secret World of Polygamy: As Toronto Mother
 Describes Her Ordeal, Imam Admits He Has "Blessed" over 30 Unions.'
 Toronto Star, 24 May.

Kamali, Mohammad Hashim. 2007. 'Shariah and Civil Law: Towards a
 Methodology of Harmonization.' *Islamic Law and Society* 14(3): 391–420.

Kennedy, Charles H. 1992. 'Repugnancy to Islam: Who Decides? Islam and
 Legal Reform in Pakistan.' *International and Comparative Law Quarterly* 41(4):
 769–87.

Laurence, Jonathan, and Justin Vaisse. 2006. *Integrating Islam: Political and
 Religious Challenges in Contemporary France.* Washington, DC: Brookings
 Institution.

March, Andrew F. 2009. 'Islamic Legal Theory, Secularism and Religious
 Pluralism: Is Modern Religious Freedom Sufficient for the Shari'a "Purpose
 [Maqsid]" of "Preserving Religion [Hifz al-Din]"?' *Islamic Law and Law of the
 Muslim World Paper* no. 09-78; Yale Law School, Public Law Working Paper
 no. 208. Accessed 12 Dec. 2010. http://ssrn.com/abstract=1452895.

Mawdudi, S. Abul A'la. 2010. 'What Is behind the Veil?' Edited by Syed
 Mumtaz Ali. Accessed 13 Dec. 2010. http://muslim-canada.org/purdah.pdf .

Mills, Rabia. 1995. 'A Review of the Muslim Personal/Family Law Campaign.'
 Accessed 12 Dec.2010. http://muslim-canada.org/pfl.htm.

Mir-Hosseini, Ziba. 1993. *Marriage on Trial: A Study of Islamic Family Law, Iran
 and Morocco Compared.* London: I.B. Tauris.

Moore, Sally Falk. 2000. *Law as Process: An Anthropological Approach,* 2nd ed.
 Oxford: James Currey with the International African Institute.

Muslim Canada Organization. 2010. 'Our President.' Accessed 13 Dec. 2010.
 http://muslim-canada.org/csm_president.html

Muslim Woman. 2010. 'Husband's Rights Concerning His Wife.' Accessed
 13 Dec. 2010. http://www.themuslimwoman.com/herrole/husbandsrights.
 htm.

Nasr, Seyyed Vali Reza. 1996. *Mawdudi and the Making of Islamic Revivalism.*
 Oxford: Oxford University Press.

National Post. 2006. 'Legalize Polygamy: Study.' 13 Jan. 13. Accessed 13 Dec.
 2010. http://www.nationalpost.com/story.html?id=8451dc17-5b5f-4ea4-
 a05f-71f7c758662a&k=52900&p=1.

Peaceful Families Organization. n.d. 'About the Peaceful Families Project.'
 Accessed 13 Dec. 2010. http://www.peacefulfamilies.org./about.html.

Peter, Frank. 2006. 'Individualization and Religious Authority in Western European Islam.' *Islam and Christian-Muslim Relations* 17(1): 105–18.

Potvin, Jean-Mathieu, and Anne Saris. 2009. 'La résolution de conflits familiaux chez les canadiennes musulmanes à Montréal : Un système de justice parallèle?' *Diversité urbaine* 9(1): 119–37. Accessed 12 Dec.2010. http://id.erudit.org/iderudit/037762ar.

Ramadan, Tariq. 2003. *Les musulmans d'occident et l'avenir de l'Islam.* Paris: Sindbad.

– 2004. *Western Muslims and the Future of Islam.* Oxford: Oxford University Press.

– 2009. *Radical Reform: Islamic Ethics and Liberation.* Oxford: Oxford University Press.

Roy. Sylvie. 2005. 'Journal des débats de l'Assemblée nationale.' Accessed 13 Dec. 2010. http://www.assnat.qc.ca/fr/travaux-parlementaires/assemblee-nationale/37-1/journal debats/20051125/2839.html.

Shachar, Ayelet . 2008. 'Privatizing Diversity: A Cautionary Tale from Religious Arbitration in Family Law.' *Theoretical Inquiries in Law* 9(2): Article 11. Accessed 13 Dec. 2010. http://www.bepress.com/til/default/vol9/iss2/art11.

Sháfi'í al-. [1402]/1982. *Kitáb al-umm,* 8 vols. Beirut: Dár al-Fikr.

Sikand, Yoginder. 2007. *Muslims in India: Contemporary Social and Political Discourses.* Gurgaon: Hope India Publications.

Sims, Jane. 2005. 'Boyd Says Ban on Shariah Law Won't End It.' *London Free Press,* 10 Nov.

Sjöqvist, Madeleine Sultán. 2007. 'Women's Conversions to Islam: Equality and Obedience.' *NIKK magazine* 2. Accessed on 13 Dec. 2010. http://nikk.no/Women's+Conversions+to+Islam%3A+Equality+and+Obedience.9UFRzGWI.ips.

Sonbol, Amira el-Azhary.1998. '*Ta'a* and Modern Legal Reform: A Rereading.' *Islam and Christian-Muslim Relations* 9(3): 285–94.

Song, Vivian. 2004. 'Sharia Law in Ontario: Proponents Insist Laws Are Misunderstood.' *Toronto Sun,* 15 June. Accessed 11 Dec. 2010. http://talk.islamicnetwork.com/archive/indhttp://talk.islamicnetwork.com/archive/index.php/t-98.html.

Stastna, Kazi. 2005. 'Muslim Leaders Liken Sharia to Canada's Arbitration System: Decry Opposition to Faith-Based Tribunal.' *Gazette,* 12 March.

Takim, L. 2009. *Shiism in America.* New York: New York University Press.

Thornback, James. 2005. 'The Portrayal of Sharia in Ontario.' *Appeal: Review of Current Law and Legal Reform* 10: 1–12.

Trilling, A. 2010. 'Wife Beating Is Not Allowed in Islam in Any Case!' Accessed 13 Dec. 2010. http://www.answering-christianity.com/beating_no.htm.

Tucker, Judith. 1998. *In the House of the Law: Gender and Islamic Law in Ottoman Syria and Palestine*. Berkeley: University of California Press.

Túsí. [1417]/2003. *Khiláf*. 14 vols. Qum, Iran.

Watson, Alan. 1983. 'Legal Change: Sources of Law and Legal Culture.' *University of Pennsylvania Law Review* 131(5): 1121–57.

Welchman, Lynn. 2007. *Women and Muslim Family Laws in Arab States: A Comparative Overview of Textual Development and Advocacy*. Amsterdam: Amsterdam University Press.

Yilmaz, Ihsan. 2003. 'Muslim Alternative Dispute Resolution and Neo-Ijtihad in England.' *Alternatives: Turkish Journal of International Relations* 2(1). Accessed 12 Dec. 2010. http://www.alternativesjournal.net/volume2/number1/yilmaz.htm.

6 Islamic Law and the Canadian Mosaic: Politics, Jurisprudence, and Multicultural Accommodation

ANVER M. EMON

The debate on the use of Sharia for family law arbitration in Ontario highlighted a few of the predicaments that arise when balancing commitments to individual rights and multiculturalism. In particular, to what extent can a liberal nation's rule-of-law system tolerate a minority group exerting autonomy within a particular area of the law, especially when individuals within the minority group may be disadvantaged by the exercise of community autonomy?[1] Certainly, scholars on issues of multiculturalism and legal pluralism have offered models by which national rule-of-law systems can accommodate community autonomy while upholding individual liberties and interests. For instance, Suzanne Last Stone has argued for a model of 'dialectical interaction' between two legal systems that may result in mutual innovation and change. Writing about New York State's use of a Get law to assist Jewish women in obtaining religious divorces, Last Stone (2000) offers a dialogic model in which multiple norm-generating systems interact with one another to foster change and development. Ayelet Shachar (2001), reviewing the extensive literature on multiculturalism and legal pluralism, offers a model of transformative accommodation to balance the interests of cultural groups with those of the state in order to uphold the liberties of its citizenry.

To determine whether to allow Sharia arbitration in family law, the Ontario government appointed the Honourable Marion Boyd, former attorney general of Ontario, to investigate the extent to which federal and provincial law could uphold the interests of their citizens while also respecting the use of religious law to arbitrate family disputes. Relying on Shachar's model of transformative accommodation, Boyd (2004) suggested that within a reformed arbitral system, religious law

(Sharia or otherwise) could be used in a way that both allows for accommodation of cultural autonomy, and does not violate the liberty interests of Canadian citizens under the Charter of Rights and Freedoms. Suggesting numerous changes to the arbitral system in Ontario, most of which involved increasing training, transparency, and accountability of arbitrators, Marion Boyd did not consider Sharia law, by its very essence, to undermine or vitiate a woman's liberty or equality interest.[2]

Boyd's report, however, did not describe or otherwise provide much substantive description of Sharia. Referring only to the use of 'Islamic principles' to govern arbitral proceedings, Boyd did not define for Muslims or others what Islamic law is or should be. Rather, that was something left to Muslims to figure out for themselves. Not surprisingly, Muslim proponents and opponents of Sharia arbitration engaged in a heated debate about what Sharia law would demand in family law arbitration settings. They hostilely debated the implications of using Sharia on the liberty and equality interests of Muslim women in Canada. In fact, some argued that the introduction of Sharia in family law arbitrations would open the door to even greater reliance on Sharia, including in the criminal sphere.[3] Of interest in this study, though, is that those involved in the debate arguably espoused a particular, shared image of the Sharia that I argue has a recent historical provenance and is the product of a particular political history. Even though the Ontario government has chosen to disallow religious arbitrations in family law, the issues that spurred the debate on Sharia arbitration have not disappeared. The concern for Muslim women's rights in the family law context remains, especially since imams can still perform Islamic divorce services under the rubric of mediation as opposed to legally enforced arbitration, as described in chapters by Julie MacFarlane and Christopher Cutting (see also Trichur 2004).

For those interested in legal pluralism in liberal rule-of-law systems such as in Canada, further investigation into the concept of Sharia that dominated the Canadian debate is essential if the meaning of a state's commitment to individual freedom and multiculturalism is to be fully understood and implemented.[4] Our understanding of what it means to uphold and preserve multiculturalism will often depend on how we understand, represent, and characterize the 'Other.' The substance and limits of one nation's multicultural commitments do not simply involve a forceful assertion of its values. Rather, to understand a nation's values and their limits, we need to properly understand the Other and how the Other fits into the existing national landscape of values and identities.

Arguably, by relying on polemic and rhetoric to understand the Other, the possibility of true understanding, both of the self and the Other, is unlikely. As I have written elsewhere, the more 'critical and honest we can be in learning about and understanding the Other, the better we can understand our own values and the limits of our multiculturalism' (Emon 2005b, 20).

In the next two sections, I address the early history of Sharia and how medieval legal doctrines were embedded within institutional frameworks that helped make the tradition meaningful and responsive to changing situations. Then I show how this early rule-of-law system was gradually dismantled, generally at the instigation of European colonial interests, and the following section illustrates how post-colonial Muslims have uncritically adopted the representations of Sharia handed to them by the former colonial powers; as subalterns they internalized the discourse of their colonial masters. In doing so, their representations of Sharia today have more to do with contested forms of political identity, rather than with creating rule-of-law systems that are responsive to Islamic values. I conclude with a proposal suggesting how liberal governments can cooperate with Muslim civil society organizations to create spaces for Muslims to engage in critical thought about the accommodation of Islamic law within national rule-of-law frameworks founded on fundamental values of liberal states.

The Concept of Sharia

The concept of Sharia that prevailed in the Ontario debates was one that viewed the tradition as an inflexible and immutable code of religious rules, based on the Qur'an and traditions of the Prophet Muhammad.[5] Various media outlets described Sharia as a 'code' of law that deterministically governs every aspect of a Muslim's life (Mackinnon 2005). In letters to the editor, readers commented on their fear of the use of Sharia in Ontario, calling it an 'archaic paternalistic code' (West 2005; Wilson 2005). The view of Sharia as a code, however, ignores the centuries of juristic literature that challenges any conceptualization of Sharia as a determinate, narrowly constructed, unchanging code of law. Sharia has a history whose normative foundations and development stretch from the seventh century to the present,[6] and which illustrates that legal rules were often the product of Muslim jurists' analytical discretion in the context of a culture and institution of education, precedent, principles, and doctrines.[7] The interpretive theory of Islamic law certainly espouses a commitment to the Qur'an and traditions of Prophet Muhammad (d. 632 CE) also called *hadīth*. These 'scriptural' sources provide an authoritative foundation for juristic analysis and interpretation. But by themselves, these sources do not constitute a legal system. The Qur'an contains 114 chapters, but only a small fraction of its verses can be characterized as 'legal.'[8] Likewise the traditions of Muhammad are often highly contextualized, and their meanings are informed by that context. Furthermore, as both Muslim jurists and Western scholars of Islam have noted, as the embodiment of an earlier oral tradition, the hadīth cannot always be relied on as authentic statements of what the Prophet said, did, or decided.[9] While both sources occupy an undeniable position of authority within Islamic jurisprudence, they alone do not constitute the Islamic legal tradition. The Sharia tradition is comprised of considerable juridical literature, much of which illustrates that jurists often went beyond scripture, utilizing their discretion in various ways to articulate the law. In the field of medieval legal theory or *usul al-fiqh*, jurists developed various interpretive methodologies that balanced the need for authority, legitimacy, and discretion in a way that ensured a just outcome under the circumstances. They extended scriptural rules through analogical reasoning (*qiyās*), balanced competing precedents in light of larger questions of justice (*istihsan*), and legislated pursuant to public policy interests where scripture was otherwise silent (*maslaha mursala*). Muslim jurists did more than simply read the Qur'an and hadīth as if they are codes and thereby transparently and determinately meaningful.[10] In other words, it is highly misleading to suggest that Islamic law is constituted by the Qur'an and traditions of the Prophet without further recourse to techniques of juristic analysis that allowed the law to remain socially responsive without at the same time undermining the legal tradition's authority.

Islamic law arose through a systematic process of juristic commentary and analysis that stretched over centuries. During this process, different interpretations of the law arose, leading to competing 'interpretive communities'[11] of the law or what are often called schools of law (*madhahib*, sing. *madhhab*) – all of which were historically deemed equally orthodox.[12] Over time, the number of interpretive legal communities or madhahib diminished, to the extent that there are now four remaining Sunni legal schools and three Shi'ite schools. The Sunni schools are the Hanafi, Maliki, Shafi, and Hanbali schools. The Hanafi school is predominant in South Asia and Turkey; the Malikis are most often found in North Africa. The Shafiis are dominant in Southeast Asia and Egypt, while the Hanbali school is found in the Gulf region. The Shii'te schools are as follows: Jaafari (mostly in Iran), Ismaili, and Zaydi. Consequently, if one wants to determine a rule of Islamic law, one will often start with a text on substantive law, rather than the Qur'an or traditions of the Prophet. One may consult a summary of substantive law (i.e., *mukhtasar*) or an elaborate encyclopedia written by a jurist within the particular madhhab to which one belongs.[13] Furthermore, if one inquires into the historical development of doctrine around a given issue, one may find that the law and legal analysis manifest distinct shifts that may be based on contexts yet to be determined by further research.[14]

For instance, under Islamic law a husband has the right to unilaterally divorce his wife through a procedure known as *talaq*, while the wife does not have this power, unless she negotiated to have this power included as a condition in her marriage contract (*'aqd al-nikah*).[15] If a wife has not done so, she must petition a court to issue a divorce. A wife can seek either a for-cause divorce or a no-cause divorce. In a for-cause divorce, she alleges some fault on the part of her husband (e.g., failure to support, abuse, impotence) and seeks a divorce while preserving her financial claims against her husband. In a no-cause or *khula* divorce, a woman asserts no fault by her husband, and agrees to forgo any financial claim against her husband to be free from the marriage.[16] The difference between a husband's right of divorce and a wife's right in this case is fundamentally a matter of the degree and scope of the power to assert one's liberty interests.

According to the Shafi jurist Abu al-Hasan al-Mawardi (d. 1058), the husband's unilateral power to divorce is based on a Qur'anic verse which reads: 'O Prophet, when you divorce women, divorce them at their prescribed periods' (Qur'an 65:1). One might ask why this verse should be read as giving men a substantive unilateral right to divorce their spouses to the exclusion of women, rather than as a mechanism prescribing the procedure a man should follow when divorcing his wife? Read as providing a procedural mechanism, the verse arguably grants implicitly the right of unilateral divorce to both men and women, while requiring men to utilize their power in a certain procedural manner. However, most jurists held that the verse substantively grants men a unilateral power of divorce. The challenge for jurists was to provide a rationale for extending the substantive right of divorce only to men (al-Mawardi 1994, 10:111). For example, al-Mawardi argued that since the duty to provide support and maintenance (*mu'una*) falls exclusively on the husband, he is entitled to certain special rights given this difference (114). Second, and most troubling, al-Mawardi stated that the power of talaq is denied to a woman because her whims and desires overpower her (*shahwatuha taghlibuha*), and hence, she may be hasty to pronounce a divorce at the first sign of marital discord. But men, he said, dominate their desires more than women, and are less likely to hastily invoke the talaq power at the first sign of discord (114).

Certainly, many readers, Muslim and otherwise, may find al-Mawardi's reasoning not only patriarchal but frankly offensive. The rationale provided for distributing the right of talaq to men and not women is hardly persuasive, given a contemporary liberal democratic context where gender equality is generally an honoured and respected norm.[17] Consequently, one might suggest that the patriarchal tone of al-Mawardi's reading was elemental to a particular context that gave meaning to this rule, but which no longer prevails. To do so need not necessitate countering the Qur'anic verse. Rather, the Qur'anic verse noted above is arguably broad and ambiguous enough to tolerate multiple readings. However, as discussed below, the challenge of reforming Islamic law today is not as simple as arguing that a particular reading or rationale is logically unpersuasive from a jurisprudential perspective.

Islamic Law and Institutions

Historically, Islamic law was immersed not only within a cultural context, but also within an institutional context that transformed what might have been moral norms into enforced legal rules. The institutional frameworks for adjudication and enforcement were the means by which Sharia was applied to actual cases in controversy. Whether deciding rules of pleading, sentencing, or litigation, for instance, the way jurists determined and at times constructed rules, individual rights, and entitlements was significantly influenced by assumptions of institutions of adjudication and enforcement.[18] The law was not simply created in an academic vacuum devoid of implications in the real world. Rather, the existence of institutions of litigation and procedure contributed in part to the determination and meaningfulness of the law.

In fact, the procedural institutions of medieval adjudication were so important that resolving a particular controversy may not have been dependent on some doctrinal, substantive determination of the law. For instance, the medieval Shafi jurist Abu al-Ma'ali al-Juwayni (d. 1098) related a hypothetical about a Hanafi husband and a Shafi wife. Suppose the husband declares to his wife in a fit of anger that he divorces her.

According to al-Juwayni, the Hanafis held that such a pronouncement is invalid and ineffective, whereas the Shafis considered it to be valid. Are the husband and wife still married? According to the husband they are married, but according to the wife they are divorced. Which view should prevail? Certainly, the two parties can insist on their respective views and claim to be justified in doing so. But to resolve the dispute, the parties must resort to a rule-of-law process, namely adjudication. They will submit their case to a *qadi* whose decision, based on his own analysis, is binding on both parties. The qadi's decision is authoritative not because it accords with one specific legal rule or another; rather, it is authoritative because of the imperium tied to his institutional position within a Sharia rule-of-law system (al-Juwayni 1987).[19]

Since the eighteenth century, the institutional structure that gave real-world significance to Islamic law began to be dismantled or modified. As discussed below, pursuant to the capitulation agreements with the Ottoman Sultan, non-Muslim Europeans were exempted from the jurisdiction of Ottoman courts. In Egypt, the use of the Mixed Court to hear cases involving non-Muslim parties and interests further eroded the extent to which Sharia was applied. When Egypt adopted the Napoleonic Code in the late nineteenth century and created national courts to adjudicate it, Sharia courts and the law they applied began to lose relevance and institutional efficacy in resolving legal disputes. The idea of Sharia today as a rule-of-law system suffers from a discontinuity between the texts that embodied the juristic tradition and the application of those texts to day-to-day situations. Without the institutions of case-by-case adjudication, we are left with texts that contain the abstract doctrine of surviving interpretive communities of Islamic law that reflect a cultural context long gone, and with few if any institutional structures that can mediate between text and context. When we speak of Islamic law today, we are not generally referring to institutions of justice, but rather to juristic doctrines reflecting the historicity of juristic subjectivity.

Certainly, one might suggest that if the cultural context has changed, then so too should the law. But part of the problem with legal reform in Islamic law is that with the progression of history came the demise of the institutional setting that made Sharia a rule-of-law system, rather than merely doctrinal rules of law existing in the abstract. As doctrine in the abstract, it has been transformed from a rule-of-law system to a system of ideology. As suggested below, with colonialism, colonial resistance, post-colonial nation building, and Islamization programs,

Muslims have often viewed Islamic legal doctrine (whether positively or negatively) in light of developing political ideologies of identity rather than as part of a rule-of-law system. As such, to change Islamic rules of law is viewed as an attack on the political identity and ideology it is made to reflect and represent.

Sharia in the Nineteenth and Twentieth Centuries

In the Ontario Sharia debate, many seemed to believe steadfastly that Islamic law is so fundamentally rigid and different from Canadian law that no synthesis would be possible. Interestingly, this view mimics the findings of Orientalist scholars of Islamic law in the late nineteenth and early twentieth centuries. Those scholars advised governments such as Britain and France on how best to understand Muslims for the purpose of managing and maintaining colonial power while keeping the indigenous peoples content. To understand Muslims and Muslim law, and perhaps to (re)present Islamic law to Muslims themselves, colonialists and their Orientalist advisers often reduced the Muslim experience to what was expressed in specific texts that they deemed authoritative. The colonial use of texts to understand Muslims and Islamic law led not only to the development of textual experts, but also to the phenomenon of the textual expert representing the Muslim and Islamic law in strict accordance with the image presented in the text. As Edward Said (1979) has argued, texts can 'create not only knowledge but also the very reality they appear to describe.' By approaching Islamic law reductively as a text-based tradition, colonialists could attempt to 'understand' the Muslim and Islamic experience by mere reference to text, while ignoring the significance of context and contingency that is often taken into account in working rule-of-law systems.[20] Deviation from the authentic text was considered dangerous, ultra vires, if not an aberration from the truth, the true Islamic law.[21] As a text-based law, Islamic law could be viewed as an unchanging, inflexible religious code, which ultimately aided colonialists in both placating their Muslim subjects' religious interests, and marginalizing the tradition in various legal sectors as contrary and incompatible with progress and modernization in the law.

Anglo-Muhammadan Law: A Reductive Concept of Law

Under the initial leadership of Warren Hastings, Governor General of India from 1773 to 1784, the British developed mechanisms by which they could both understand their Muslim subjects, as well as accommodate their religious preferences through the implementation of British-inspired Sharia courts. These courts ultimately created what has come to be called 'Anglo-Muhammadan Law,' a body of law in which Islamic legal principles were fused with common law principles to provide a system of legal redress for Muslims living in British India concerning issues such as marriage, divorce, and inheritance.

Often staffed by British judges, the first task of this court was to determine authoritative sources of Islamic law that they could easily access. To understand the Sunni tradition, British judges in Anglo-Muhammadan courts relied on a translation of the four-part Hanafi legal text (n.d.) al-Hidaya by al-Marghinani (d. 1197). Notably, in the larger context of medieval Hanafi fiqh texts, *al-Hidaya* is a short manual of Hanafi law that does not consistently provide the underlying logic or reasoning for the rules of the school. Badr al-Din al-'Ayni's (d. 1451) multi-volume commentary on al-Marghinani's work, al-Binaya: Sharh al-Hidaya (2000), provides greater jurisprudential insight into the Hanafi legal tradition. However, al-'Ayni's work was not translated and generally was not referred to in the Anglo-Muhammadan courts.[22] Rather, Anglo-Muhammadan judges were content to rely on Charles Hamilton's flawed translation of al-Hidaya (1982). Notably, Hamilton did not translate directly from the original Arabic text. Instead, Hastings commissioned three Muslim clerics to translate the Arabic text into Persian, which Hamilton then translated into English in 1791 (Anderson 1989). This translated legal treatise provided a textual foundation for the British to understand and apply Islamic law, and thereby build relations with their Muslim subjects.

Originally, Hamilton's translated text comprised four volumes. However, as a large and voluminous work that was often not easily available by the late nineteenth century, the translated Hedaya proved very costly for students at the Inns of Court in Britain who wanted to practise law in India and needed to purchase the text to qualify themselves for the Indian bar. Consequently, in 1870, the editor of the second edition of the Hedaya, Standish Grove Grady, removed whole sections of Hamilton's version of al-Hidaya. Certainly, students training for their legal exams and seeking admission to the English bar might find the reduction in price a relief. But Grady's hope was not solely about the financial wherewithal of law students. He states:

Although the present Edition has been published with a view of assisting the student to prosecute his studies, yet the hope is entertained that the

Judge, as well as the Practitioner, will find it useful, particularly in those provinces where the Mahommedan law demands a greater portion of the attention of the judiciai, as well as that of the practitioner. It is hoped, also, that it may be found useful in promoting the study of the law in the several Universities in India, it being advisable to assimilate the curriculum in both countries as much as possible. (Grady 1982)

The hope, therefore, was that Hamilton's translation of a Persian version of al-Marghinani's Arabic text, as edited and shortened in the second edition, would be a useful source for judges and practitioners in India adjudicating Islamic legal concerns for Muslims. That Muslims would be subjected to this doubly reductive conception of Islamic law, without reference to custom or context, was further emphasized in the Muslim Personal Law (Shariat) Application Act, 1937, in which the British enacted that Muslim personal law would apply to all Muslims throughout India, to the full and complete exclusion of customary practice. In fact, section 2 of the act states that 'notwithstanding any custom or usage to the contrary' in matters involving inheritance, marriage, dissolution, financial maintenance, dower, gifts, and other matters of personal status and finance, 'the rule of decision in cases where the parties are Muslim shall be the Muslim Personal Law (Shariat).'[23] Nowhere in the act does the government state how it defines Islamic law or 'Shariat.' But given the prominent usage of texts such as Hamilton's *Hedaya*, the notion of Islamic law used to represent their own law to Muslims was reduced to codelike notions of it, without recourse to discretionary approaches that might take non-textual factors into account.

This reductive view is best illustrated in the way British judges adjudicated Islamic law in Anglo-Muhammadan courts. British judges often took a narrow view of what counted as proper and applicable Islamic law. For instance, in the 1903 case *Baker Ali Khan* v. *Anjuman Ara*, the decision written by Arthur Wilson of the Judicial Committee of the Privy Council illustrates how hesitant British judges were in going beyond the confines of translated texts and in analysing and choosing between conflicting Islamic precedent.[24] Yet despite that hesitation, these same British judges did not seem troubled if they modified the dominant Islamic legal ruling where they felt the Islamic tradition made little meaningful sense in light of their own common law training. The *Baker Ali Khan* case involved a testatrix who created a charitable trust (*waqf*) by a will (*wasiyya*). The testatrix was the daughter of the former king of Oudh and a member of the Shi'ite faith. She had three great grandchildren through her son, including one Baker Ali, a minor.

Before she died, the testatrix had executed a document deemed to create a charitable trust (waqf) for religious purposes. Pursuant to the document Baker Ali and his guardian Sadik Ali were to be executors and trustees of the waqf. The other two great grandchildren argued that all three were equally entitled to one-third of the testatrix's estate, including that contained within the waqf document.

To decide the case, the Privy Council judges had to contend with an 1892 precedent decided by Mahmood J. of the Allahabad High Court in *Agha Ali Khan* v. *Altaf Hasan Khan*, in which the learned Muslim justice held that under the Shia law, one cannot create a waqf through a bequesting instrument like the wasiyya.[25] He argued that such a waqf was invalid under Shia law, although valid under Hanafi law of the Sunni tradition. Mahmood J. criticized early nineteenth century courts that had failed to apply Shia law to Shia parties, instead assuming that the Sunni and Shia law on this issue were identical (*Agha Ali Khan*, 449). Mahmood J. said: 'I seriously doubt whether in those days the Shia law was ever administered by the Courts of British India as the rule of decision, even when Shias were concerned' (449). Mahmood J. stated that the Privy Council began to apply Shia law to Shi'ite Muslims only by the mid-nineteenth century (449).

Having established the central relevance of Shia law, Mahmood J. began to analyse the Shia law on waqf and the extent to which a Shi'ite Muslim could grant a waqf through a testamentary bequest enforceable on his death. Central to his discussion is a review of various Shia legal sources. He started with an analysis of the 'Sharáya-ul-Islám' written by al-Muhaqqiq Hilli (d. 1277 or 1278), an early Shia text that was translated by Neil Baillie as Imameea Law.[26] The problem for the later *Baker Ali* court was that Mahmood J. also cited the following significant commentaries on Hilli's text not translated into English:[27] Masálik-ul-Afhám,[28] Jawáhir-ul-Kalám,[29] Jámi-ul-Shattát,[30] Sharah Lumah Dimashkia,[31] and Jámi-ul-Maqásid (al-Karaki 1991).

After analysing these sources, Mahmood J. argued that under Shia law, as opposed to Sunni law, a waqf is considered a contract (*aqd*) (*Agha Ali Khan*, 450). As a contract, it has various conditions precedent that must be satisfied before it can be considered valid, in particular offer and acceptance. Under Shia law, a waqf is not a unilateral disposition of property; rather, it is a 'contract inter pares,' requiring the two parties involved to make an inter vivos exchange. In other words seisin of the waqf property must be delivered (450–6). In cases where the waqf is for the benefit of the poor and mendicant, the requirement of acceptance is relaxed as no specific party can effectuate acceptance (453–4). But in all other cases, there must be an actual exchange, or what Mahmood J.'s Arabic sources call *tanjíz*. Under this doctrine, any contract, waqf or otherwise, must take effect immediately and not be conditional on some future event (455–7). Citing various Shia sources, Mahmood J. argues that since a waqf is a contract that requires offer and acceptance, and since a valid contract must meet the condition of tanjíz, a waqf created by a testamentary instrument that takes effect only on one's death is invalid.

Mahmood J.'s decision was the leading case on the creation of waqfs by testamentary bequests in Shia law until the Judicial Committee of the Privy Council decided *Baker Ali*, the facts of which were described above. They were faced with a lower court decision written by a judge well-versed in Arabic and in the Shia sources, and who went beyond the sources translated into English. Despite including both the Arabic and English translation in the opinion, Mahmood J.'s ruling raised concerns for the Privy Council about how to define authoritative sources of Islamic law and delineate the bounds of judicial activity and interpretation amidst an inherited tradition of religious law.

To argue against Mahmood J.'s decision, the Judicial Committee attacked his reliance on the untranslated Arabic sources. It did not matter that the sources themselves were (and still are) significant within the Shia tradition, or that they reflected a general agreement on the conception of a waqf as a contract requiring offer, acceptance, and an inter vivos transfer. Despite Mahmood J.'s argument, translation of texts, and inclusion of the original Arabic in the footnotes, the British judges argued that the untranslated sources led to more ambiguities than determinate answers.

As a general principle, the British judges believed prudence and caution required recognition of the dangers of 'relying upon ancient texts of the Mahomedan law, and even precepts of the Prophet himself, of taking them literally, and deducing from them new rules of law' (*Baker Ali Khan*,14). For the justices, there was a very real danger of straying too far from the 'authentic' tradition of Sharia. The idea of expanding analysis of Islamic law to older texts threatened the justices of the Privy Council, despite the authority of those texts within the Shii'te tradition.

The contest between Mahmood J. and the Judicial Committee seemed to centre on defining authoritative sources, and whether one must limit them to those sources that have been translated into English. The Privy

Council Law Lords were content to rely on the 'more important of those [Shia] texts which have long been accessible to all lawyers' (*Baker Ali Khan*,14–15). But accessibility here has more to do with translation than with the significance of texts to the legal tradition being analysed. Certainly, the Sharáya-ul-Islám is an important Shia text; but for the British judges, it was also accessible because it was translated into English. According to Mahmood J., another Shia text, Jámi-ul-Shattát, was also widely accessible. But the latter text was not translated into English (*Agha Ali Khan*, 451). Certainly, for British judges to rely on un-translated texts of Islamic law would have introduced administrative problems of accessibility given that not all lawyers practising in Anglo-Muhammadan courts necessarily knew Arabic, let alone Persian.

The Lords of the Privy Council were also concerned about the extent to which one should interpret from the early sources to find legal reso-lution in contemporary disputes. They criticized Mahmood, J. for utiliz-ing too much discretionary analysis in his critical reading of the 'ancient' texts. While they recognized that Mahmood J.'s analysis of those texts on some issues might be directly relevant to the case at hand, they were concerned that the texts themselves presented no unanimity. However, from the analysis above, it seems that Mahmood J. was convinced that the texts demonstrated that *awqaf* (sing. *waqf*) created by testamentary bequests were invalid because of the lack of immediate acceptance by the beneficiary pursuant to basic principles of Islamic contract law. But the Judicial Committee was not interested in how awqaf are contracts under Shia law, and thereby subject to certain rules of formation. Instead they argued Mahmood J. exceeded the bounds of judicial analysis by excessive interpretation of the early texts (*Baker Ali Khan*, 15).

But what was particularly remarkable about the Judicial Committee's judgment was that although Shia precedent invalidated a waqf created by a testamentary bequest, the Committee nevertheless held that a Shia could indeed use a will to create a waqf. They argued, using common law logical analysis, that a Shii'te can make an inter vivos gift, whether as a waqf or not. A Shi'ite can also make a gift by will. Logically, they argued, a Shii'te should also be able to make a waqf by will. Completely ignoring Shia jurisprudence that a waqf is a contract, the Judicial Committee recharacterized the waqf as a gift. But even more, it used this case as an opportunity to reduce the scope of Islamic law and the extent to which one could investigate competing sources for conflicting precedent.

The effect of the *Baker Ali* decision was not only to create a doctrine of limited interpretation, but also to fundamentally affect the way Muslims themselves conceptualized and understood their own religious tradition. Even Muslim Indians, as subalterns under colonial rule, seemed to adopt colonial discourses of Islamic law and reduced the tradition to a doctrine of prior precedent while denying the possibility of innovative analysis and reasoning.

Dismantled Institutions and Diminished Jurisdiction

From a colonial perspective, Islamic law was not only a tool of administration and control, but at times could be an obstacle that had to be removed in order to facilitate colonial interests. When Western powers developed strong economic ties with the Ottoman Empire, they often negotiated 'capitulation' agreements with the sultan by which both parties secured an acceptable trading relationship while preserving their own domestic interests. Importantly, under such agreements, European foreigners were immune from the jurisdiction of the Ottoman courts of law (Brinton 1968). Their cases were adjudicated by consuls representing the different European countries. Commercial disputes between foreigners and natives were heard before special tribunals adjudicated by both foreign and Ottoman judges, or were heard before ordinary Ottoman courts generally with the presence of a consular official (ibid.). As local leaders looked to Europe for financial investment and deeper economic relations, they were asked to grant foreigners greater immunities from the application of Sharia law, thereby expanding consular jurisdiction in managing the legal affairs of foreigners.

From the chaos of venues that arose with consular jurisdiction, the Mixed Court was established in Egypt to adjudicate cases involving foreign interests, that is, where one of the parties was a foreigner or where a foreign interest was implicated, even if both parties were native Egyptians. Gradually, the Mixed Court acquired greater jurisdiction.[32] Furthermore, the Egyptian government in 1883 adopted the Napoleonic Code as its civil law and created national courts to administer that code. The result was three Egyptian court systems: the Mixed Courts, the secular National Courts, and the Sharia courts.[33]

For colonial powers, Islamic law was considered an obstacle to orderly legal and market systems, and an impediment to progress and modernity. In much of the Muslim world in the nineteenth century,

> modern scientific and technical culture ... came to the Muslim world in
> the nineteenth century as an essentially European import. Often one found
> that either foreigners or local non-Muslim minority groups had privileged
> access to modern education and the modern sector of the economy, while
> the Muslims, although they were politically dominant, were mainly con-
> fined to traditional education, to the traditional sector of the urban econo-
> my, and to landed wealth. For a Muslim, gaining a position in the modern
> economic or technical spheres thus involved a departure from traditional
> roles, as well as competition with foreign or minority groups, who in
> many cases could manage to be modern without great sacrifice to their
> social identity. (Christelow 1985)

In time, colonial officials and native collaborators considered Sharia not
only fixed and rigid, but also an obstacle to progress, modernity, and
civilization. They justified their efforts to marginalize the jurisdiction of
Islamic law as necessary to bring 'civilization' to the Muslims.

In the late nineteenth century, the Ottoman Empire initiated a series of
legal reforms that involved adopting and mimicking European legal
codes as substitutes for Islamic legal traditions.[34] In many ways, this
indigenous response to colonial advancement and legal imposition can
be viewed as a subaltern resistance against colonial domination. In offering their own interpretations and codifications of Islamic law,
Muslim elite members challenged the occupier's treatment of Islamic
law, but only by attempting to fit Islamic law into a European mould.[35]
Medieval Islamic law was characterized by a multiplicity of opinions,
different doctrinal schools, and competing theories of interpretive analysis. In the Ottoman reform period, this complex substantive and theoretical diversity was reduced through a selective process of codification.
For instance, when Muslims began to codify Islamic law, such as when
the Ottomans drafted the first Islamic code the Majalla,[36] they had to
decide which rules would dominate. Would they create a Hanafi,
Maliki, Hanbali, or Shafi code for those countries that were mostly
Sunni? And what would they do about their Shia population? Often,
these reformers would pick and choose from different doctrinal schools
to reach what they felt was the best outcome. This process of selection
(takhayyur) and harmonization (talfiq) of conflicting aspects of medieval
opinions allowed reformers to present a version of Islamic law that paralleled the European model of law in form and structure; but in doing
so, they reduced Islamic law to a set of positivist legal assertions divorced from the historical, institutional, and jurisprudential context

that contributed to its flexibility.[37] As another example, in 1949 Egypt adopted a civil code borrowed mostly from the French Civil Code, and which also incorporated minimal elements of Islamic law. Subsequently, in 1955 the Sharia courts were disbanded in the country.[38] One exception to this dislocation of Sharia was in the area of family law. Both colonial administrators and Muslim nationalist assemblies preserved Islamic family law in codified form while modernizing other legal areas such as commercial law. This reduction in jurisdiction and application arguably placated Islamists who felt threatened by modernization and considered the preservation of traditional Islamic family law to be necessary to maintain an Islamic identity in the face of an encroaching modernity.[39] This phenomenon was widespread across the Muslim world where colonial powers exerted force, and had a profound effect on the Muslim and European understanding of Sharia. In redefining Sharia, reducing its scope, and considering it without reference to history, institution, or context, colonial powers reified the way Sharia was applied and even understood by European powers and Muslims themselves.[40]

The Muslim Response: From Reified Sharia to Identity Politics

As Muslim nations became independent after the Second World War, and later embraced Islamization campaigns in the 1970s, the assertion of Islamic law in its traditional form began anew. Faced with the challenges of modernity and increasing globalization, Muslims in these countries asked themselves how far they could modernize without compromising their Islamic commitments. For those Muslims who saw modernization as associated with the hegemonic 'Other' and as challenging Islamic identity, the historical Sharia in codelike form provided a symbolic and determinate anchor for delineating a monist vision of 'Islamic identity.' The idea of Islamic law as fixed, unchanging, and closed to de novo analysis, operates among Muslims as a device to assert political, cultural, and religious identity.[41] The reductive reading of Islamic law by colonial administrators as fixed and unchanging has affected the way in which those living in the twenty-first century understand and conceptualize the Islamic tradition.

For instance, in an attempt to situate the development of Islamic law historically, the late Orientalist scholar of Islamic law, Noel Coulson, argued that in its traditional form Muslim jurisprudence 'provides a[n] ... extreme example of a legal science divorced from historical considerations. Law, in classical Muslim theory, is the revealed will of God, a divinely ordained system preceding and not preceded by the Muslim state, controlling and not controlled by Muslim society ... Since direct access to revelation of the divine will had ceased upon the death of the Prophet Muhammad, the Shari'a, having once achieved perfection of expression, was in principle static and immutable' (1964, 1–2).

For Coulson, Islamic law, in its ideal form, is the embodiment of God's will. That will is captured forever in scripture – scripture that precedes the Muslim state and governs it and its actions. The role of the jurist in Islamic law is not to construct or fashion laws, but rather to discover the divine law: 'The role of the individual jurist is measured by the purely subjective standard of its intrinsic worth in the process of discovery of the divine command' (Coulson 1997, 2). Islamic law does not grow and develop through a jurisprudentially legitimized use of critical analysis; instead it stagnates in the form of inherited scriptural texts provided by God's divine will. Sharia provides for Coulson a unifying standard to which Muslims adhere, and stands against 'the variety of legal systems which would be the inevitable result if law were the product of human reason based upon the local circumstances and the particular needs of a given community' (ibid.). With this image of Islamic law, Coulson considers the Sharia tantamount to a *ius naturae* or natural law as against all other humanly contrived legal systems (ibid.). But by natural law, he means a universal standard, rather than a system of law that accounts for historical contingencies. His conception of the classical theory of Islamic law is not one that grants legitimacy to unaided reason and the needs of society as building blocks of the law. This conception of Islamic law does not allow for considerable discretionary judgment, legal innovation, or legal change.

Coulson was writing as an observer and scholar of Islamic law. But for Muslims contending with post-colonial controversies over political identity, the idea of changing or modernizing Islamic law in a way that does not adhere strictly to the textual tradition is perceived as surrendering to the cultural hegemony of the West and the values it enshrines. For instance, the Islamist conception of Sharia as unchanging and inflexible rules of God has been understood by some scholars, such as Roxanne Euben, to be a response to the onset of liberal modernity. The reductive and reified conception of Sharia, with its determinacy, provides a foundation for defining notions of identity through tradition, and thereby counters the atomistic notion of the liberal individual disconnected from tradition and community.[42]

As an example, in 2000, Abderrahman Youssoufi, Morocco's socialist prime minister, proposed reforms to the nation's personal status law (*Moudawwana*), which governed issues such as marriage, divorce, and other matters related to family law. Under the original Moudawwana promulgated in 1958, women were declared legally inferior to men (Rachidi 2003). When Youssoufi proposed his reforms, hundreds of thousands of supporters rallied in Rabat. However, as Ilhem Rachidi reports, 'Islamists organized a counterprotest the same day in Casablanca, with at least as many marchers denouncing what they called the Western nature of the project' (ibid., 9). To promote the reforms, while undermining Islamist opposition, King Mohammad VI invoked his authority as supreme religious commander (*amir al-mu'minin*) and created a council of religious scholars and other academics to ensure that the reforms did not violate Islamic law principles. Subsequent to this action, Islamist parties such as the Justice and Development Party (PJD) have heralded the reforms as consistent with Islamic law and have embraced the reformative endeavours. However, it is not clear to what extent the PJD truly believed in the Islamicity of the program. It is suspected that the PJD tempered its rhetoric out of respect for the king's religious authority as amir al-mu'minin, and out of concern over its suspected role in the May 2003 Casablanca bombings (ibid.).

As suggested by both the Saudi and the Moroccan examples, the challenge posed by reform and modernization is very much tied to political questions of identity in a post-colonial struggle for independence and autonomy despite continued Western influence in the region.

This single example illustrates how Islamic law is used in political strategies to support regimes and to construct national, cultural, and religious identities in a post-colonial context in which Western hegemony – whether in physical, economic, or cultural terms – is considered a threat to Islamic identity. Islamic law, reduced to a code-like system of rules, is arguably believed to be the basis for that identity, and any reform of it will be viewed as a threat to a political identity often defined in opposition to Western liberal values.

Ontario's Sharia Debate: The Politics of the Discourse

In the public debates about the use of Sharia to arbitrate family law disputes in Ontario, Muslim groups supporting the use of Sharia often relied on notions of the tradition that were reductive, and in effect, mimicked the conceptions used and proffered by colonial powers in India, North Africa, and the Ottoman regions. Arguably, they relied on a concept of Islamic law that is not new, but rather is the product of a political history of reductivism, essentialism, and colonial aggression. For instance, in promoting the use of Sharia in family law arbitrations, the website for Syed Mumtaz Ali's organization, the Islamic Institute for Civil Justice (IICJ), states that one can either opt to arbitrate under Islamic law or follow Ontario civil law. But if a Muslim chooses to follow Ontario law, 'you cannot claim that you believe in Islam as a religion and a complete code of life actualized by a Prophet who you believe to be a mercy to all.'[43] In its submission to Marion Boyd, who consulted various parties prior to drafting her report, the Council on American-Islamic Relations Canada (CAIR-CAN) defined Sharia as 'a religious code for living covering all aspects of a Muslim's life from prayers, to financial dealings, to family relations, to caring for the poor' (CAIR-CAN 2004, 3). In other words, those proposing and supporting the use of Sharia relied on a conception of the tradition in which it is deterministically structured as a comprehensive code.

Many who opposed the use of Sharia arbitration seemed keenly aware of its historical diversity. However, they asserted that Islamic law is so radically indeterminate that it is vulnerable to political control and manipulation. They argued that Islamic law is a tool used by Islamists and autocratic governments to establish political control and legitimacy, and poses a danger to cherished liberal values. For instance, Alia Hogben, president of the Canadian Council of Muslim Women (CCMW), wrote that those Muslims who promote the use of Sharia arbitration were using the issue to argue 'that we need identity markers to remain Muslim' (Hogben 2004, A19) in a multicultural Canadian context. In other words, Islamic law becomes the means by which a minority group in a pluralistic country can maintain their identity, religious and otherwise. Homa Arjomand, originally from Iran and a vocal opponent of Sharia arbitration, argued that the proposal for Sharia arbitration has nothing to do with Islam. Rather, 'it has something to do with political Islam' (Jeffs 2005).

Whether one was an opponent or proponent of Islamic law, however, there was little effort by either party to think of Islamic law historically, methodologically, or as a rule-of-law system. The views were based on relatively synchronic, colonial and post-colonial paradigms of Islamic law without serious reference to Sharia as a rule-of-law system sensitive to doctrine, institution, and context. Like the colonists and administrators of the British Empire, Muslims debating about Sharia in Ontario did not seem interested in the history, jurisprudence, or diachronic development of Islamic law. They simply saw it as an all-or-nothing system of decontextualized rules, which for some were amenable to Charter values, but for others directly contravened human rights norms. And yet, among the commentators on Sharia, there was little detailed legal discussion about the kind of jurisprudence that could lead to a mutual accommodation of Sharia and Charter values.

The debate on Sharia in Ontario never actually addressed Sharia as a rule-of-law system or recognized the potential for legal change in a way that is consistent with Sharia values. Muslim proponents and opponents of Sharia were often those who left countries like Pakistan and Iran, where the concept of Sharia is embedded in the political discourses of post-colonial nation state identity. Some simply held that Sharia law is so diverse and inconsistent that to make reference to it at all would lead to an unworkable system of law and justice (see Kamlani and Keung 2004). There was little effort by opponents to offer alternative paradigms of jurisprudence, to understand the strengths and weaknesses of family law in Ontario, or to balance multiculturalism with liberal values of equality.[44] Likewise, proponents of Sharia arbitration provided no systematic analysis or jurisprudential treatment of how medieval Islamic legal doctrine, preserved over centuries, could be reconsidered, restructured, and made to accommodate competing Canadian legal and cultural values.

Some may deny that Sharia can accommodate liberal values, but a reference to Tunisia's approach to Islamic law provides evidence to the contrary. Attempting a balance between liberal and Islamic values, Tunisia adopted provisions in its family law code that conflict with historical Sharia, but which the country nonetheless justifies on Islamic grounds. Most notable is Tunisia's ban on polygamy. Islamic law allows a man to marry four women concurrently. However, Tunisia banned polygamy on Islamic grounds by relying on a Qur'anic verse that provides: 'You will never be able to be just among women even if you desired to do so' (Qur'an 4:129). The verse is read as providing a moral trajectory away from polygamy towards monogamy as an ethical value underlying Islamic marriage. Muslim reformers such as the late Fazlur Rahman (1989) also adopted this reading of the Qur'an to counter the licence for polygamy within an Islamic framework. Furthermore, Tunisia requires a divorcing couple to pursue their divorce by petitioning the courts (Women Living under Muslim Laws 2003, 245). By requiring divorcing couples to utilize the judicial machinery of the state, Tunisia has effectively undermined the husband's substantive right to unilaterally divorce his wife under Islamic law.

Conclusion: A Proposal for Accommodation

The characterization of Sharia by all parties in the Ontario debate was not entirely new. Rather, it paralleled the rhetoric on Sharia that has existed in the Muslim world since the era of European colonization and Muslim state formation, and is now embraced both by Muslim fundamentalists as a critique against modernity, and by secular Muslims who consider Sharia to be an obstacle to liberal equality. Regardless of which position one took in the debate, the concept of Sharia was of a rigid code of abstract rules.[45] This particular view dominated the discourse in Ontario, and arguably influenced the government's decision to apply one law for all Ontarians to ensure individual liberties and protections.

Yet, even though religious arbitration may have no legal force in Ontario, mediation remains a viable method for those wishing to use religiously based dispute resolution mechanisms.[46] The option to mediate marital disputes, based on the rights of the parties to contract freely, suggests that nothing has fundamentally changed for Muslim women whose vulnerability to bad-faith husbands and patriarchal imams was the central concern of opponents to Sharia arbitration. Muslim women under pressure to conform to their religious community's standards remain vulnerable to being pressured to have their marital disputes mediated in accord with what is presented to them as Islamic law. If opponents of Sharia arbitration aimed to eliminate a Muslim woman's vulnerability, they failed in their campaign.

Few who were vocal in the debate seemed to understand fully the nature of family law adjudication in Ontario or the extent to which the relevant family law codes allow parties to resolve matters privately. Additionally, opponents of Sharia arbitration were sceptical of Boyd's suggestions to amend the arbitration act to ensure greater responsibility, transparency, and accountability of arbitrators and the arbitral process. Yet, when Ontario Attorney General Michael Bryant announced the amendment to the arbitration act, many of its provisions reflected Boyd's reform proposals concerning the training of arbitrators, and the transparency and accountability of their decisions (Attorney General 2005, 2; copy available from author). In retrospect, it seems that the debate in Ontario did not result in a ban on private resolution of family disputes. People can still arbitrate and mediate divorces under the proposed amendments within the context of provincial and federal family law. Rather, the rejection of religious family dispute arbitration in Ontario was based on a vocal and vociferous debate about Sharia specifically, and its ability to change and to accommodate the values and aspirations of Canadian citizens. But before members of a liberal democratic polity such as Canada can truly understand what the values of liberty, equality, and multiculturalism can and cannot accommodate, they must also make an effort to understand the Other that seeks accommodation.

Admittedly, Sharia has been codified in a form that limits the extent of substantive change and adaptation. Likewise, there are few critical centres and institutions to study and analyse Sharia; those that do exist often have been coopted by state governments to promote their own legitimacy before a rising tide of Islamic movements.[47] But to see the tradition exclusively as reified is to reemphasize certain conceptions of Sharia that were products of varied political forces. The fact that few considered Sharia in terms of a rule-of-law system is largely a function of the political history discussed above and its effect on transforming Sharia into a building block of identity construction.

This analysis is meant to set the stage for an institutional model that links government and civil society in a way that balances respect for religious commitments and liberal democratic values. The model I present borrows from the doctrinal pluralism and legal institutions that at one time allowed Sharia to be a dynamic and diverse rule-of-law system. I suggest that in liberal democratic states where Muslims wish to observe Sharia values in the area of family relations, the government can regulate non-profit Muslim family service organizations that offer arbitration services for a fee. By utilizing existing legislation and the power of judicial review, the government can create venues for Muslims to create their own civil society institutions through which they can critically evaluate the historical Sharia doctrine, determine how it fits within the state's legal system, and arbitrate family disputes in light of their de novo analysis of Sharia.

Because arbitration decrees are legally enforceable in ways that mediated settlements are not, the state has a legitimate interest in regulating arbitrations that justifies its use of legislative power to regulate family dispute arbitration services, whether religious or not. Using existing legislation governing non-profit and charitable organizations, the state can provide incentives to facilitate the development of such civil society organizations, such as granting tax exemption to the organization for providing its services, and tax credits or deductions for donations from members of the public. Organizations seeking to arbitrate family disputes may be required to organize as a tax-exempt organization in order to emphasize their commitment to community service.[48]

To ensure that the organization both reflects and serves community interests, the government can require an annual audit to ensure that the family service organization receives its financial support from an actual community of users, whose diversity and scope justifies the organization's existence. To avoid the possibility that a single party could use its financial power to monopolize or dominate the discourse, other legislative requirements might include a cap on any single private donation, or gradually decreasing tax relief as the donation amount increases. Furthermore, the government can require arbitrators to receive training and certification as arbitrators to ensure that the arbitral process is transparent and accountable. Finally, government legislation must preserve the parties' right to appeal the arbitral decree in a court of first instance. The appeal process would operate as the field of dialogue where state values and the values of a religious community, for instance, are balanced. The judicial standard of review certainly will differ depending on the national, cultural, and constitutional context. There is no set formula that could be applied uniformly across different nation-states, constitutional orders, and cultural context. However, it should be noted that the real test of the dialogue will lie in how thickly or thinly the judiciary defines the standard of review. The thicker the standard of review, the more the state will meddle with religious communities and perhaps be seen as imposing its values on religious communities. The thinner the standard, the more religious communities will enjoy autonomy within the state, but possibly to the detriment of the state's liberal values.

There may be some Muslims who believe that to have their vision of Islamic law subjected to the state's standards of judicial review will unduly interfere with their religious freedom. These Muslims are not compelled to form or seek the services of a state-regulated family service organization. If they wish to resolve family disputes on their own terms, they can use private mediation. But they will not enjoy the benefit the state confers through arbitral decrees. The state bestows a benefit by allowing arbitration because of the presumed efficiency that arbitration decrees offer to the parties. Mediated settlements arguably are less efficient than arbitrated ones because the former are not automatically legally enforceable, but instead require the parties to petition the court for review and enforcement. The efficiency of arbitration theoretically would provide an incentive for Muslims to create family service organizations and thereby enter into dialogue with the state. Those who opt out of the arbitration regime would not enjoy the benefit, but also would not engage in the dialogue. They might reconsider their position if another family service organization develops an approach to Islamic family law that appeals to their values, is economically efficient, and does not violate the prevailing standards of judicial review.

This proposal arguably would allow multiple voices to express competing visions of Islamic commitments in liberal polities. Imagine a political spectrum of Muslim family service organizations. Those on the left might critically engage the Islamic legal tradition, concluding, for instance that Sharia can accommodate same-sex marriage and divorce and offer those services to gay and lesbian Muslims. Those on the right might instead follow a more traditional or even patriarchal Sharia law regime. Other Muslim family service organizations might advocate positions between these poles. Ultimately, Muslims who desire religiously based family law services would have different organizations to choose from, thereby giving them a choice between competing visions of Islamic law. By advertising their services, reaching out to the community, and disclosing their philosophical approaches to Islamic law, the family service organizations will contribute to a 'marketplace' of Islamic legal ideas.[49] Furthermore, if one of the parties to the arbitration considers the arbitral decree unfair or unjust given the liberal values of the state, he or she can appeal the decision to the courts. The Islamic legal philosophy adopted by the family service organization will then be presented in dialogue with the state and its values. As the courts develop a doctrine of review over time, the family service centres and the government will gradually develop a mutually shared understanding of how to observe religious values within a liberal state.

In the process of regulating Muslim civil society, the government would consequently provide an equal playing field for diverse voices in the Muslim community to articulate competing visions of Sharia. With a critical mass of family service groups, service providers would compete for customers by advertising their services. In doing so, they would engage in a deliberative discourse about the role of Islamic values in a liberal pluralist state, and would inform and educate the Muslim consumer about the different organizations' respective presumptions, first principles and critical analyses of Sharia as a rule-of-law system. This competition would not be geared towards determining a new orthodoxy using market principles. Rather, it would be meant to move the current Islamist debate away from authoritarian absolutist claims.

Admittedly, this model for dialogue between Muslims with each other and with the state relies on fundamental assumptions about the nature of faith and Islamic law. The first assumption is that one can be a rational actor within the context of faith commitments. In other words, faith does not preclude one from using economic efficiency to evaluate and select among alternative religious commitments. The second assumption is that no specific Islamic legal view has ontological priority over any other. A corollary to the second presumption is that no Islamic legal position enjoys absolute protection from falling into disuse. Islamic legal history is full of examples of how different legal schools and opinions met their demise for reasons ranging from their lack of substantive persuasiveness to historical factors involving the economics and politics of patronage (see Makdisi 1981; Bulliet 1972).

By creating space for deliberation via private sector assistance and government regulation, the long-term hope is that Muslim family service groups will be able to provide a spectrum of choices for Muslim consumers who desire an Islamically inspired dispute resolution service as an alternative to costly civil litigation. In the process, the civil society groups will engage in a dialogic process concerning the substance and form of Sharia in light of competing and complex notions of political, social, and cultural identity. With a regulated and operational 'marketplace' of Islamic law ideas, the ultimate victor will not be one group over another, but rather the Muslim consumer who will have a chance to make a choice.

ACKNOWLEDGMENT

This chapter is based on an earlier version published in the *Singapore Journal of Legal Studies*, December 2006, 331–55. I am grateful for their support of my work and their permission to develop the piece into the form presented here. This study benefited from comments at the following symposia: Ontario Bar Association, 'Family Law: The Charter, Religious Values and Legal Practice,' 3 Nov. 2005; York University's Centre for Feminist Research, 'Racialized

Gendered Identities,' 18 Nov. 2005; The Munk Centre (with the patronage of the Lieutenant Governor of Ontario), 'Religion and Shared Citizenship,' 10 Feb. 2005; University of Toronto, Faculty of Law, Constitutional Roundtable, 14 Feb. 2006; and National University of Singapore, Faculty of Law, 'Law and Multiculturalism,' 22 Feb. 2006. I would like to thank the participants at those events for their thoughts, comments, and criticisms. I also want to gratefully acknowledge and thank my colleagues at the University of Toronto whose generosity and support of this work was a source of inspiration and strength. In particular, I want to thank Bruce Chapman, Rebecca Cook, David Duff, Jean-Francois Gaudreault-DesBiens, Robert Gibbs, Andrew Green, Audrey Macklin, Denise Reaume, Arthur Ripstein, Kent Roach, Carol Rogerson, Ayelet Shachar, Lorne Sossin, Ernest Weinrib, and Lorraine Weinrib.

I want to acknowledge the Hon. Marion Boyd for her commitment to justice in a multicultural society, for her courage in the face of criticism and, on a personal note, for her enthusiasm for my research.

I want to extend my thanks and gratitude to the staff of Bora Laskin Law Library, in particular research librarian Sooin Kim, who was instrumental in locating hard to find sources.

I also want to thank Nafisah Chaudhary and Amy Smeltzer for their research assistance.

All of these people helped me to make this chapter, but they are in no way responsible for any of its faults. All errors remain the responsibility of the author.

NOTES

1 For a survey of literature addressing the predicament of vulnerable individuals within minority groups, see Shachar (2001).
2 For possible legislative and procedural mechanisms that Ontario could have used to regulate religious arbitration, see Boyd (2004).
3 For concerns about how allowing Sharia family law arbitration would lead to a slippery slope that would lead to the use of Islamic penal measures, see Trichur (2004).
4 See Charter of Rights and Freedoms, Art. 27: 'This Charter shall be interpreted in a manner consistent with the preservation and enhancement of the multicultural heritage of Canadians.'
5 For media accounts reporting this conception of Islamic law, see Trichur (2005), Jeffs (2005), and Syed Mumtaz Ali (2004), who as, one of the early proponents of the Sharia tribunals, held that appearing before the

Sharia tribunals allows Muslims to abide by the Qur'an and would be so
central to one's faith that to avoid them would be blasphemy; Harvey
(2005, 1).

6 For historical introductions to Islamic law, its origins and evolutions, see
Schacht (1993); Coulson (1997); Melchert (1997); Dutton (1999); Hallaq (2005).

7 For a discussion of the curricula that were characteristic of Islamic legal
education in the medieval Muslim world, see Makdisi (1981).

8 Various commentators suggest that there are anywhere from 80 to
600 verses of the Qur'an that have content that can be called legal. For
instance, Kamali (2003, 26), states that the Qur'an contains 350 legal verses.
An-Na'im (1990, 20), notes that some scholars consider 500 or 600 of the
over 6,000 verses in the Qur'an to be legally oriented. However, of those,
most deal with worship rituals, leaving about 80 verses that deal with
legal matters in a strict sense.

9 Many authors address the oral tradition that culminated in the *hadīth*
literature, and provide alternative methods of understanding their historical import. Some such as Schacht (1993) argue that the hadīth are complete
forgeries and cannot be relied on for knowing anything about what the
Prophet Muhammad said or did during his lifetime. Others such as Fazlur
Rahman (1965) suggest that the hadīth tradition reflects the collective
memory of Muslims about the Prophet, although some certainly reflect
later historical, political and theological controversies. Khaled Abou El
Fadl (2001) suggests that the hadīth literature represents an 'authorial enterprise' and the challenge is to determine the extent and degree to which
the Prophet's voice has been preserved.

10 For general treatments of the principles of legal analysis in Islamic law, see
Kamali (2003), Hallaq (1997), Weiss (1992, 1998), Masud (1989).

11 The phrase 'interpretive community' is borrowed from the work of Fish
(1980).

12 For the history of the legal *madhhab*, see Melchert (1997). For the
curriculum often taught at these legal schools, see Makdisi (1981).

13 For a bibliographical listing of medieval Arabic fiqh sources from the
various Islamic legal schools, see J. Makdisi (1986).

14 For an illustration of how jurists utilized their own discretion to construct
and create rules of law, see Emon (2004–05). The idea that the meaningfulness of one's norms is contingent on background factors too variegated
and implicit to begin quantifying is one that has been adopted by commu-
nitarian theorists as well as hermeneutic philosophers to give a sense of
limited determinacy to the use of discretion in the creation and construction of norms, legal or otherwise. Taylor (1989), for instance, relies on the

concept of 'moral frameworks' that provide an individual a sense of meaningfulness and identity in his world. Gadamer (1989), when writing about the hermeneutic interaction between reader and text speaks of the reader's historical horizon which must fuse with the text's horizon in order to generate meaningfulness. In a similar vein, Habermas (1998), writes about the implications of 'life worlds' that provide a basis by which one finds meaning and normative value in the world.

15 One of the formalities of a valid Islamic marriage is that the parties have a marriage contract, which can be analogized to a pre-marital agreement. There is a lengthy juristic tradition of allowing parties to a marriage to negotiate certain provisions and create conditions in a marriage contract. One such condition is for the husband to grant his wife the power to unilaterally divorce herself. This procedure is known as *tafwid al-talaq* (Jawad 1998; Carroll 1996). For a general discussion on marriage law and the marriage contract, see Spectorsky (1993).

16 For discussions on this distribution of rights scheme concerning the right of divorce, see Spectorsky (1993, 27–39, 50–2), Jawad (1998), and An-Na'im (2002).

17 See, e.g., Art. 15 of the Canadian Charter, providing: 'Every individual is equal before and under the law and has the right to the equal protection and equal benefit of the law without discrimination and, in particular, without discrimination based on race, national or ethnic origin, colour, religion, sex, age or mental or physical disability.'

18 For examples of how jurists created rules of pleading, litigation, and sentencing in light of presumptions of an efficacious institutional framework, see my discussion of juristic discretion and rights in Emon (2005a, 2005b, 2006).

19 For a discussion of al-Juwayni's hypothetical, see Abou El Fadl (2001, 149–50). Elsewhere El Fadl argues that in the hypothetical situation above, if the judge decides in favour of the husband, the wife should still resist as a form of conscientious objection (2002, 60n11). However, this position seems to ignore the fact that Sharia as a rule-of-law system is more than an abstract doctrine of fundamental values that governs behaviour. Rather, as suggested in this study, a Sharia as rule-of-law system implies the existence of institutions to which members of a society may grant authority either through certain social commitments or even through the very act of seeking the court to adjudicate disputes.

20 For illustrations of how legal substance and contextual analysis contributed to legal determinations in medieval Islamic law, see Powers (2002). For commentary on how even sophisticated textual approaches

were subject to grave error in the British Indian context, see Anderson (1993, 165–85, 173).

21 For instances of this attitude, see the discussion below on Anglo-Muhammadan case law.

22 The Anglo-Muhammadan courts utilized very few Islamic sources in translation. For a discussion on the use of limited translations of Islamic texts in the Anglo-Muhammadan courts, see Anderson (1989, 205–23, 213–14).

23 The Muslim Personal Law (Shariat) Application Act, 1937, reproduced in . Fyzee (1964, 460–2, 460).

24 *Baker Ali Khan* v. *Anjuman Ara* (1903) 30 IA 94, in Fyzee (2005, 4–16).

25 *Agha Ali Khan and another* (Plaintiffs) v. *Altaf Hasan Khan and another* (Defendants), ILR 14 All. 429–97 (1892). For those not familiar with legal citation, the source citation indicates that this case was decided in 1892 and is contained in the *Indian Law Reports*, Allahabad Series, vol. 14 and starts on page 429. I would especially like to thank Sooin Kim, research librarian at the Bora Laskin Law Library, Faculty of Law, University of Toronto, for locating this case in the ILR.

26 For a reference indicating that Baillie's work is a translation of the Sharáyi-ul-Islám that Mahmood J. reviews, see *Agha Ali Khan*, ILR 14 All at 447, where he quotes Baillie's translation and identifies it as being from Hilli's text. For the Arabic version of the text, see al-Muhaqqiq al-Hilli (1998).

27 The transliterated spelling of the texts is that used by Mahmood J. Where I provide bibliographical information for each source, the transliteration follows the *International Journal of Middle East Studies* style. Mahmood J. refers to another text that he calls Durus and considers to be a work of higher authority than the Jámi-ul-Shattát. *Agha Ali Khan*, ILR 14 All at 452. A bibliographical reference for this cite was not found during my research.

28 Zayn al-Din b. 'Ali al-Shahid al-Thani, Masalik al-Afham – for bibliographical and manuscript information, see Modarressi (1984, 80–1).

29 For a 43-volume edition of this text, see al-Najafi (n.d.).

30 Mahmood J. states that he used the Tehran edition of Jámi-ul-Shattát, that it is in print and widely available. Consequently he chose not to quote extensively from the text. For a copy of the text, see al-Qummi (2000–01).

31 For a 10-volume edition of this text, see al-Amili (n.d.).

32 For a history of the Mixed Courts of Egypt, see Brinton (1968).

33 For a discussion of the gradual demise of Sharia courts in Egypt, see Brown (1997).

34 The reforms emanating from this period are called collectively, the
   Tanzimat. For a history of the reforms in this period, see Liebesny (1975,
   46–117).
35 For a brief study of how subaltern communities might fit their indigenous
   custom or law within models or frameworks that put their respective traditions in at least the same form as the imposed law of the colonialist, see
   Merry (1991).
36 For an English translation of the Majalla, see Tyser et al. (2001).
37 On the process of doctrinal selectivity and its effect on the nature of Sharia,
   see Hallaq (1997, 2004).
38 For a historical account detailing the move from Islamic to secular law in
   Egypt, see Brown (1997, esp. 61–92).
39 Locating an authentic past on the bodies of women within the family has
   been used to construct modern national identities in post-colonial societies
   where the past provides an authentic basis for the national identity of new
   states immersed in a modern world. Traditional family law regimes may
   be used to bring the values of the past into the present national consciousness to provide a sense of identity in opposition to the norms perceived to
   emanate from the colonizing world. For an excellent analysis of women,
   family, and nationalism, see McClintock (1993). One exception to this colo-
   nial-inspired narrative about the narrowing of Sharia is the case of Saudi
   Arabia. Colonial powers did not seem to exert much control over Saudi
   Arabia, and consequently, the colonial narrative does not universally
   apply across the Muslim world. However, I would suggest that the narrative about the reduction of Sharia is not dependent on colonization as its
   only topos. Rather, the colonial topos is only part of the narrative, which
   fundamentally involves a relationship between power, law, and the
   formation of political/nationalist identities.
40 For a discussion of the impact the reified and static version of Islamic law
   had on Muslims under colonial occupation, see the excellent study by
   Kugle (2001).
41 There are many who have argued that the restriction on interpretation in
   Islamic law occurred much earlier and by Muslims themselves. This
   'moment' in history when jurists decided that all interpretation would end
   is termed the 'closing of the doors of ijtihad.' For those who espouse this
   view, see Schacht (1993) and Coulson (1964). However, Wael Hallaq (1984)
   has argued persuasively that the doors of ijtihad were never, in fact,
   closed, and legal interpretation continued unabated (see also Ali-Karamali
   and Dunne 1994). This fundamentally historical and jurisprudential debate

is completely ignored by self-proclaimed Canadian Muslim reformists like Irshad Manji (2004) who want to reopen the gates of ijtihad.

42 The fundamentalist conception of Sharia as unchanging and inflexible, as a rigid system of God's law, has been understood by some to be a response to the onset of modernity and the values for which it stands (see Euben 2004). For similar Western critiques of liberal atomism, see MacIntyre (1984) and Taylor (1989).

43 A copy of the webpage is on file with the author.

44 See, e.g., the following media accounts: Jeffs (2005) and Harvey (2005), referring to Alia Hogben, executive director of the Canadian Council of Muslim Women (CCMW), who wants nothing to do with Muslim courts and Sharia law.

45 In her discussion of the arbitration debate, Natasha Bakht, writing for Canadian women's groups such as the CCMW, adopts uncritically the stereotype of Islamic law as a code. Citing the view of Syed Mumtaz Ali, she writes how Sharia is meant to be a universal system that governs every aspect of a Muslim's life. And while she recognized the complexity of the tradition, she expressly refuses to investigate its history, development, and theoretical contours (Bakht 2004).

46 See Ontario's Family Law Act, s. 52.

47 For instance, in the medieval period, the mufti often occupied a position of authority and preeminence in towns, and was consulted by lay people and judges alike for his legal opinions. However, during the Ottoman period, and later with the rise of new nation states, the office of the mufti soon fell within the larger structures of government. Consequently, currently appointed state muftis are often viewed with scepticism given their connection to the government and the pressures they are presumed to face to support government policy. For a discussion on state muftis, which upholds the view that their independence is quite limited, see Skovgaard-Petersen (2004).

48 I want to thank my colleague David Duff for sharing his thoughts on the nuances of institutional design, and the capacity and limits of tax legislation to affect economic behaviour.

49 To use 'market' and 'Islam' in the same sentence might strike some as odd if not inappropriate. The idea here, though, is not to reduce religious practice and belief to some vulgar capitalist free market system. Rather, the 'market' is a metaphor used to understand how institutional development of a civil society sector can avoid current pitfalls by ensuring a regulatory design meant to foster an open Muslim society through various incentive structures

that also protect against monopolistic control. Furthermore, use of the market metaphor is an important check against the tendency to reduce religious argument and belief as based on authority and not reasoned deliberation. The use of 'market' is not, however, meant to gloss over the ongoing challenges that will exist for those seeking to choose their venues for themselves. For a study on the religious marketplace, see Ahdar (2006).

REFERENCES

Abou el Fadl, Khaled. 2001. *Speaking in God's Name: Islamic Law, Authority and Women*. Oxford: Oneworld Publications.
– 2002. *The Authoritative and Authoritarian in Islamic Discourses: A Contemporary Case Study*, 3rd ed. Alexandria: al-Saadawi Publications.
Ahdar, Rex. 2006. 'The Idea of "Religious Markets."' *International Journal of Law in Context* 2(1): 49–65.
Ali, Syed Mumtaz. 2004. 'YWCA Toronto Takes Stand on Sharia Law.' *Canada News Wire*. Ottawa. 21 Dec.
Ali-Karamali, Shaista, and Fiona Dunne. 1994. 'The Ijithad Controversy.' *Arab Law Quarterly* 9(3): 238–57.
Amili, Muhammad al-, b. Jamal al-Din Makkij. n.d. *Sharh al-Lum'a al-Dimashqiyya*. Beirut: Dar Ihya' al-Turath al-Arabi.
Anderson, Michael R. 1989. 'Islamic Law and the Colonial Encounter in British India.' In Chibli Mallat and Jane Connors, eds., *Islamic Family Law* . London: Graham and Trotman.
– 1993. 'Islamic Law and the Colonial Encounter in British India.' In David Arnold and Peter Robb, eds., *Institutions and Ideologies: A SOAS South Asia Reader*. Surrey: Curzon Press.
An-Na'im, Abdullahi A. 1990. *Toward an Islamic Reformation: Civil Liberties, Human Rights, and International Law*. Syracuse: Syracuse University Press.
–, ed. 2002. *Islamic Family Law in a Changing World: A Global Resource Book*. London: Zed Books.
Attorney General, Ministry of. 2005. 'Background Statement.' *The Family Statute Law Amendment Act, 2005*. 15 Nov. Copy in author's files.
'Ayni, Badr al-Din al-. 2000. *Al-Binaya Sharh al-Hidaya*. Ed. by Amin Salih Sha'ban. Beirut: Dar al-Kutub al-'Ilmiyya.
Bakht, Natasha. 2004. 'Family Arbitration Using Sharia Law: Examining Ontario's Arbitration Act and Its Impact on Women.' *Muslim World Journal of Human Rights* 1(1): 1–24.

Boyd, Marion. 2004. *Dispute Resolution in Family Law: Protection Choice, Promoting Inclusion.* Accessed 21 Jan. 2011. http://www.attorneygeneral.jus. gov.on.ca/english/about/pubs/boyd/.

Brinton, Jasper Y. 1968. *The Mixed Courts of Egypt,* rev. ed. New Haven: Yale University Press.

Brown, Nathan. 1997. *The Rule of Law in the Arab World: Courts in Egypt and the Gulf.* Cambridge: Cambridge University Press.

Bulliet, Richard. 1972. *Patricians of Nishapur.* Cambridge, MA: Harvard University Press.

CAIR-CAN. 2004. 'Review of Ontario's Arbitration Process and Arbitration Act: Written Submissions to Marion Boyd.' 10 Aug. Copy in author's files.

Carroll, Lucy. 1996. *Talaq-i-Tafwid: The Muslim Woman's Contractual Access to Divorce.* London: Women Living under Muslim Law.

Christelow, Allan. 1985. *Muslim Law Courts and the French Colonial State in Algeria.* Princeton: Princeton University Press.

Coulson, N.J. 1964. *A History of Islamic Law.* Edinburgh: Edinburgh University Press.

– 1997. *A History of Islamic Law.* Edinburgh: Edinburgh University Press.

Dutton, Yasin. 1999. *The Origins of Islamic Law: The Qur'an, the Muwatta,' and Madinan 'Amal.* Surrey: Curzon Press.

Emon, Anver M. 2004–05. 'Natural Law and Natural Rights in Islamic Law.' *Journal of Law and Religion* 20(2): 351–95.

– 2005a. 'The Natural Law and Natural Rights Tradition in Islamic Law.' Doctoral dissertation, University of California at Los Angeles.

– 2005b. 'Minority Rights in a Multicultural Society.' *Nexus* (Fall–Winter): 37–9.

– 2006. 'Huquq Allah and Huquq al-'Ibad: A Legal Heuristic for a Natural Rights Regime.' *Islamic Law and Society* 13(3): 325–9.

Euben, Roxanne. 2004. *Enemy in the Mirror.* Princeton: Princeton University Press.

Fish, Stanley. 1980. *Is There a Text in This Class? The Authority of Interpretive Communities.* Cambridge, MA: Harvard University Press.

Fyzee, Asaf A.A. 1964. 'The Muslim Personal Law (Shariat) Application Act, 1937.' In Asaf A.A. Fyzee, ed., *Outlines of Muhammadan Law,* 3rd ed. Oxford: Oxford University Press.

– 2005. *Cases in Muhammadan Law: India, Pakistan and Bangladesh.* Oxford: Oxford University Press.

Gadamer, Hans-Georg. 1989. *Truth and Method.* 2nd rev. ed. Translated by Joel Weinsheimer and Donald G. Marshall. London: Continuum International.

Grady, Standish Grove. 'Advertisement to the Second Edition.' In Charles
    Hamilton, trans.,*The Hedaya*, 2nd ed. Delhi: Islamic Book Trust, 1982, iv.
Habermas, Jurgen. 1998. *Between Facts and Norms*. Translated by William Rehg.
    Cambridge, MA: MIT Press.
Hallaq, Wael. 1984. 'Was the Gate of Ijtihad Closed?' *International Journal of
    Middle East Studies* 16(1): 3–41.
– 1997. *A History of Islamic Legal Theories*. Cambridge: Cambridge University
    Press.
– 2004. 'Can the Shari'a Be Restored?' In Yvonne Yazbeck Haddad and
    Barbara Freyer Stowasser, eds., *Islamic Law and the Challenge of Modernity*,
    21–53 . New York: Altamira Press.
– 2005. *The Origins and Evolution of Islamic Law*. Cambridge: Cambridge
    University Press.
Hamilton, Charles, trans. 1982. *The Hedaya*. Delhi: Islamic Book Trust.
Harvey, Bob. 2005. 'Sharia Law Debate Divides Ontario's Muslims.' CanWest
    News. Ontario. 17 Jan.
Hogben, Alia. 2004. 'Should Ontario Allow Sharia Law? NO: The Laws of the
    Land Must Protect All of Us, Irrespective of Gender or Religion.' *Toronto
    Star*, 1 June.
Jawad, Haifaa A. 1998. *The Rights of Women in Islam*. New York: St Martin's
    Press.
Jeffs, Allyson. 2005 'Iranian Activist Warns against the Hammer of Sharia
    Law.' *Edmonton Journal*, 30 Jan.
Juwayni, Abu al-Ma'ali al-. 1987. *Kitab al-Ijtihad min Kitab al-Talkhis*. Damascus:
    Dar al-Qalam.
Kamali, Mohammad Hashim. 2003. *The Principles of Islamic Jurisprudence*,
    3rd ed. Cambridge: Islamic Texts Society.
Kamlani, Tarannum, and Nicholas Keung. 2004. 'Muslim Group Opposes
    Sharia Law; Argues It Does Not Protect Women; Islamic Body Presents Case
    to Boyd.' *Toronto Star*, 28 Aug.
Karakii, Ali b. al-Husayn al-. 1991. *Jami' al-Maqasid fi Sharh al-Qawa'id*. 13 vols.
    Beirut: Mu'assasat Al al-Bayt li Ihya' al-Turath.
Kugle, Scott Alan. 2001. 'Framed, Blamed and Renamed: The Recasting of
    Islamic Jurisprudence in Colonial South Asia.' *Modern Asian Studies* 35(2):
    257–313.
Last Stone, Suzanne. 2000. 'The Intervention of American Law in Jewish
    Divorce: A Pluralist Analysis.' *Israel Law Review* 34: 170–210.
Liebesny, Herbert J. 1975. *The Law of the Near and Middle East: Readings, Cases
    and Materials*. Albany: State University of New York Press.

MacIntyre, Alisdair. 1984. *After Virtue*. 2nd ed. Notre Dame: University of Notre Dame Press.

Mackinnon, Mark. 2005. 'For Muslims, Investing by the Book Increasing, and Increasingly Profitable.' *Globe and Mail*, 18 Nov.

Makdisi, George. 1981. *The Rise of Colleges: Institutions of Learning in Islam and the West*. Edinburgh: Edinburgh University Press.

Makdisi, John. 1986. 'Islamic Law Bibliography.' *Law Library Journal* 78(1): 103–89.

Manji, Irshad. 2004. *The Trouble with Islam Today: A Muslim's Call for Reform in Her Faith*. New York: St Martin's Press.

Marghinani al-. n.d. *Al-Hidaya: Sharh Bidayat al-Mubtadi'*. Ed. by Muhammad Darwish. Beirut: Dar al-Arqam.

Masud, Muhammad Khalid. 1989. *Islamic Legal Philosophy: A Study of Abu Ishaq al-Shatibi's Life and Thought*. Delhi: International Islamic Publishers.

Mawardi, Abu al-Hasan al-. 1994. *Al-Hawi al-Kabir*. Beirut: Dar al-Kutub al-'Ilmiyya.

McClintock, Anne. 1993. 'Family Feuds: Gender, Nationalism and the Family.' *Feminist Review* 44: 61–80.

Melchert, Christopher. 1997. *The Formation of the Sunni Schools of Law, 9th–10th Centuries, CE*. Leiden: Brill.

Merry, Sally Engle. 1991. 'Law and Colonialism.' *Law and Society Review* 25(4): 89–92.

Modarressi, Hossein. 1984. *An Introduction to Shi'i Law*. London: Ithaca Press.

Muhaqqiq al-Hilli al-. 1998. *Shara'i' al-Islam fi Masa'il al-Halal wa al-Haram*. 2 vols. Beirut: Markaz al-Rasul al-A'zam.

Najafi. Muhammad Hasan al-. n.d. *Jawahir al-Kalam fi Sharh Shara'i' al-Islam*. Beirut: Dar Ihya' al-Turath al-'Arabi.

Powers, David. 2002. *Law, Society, and Culture in the Maghrib, 1300–1500*. Cambridge: Cambridge University Press.

Qummi, Abu al-Qasim al-, b. Muhammad Hasan. 2000–01. *Jami' al-Shattat*. 3 vols. Tehran: Danishkadah Huquq va 'Ulum-i-Siyasi-I Danishgah-I Tihran.

Rachidi, Ilhem. 2003. 'After Struggle, New Equality for Moroccan Women.' *Christian Science Monitor*, 24 Oct.

Rahman, Fazlur. 1965. *Islamic Methodologies in History*. Karachi: Central Institute of Islamic Research.

– 1989. *Major Themes of the Qur'an*. Biblioteca Islamica.

Said, Edward. 1979. *Orientalism*. New York: Vintage Books.

Schacht, Joseph. 1967. *The Origins of Muhammadan Jurisprudence*. Oxford: Clarendon Press.

– 1993. *An Introduction to Islamic Law*. Oxford: Clarendon Press.

Shachar, Ayelet. 2001. *Multicultural Jurisdictions: Cultural Differences and Women's Rights.* Cambridge: Cambridge University Press.

Skovgaard-Petersen, Jakob. 2004. 'A Typology of State Muftis.' In *Islamic Law and the Challenge of Modernity*, 81–98, eds. Yvonne Yazbeck Haddad and Barbara Freyer Stowasser. California: Altamira Press.

Spectorsky, Susan. 1993. 'Introduction.' In *Chapters on Marriage and Divorce*, 1–59 . Austin: University of Texas Press.

Taylor, Charles. 1989. *Sources of the Self: The Making of the Modern Identity.* Cambridge, MA: Harvard University Press.

Trichur, Rita. 2004. 'Muslims Divided over whether Sharia Belongs in Ontario Arbitration Law.' *Canadian Press Newswire.* 22 Aug.

– 2005. 'Iranian Activist Fears Ontario Passage of Sharia Law for Family Disputes.' *Canadian Press Newswire.* 22 Jan.

Tyser, C.R., D.G. Demetriades, and I.H. Effendi, trans. 2001. *The Mejelle: Being an English Translation of Majallah El-Ahkam-I-Adliya and a Complete Code on Islamic Civil Law.* Kuala Lumpur: The Other Press.

Weiss, Bernard G. 1992. *The Search for God's Law: Islamic Jurisprudence in the Writings of Sayf al-Din al-Amidi.* Salt Lake City: University of Utah Press.

– 1998. *The Spirit of Islamic Law.* Athens: University of Georgia Press.

West, Ken. 2005. 'Shinaz and Sharia.' Letters to the Editor. *Globe and Mail*, 9 Sept.

Wilson, Lois. 2005. 'Which Sharia?' *Globe and Mail*, 2 Sept.

Women Living under Muslim Laws. 2003. *Knowing Our Rights: Women, Family Laws and Customs in the Muslim World.* London: Author.

PART FOUR

Negotiating the Politics of
Sharia-Based Arbitration

7 The 'Good' Muslim, 'Bad' Muslim Puzzle? The Assertion of Muslim Women's Islamic Identity in the Sharia Debates in Canada

NEVIN REDA

The title of this chapter 'The "Good" Muslim, "Bad" Muslim Puzzle?' refers to the Islamic Institute of Civil Justice's (IICJ) website, in which the Muslim community is classified into 'good' and 'bad' Muslims, according to their support or opposition to the IICJ plan to implement Sharia law in Ontario (Ali 2004).[1] The debate at its very conception was thereby set up as a dialectic, where two groups are at opposing ends, each arguing with the other with a distinct outcome in sight. This discourse has important implications. For one, it reflects an understanding of Islam by the IICJ (and others) that tends to be authoritarian,[2] not recognizing the legitimacy of the mosaic of voices that form the Muslim community in Canada. The identity of each group was imposed in advance, one group alone having the privilege of being in accordance with Islam, with the authority to pass moral judgment on the other. In this framework, one of the main voices to disrupt the dialectic imposed by the IIJC is the voice of the Canadian Council of Muslim Women (CCMW), which argued for one law for all Canadians. In the ensuing debates, proponents of faith-based arbitration were associated with a prevailing Islamic identity, while insufficient credence was given to the identity of CCMW as women of faith, profoundly moved by their religiosity and their understanding of Islam. It is this marginalized aspect which is the concern of this chapter.

To respond to the way in which the IICJ framed this dialectic, I explore the religious dimension of the CCMW's discourse,[3] and propose an alternative, non-dialectical framework for future debates, based on a new understanding of the term 'Islam.' The first section contextualizes the debates within the broader movement known as 'political Islam,' exploring its theoretical connections to the Canadian debates.

My critique of the IIJC's plan is a theological, Qur'an-based critique, since the implementation of Sharia would compromise some of its foundational principles. The second section presents a more comprehensive interpretation of the meaning of 'Islam,' suggesting how this understanding may change our approach to future debates. In conclusion, I sum up the legacy of the Sharia debate experience and discuss its effect on various present-day intellectual trends within the Canadian Muslim community. My own location within this debate is as a Muslim woman scholar-activist, whose voice found expression in the CCMW position. In addition to textual and theoretical analyses, I draw on my lived experiences, highlighting the connection between scholarship and activism, and showing how our lived experiences in Canada contribute to how we negotiate our identity as Canadian Muslims.

Background

The call for Sharia law is not unique to Canada, but a well-known phenomenon in the Muslim world, since it is an established item on the political agenda of groups such as the Muslim Brotherhood, founded by Hasan al-Banna (d. 1949) in Egypt,[4] and the Jamaat-e-Islami, founded by Abūal-A'lā Mawdūdī (d. 1979) in Pakistan. Adherents, particularly in Egypt, point to the Qur'anic *hudūd* punishments,[5] judging governments, which fail to implement them as heretical.[6] This argument is based on the verse (Qur'an 5:44) : 'Whoever does not "govern" in accordance with what God has sent down, these are the ungrateful ones (heretics),'[7] where the word *yahkum* is interpreted to mean 'govern' and not 'judge,' in keeping with the modern standard Arabic term for government, *hukūma*.

The intellectually vibrant cradle of this ideology also saw the birth of a lively critique, led by a foremost Egyptian justice and intellectual, Muhammad Sa'īd al-'Ashmāwī. In his ground-breaking *al-Islām al-Siyīsī* (1992), 'Ashmāwī identified the political dimension of the discourse, and was the first to widely disseminate the term *al-Islām al-Siyīsī*, or 'political Islam,' in connection with this movement.[8] He pointed out that the conditions for implementing the hudūd are absent within Egyptian society, necessitating alternative punishments or *hukm ta'zīrī* (1996, 132–3). This eminent Islamic law professor thereby used Islamic law to argue for the accordance of Egyptian state laws with Islamic law. 'Ashmāwī also showed that the Qur'anic word for government is *amr* and not the modern hukūma, thereby countering his opponent's claim that the Egyptian government is 'heretical' (1992: 45–7). Thus, even within the birth-lands of political Islam, calls for Sharia law do not go undisputed, and no single voice speaks for Islam.

While there are some transnational connections, the Canadian experience has its own intricacies. Here too, the call for Sharia has its theoretical basis in the well-established discourse of political Islam, depending on the works of key thinkers such as Sayyid Qutb (d. 1966) and Abū al-A'lā Mawdūdī, for its intellectual clout. Here too, the pervasiveness of this discourse made it particularly challenging for oppositional voices to articulate their disagreement. However, within the Canadian context, proponents of faith-based arbitration had an additional tool with which to attempt to silence opposing voices: fear of negative media images of Islam and Muslims, which vocal critique of the IIJC plan would inadvertently reinforce. In the ensuing media frenzy, sensationalism contributed heavily to the already existing polarization set up by the 'good Muslim, bad Muslim' parameters of the debate. Thus, one of the biggest challenges faced by participants in the Ontarian debate was how to navigate these various currents, while maintaining the dignity and legitimacy of all voices.

Negative media images are not the only differences that distinguish the Canadian debates from others elsewhere. The contributions of individual scholars also played a part in shaping the Ontarian debate. For instance, in the CCMW's careful articulation of its position, I was but one among many academics consulted by the CCMW board. While in the Egyptian context al-'Ashmāwī based his arguments on his knowledge and expertise in Sharia and Egyptian law, my own position on Sharia is based in my area of scholarly expertise, the Qur'an and the Islamic faith tradition, mingled with study of Arabic and biblical Hebrew language and literature. What follows underscores some of the points I raised in the Ontario debates.[9] This reasoning was then included on the CCMW website as part of a discussion forum in an attempt to build bridges with other faith-based voices and overcome the polarization.

In my understanding of Sharia in the Ontarian context, I focus on three main Qur'anic principles, which I argue the initial IIJC plan compromised: monotheism, freedom of religion, and consultation (shūra). I then address the main practical aspect at stake in the Sharia debates. When there is a conflict in the interpretation of key verses, I follow an intertextual method of interpretation, known as tafsīr al-qur'ān bi'l-qur'ān (interpreting the Qur'an by means of the Qur'an). This method is also well known in the Islamic tradition, as can be noted in the works of scholars such as Ibn Taymiyya (d. 728/1328) (1998, 93–105), al-Zarkashī (d. 794/1391) (n.d., 2: 175–6), and al-Suyūtī (d. 911/1505) (n.d., 4:174). These thinkers classify methods of interpretation into four epistemological categories, of which the most superior is considered to be interpreting by means of the Qur'an. Intertextuality in its various forms is also a rising trend among scholars in the West.[10] Thus, the method of interpretation used in the analysis that follows is accepted and well recognized in both the tradition and in contemporary studies.

Monotheism

Monotheism is generally recognized as the central principle of Islam, indispensable for attaining salvation. Verse 4:48 of the Qur'an implies that polytheism, or taking up partners with God, is the one unforgivable sin,[11] while lesser sins may or may not be forgiven.

While polytheism was not an issue in the debates, a related practice, which also compromises the distinctive Qur'anic concept of monotheism, is the focal point here. I argue that the IICJ's proposal undermines this distinctive understanding of monotheism, as portrayed in the Qur'an. Verse 3: 64 best expresses this understanding: 'Say: "O People of the Book, let us come to a common word between us and you: that we worship none but God, that we do not associate anything with him, and that we do not take each other up as rabbis (arbāb) besides God." If they turn away, then say: "Bear witness that we are Muslims."'[12]

Of interest to the discussion of this chapter is the meaning of the word arbāb, which I have translated as 'rabbis.' This translation differs from the more usual 'lord,' which is made evident by certain insights from the Arabic and Hebrew languages and the application of the Qur'an-based, intertextual method of interpretation. Arabic and Hebrew belong to the same Semitic family of languages. They share many roots and grammatical and morphological structures, as well as common words, known as cognates. One such cognate is the word rabb. The final 'i' in the English 'rabbi' is the first person singular pronominal suffix in both Arabic and Hebrew, meaning 'my rabb.'[13] The Arabic arbāb is the plural form of rabb.

In Hebrew, the word means teacher, master, chief, commander, and authority figure (Koehler and Baumgartner 1994, 1172–3), similar to the Arabic meaning of master, lord, owner, commander, authority figure, teacher, nurturer, and cherisher (Wehr 1994, 370; Ibn Manzūr 1994, 14:304–7; al-Zabīdī 1994, 2:4–5).[14] Within the Jewish and Christian milieus of the revelation, as well as in our Canadian understanding today, the term 'rabbi' has legal implications: a rabbi is a highly trained specialist in Jewish law, who is qualified to expound and apply it for the Jewish people (Bornstein-Makovetsky et al. 2007, 17:11–19; *Webster's New Collegiate Dictionary* 1980, 942). Many such experts devote their lives to the pursuit of knowledge and to the service of their communities. Some Christian speakers of other Semitic languages, such as Syriac, also use the word *rabbi* in connection with their religious leaders or teachers. Jesus is also portrayed as a rabbi, since his disciples address him as such in the Gospels.[15] The association of the term *arbāb* with this religious-legal authoritative elite is underlined intertextually in other verses in the Qur'an, such as verse 9:31: 'They took up their scribes and monks as rabbis besides God, and Christ the son of Mary, while they were commanded to worship but one God – there is no God but him – may He be exalted from what they associate with Him.'

The connection of the rabbis with religious law was also known to early Muslims, as can be noted in the commentary tradition on this verse. The tradition depicts the following anecdote. A well-known Christian, 'Udayy ibn Hātim al-Tā'ī, entered upon the prophet as he was reciting the verse and objected, pointing out that Christians and Jews did not worship their scribes and monks. The prophet responded in the following report: 'They [the rabbis] prohibited them from what is allowed (*halāl*), and allowed them what is prohibited (*harām*) and they [the people] followed them, so this is their worship of them.'[16] Thus, blindly following the religious-legal rulings of a scholarly elite is portrayed as a form of worshipping this elite, compromising the distinctive monotheism taught in the Qur'an. It thereby becomes the responsibility of every Muslim to ensure that what they are following is in accordance with the Qur'an.

It is noteworthy that while the above religious-legal interpretation is quite prevalent in both classical and modern works, in the discourses of political Islam it has been supplanted by the political interpretation. For example, reading the above two verses (vv. 2:64, 9:31) together and with the 'Udayy tradition can be noted in the works of scholars such as Muhammad Sayyid Tantāwī (1997, 2:133–4), Muhammad Rashīd Ridā (d. 1935) (1973, 3:268–9), al-Biqā'ī (d. 885/1480) (2006, 2:108–9), Abū Hayyān al-Andalusī (d. 754/1353) (2005, 3:195–6), al-Qurtubī (d. 671/1272) (2006, 5:162–3), al-Tabarsī (548/1154) (1333 AH, 1:455), and al-Zamakhsharī (d. 538/1144) (n.d., 1: 326–7). Al-Qurtubī, probably the most popular sunnī commentary of the legal genre, goes so far as to identify specific groups. His commentary mentions aspects of Hanafī legal practice and that of the Rāfidites (Shī'ites), when explaining that no human being has the authority to forbid what God has not forbidden or to permit what God has not permitted (al-Qurtubī 2006, 5:162–3).

On the other hand, Sayyid Qutb does not understand the word *arbāb* in verse 3:64 of the Qur'an to mean a religious-legal scholarly elite, but rather political systems, such as democracies and dictatorships (Qutb 1972, 1:406–7). His interpretation may seem unusual, but it has a basis in another method of interpretation, known as interpretation by transmission, *al-tafsīr bi'l-ma'thūr*. In this method, exegetes look to a limited selection of explanations attributed to first and early second–century (AH)[17] authority figures via a chain of transmission and limit themselves to choosing one or more of these interpretations. The best-known work of this genre is probably that of al-Tabarī (d. 310/923) (al-Tabarī n.d.). He also does not mention a rabbinic-like religious-legal elite or associate this verse with 9:31, but uses chiefs/heads (*ru'asā'*), leaders (*qāda*) and lords (*sāda*) to explain *arbāb* (ibid., 6: 483–9).[18] While Sayyid Qutb's commentary is quite extensive, Jamaat-e-Islami's founder Mawdūdī's is somewhat brief, and does not address the meaning of *arbāb* (Mawdūdī 1988, 1:262).[19] Another famous modern commentary is that of al-Tabātabā'ī (d. 1981), who mentions 9:31 in passing among other verses (n.d., 3:248–9). He also seems to understand the meaning of *rabb* to be an exclusive characteristic of the deity and does not explicitly associate it with a religious-legal scholarly elite (ibid., 3:246–50). All of these commentators do not interpret *arbāb* in verse 3:64 to mean 'rabbis,' thereby paving the way for the establishment of a religious authoritative elite.

Thus, there are two competing interpretations for the meaning of *arbāb*, both of which are bolstered by tradition and the classical commentaries. They are not mutually exclusive, since religious-legal authorities may also coincide with state authorities, as for example, in a theocracy or in the Sharia-based system that Sayyid Qutb advocates, since it will necessitate establishing a clergy-like religious elite to expound and implement the law. However, both have diametrically opposed implications for the call for divine law: the religious-legal interpretation hinders it, while the political interpretation supports it. This curious dilemma may explain the absence of the religious-legal interpretation in Qutb's work.[20]

The religious-legal interpretation relies on further evidence from other verses that also reinforce the notion that it is God's exclusive right to outline what is legally allowed and what is prohibited. Verse 16:116

of the Qur'an states: 'Do not say about what your tongues falsely describe: "This is allowed and this is prohibited," so as to ascribe false things to God. For those who ascribe false things to God will never prosper.'

Thus, Muslims are warned against falsely giving pronouncements of 'allowed' and 'prohibited,' since such actions are considered attributing false things to God. This warning is addressed to Muslims in general, and therefore extends to would-be rabbinic-like authority figures and those who follow and propagate their pronouncements.

In order to complete the intertextual analysis of the word *rabb*, I will briefly summarize its occurrences in the Qur'an. The word appears in the singular a total of 971 times, of which 962 refer to God.[21] In one occurrence, the reference could either be to God or to the Egyptian man who raised Joseph (v. 12:23), and in eight occurrences it refers to an alternate cultic deity or human authority: the planet (6:76), the moon (6:77), the sun (6:78), the king of Egypt (12: 41, 42 (twice)), 50), and Pharaoh (79:24). The word appears in the plural as *arbāb* four times (3:64, 80; 9:31; 12:39). In all these occurrences, the role of God as *rabb* is affirmed, while that of others is rejected.

In this section I have argued that the Arabic *arbāb* (sing. *rabb*) refers to a religious elite, who expound and apply religious law. Setting up a Muslim scholarly elite, with this kind of religious-legal authority is tantamount to condoning Muslim rabbis. Such a structure lies outside the purview of the distinctive Islamic monotheism described above, where not taking up rabbis other than God becomes a distinguishing characteristic of a Muslim. As we see it in verse 3:64, this feature is central to the very definition of what it means to be a Muslim. In my view, it is the responsibility of Muslims to know and to decide for themselves when such rulings conflict with the Qur'an and to ensure they have the freedom to refrain from following aberrant rulings.[22] Thus, with regards to the debate in Ontario, if an arbitrator were to issue a conflicting ruling for an individual, it is up to the individual to decide not to follow it, and it is up to the community to ensure individual freedom. In a faith-based arbitration framework as advocated by the IIJC, this freedom is not guaranteed. For the IICJ, 'good Muslims' may not decide for themselves if an arbitrator's ruling is in accordance with the Qur'an, choosing whether or not to implement it.

Freedom of Religion

Freedom of religion is a well-known concept in the Qur'an. Verse 2: 256 affirms: 'Let there be no compulsion in religion.' This principle is also compromised in the IICJ's proposed faith-based arbitration framework, since it uses the force of law to implement religious rulings. While there is some degree of choice at the beginning of the arbitration process, there is none in the middle or at the end. Once a person has agreed to undergo arbitration and has signed the agreement, then that person is bound to comply by force of law, which is why it is known as *binding* arbitration. He or she may not withdraw either before or after the arbitrator has issued a ruling, even if that person is not satisfied with the arbitrator's understanding of the Islamic faith. There are possible moral implications, as well. In one of the frequently asked questions on the IIJC's website, withdrawing in the middle of the process is likened to blasphemy-apostasy (Mills 1995), an accusation which can have severe repercussions in some applications of Islamic law.

In light of the binding nature of arbitration, using force of law to implement religious rulings constitutes compulsion in religion. The only way to safeguard freedom of religion in a faith-based arbitration framework is if it is non-binding. Consequently, the CCMW has not opposed the use of Sharia in a framework of non-binding arbitration or mediation, and this option remains open for those who wish to enrich their negotiations with insights from the Sharia tradition. In a non-binding arbitration or mediation process, if both parties are satisfied with the outcome, they may implement it of their own free will and have a contract drawn up. In a non-binding scenario, persons wishing to exercise their freedom of choice have the opportunity to do so at the beginning, middle, and end of the process. Women will know exactly what they are signing onto: they will not have their hopes dashed, imagining that the arbitrator will rule in their favour, giving them adequate, Qur'an-mandated provisions from their ex-husbands, and find themselves being forced to comply with minimal 'Sharia'-mandated allotments instead.

Consultation (*Shūra*)

The third Qur'anic principle to be compromised by the IICJ's proposed faith-based arbitration is the concept of *shūra* or public consultation, generally associated with good government. Verse 42:38, which is usually cited in this context, contains: 'their [Muslims'] affairs are [to be] conducted through [mutual] consultation among them.' The word for 'affairs' here is *amr*, the same word that al-'Ashmāwī has shown to be the Qur'anic word for 'government' (1992: 45–7). Since the development and implementation of the justice system fall under the purview of government, this verse delineates that this process be based on consulting the people who are subject to these laws. In my understanding of the Qur'an, it is this process of consultation which legitimizes state laws and their enforcement.

In order to see if this principle of consultation is present in a Sharia framework, it helps to take a closer look at what is generally meant by 'Sharia.'[23] The term is used very ambiguously, often confusing divine law as delineated in the Qur'an, and classical Muslim jurisprudence, better known as *fiqh*. The latter was produced by at least five different groups of men, largely in medieval times. The names of these men are known, as are the names of the schools to which they belonged: the Hanafī, Mālikī, Shāfi'ī, Hanbalī, and Ja'farī schools among others.[24] While in theory the Qur'an is the primary source of this law, in practice the consensus of a male scholarly elite tends to carry more weight (see Hourani 1996, 155–201; Hallaq 1986, 427–54). In cases where the two conflict, consensus can override the Qur'an and the Qur'an is thereby disregarded.[25]

While a process of public consultation may have taken place in medieval times, in Canada today Muslims have not had a say in it, but have merely inherited this law.[26] Therefore, the principle of *shūra* is absent in the contemporary Canadian Sharia framework. It is noteworthy, that in secular Canadian law today, the people have a say in its development in the form of parliament and a system of public involvement. Thus, according to the Canadian legal context and the centrality of consultation implicit in Islamic law, it is legitimate to apply and enforce Canadian law, while doing the same for inherited principles of Sharia law would be questionable.

From a text-based, theological perspective, there is one more advantage to using secular law to adjudicate disputes over 'divine' law: the attribution of mistakes. The Qur'an contains dire warnings against lying about God, attributing falsehood to God (3:94; 4:50; 5:41, 42, 103; 6:93, 144; 7: 37, 89; 10:17, 60, 69; 11:18; 16:62, 105, 116; 18: 5, 15; 20:61; 29:68; 39:3; 40:28; 61:7), or even sitting with persons who are mocking the Qur'an or Islam (4:140, 5:58), precepts which come into question in a Sharia framework. Canadian Muslims need to ask: What happens in cases of miscarriages of justice? Do we want these mistakes to be attributed to the will of God, or do we want them to be attributed to the will of the people? Judges, whether Muslim or otherwise, are human and are bound to make mistakes and/or offend someone's sense of justice, since no legal system is perfect. What happens to a person's relation-ship with God when that person submits to Sharia law and receives an oppressive judgment, as in the Shah Bano case (below)? Will it not cross that person's mind that God may be somehow unjust or unmerciful? What happens to that person's sense of self-worth? For those like the IICJ, who have used the aforementioned 'blasphemy-apostasy' argu-ment, what really constitutes blasphemy? Is it to reject the imposition of a man-made law masquerading as divine, or is it to mete out injustice in the name of God?

These are troubling questions, many of which have not been answered in the course of the debates in Ontario. I find injustices that occur in the name of Islam to be doubly offensive – not only because of the inherent sense of wrong, but also because of the affront to Islam and Muslims. For Canadian Muslims who sometimes feel that we are being inundat-ed by horror stories about the treatment of women in parts of the world that claim to be governed by Sharia law, I ask: Do we really want to open the door for yet another source of negative images – a homegrown source?

From the above analysis, the answers to these questions reinforce the wisdom of making a clear distinction between what is divine law and what is human law. In my view, the solution to these problem stems from the shūra verse (42:38): a rule of law should only be considered legitimate if the people on whom this law is to be applied have a say in its development. A shūra-based system, such as the secular Canadian legal system, not only conforms to the Qur'an's guideline, it also avoids confusion between the divine and the human.

The Practical Aspect

While the above aspects of my critique of the IIJC discourse tend to be theoretical, in this section I turn to significant practical issues: the ques-tion of alimony and divorce settlements. Under Canadian law, divorced women often receive half of the couple's assets, irrespective of who ini-tiates the divorce. Under most applications of Sharia law, if a woman requests the divorce, she receives nothing, while if it is initiated by the husband, she receives maintenance ranging from three months to a year. She may also receive additional sums, mainly the divorce settle-ment (*mu'akhkhar sadāq*), if it has been specified in the marriage con-tract. Thus, divorced women generally benefit more under Canadian law than under classical Muslim law.

The Shah Bano case is a good example of what is at stake for women in the application of Sharia law (CCMW 2004, 18). Divorced by her husband at the age of sixty-two and denied maintenance, this Indian mother of five was left destitute and unable to secure financial provision for herself and her children under the auspices of Sharia law in India.[27] In this framework, women are at the financial mercy of men, since they can be divorced anytime with comparatively little provision.

The Shah Bano case illustrates a disconnect between classical Muslim law and certain Qur'anic verses that enjoin divorced women's financial rights (2: 229, 231, 236, 241; 65:1-7; 33:49). While the Qur'an does not specify the amount of divorce settlements, the word used, *matā'* (2:241),[28] carries the nuance of goods, commodities, property, enjoyment, pleasure, and even luxury. In verse 4:34, men are generally designated as financial providers for women.[29] Other than the husband, the Qur'an does not specify who these men are, and they can include fathers, brothers, or other kin. While in an ancient tribal society, a father or brother may have been a more sensible choice, the Canadian Muslim community is largely composed of immigrant nuclear families and this financial responsibility generally falls to the husband. It is problematic that classical Muslim law, which was developed under different conditions, is one way for recalcitrant husbands to get out of their obligations. While in the distant past, Sharia did improve the situation of women, granting them rights to divorce, independent ownership of property, and otherwise, it is ironic that secular Canadian law today with its generally more favourable provisions for divorced women is more in keeping with the Qur'anic injunction to provide for women (verse 4:34) than Sharia law and that Sharia law is used as an excuse to do away with the Qur'anic injunction.

In my view, given this financial disparity, it is hardly surprising that men should seek recourse to Sharia notions of maintenance and divorce settlements, since the thought of handing over half their financial assets under the current Canadian divorce model can hardly be welcome. Some choose to enter into common-law relationships under the guise of *nikah*, a common-law 'religious' marriage, in order to overcome alimony and other financial liabilities. Such unions would have been recognized as legitimate marriages by the courts in medieval times, when Sharia was being formulated. However, today, the situation has changed and women who enter into nikāh-type arrangements no longer have recourse to the courts to obtain a divorce, alimony, or other rights of a wife.[30] Ironically, Sharia law defines marriage as a civil contract, and these relationships do not pass muster as civil marriages today.[31] Such unions also exist elsewhere, for example, the '*urfī* marriage in Egypt. However, while in Egypt such marriages are usually frowned on, here in Canada, they seem to have acquired a sacrament-like quality. Some women are under the impression that God blesses nikāh/'urfī–type unions, a blessing that is absent in a civil contract. It is unclear whether this new sacrament-like quality is a Christian influence, or whether it is yet another invention to deprive women of their financial rights.

To avoid Shah Bano–like outcomes in the midst of the Ontarian debate, some Sharia proponents suggested an evolved Sharia. While it is not inconceivable that Sharia law be codified and made congruent with Canadian notions of justice and equality, such endeavours remain hypothetical. We have seen no tangible proposal, feasability study, or serious commitment to undertake such a project. Rather, it was the classical Muslim law that was to be applied, albeit in its modern, static interpretations, bolstered by the authority of 'religion.' An evolved form of Sharia would not have guaranteed the same financial benefits for men, thereby perhaps defeating the purpose of those who felt they would benefit financially from the proposed arbitration tribunals

While in the end, the CCMW managed to uphold the three principles of Qur'anic monotheism, the freedom of religion, and public consultation and to avert the application of Sharia law in a binding arbitration framework, this success was tempered by the misunderstandings and polarization prevalent in the community. In my view, even though both CCMW and proponents of Sharia tribunals are faith-based groups, there was a failure to get together and discuss the issue from a faith-based perspective, and to achieve some kind of rapprochement.[32] The Ontario faith-based arbitration debate has led to the realization that the Canadian Muslim community is in dire need of improving internal channels of communication and of developing a more inclusive approach to different voices. Thus, in the aftermath of the debates, one of the most important challenges that has surfaced is how to overcome hostilities and fragmentation within the community. I suggest that developing a better understanding of what it means to be a Muslim may contribute to a friendlier environment, in which Muslims from opposite ends of the intellectual spectrum may sit down and discuss rather than having such conversations mediated through the media. It is this burgeoning understanding to which I will turn to in the next section.

What Does It Mean to Be a Muslim?

The question of 'good' and 'bad' Muslim is intimately related to the question of what the words 'Muslim' and 'Islam' mean and how these Arabic words are translated and expressed in the English language. While Islam is usually translated as 'submission,' I would like to present a new understanding here, shaped by my study of the Arabic language and my own life experiences in Canada. In the following, I suggest that the meaning of 'Islam' is better conveyed by the terms wholeness making, peacemaking, well-being making, and safety making. This understanding is based on an analysis of the word's grammatical form,[33] in conjunction with its root (*jadhr*), which together shape the meaning.

To illustrate the finer nuances of form and highlight the meaning of 'Islam,' I will translate 'submission' back into Arabic and compare the resulting word with the original. This method is well known for checking the adequacy of a translation. The closest Arabic translation for 'submission' is *istislām*, and not *islām*. Both words are gerunds or infinitives, and are derived from the same root (*s-l-m*), which in its most basic form (Form I) has the meaning of wholeness, peace, well-being, and safety.[34] The words have different forms, which are given Roman numerals in order to tell them apart – *islām* is a Form IV (*aslama yuslimu islāman*), while *istislām* is a Form X (*istaslama yastaslimu istislāman*). These forms generally modify the meaning by giving it a different nuance. Form IV of any verb or verbal noun, as in *islām*, generally lends the basic meaning a causative sense, while a Form X, as in *istislām*, gives it a quasi-passive meaning. This form implies that the subject seeks to perform the action, generally by deferring the agency to someone else, while receding into the background. Form X thereby has an initial causative spurt, and then the action peters out.

Thus, on one hand, the Form IV, *islām* – the causative of wholeness, peace, well-being, and safety – means wholeness making, peacemaking, well-being making, and safety making. On the other hand, the quasi-passive Form X, *istislām*, has the nuance of initiating wholeness, peace, well-being, and safety while deferring the agency to someone else, which is best translated by 'submission.' For example, one might submit to God, by initiating the action of making whole one's devotions to Him (not taking up other Gods), and subsequently deferring the agency to Him, after which the action peters out. The wholeness-making action thereby has an initial causative impetus, but no continuous activity. One submits to someone else, by initiating peace with that person, and deferring the agency to that person. This quasi-passive nuance of an initial peace-making action and then no action is adequately conveyed by 'submission.'

In my experience, the attention to form is not as prevalent in the study of Arabic as it is in Biblical Hebrew, so further examples may help clarify these distinctions, particularly for native speakers. I will provide two. The first is the root *n-z-l*, which in the basic Form I means 'to descend/go down,' for example, the subject going down the stairs. Form IV (*anzala*) becomes 'to bring down,' for example, the subject actively bringing a book down the stairs.[35] On the other hand, Form X (*istanzala*) has the meaning of 'to seek the descent of,' for example, the subject seeking someone else to bring down the book. The subject's agency tends to be short-lived: their sole contribution to bringing down the book is in the beginning, when they initiate the action by empowering someone else to do it.

The second example is derived from the root *n-j-d*. Form IV (*anjada*) means 'to rescue,' for example, the subject actively pulling someone else out of the water to save them from drowning. On the other hand, Form X (*istanjada*) means 'to seek the rescue' or 'to call for help,' for example, the subject seeking someone else to rescue the drowning person. Here, too, their role ends in the initiation stage and is not sustained till the end of the action; they may stand passively by while someone else jumps into the water. Thus, the biggest difference between the two forms is that of agency and continuity: in a Form IV, the subject of the action is actively causing it from the beginning to the end, while in a Form X, the subject does not retain the agency nor do they perform the action; rather they delegate it to someone else and fade into the background.

In light of the above, a Form X is not equivalent to a Form IV in meaning. A Form IV lends the action a sustained causative sense, while a Form X tends to initiate the action, while delegating the agency else-where. 'Submission' fails to convey the sustained causative nuance of the action implied in *islām*. Therefore, this word is best translated as wholeness-making, peace-making, safety-making and well-being-making.

While the above four meanings were clearly represented to me in the Qur'an, the relationship between the idea of wholeness-making and peacemaking remained unclear, and it took personal experience for me to develop an understanding of the connection. For example, the meaning of wholeness-making alone is evident in verse 39:29, which contains the similitude of a servant who is wholly devoted to one master. The word used for 'wholly' is *salam*, a basic Form I of the word. This example is contrasted with someone who serves several masters, who are at odds with one another. Here, wholeness making means being an active monotheist, as opposed to someone who serves several deities.[36] While this example clarified the meaning of wholeness making for me, I could not see a clear connection to the idea of peacemaking.

The meaning of Islam as peacemaking can be noted in verse 41:33–5, where Muslims are encouraged to repay unkindness with kindness, and to have patience, so that their enemy may become their friend. Here, although peacemaking seems obvious, wholeness making is not.

The connection between these two very different meanings came out clearest to me during an interfaith dialogue seminar,[37] which I co-led together with Susan Harrison and Shari Golberg. In these scriptural reasoning sessions, Muslims, Christians, and Jews sat down together to read scriptures from all three faith traditions. At the time, I was writing my doctoral dissertation, and exploring the ideas of the Russian philosopher and literary theorist, Mikhail Bakthin, particularly dialogism (see Holquist 1990). It is through dialogism that I made the connection between wholeness making and peacemaking. Wholeness making also means peacemaking, because one makes peace with the other, with the understanding that all of us together form the whole. One converses with the other, in order to better understand oneself, as a part of that whole. The other is thereby a dignified entity, integral to the process of self-identification, and integral to the whole. Dialogism is often contrasted with dialectic, where the other is an opponent, and the relationship can be hostile, each party attempting to prove itself right and the other wrong (ibid.).

Thus, a deeper understanding of what it means to be a Muslim can contribute towards developing a non-hostile, more inclusive, dialogic framework for engaging in conversations and future communal deliberations, as opposed to the dialectical framework established in the debates.

Paradigm Shift?

One of the questions that emerge from this experience is whether there is enough to suggest a paradigm shift from an understanding of Islam as submission to an understanding of Islam as wholeness making,

peacemaking, well-being making, and safety making.[38] Can we collectively agree that there is more to Islam than to submit to an inherited,
manmade law, which is not always accurately called Sharia, in the hope
that it is somehow the will of God? Can we agree that God is fathom-
less, and that all we can do is to try our best to follow his word and to
respect the efforts of others?

Although it is too soon to suggest that we are experiencing a paradigm
shift in interpreting Islam, there is hope for the future. One of the most
encouraging experiences in the aftermath of the debates has been the
coming together of people from various parts of the Muslim spectrum,
together with Christians, to help develop a program at Emmanuel
College at the University of Toronto that will serve the Muslim community.[39] The idea arose in the context of my interfaith friendship with
Susan Harrison, the Christian co-leader in my interfaith dialogue experience, whereupon Susan contacted the Toronto School of Theology
and I, with some help, contacted the Canadian Council of Imams.

My choice of the Canadian Council of Imams was not a coincidence,
but was based on another fairly positive experience: that of women-led
congregational prayers in Canada. The debate ensued when a young
woman, Mariam Mirza, delivered part of an Eid sermon at the United
Muslim Association (UMA) mosque in Etobicoke in 2004. This event was
followed by a full congregational Friday prayer in 2008, led by Pamela
Taylor at the UMA mosque on Canada Day. Here, there were no death-
threats, picketing, or verbal abuse, which accompanied a similar experience south of the border. I attribute this relative success in part to a
widely distributed email dialogue between a member of the Council of
Imams and myself, under the aegis of CCMW.[40] In this dialogue, I pointed out the textual basis for women-led prayers and addressed opposing
arguments one by one, while Mubin Shaykh argued against women
Imams, also based on the classical sources. While neither side was convinced of the other position, the dialogue resulted in an understanding
of sorts. It is this experience that has led me to recognize the value of
internal dialogue and to contact the Council of Imams a second time.

Comparing these fruitful community-based experiences with the faith-
based arbitration media fiasco, I wonder: Had we as a community approached our differences less judgmentally and been readier to listen to
one another at an early stage, could we have averted the subsequent misunderstandings and polarization in the community? Can we learn from
the past and avoid similar mistakes in the future? There is no easy answer
to these questions, but small successes give us hope. By engaging in these
initiatives, we have taken a decisive step towards building bridges and

towards developing a more dignified and inclusive paradigm. While the CCMW is but one voice among a plurality of voices within the Muslim community, it is our hope that similar efforts will continue.

Conclusion

As we sit poised for the future, we can sense the effect the 2003–05 Sharia debates have had on a number of intellectual trends. While the experience has spurred intellectual growth, the resulting polarization has brought to light the divide between competing directions. I suggest that one such leaning is conservative, often informed by the intellectual giants who also inform political Islam, such as Sayyid Qutb[41] and Abū al-A'lā Mawdūdī.[42] And, at the other end of the spectrum is a progressive leaning, interacting with the Canadian environment and the sources of Islam in ways which tend to give credence to both.

In the wake of the debate, Muslim women have also emerged with strong independent voices, with some influence within progressive circles and Canadian society at large. Within conservative circles, women's voices tend to be highly marginalized, since they are denied pulpits, most instructorships in religious institutions, and speaking opportunities for mixed-gender gatherings. However, conservative women have a strong voice within women-only circles.

The polarization that resulted from the Sharia debate has also given rise to another trend, mostly among women, a trend that attempts to bridge the gaps and make peace among opposing groups. In addition to the Muslim community, this trend tends to be also active among Jewish and Christian circles, building interfaith friendships and other bonds. I have broadly outlined four intellectual trends which have been affected by the Sharia debates, but it is difficult to compartmentalize persons or organizations in this manner, since they may be inspired by ideas from any or all of them. It is also difficult to judge any or all of these trends as contributing to the development of 'good' or 'bad' Muslims, in whichever way one may choose to interpret what constitutes a 'good' or a 'bad' Muslim.

NOTES

1 For an alternative use of 'good' Muslim, 'bad' Muslim, see Mamdani (2004).
2 For more on the authoritarian and its distinction from the authoritative, see Abou El-Fadl (2001).

3 CCMW is not the only Muslim organization to oppose the implementation of Sharia law in Canada. Many of the arguments below may equally hold true for other faith-based voices.

4 The al-Banna family has produced other leading intellectuals of profound influence within their respective time-frames. For a very liberal, contemporary thinker, see the work of Jamāl al-Banna (2008a, 2008b, 2008c, 2008d).

5 The *hudūd* are punishments of serious crimes derived from the Qur'an and Islamic history. In Pakistan, some of these punishments were implemented under General Zia ul-Haq (d. 1988). For more, see the work of Khan (2003, 2004, 2006).

6 The word *kāfir* in the Qur'anic context has a meaning closer to 'ungrateful.' However, in this context, 'heretical' is closer to the Arabic nuance.

7 See n6. For more, see Wild (2006, 282–3).

8 While al-'Ashmāwī's discourse is indigenous, addressing the local situation in Egypt, the epithet 'political Islam' has circulated beyond the Egyptian borders and has been used in different contexts, receiving various nuances. See, e.g., Mandaville (2007), Ayoob (2008), and Roy (1994).

9 The first three points were previously articulated at a panel discussion organized by the Canadian Voice of Women for Peace. See Raza et al. (2005).

10 For more on intertextuality, see Reda (2008, 31–5; 2010, 62–4). See also Neuwirth (2000, 2008).

11 Compare also the Ten Commandments, of which the first are also centred on monotheism. See Exodus 20:2–17 and Deuteronomy 5:6–21.

12 All translations from the Arabic are mine, unless otherwise stated. Compare this verse with the Gospel of Matthew 23:8 and the Letter of James 3:1 in the New Testament, where Christians are warned against calling anyone 'rabbi.'

13 See *Webster's New Collegiate Dictionary* (1980, 942).

14 Al-Zabīdī (1994, 2:4) explains *rabb* also as *murabbī*, derived from a related root, *r-b-w*. Compare also Ibn Manzūr (1994, 1:399–403), particularly *murabbī* (399) and *rabbā waladahu* (401). The root of the word in both Arabic and Hebrew is *r-b-b*, and seems to be connected to a Form II/Piel of the final weak root *r-b-w/h*, meaning to raise, rear, make grow, make more, make greater, cultivate, breed, etc. See also Wehr (1994, 374), Koehler (1994, 2:1176), Ibn Manzūr, (1994, 14:304–7), and al-Zabīdī (1994, 19:441–4).

15 See Mark 9:5, 10:51, 11:21, 14:45; Matthew 26:25 and 49; John 1:38 and 49; 3:2 and 26 (John the Baptist); 4:31, 6:25, 9:2, 11:8, 20:16. Compare also

Qur'an 3:80, where the taking up of prophets as rabbis is declared *kufr*, in opposition to what constitutes a Muslim. For the portrayal of Jesus as a rabbi, see in particular the work of Chilton (1984, 1989, 2000). See also Phipps (1993) and Kolbell (2007). This aspect of Jesus has caused a rapprochement between the Christian Jesus and the Jewish approach to Jesus. See, e.g., Hoffman (2007) and Maccoby (2003).

16 Translated and summarized from Ibn Kathīr (1994, 2:348–9).

17 Anno Hegirae (AH) is a reference to the Islamic calendar, which is lunar and begins with the Prophet's emigration from Mecca to Medina.

18 Another well-known work in the *ma'thūr* tradition is that of Ibn Abī Hātim al-Rāzī (d. 327/938) (2006). His explanation recalls al-Tabarī's, since he also understands *arbāb* to mean lords (*sāda*) and other meanings similar to al-Tabarī's (ibid., 2:166).

19 While Mawdūdī's commentary does not directly address the meaning of *arbāb*, he restricts the addressees in this verse to the Jews, and does not give a reason. This restriction may be a hint that he has somehow connected this meaning with the Jewish rabbis.

20 It is noteworthy that al-Tabarī's early interpretive authorities can also be viewed as a kind of rabbinic-like religious elite, unless modified to make room for new interpretations and a more egalitarian approach to Qur'an interpretation.

21 For each individual occurrence, check a concordance, such as 'Abd al-Bāqī (1996, 350–67).

22 In contemporary religious discourses, three verses are generally used to argue for the exclusive right of a religious scholarly elite to issue *fatwas* and other religious-legal rulings and pronouncements: Qur'an 4:59, 16:43, and 21:7. The last two are almost identical and direct the Muslim community to ask Jews and Christians if previous messengers had been human beings. It does not direct them to ask for religious-legal rulings from Jews and Christians or otherwise. Verse 21:7 reads: 'O you who believe! Obey God and obey the messenger and the ones who have the command (*amr*) among you.' 'The ones who have the command' *ulī al-amr* is sometimes interpreted to refer to a rabbinic-like religious elite. However, al-'Ashmāwī has shown that it refers to government authorities, since 'amr' is the Qur'anic word for government' (1992: 45–7). For more, see Reda (2010, 161n494).

23 Sharia literally means way to water. For more on Sharia, see CCMW (2004, 17).

24 For manuals of *fiqh*, see Ibn Rushd (2004), al-Jazīrī et al. (1998), Sābiq (1994).

25 For example, the first Qur'anic condition for polygamy – fear of injustice towards widows and their children – is dropped on the authority of the consensus of a male scholarly elite. See *sāqit bi'l-ijmā'* in Ibn al-'Arabī's commentary on verse 4:3 (198?, 1:310). See Reda (n.d., 5–6).

26 For the most commonly used general manuals of Sharia today, see n24.

27 For more on the Shah Bano case, see Mody (1987, 935–3), Engineer (1987), Hasan (1989, 44–50), Pathak and Rajan (1989), and Jenkins (2000)

28 It appears in an alternate grammatical form in 2:236.

29 The word *qawwāmūn* literally means 'provide for,' *mā'in* in Ibn Manzūr et al. (1994, 12:503); *mutakaffil* in al-Zabīdī (1994, 598; see also 594, 596). This meaning is further affirmed by the rest of the sentence: 'men are providers for women with what (*bimā*) God has preferred some of them over others [a reference to their inheritance portions in the previous verse] and with what they spend of their money.'

30 The situation changes if these women also have a legitimate marriage certificate. In some cases when the common-law union has lasted a certain number of years, common-law spouses may also receive provisions upon the dissolution of the union.

31 For more on the marriage contract, see Mir-Hosseini (2009, 23–63; 2010, 17–19).

32 See also Wielandt (1996, 257–82).

33 While in English, 'form' is the appropriate word to use, in Arabic the closest widely disseminated equivalent is *wazn*. The terms are not identical. 'Form' indicates a paradigm consisting of several patterns, which generally include the respective present and past tense verbs in their various conjugations, the gerund (*masdar*), the active participle (*ism al-fā'il*), and the passive participle (*ism al-mafʿūl*). The Arabic *wazn* is generally used to refer to any one of these various patterns that constitute the paradigm. The paradigm is usually conveyed by giving three of its patterns: the third person masculine singular past tense verb, the third person masculine singular present tense verb, and the gerund.

34 See also Wehr (1994, 495–6).

35 There is a second form, Form II, which is also causative, but has a difference nuance. Here it tends to be distributive, so that *nazzala*, Form II of *n-z-l*, means to bring down in a piecemeal fashion, while with *anzala*, the focus is on the book in its entirety. For more on the use of these two words in connection to the Qur'an, see al-Zabīdī (1994, 15:728–9). This nuance is usually lost on contemporary native speakers who read the Qur'an, but have not studied this particular linguistic aspect. Compare also with the

meaning of the piel stem, e.g., in Seow (1995, 173–5). For more, see Wild (1996, 137–53).

36 See also Baneth (2001, 85–92).

37 This scriptural reasoning seminar was called 'Reading Abrahamic Scriptures Together.' It was supervised by Paul Gooch, Robert Gibbs, and Anver Emon, also a contributor here, and was made possible by a grant from the University of Toronto's Student Experience Fund. It took place at the Victoria University in the University of Toronto from the fall of 2006 to the spring of 2009. It continued under the leadership of Susan Harrison in the Multi-Faith Centre at the University of Toronto.

38 The meaning of Islam as wholeness-making, peace-making, well-being-making, and safety-making was widely accepted among the women who form the Women's Islamic Initiative for Spirituality and Equality (WISE) Shura Council, a transnational network of leading Muslim women. It was used in the Jihad Against Violence Digest (2009) presented at the WISE conference in Kuala Lumpur, 18 July 2009.

39 For more, see Emmanuel College (2010). See also Halfnight (2010, 14–16). For another use of the 'good Muslim' description, see Laidlaw (2010).

40 The results of this dialogue were summarized and placed on the following websites, but have since been removed:
http://www.muslimwakeup.com/main/archives/2005/03/women_imamat.php
http://www.pmuna.org/archives/2005/04/hina_azams_crit.php#more
http://www.salaamcanada.org/femaleimam.html
An earlier version is available on:
http://www.ccmw.com/documents/NevinReda/Women_Leadership1.pdf.

41 His most famous work is probably his commentary on the Qur'an (Qutb 1972).

42 His most famous work is probably Mawdūdī (1962–73).

REFERENCES

'Abd al-Bāqī, Muhammad Fu'ād. 1996. *al-Mu'jam al-Mufahras li-alfāz al-Qur'ān al-karīm.* al-Qāhira: Dār al-Hadīth.

Abou El-Fadl, Khaled. 2001. *Speaking in God's Name: Islamic Law, Authority and Women.* Oxford: Oneworld Publications.

Ali, Syed Mumtaz. 2004. 'The Good Muslim/Bad Muslim Puzzle.' 14 June. Accessed 30 May 2010. http://muslim-canada.org/goodbad.html.

Andalusī, Abū Hayyān Muhammad ibn Yūsuf al-Ghirnātī al-. 2005. *al-Bahr al-muhīt fī al-tafsīr*. Beirut: Dār al-Fikr.

'Ashmāwī, Muhammad Sa'īdal-. 1992. *al-Islām al-siyāsī*. 3rd ed. al-Qāhira: Sīnā li'l-Nashr.

– 1996. *Usūl al-sharī'a*. 4th ed. [al-Qāhira]: Maktabat Madbūlī al-Saghīr.

Ayoob, Mohammed. 2008. *The Many Faces of Political Islam: Religion and Politics in the Muslim World*. Ann Arbor: University of Michigan Press.

Baneth, D.Z.H. 2001. 'What Did Muhammad Mean When He Called His Religion Islam? The Original Meaning of Aslama and Its Derivatives.' In Andrew Rippin, ed., *The Qur'an: Style and Contents*, 85–92. Burlington: Ashgate.

Banna, Jamāl al-. 2008a. *Hal yumkin tatbīq al-sharī'a*. al-Qāhira: Dār al-Shurūq.

– 2008b. *al-Islām wa-hurriyyat al-fikr*. al-Qāhira: Dār al-Shurūq.

– 2008c. *al-Mar'a al-muslima bayna tahrīr al-Qur'ān wa-taqyīd al-fuqahā*. al-Qāhira: Dār al-Shurūq.

– 2008d. *al-Islām dīn wa-umma wa-laysa dīn wa-dawla*. al-Qāhira: Dār al-Shurūq.

Biqā'ī, Burhān al-Dīn Abū al-Hasan Ibrāhīm ibn 'Umar al-. 2006. *Nazm al-durar fī tanāsub al-Āyāt wa'l-suwar*. Ed. by 'Abd al-Razzāq Ghālib al-Mahdī. 3rd ed. Beirut: Dār al-Kutub al 'Ilmiyya.

Bornstein-Makovetsky, Leah, Alexander Carlebach, Wolfe Kelman, Judith Baskin, and Louis Rabinowitz. 2007. 'Rabbi, Rabbinate.' In *Encyclopaedia Judaica*, 17: 11–19. Ed. by Michael Berenbaum and Fred Skolnik. 2nd ed. Detroit: Macmillan Reference.

Canadian Council of Muslim Women (CCMW). 2004. 'Position Statement on the Proposed Implementation of Sections of Muslim Law [Sharia] in Canada.' Revised 5 May. Accessed 30 May 2011. http://www.ccmw.com/activities/act_arb_muslimlaw_sharia.html.

Chilton, Bruce. 1984. *A Galilean Rabbi and His Bible: Jesus' Use of the Interpreted Scripture of His Time*. Wilmington: Michael Glazier.

– 1989. *Profiles of a Rabbi: Synoptic Opportunities in Reading about Jesus*. Atlanta: Scholars Press.

– 2000. *Rabbi Jesus: An Intimate Biography*. New York: Doubleday.

Emmanuel College. 2010. *Canadian Certificate in Muslim Studies*. Accessed 30 May 2010. http://www.emmanuel.utoronto.ca/coned/muslimstudies.htm.

Engineer, Asghar Ali, ed. 1987. *The Shahbano Controversy*. Hyderabad: Orient Longman.

Halfnight, Drew. 2010. 'A Study in Diversity: A New Muslim Studies Program at the United Church's Largest Seminary Pushes the Envelope of Theological Education.' *United Church Observer* (Sept.): 14–16. Accessed 8 Jan. 2011. http://www.ucobserver.org/faith/2010/09/muslim_studies/.

Hallaq, Wael. 1986. 'Authoritativeness of Sunni Consensus.' *International Journal of Middle East Studies* 18: 427–54.

Hasan, Zoya. 1989. 'Minority Identity, Muslim Women Bill Campaign and the Political Process.' *Economic and Political Weekly* 7: 44–50.

Hoffman, M. 2007. *From Rebel to Rabbi: Reclaiming Jesus and the Making of Modern Jewish Culture.* Stanford: Stanford University Press.

Holquist, Michael. 1990. *Dialogism: Bakhtin and His World.* London: Routledge.

Hourani, G.F. 1996. 'The Basis of Authority of Consensus in Sunnite Islam.' In I. Edge, ed., *Islamic Law and Legal Theory,* 155–202. Aldershot: Dartmouth.

Ibn al-'Arabī, Abū Bakr Muhammad ibn 'Abdillāh al-ma'rūf b-. 198?. *Ahkām al-Qur'ān.* Beirut: Dār al-Ma'rifa.

Ibn Kathīr, 'Amād al-Dīn, Abū al-Fidā' Ismā'īl. n.d. *Tafsīr al-Qur'ān al-'azīm.* [al-Qāhira]: 'Isā al-Bābī al-Halabī.

Ibn Manzūr al-Ifrīqī al-Misrī, Abū al-Fadl Jamāl, and al-Dīn Muhammad ibn Makram. 1994. *Lisān al-'arab.* 3rd ed. Beirut: Dār Sādir.

Ibn Rushd, Muhammad ibn Ahmad (Averroes). 2004. *Bidāyat al-mujtahid wa nihāyat al-muqtasid.* Ed. by Farīd 'Abd al-'Azīz al-Jindī. al-Qāhira: Dār al-Hadīth.

Ibn Taymiyya, Taqī al-Dīn Ahmad ibn 'Abd al-Halīm. 1988. *Muqaddima fī usūl al-tafsīr.* al-Qāhira: Maktabat al-Turāth al-Islāmī.

Jazīrī, 'Abd al-Ramān al-, Muhammad al-Gharwī, and Yāsir Māzih. 1998. *Kitāb al-fiqh 'ala al-madhāhib al-arba'a wa madhhab ahl al-bayt.* Beirut: Dār al-Thaqalayn.

Jenkins, Laura Dudley. 2000. 'Shah Bano: Muslim Women's Rights.' Accessed 30 May 2010. http://homepages.uc.edu/thro/shahbano/allshahbano.htm.

Jihad Against Violence Digest. 2009. Presented at the WISE Conference, 18 July, Kuala Lumpur. Accessed 30 May 2010. http://dfint.ua.es/es/documentos/congresos-cursos-y-actividades/jihad-against-violence.pdf.

Khan, Shahnaz. 2003. 'Zina and the Moral Regulation of Pakistani Women.' *Feminist Review* 75: 75–94.

– 2004. 'Locating the Feminist Voice: The Debate on Zina Laws in Pakistan.' *Feminist Studies* 30(3): 660–85.

– 2006. *Zina: Transnational Feminism and the Moral Regulation of Pakistani Women.* Vancouver: UBC Press.

Koehler, Ludwig, and Walter Baumgartner. 1994. *The Hebrew and Aramaic Lexicon of the Old Testament.* Translated by M.E.J. Richardson. Leiden: Brill.

Kolbell, E. 2007. *What Jesus Meant: The Beatitudes and a Meaningful Life.* Louisville: Westminster John Knox.

Laidlaw, Stuart. 2010. 'A Good Muslim, and a Good Canadian.' *Toronto Star,*
8 Feb. Accessed 8 Jan. 2011. http://www.thestar.com/living/religion/
article/761857--a-good-muslim-and-a-good-canadian.

Maccoby, H. 2003. *Jesus the Pharisee.* London: SMP.

Mamdani, Mahmood. 2004. *Good Muslim, Bad Muslim: America, the Cold War
and the Roots of Terror.* New York: Pantheon Books.

Mandaville, Peter. 2007. *Global Political Islam.* New York: Routledge.

Mawdūdī, Abū al-A'lā. 1962-1973. *Tafhīm al-Qur'ān.* Lāhūr: Maktabah-i
Ta'mīr-i Insānīyat : Idārah-i Tarjumān al-Qur'ān.

– 1988. *Towards Understandong the Qur'ān.* English version of Tafhīm
al-Qur'ān. Translated and edited by Zafar Ishaq Ansari. Leicester: Islamic
Foundation.

Mills, Rabia. 1995. *Interview: A Review of the Muslim Personal/Family Law
Campaign.* Islamic Institute of Civil Justice. Accessed 30 May 2010. http://
muslim-canada.org/pfl.htm#23.

Mir-Hosseini, Ziba. 2009. 'Toward Gender Equality: Muslim Family Laws and
the Shari'a.' In Zainah Anwar, ed., *Wanted: Equality and Justice in the Muslim
Family,* 23–63. Kuala Lampur: Sisters in Islam.

– 2010. 'Criminalizing Sexuality: Zina Laws as Violence against Women in
Muslim Contexts.' In Rochelle Terman, ed., *The Global Campaign to Stop
Killing and Stoning Women and Women Living under Muslim Laws,* 17–19.
Accessed 30 May 2010. http://www.stop-stoning.org/node/882.

Mody, Nawaz B. 1987. 'The Press in India: The Shah Bano Judgment and Its
Aftermath.' *Asian Survey* 27(8): 935–53.

Neuwirth, Angelika. 2008. 'Die Psalmen – im Koran neu gelesen (Ps 104 und
137).' In Dirk Hartwig, Walter Homolka, Michael J. Marx, and Angelika
Neuwirth, eds., *Im vollen Licht der Geschichte: Die Wissenschaft des Judentums
und die Anfänge der kritischen Koranforschung,* 157–90. Wurzburg: Ergon.

– 2000. 'Referentiality and Textuality in Sūrat al-Hidjr: Some Observations on
the Qur'ānic "Canonical Process" and the Emergence of a Community.' In
Issa J. Boullata, ed., *Literary Structures of Religious Meaning in the Qur'ān,*
143–72. Richmond: Curzon.

Pathak, Zakia, and Rajeswari Sundar Rajan. 1989. 'Shahbano.' *Signs: Journal of
Women in Culture and Society* 14(3): 558–82.

Phipps, W.E. 1993. *The Wisdom and Wit of Rabbi Jesus.* Louisville: Westminster/
Knox.

Qurtubī, Muhammad ibn Ahmad ibn Abī Bakr al-. 2006. *al-Jāmi' li-Ahkām
al-Qur'ān.* Ed. by 'Abdullāh ibn 'Abd al-Muhsin al-Turkī and Muhammad
Ridwān 'Irqsūsī. Beirut: Mu'assasat al-Risāla.

Qutb, Sayyid. 1972. *Fī zilāl al-Qur'ān.* 25th ed. al-Qāhira: Dār al-Shurūq.

Raza, Raheel, Nevin Reda, and Mubin Shaykh. 2005. 'The Effect of Faith-Based Arbitration on Women's Rights.' Panel presentation, Canadian Voice of Women for Peace, 20 Oct., Toronto.

Rāzī, 'Abd al-Rahmān ibn Abī Hātim Muhammad ibn Idrīs al-Tamīmī al-Hanzalī al-. 2006. *al-Tafsīr bil-ma'thūr*. Ed. by Ahmad Fathī 'Abd al-Rahmān Hijāzī. Beirut: Dār al-Kutub al-'Ilmiyya.

Reda, Nevin. n.d. 'How "Islamic" Is "Sharī'a" Law in Relation to Women?: Three cases in which the Qur'ān Was Overruled by Sunna, Ijmā' or Qiyās.' Accessed 30 May 2011. http://www.ccmw.com/documents *fiqh*/ NevinReda/MethodologyofIslamicLaw4.pdf.

– 2008. 'The Qur'anic T'ālūt and the Rise of the Ancient Israelite Monarchy: An Intertextual Reading.' *American Journal of Islamic Social Sciences* 25(3): 31–51.

– 2010. 'Textual Integrity and Coherence in the Qur'an: Repetition and Narrative Structure in Surat al-Baqara.' Doctoral dissertation presented, University of Toronto.

Ridā, Muhammad Rashīd. 1973. *Tafsīr al-manār*. al-Qāhira: al-Hay'a al-Misriyya al-'āmma li'l-Kitāb.

Roy, Olivier. 1994. *The Failure of Political Islam*. Translated by Carol Volk. Cambridge, MA: Harvard University Press.

Sābiq, Sayyid. 1994. *Fiqh al-sunna*. al-Qāhira: Dār al-Fath li'l-I'lām al-'Arabī.

Seow, C.L. 1995. *A Grammar for Biblical Hebrew*. Nashville: Abington Press.

Suyūtī, Jalāl al-Dīn 'Abd al-Rahmān al-. n.d. *al-Itqān fī 'ulūm al-Qur'ān*, Ed. Muhammad Abū al-Fadl Ibrāhīm. al-Qāhira: Dār al-Turāth.

Tabarī, Muhammad ibn Jarīr al-. n.d. *Jāmi' al-Bayān 'an ta'wīl āy al-Qur'ān*, Ed. by Mahmūd Muhammad Shākir and Ahmad Muhammad Shākir. Misr: Dār al-Ma'ārif.

Tabarsī, Al-Fadl ibn al-Hasan al-. 1333 A.H. *Majma' al-bayān fī tafsīr al-Qur'ān*. Qum: Makatbat Āyatillah al-'Uzmā al-Mar'ashī al-Najafī.

Tabātabā'ī, Muhammad Husayn al-. n.d. *al-Mīzān fī tafsīr al-Qur'ān*. Beirut: Mu'assasat al-A'lamī.

Tantāwī, Muhammad Sayyid. 1997. *al-Tafsīr al-wasīt li'l-Qur'ān al-karīm*. Madīnat al-Sādis min Uktūbar: Nahdat Misr.

Webster's New Collegiate Dictionary. 1980. Ed. by Henry Bosley Woolf. Springfield, MA: G. and C. Merriam Co.

Wehr, Hans. 1994. *The Hans Wehr Dictionary of Modern Arabic*. 4th ed. Ed. by J.M. Cowan. Ithaca: Spoken Languages Services.

Wielandt, Rotraud. 1996. 'Wurzeln der Schwierigkeiten Innerislamischen Gesprächs über Neue Hermaneutische Zugänge zum Korantext.' In Stefan Wild, ed., *The Qur'an as Text*, 257–82. Leiden: Brill.

Wild, Stefan. 1996. 'We have sent down to thee the book with the truth.' In Stefan Wild, ed., *The Qur'an as Text*, 137–53. Leiden: Brill.

– 2006. 'Political Interpretation of the Qur'an.' In Jane Dammen McAuliffe, ed., *The Cambridge Companion to the Qur'an*, 273–89. Cambridge: Cambridge University Press.

Women's Islamic Initiative for Spirituality and Equality (WISE) Shura Council. Accessed 30 May 2010. http://www.wisemuslimwomen.org/about/shuracouncil/

Zabīdī, Muhammad Murtadā al-. 1994. *Tāj al-'arūs min jawāhir al-Qāmūs*. Beirut: Dār al-Fikr.

Zamakhsharī, Jārallah Mahmūd ibn 'Umar al-. n.d. *al-Kashshāf*. Ed. by Yūsuf al-Hammādī. al-Fajjāla: Maktabat Misr.

Zarkashī, Badr al-Dīn Muhammad ibn 'Abd Allāh al-. n.d. *al-Burhān fī 'ulūm al-Qur'ān*. Ed. by Muhammad Abū al-Fadl Ibrāhīm. al-Qāhira: Dār al-Turāth.

8 'The Muslims Have Ruined Our Party': A Case Study of Ontario Media Portrayals of Supporters of Faith-Based Arbitration

KATHERINE BULLOCK

This chapter analyses the biases present in the media discourse of faith-based arbitration (FBA) through my experiences as an activist and an academic. During the 2005 debate I was working part-time for the Islamic Society of North America–Canada (ISNA–Canada) as the executive director of education, media, and community outreach. As such, I received many calls from journalists to give comments on the debate. In this chapter, I consider the often nerve-wracking and mostly disheartening experience in which the media tainted the perspectives of those who were in favour of faith-based arbitration. Relying on Paul Nesbitt-Larking's (2001) study of politics, the media, and society and Edward Said's (1979, 1981, 1993) reading of Orientalism, I show how the media celebrated 'good' Muslims for opposing FBA, and allowed those of us who supported it to be denigrated (see also Karim 2003; Mamdani 2005; Razack 2008).

As a representative of ISNA, I was positioned by a variety of Canadian media to defend FBA and to explain why it would not undermine Canadian values. To consider this experience, in the next section I examine the barriers I observed related to the news production process. The constraints of short deadlines, an emphasis on entertainment, and the necessity of speaking in sound bites made communicating the profundity of the issue impossible. Related to these structural constraints, in the section that follows I turn to more ideological considerations to think about the way the media framed and 'balanced' stories, used labels, and conceptualized 'choice.' I conclude by highlighting significant complexities that were lost in a debate where voices like popular right-wing radio host John Oakley's dominated, bemoaning that 'the Muslims have ruined our party … not all religious arbitration is equal … Jews and Christians were doing just fine till fundamentalists started clamouring for Sharia so they can stone adulterous women' (Oakley 2005).[1]

Before I turn to this analysis, let me briefly describe my participation in the FBA debate. When the issue first assumed prominence in the media in late 2003, I was not motivated to initiate a grassroots Muslim campaign in support of the legislation.[2] The noise in the media against the proposal was from my perspective standard anti-Muslim fare. I thought the Liberal government would be above it when it came to formulating policy, because other faith groups were already conducting faith-based arbitration. From my understanding of the law, Muslims were already legally entitled to refer to faith-based arbitration, and the Islamic Institute of Civil Justice (IICJ) had created unnecessary public hype by making such public pronouncements. There was no need to seek government or public 'approval.' Even the appointment of Marion Boyd in response to the growing criticism in 2004 did not push ISNA–Canada into an activist direction, based on the same estimation. The eventual decision in 2005, to ban FBA for all,[3] did not cross our minds – we could not imagine that the government would take away an accommodation that was already present in the law. My activities increased marginally after I met a lawyer, Faisal Kutty, at the annual ISNA–Canada conference in May 2005, who seemed to confirm our assumptions, yet who told me that he had heard from the attorney general's office that they were preparing the legislation to reflect Boyd's recommendations, but they needed more vocal support from the Muslim community to justify this position to their colleagues and the general public. In response to this request, I met with Marion Boyd to present ISNA–Canada's position in support of FBA, sent a letter to the premier, and publicly supported Boyd's recommendations.

There are at least two voices through which I interpret my interaction with the media during this time. The 'ISNA–Canada Katherine Bullock' could only conclude that the media were biased against traditional Muslims – an observation strengthened by the media celebration of the 'progressive Muslims' who spoke up against the proposal. The 'academic Katherine Bullock,' having studied and written about the largely negative stereotypical media representation of Muslim women's veil, understood perfectly well what was happening (Bullock 2002; Bullock and Jafri 2000). And yet, that academic knowledge was unable to prevent the 'ISNA–Canada Katherine Bullock' from being portrayed negatively in the media. I say that I had at least two voices, because as the ISNA–Canada spokesperson, I was a 'corporate personality' (speaking on behalf of the organization ISNA–Canada), and yet, I also held personal perspectives on the issue that were not necessarily articulated while I was wearing the corporate hat. The complexity of my multifaceted persona, as a *hijabi*, professor, executive director, a (mostly) traditional Muslim in modern Canada, a mother: none of this complexity was captured by the media which had slotted me into the role of 'fundamentalist in support of regressive legislation.' Journalists contacted me to provide 'balance' to their stories – an interview with the pro and an interview with the con – I could be no more than this, otherwise I would disturb their neat dichotomies: 'sensible' people con, 'fundamentalists' pro-'Sharia' (Sharify-Funk 2009).

This portrayal erased the fact that I saw myself as a progressive and feminist, rather than a conservative or traditional, on many social, political, and economic issues. At risk of failing properly to convey such complex points, if I had been able to communicate these multiple messages, I would have talked about: my admiration for Sharia in its ideal form (though not always in its practice) and its finely tuned balance of rights and duties between men and women; why I accept and appreciate some of the rulings that were considered by critics as against women's equality, and why I do not see them as unequal; my appreciation for the growth of legal pluralism in Canada, which reflects the legal pluralism of traditional Islamic law; an admiration for Canadian multiculturalism for being flexible enough to encompass Muslim legal traditions within its legal system, and thus allowing those who wanted to, to have their family situations dealt with according to their understanding of divinely inspired legal traditions; my concerns about how a few male-biased imams currently disadvantage women, and how I saw the FBA initiative as assisting in that regard; the need for creative, flexible, and woman-friendly interpretations of the law; imams in the GTA who do make an effort to safeguard women's rights and interests; how patriarchy still exists in Western culture, and that the court system is not an automatic guarantee of a non-Muslim woman's rights; the bias and discrimination possible against Muslim women in the court system; the need for domestic violence training, transparency, and community oversight that over time would help weed out male-biased imams, and how the educative process in the long run would be beneficial for the Muslim community; how religious Muslim women have agency and are no more or less inclined to suffer from negative family pressure than any other women; the range of views about women's roles within the Muslim community, from traditional to progressive; and, how since the FBA initiative was voluntary, it was important to support an initiative that would be meaningful for those men and women in our community who wanted to go that route, even if that choice sometimes reflected a more traditional understanding of women's roles than I personally might accept. In the end, the media did not convey any of my messages, whether personal, academic, or corporate. As I will describe in what follows, they used my position as a supporter of faith-based arbitration in a one-dimensional way to give their stories the illusion of 'balance.'

Structural Media Constraints

It is fairly easy, using critical discourse analysis, to show how Western media texts perpetuate negative stereotypes of Muslims. A great deal of scholarship has been done in this area for more than twenty years (see Bullock 2002; Bullock and Jafri 2000; Henry and Tator 2002; Karim 2003; Poole 2002; Said 1979, 1981, 1993; Shaheen 2007). In the remainder of this chapter, unlike Anna Korteweg's chapter in this volume, I do not undertake critical discourse analysis of those newspaper or magazine articles in which I am quoted. Rather, I demonstrate how the interplay between two factors, structure and ideology, skewed the position of those who were in favour of FBA. I begin by examining barriers embedded in the news production process. Paul Nesbitt-Larking (2001, 336, 343, passim) argues that news reporting is not an objective, impartial summary of the day's events. It is a highly structured production, in which the good intentions of professionally trained journalists are constrained by many factors, including the profit motive, entertainment value, political regulation, and the news production process. Here I highlight the impact of deadlines, entertainment value, and sound bites in my experience throughout the FBA debate.

Deadlines

As Korteweg's Table 10.2 (Chapter 10, this volume) demonstrates, I did not actually do a lot of media interviews with respect to this topic. In the media debate over FBA, nine people who were against it were quoted more than twice in a total of seventy-two articles; and eight people who were for it more than twice in forty-two articles. Of the nine against FBA, three people, Tarek Fatah, Homa Arjomand, and Alia Hogben, were quoted in twenty-two, fourteen, and fourteen articles, respectively. Of the eight people who supported FBA, Syed Mumtaz Ali was cited

sixteen times and Mohamed Elmasry seven. I was quoted in three articles (and not recorded on Korteweg's table; I also did one radio and two
television panels). This relative inactivity was not because I was unwilling to speak to journalists but rather due to time restrictions related to
childcare, which made it impossible for me to be available for afternoon
or evening interviews. I went on maternity leave at the end of August
2005 which further limited my involvement.[4] Sometimes a television
crew just shows up expecting on the spot interviews. If you are out or
busy, they do not wait. They just keep trying until they find someone
who is free. This method means that news interviews often reflect
simply who happens to be available on short notice.

Another part of 'availability' is being in a journalist's rolodex. If they
call you once for an interview and you are unavailable, they tend not to
call again. If they call you and you do an interview, it creates a spin-off,
as they will pass your number on to others, who also will call you. So,
again, who is interviewed on a topic is not necessarily related to their
expertise or their relationship to the 'news' issue. Neither is it always
reflective of the journalist producing a fine balanced account – it is who
the journalist could find to interview within the constraints of deadlines – never mind people who wanted to say something to the media
but who could not get a journalist interested in interviewing them.

This pressure to interview people within deadlines is not a good way
to ensure that multiple viewpoints on issues are captured. Ultimately,
this method produces a skewed news product not representative of the
range of perspectives in the citizenry. Not being freely available was a
structural constraint that blocked and/or impeded my messages reaching the public forum via the media. Clearly those against FBA had
greater access to the media, facilitated partly by their availability.

Entertainment

The sixty-minute panel discussion is presented as a media organization's attempt to provide 'depth,' 'balance,' and 'analysis' of topical
news issues. However, a structural feature of television greatly sculpts
and inhibits true depth or analysis: the television show must be interesting to viewers, who will otherwise switch channels or turn the set off
if it becomes boring (Nesbitt-Larking 2001, 170, 177). Thus, television is
ultimately entertainment, and the panel show is no different.

The way panel shows create and keep interest is to ensure lively conflict and disagreement between panellists. They cannot be too intellectual either, or the audience will get bored. It is a modern version of the

Roman gladiator sport. Panellists are carefully put together based on availability, and on what answers are provided to a set of questions predetermined by the host and his or her research team and responded to beforehand. In short, they have already decided which perspectives they wish to air – we've got A who will say this about Sharia, B who will say this, and C who will say this. Based on their assumption that you might fit into one of these three or four categories (a panel is usually three or four people), a screening interviewer will call you to sound out your answers to the preset questions. If they like what you say, you are on. If they don't, you are not.

In my experience on such programs, the host will try to create conflict even if the participants agree with each other to some degree, either by asking a panellist a 'challenging' question (to which they already know your answer through the screening interview), or by pitting one panellist's opinion against another's, casting panellists' perspectives in the most polarized way. A panelist cannot shape the debate, to say what the most important issues are for her (you might be asked about a topic that they think is crucial, like why you are wearing the veil, that you don't think is particularly relevant). You cannot bring your own questions to bear on the topic nor can you ask other panellists your own questions.[5]

During the FBA debate, I was called on to represent the 'I am in support' position. The fact that I was a woman, a woman in hijab, a convert, and an employee at ISNA cemented me into the pre-existent stereotype of the 'fundamentalist' Muslim. For instance, on a panel for the Michael Coren show, I was seated next to Tarek Fatah and across from journalist Sally Armstrong, both vocal opponents; next to me was a Jew representing the 'we are already doing FBA' experience. We all were typecast and expected to stay in character – analysis, nuance, context, caveats, grand discourses about Islam and the West, Islam and modernity, Islamic law, the difference between Sharia and faith-based arbitration, how to be Canadian and Muslim and traditional – none of these topics could be conveyed in this panel. We all played our parts fairly well, but unfortunately the on-screen performance did not cover some of the nuances and lines of agreement, as well as genuine disagreement that had emerged while we had socialized with each other in the guest/make-up area both before and after the show. There is nothing wrong with disagreement; in fact, the best learning and most creative synthesis often comes about through genuine discussion between people with initially opposing views. However, in a polity where citizens are debating policy-relevant issues, such discussions should be contextualized, and allow for shifting positions, caveats, compromises, and nuances. Television panel shows, in spite of how they are advertised, are not constructed to bring about such dialogue, given the structural requirements to keep viewers entertained lest they switch channels.[6] The two panels in which I participated did not provide a way to make my case to the general public.

Sound Bites

The last structural condition of news-making is the need to speak in ten- to thirty-second sound bites so that you can get your point across in a short newspaper quotation, or before you are cut off by a radio or television host, advertisements, or other guests. One of the first lessons in doing a media interview is to develop between two to five short 'talking points.' You have to learn how to move from an interviewer's question to the 'talking point' you wish to make; you have to be careful and watch your words; and you need to talk in 'quotable quotations' – that is, in short sound bites. It requires considerable skill. It is in this sound bite forum that I think my somewhat naive desire to be the 'academic,' 'knowledgeable voice,' the 'expert' we see in the media – to explain and interpret what was going on, to analyse – got in the way of my corporate role.[7] For instance, during interviews I sometimes gave mini-lectures like the ones I was giving in my university political science class about the history of West/Islam relations, colonialism, media portrayal of Islam/Orientalism, and so on. I would interpret and explain to the journalist why some Muslims acted in odd ways (to a non-Muslim Westerner), only to have my academic explanation of others' behaviours used as a quotation as if it was something I myself believed.

I was inexperienced with the media and believed that I could rise above the structure of news production. I was wrong. The journalists who came to interview me sought me out not to do stories to transcend Orientalism, but to provide the 'pro side' of the 'debate,' relying on Orientalist stereotypes of what I was supposed to represent.[8] Neglecting my talking points and not being careful with my sound bites was detrimental to my attempts to convey my perspectives on FBA policy issues.

Nesbitt-Larking points out that on an issue there may be one side or thirteen sides, but by pretending to be objective, and to simplify things, the media tend to present only two sides of an issue as if they have not filtered out other perspectives (Nesbitt-Larking 2001, 373–4, 376). This observation is relevant to the range of responses from the Muslim community – from those supportive of FBA but not within the purview of the state; to those supportive of FBA, but not necessarily because they would use FBA themselves, but in defence of the right of others to use it if they chose; to those supportive under certain conditions; to those opposed to FBA but concerned over Islamophobia; to a secular humanist opposition to any influence of faith in the public arena. This range of positions did not emerge through media reportage. The media is meant to air all sides of a debate, to be neutral and objective and to present the facts so that the public can decide for themselves. But because the industry rewards the 'scoop,' the exposure of 'dirt,' gossip, or sensational controversy, journalists often slant and twist words to find the dirty story, or to sensationalize. Many journalists seem to have no qualms about pretending to be warm and friendly while they set up their camera or tape recorder to set you at ease, and then write an article, or present a documentary with quotations from you that cast you in a bad light. The reading/viewing public is also culpable in this cycle, as they are the ones that respond positively (i.e., make it financially rewarding) to undertake this kind of news reporting.

The gravity of this situation is highlighted by the fact that companies, politicians, and non-profit organizations often hire special media spokespeople to interact with the media to minimize the media's chances to do damage. There are people who make a living out of *teaching others how to interact with the media*. Instead of reasoned debate, we are reduced to being spin-doctors, producing sound bites, and a media waiting to pounce.

Two of my experiences capture the difficulty of producing sound bites. The first pertains to an interview with a radio station in southern Ontario. It was a 'news talk' show where you get about ten seconds to make a point, and the whole interview is over in about two minutes. I literally felt as if the interviewer did not breathe while we spoke. Once again I was called on to defend the position of being a Muslim woman in support of FBA, given its oppression of women. How on earth can one make any kind of intelligent point on such a complex matter in a two minute interview? In this circumstance, one must flatten oneself to the most important 'talking point.' In this case, my point was not related to the actual policy issue itself, but to persuade the listeners my values were not a threat to Canada: again, a thirty-second talking point has to adopt a 'position' to be eye catching, and not be reflective or analytical.

In a second instance, I agreed to come out of maternity leave to do an interview with a journalist for a prominent newspaper who had been writing about the topic for more than a year. I had found her articles extremely biased against FBA and its supporters. She said she had asked supporters repeatedly to find her someone with positive experiences, and they had never been able to find one. So now she was reaching out to understand the other side and was happy to report the positive perspective. I consented because I knew that not many Muslims were being interviewed for the 'pro side' and I thought this might be a chance to provide 'balance' to the coverage. I took her at her word. We had a two hour long interview in the ISNA–Canada boardroom. Perhaps it was the layout of the room, with a big round table that reminded me of graduate seminars, but instead of sticking to my 'talking points,' I engaged in a discussion about issues to do with Islam and the West, colonialism, Orientalism, Muslims in Canada, traditional Muslims, and so on. I remember telling her the media were using me as a negative and Orientalist 'foil' to the 'progressive' Homa Arjomand, the secular-humanist leader of the International Campaign against Shari'a Court in Canada, and how this was a misrepresentation.

I realized that the interview was not going well when she called the way I was dressed a 'threat' to Canadian values, along with a discussion about why some Muslims do not eat in restaurants that serve alcohol. I was wearing a black *abaya* (a long black dress that is worn over everyday clothes), acceptable 'office attire' at ISNA, my workplace. I forgot, however, how it was viewed by outsiders as proof of a 'fundamentalist' mind-set.

As I left ISNA, I had a sinking feeling I had not done a good job – I'd discoursed instead of given 'talking points.' A colleague called to alert me to the journalist's real agenda: to try and discredit ISNA–Canada (not to 'present the positive side' of FBA) by linking it to Saudi money (a media stereotype used to imply someone is part of a supposed global 'Wahabbi funders of terrorism' network). I was advised to email her immediately with some official responses to clarify some issues she had raised that I hadn't been sure of during the interview, which I did. She was purportedly furious, but she could not proceed with her story as she had planned it based on these emails. I believe I was saved from severe misrepresentation by this intervention, and it demonstrated to me both my naiveté and how journalists can lie while pursuing an agenda through the guise of 'balance.'

If the media really were objectively and neutrally reporting the news and fairly presenting both sides of the debate, my failure to stick to talking points and sound bites would not have been an issue, nor would the fear that the media would cut and paste your words into a negative stereotype or 'catch you out' on topics not relevant to the issue at hand. It is precisely this fear, of having their words cut and pasted into a pre-existent anti-Islamic frame that deters many Muslims in Canada (indeed many people in general) from being interviewed by journalists. My failure to be a 'good' sound bite producer enabled reporters to distort my words and exposes the prejudice against those supporting FBA. Supporters of the FBA need not have had such a fear, and this is perhaps another reason that Korteweg's table shows a disproportionate number of interviews were with the con side.

Ideological Issues

In this section, again with reference to Nesbitt-Larking (2001) and Said (1979, 1981, 1993), I turn away from these structural constraints to discuss how ideological issues like framing, the artifice of balance, and labelling contributed to distorting the perspective on those who supported FBA.

Framing and Balancing

Nesbitt-Larking's (2001) study of politics, the media and society argues that comprehensive research demonstrates that the media have an influence on how people understand issues. This power is best demonstrated through the concept of 'framing' or 'priming.'[9] Nesbitt-Larking builds on Tuchman's metaphor of a window to explain what we see and what we don't see. The media provide a window and are the lenses through which the world's stories are interpreted to us: 'For example, a newspaper might frame an election as "the immigration election," even though it is about more than that. Readers might then be primed to regard immigrants as a social, economic, and criminal "problem"' (Nesbitt-Larking 2001, 357). Without independent understanding or analysis, the general public can be heavily influenced by the media's portrayal of events. Nesbitt-Larking highlights how this framing dynamic works to create and perpetuate stereotypes, particularly because journalists facing deadlines do not have time to delve into context or history over an issue: 'The job of the news media in making the news is to render a complex series of events into a news package that audiences can understand. This means that the story must be placed within a frame of meanings familiar to the audience' (170).

When it comes to Muslims in the West, the 'frame' of meanings familiar to most Western audiences is a negative stereotype with roots in medieval Christian apologetics of Muslim men as violent barbarians, uncivilized and oppressive of women (Razack 2008). Said's *Orientalism* and *Culture and Imperialism* demonstrate what, following Raymond Williams, he calls Eurocentric 'structures of attitude and reference,' or, following Platt, the 'departmental view' of Islam, Muslims and their culture (Said 1993, 52–3, 72). Basically these views entail perceiving Islam/Muslims as inferior subject races, whose barbaric civilizations are in need of the blessings of Westernization (Said 1993; Razack 2008). Contemporary studies of media representation such as Karim Karim's show little change (Karim 2003, 2, 11, passim). The 'good' Muslim versus the 'bad' Muslim (Mamdani 2005) serves to shore up the negative stereotype of traditional Muslims.

It is in this context of the negative framing of traditional Muslims that the concept of balance must be re-examined. 'Balance' is the notion that all sides of the debate are presented objectively and fairly. During the FBA debate, journalists contacted me out of this sense of balance, so that my 'pro-side' quotation could be matched with a 'con-side' quotation. Despite the fact that the editorial boards of the two national papers and the main Toronto paper were not against FBA,[10] the media coverage disproportionately represented the issue of FBA as a threat to Muslim women and to Canadian values (see Korteweg, in this volume). Moreover, other issues irrelevant to the actual policy issue of faith-based arbitration, such as polygamy or stoning, were used by the media to sensationalize and cloud the issue. In my experience, interviewing me to provide 'balance' to an individual story did not provide overall 'balance' to the public deliberation over the FBA policy issue. 'Balance' would allow traditional Muslims and their points of view across, unfiltered through Orientalist lenses. Articles which provide a 'balance' of quotations are not a strong enough counter to the Orientalist frame; as Nesbitt-Larking says in relation to a different news story, 'the framework for contextualization [is] already in place' (2001, 345). In short, the largely secular Ontario public were primed by Western culture's long history of framing Muslims in a negative way. The perspective of the supporters of FBA was distorted through this lens into the image of medieval groups trying to turn back the clock for women in Ontario.

The framing issue, combined with the problems of deadlines, entertainment value, and sound bites, made it a gargantuan task to convey certain messages through the media.

Labelling

Labels allow human beings to interpret the world around them. They simplify and categorize the complex world in which we live, even as they (re)produce stereotypes. I turn to two important labels: those involving the term 'Sharia,' and characterizations of those in support of FBA as 'fundamentalists.'

In the first place, one of the most important symptoms of being framed through an Orientalist lens was the inability of supporters of FBA to have the public debate conducted over the specific policy question, 'Should faith-based arbitration under the auspices of Canadian law be allowed?' rather than the broader question 'Should Sharia law be allowed in Ontario?' Without going into any discussion of defining Sharia,[11] in understanding the power of labels, supporters of FBA tried in vain to remove the word Sharia from the debate, advising each other in our consultations to avoid using the word Sharia and instead using FBA. This point was not picked up on by the media, which, not surprisingly, continued to use the word Sharia (see Macklin, in this volume). For the general public, the word brought up impossible connections to polygamy, stoning, and cutting off hands. At stake was not an introduction of Sharia law into Canada, but the possibility of allowing Muslims the choice of having certain family disputes arbitrated privately through state-enforceable faith-based arbitration. The impossibility of utilizing the term 'faith-based arbitration' instead of Sharia was symptomatic of how the media prevented our viewpoint from coming across and negatively framed the language of the public debate.

In the second place, related to this same issue was the problem of how to label myself. I sought to counter having the 'fundamentalist' label applied to myself and those who supported FBA. I see this label as derogatory and rooted in Christianity, and thus inapplicable to Muslims. The problem was that I couldn't come up with an alternative label that would make sense both to me and to the general public: I think of myself as a 'traditional, progressive feminist,' who adheres to the Qur'an and *sunnah*, defined either through classical and/or modern schools of law, depending on the issue at hand. This entails a certain balancing act when these disparate orientations may be in conflict. I do not follow traditional Islamic law all the time, so I am not strictly speaking as a 'traditionalist.' While I consider myself a feminist, I do not agree with all of feminism's assumptions. Finally, I nearly always disagree with the Conservative Party in Canada, so I eschew the word 'conservative.' And yet, because I do adhere to older, more traditional understandings of modesty, male/female differences (which are often in accord with historical Western understandings, and therefore rooted in Western culture as well as Muslim culture), I decided that the label 'conservative' would be the best way to portray myself and fellow Muslims who supported FBA. When I spoke to the CCMW (Canadian Council of Muslim Women) conference in April 2005 on FBA outlining my support for it,[12] and seeking to demonstrate why the CCMW was wrong in its critique of FBA, I presented myself as a 'conservative Muslim' despite my distaste for the label (see also Kutty, this volume, where he describes the same conference). A fellow panellist, also speaking in support of FBA, quipped to me before we spoke about not being a 'conservative' – which gave me a liberating clue that I did not have to put myself into another box into which I did not feel I belonged. However, given that the media rely on stock images and stereotypes to carry their stories (Nesbitt-Larking 2001, 170; Karim 2003, 29), being without a stereotypical label left me without an easy way to convey my messages through the media, especially given the pre-set stereotype of the 'Islamic fundamentalist:' violent, irrational, oppressive, anti-woman, and anti-Western (Karim 2003, 68).

The Presentation of 'Choice'

The final point I consider in this section on how the media's dominant representation of Muslims through an Orientalist lens hampered supporters of FBA to receive a fair hearing in the public debate can be explored through the concept of 'choice.' FBA was meant to be set in a legal framework of volunteerism. If the parties wished to arbitrate their dispute outside the courts guided by principles of their faith, the state would allow it, and make arbitral decisions by faith leaders legally binding. But the concept of 'choice' was mocked during the FBA debate as another stock Orientalist stereotype of the 'imperilled Muslim woman' needing a 'Western saviour' came into play (Razack 2008, 5; Bullock 2002, Ch. 1). There is no doubt that some Muslim women live in coercive family situations and may not have chosen freely to access such a system. However, many Christian, Jewish, Hindu, Sikh, secular, and atheist women live in coercive family situations. I have yet to hear that non-Muslim Canadian women no longer face verbal, emotional, or physical abuse in their homes. Coercion is a factor that would come into play in a secular court or an FBA environment. FBA arbiters could be trained to recognize such power issues (see Macklin, in this volume).

In her chapter Korteweg demonstrates that the very ideas of volunteerism and choice were considered problematic for devout Muslim women who could not be conceived of as agents capable of making independent choices. Korteweg demonstrates how this doubt has roots in secular feminist concept of agency wherein agency reflects a resistance to religion. Religious women are thus deemed to be without agency.[13] In my experience of the debate, I felt paternalism from the general public, as well as from the CCMW and other Muslims opposing FBA, as did other Muslim women who supported FBA. At ISNA's press conference on Wednesday, 14 September 2005 in response to Premier McGuinty's announcement to ban FBA, Hoda Fahmy, a Federation of Muslim Women member with a Ph.D. and a post-doctoral fellowship in Computer Science, said: 'The fact that I've been [characterized as being] unable to make a sound judgment in this matter, I find deeply offensive ... This is something that is a loss to all Canadians. A decision like this erodes the spirit of the [Canadian] Charter [of Rights and Freedoms]' (Leong 2005, A12).

In a context in which Muslim perspectives supportive of FBA were not feared or derided, in an alternative world not dominated by the 'argument culture' (Tannen 1999), a balanced media account would have presented the views of Muslims who were against FBA because they were worried about women's position in traditional family law; Muslims who were against FBA because they believed it should remain outside the purview of the state; and Muslims who supported the initiative and felt that the concerns of (at least) the first group could be alleviated. Non-Muslim voices concerned about women and Islamic family law could have been expressed, alongside legal experts and others to discuss policy – ways such concerns could be mitigated or were in fact misplaced. Real debate could have occurred on the specific policy question, and if the wishes of those who wanted to use FBA were treated sincerely, a truly creative policy synthesis could have emerged.[14]

In the current environment, however, in which Muslims are framed by a long history of negative stereotypes as barbaric, oppressive, and anti-Western civilization, in which the artifice of balance is used to perpetuate such stereotypes and negative labelling persists, such a vision seems far-fetched. I conclude that these factors thus distorted the perspectives of those who supported FBA.

Conclusion

This chapter has examined both structural and ideological biases present in media representations of the faith-based arbitration debate. I have turned to my own experience as an activist, a representative of ISNA–Canada and an academic. I have not analysed why the provincial government decided to ban all FBA, nor why my lobbying efforts on the part of ISNA–Canada failed. I have not sought to give an extended discussion as to why I supported the proposal; why I believe the critics were wrong, especially about the impact on Muslim women; and why I continue to think I did the right thing, and feel saddened by the prevalent media discussion and the McGuinty government's decision.

Sometimes I think about alternative scenarios. Perhaps if I had initiated a grassroots campaign in support early on we could have swung the public around. Or perhaps McGuinty could have been persuaded to rescind the legislation under a landslide protest movement. But then I recall the bitter debate about public funding of faith-based schools in the 2007 Ontario election, in which Progressive Conservative John Tory lost his seat because of his support for extending such funding to non-Catholic religious schools (see Jennifer Selby, in this volume), I am not sure it would have made a difference in the end. I am convinced the cards were stacked against us. The media played on pre-existent fears about Muslims; fears present in the general public as well as amongst politicians and bureaucrats whose own knowledge of Muslims does not always transcend traditional negative Orientalist stereotypes.[15] The level of Islamophobia was extremely worrying and ultimately prejudicial to the inclusion of 'traditional' Muslims into the debate. The roles of the Canadian Muslim Congress (whose then president, Tarek Fatah agreed with radio host John Oakley that morning, claiming: 'this is the same Sharia that bin Laden is trying to promote'), the Canadian Council of Muslim Women, and secular humanist Iranian immigrant Homa Arjomand[16] as Muslim opponents of FBA does not alter this exclusion – it only highlights the distinction developed after the 1979 Iranian revolution that there are 'good' Muslims and 'bad' Muslims as far as Western media is concerned (Karim 2003, 121; Mamdani 2005).

We were also placed in a weak position. Those who spoke in favour of FBA were on the defensive.[17] Supporters of FBA had to work against the dominant Orientalist tropes that were mobilized to defend why they would support such legislation. Hence 'talking' points could not be about why FBA was beneficial, satisfying, or positive. 'Talking points' had to relate to why the proposal was not undermining Canadian values. To effectively defend and demonstrate the benefits of FBA, given the interplay of structural (deadlines, entertainment value, sound bites), and ideological barriers (framing, balance, labelling, freedom of choice) required a next-to-impossible skill-set on the part of Muslims doing media interviews. Given the largely immigrant pool with foreign accents, and lack of training in dealing with the media, these were (and remain) stupendous barriers.

Much of what I have described about my interaction with the media is well known. Many different kinds of groups accuse the media of bias. In fact I have seen journalists dismiss Muslim concerns over negative media representation of Muslims with this truth, 'Oh that is what the [unions, politicians, insert name of any lobby group] say' meaning: 'you all complain about media bias, so that's just the media doing its job, and there isn't really any special bias towards Muslims.' However, based on my experience, it is clear that supporters of FBA faced media biases and barriers to having their perspectives treated with open mindedness and due consideration.

A truly multicultural Canada cannot push out more traditional Muslims, while welcoming less traditional ones. To do so is to give an inappropriate 'editorial' perspective on how citizens should live the 'good life.' Moreover, many of the traditional values shared by Ontario's multilayered Muslim communities are shared by traditional Christians, Jews, Sikhs, and Hindus. It is through a reading of anti-Muslim discrimination, best analysed by way of Edward Said's concept of Orientalism, that we can capture why Muslim traditionalism is considered a threat to Canada when other traditionalists are not. Clearly FBA brings up complex issues. In this chapter I have tried to demonstrate that in spite of a professional call for 'balance,' the media gave approval to those Muslims who opposed FBA and not to those that supported it. Those who supported FBA were not portrayed positively for 'bravely speaking out in spite of rampant Islamophobia.' We were admonished for our support. I lament that Edward Said's analysis of how the media cover Islam has changed little in the twenty years since he wrote *Covering Islam: How the Media and the Experts Determine How We See the Rest of the World* (1981).

ACKNOWLEDGMENT

Many thanks to editors Anna Korteweg and Jennifer Selby for their editorial work, which vastly improved this chapter, and to media expert George Wooten and legal expert Julie Macfarlane for their insightful comments on an earlier draft of this chapter.

NOTES

1 Oakley is supportive of a right-wing agenda that includes supporting the Conservative party, criticizing the Left, 'political correctness,' 'multiculturalism,' being 'tough' on crime, immigrants, and 'defending' Canadian values like freedom of expression and secularism.

2 In fact, I knew some Muslims, who were likely to use FBA, but who were not in favour of the proposal, because they viewed it as Islamically illegitimate to have a non-Muslim state oversee the application of Islamic law; they wanted FBA to remain a private affair (see, e.g., Reda, this volume).

3 Julie Macfarlane (personal correspondence) points out that even though McGuinty used the word 'ban,' the government could not really 'forbid particular ways of resolving disputes between consenting adults, which would infringe the Charter and be practically speaking quite impossible ... what they did was to remove FBA from court recognition.'

4 I came out of leave twice: once to organize the press conference to express our objection to the McGuinty government's decision, and a second time to do an interview with a journalist from a major daily on the topic.

5 Thanks to George Wooten (personal correspondence, 11 Aug. 2010) for 'naming' this experience for me from a media expert's point of view as '"game framing" – essentially news stories are portrayed as contests between rival points of view. Very much like gladiatorial combat. The news builds a meta-narrative about which side is "winning" or has the advantage and why, etc. This type of frame builds drama into story-lines (i.e., entertainment value) but does little to inform or educate viewers.'

6 Tannen (1999) argues that the problem is more widespread, at least in U.S. culture, and surely transferrable to Canada, where a 'debate' means that there are only two sides of an issue positioned to each other as diametrical opposites. The media push this cultural trend to its limit by casting 'debate' into two positions as polarized as possible. Tannen argues that the

'argument culture' prevents Americans from being well-informed. Thanks to Julie Macfarlane for bringing her work to my attention.

7 Nesbitt-Larking (2001, 173) alerts us to the way in which the media reliance on 'experts' is attached to the artifice of objectivity. Karim's study (2003, 23–4) makes me realize I could never have played that role anyway, as an 'expert' in the media is one who is part of the dominant discourse that sustains the status quo (secular, Western hegemony, liberal-capitalism), not a role a convert to Islam in a headscarf can play, at least not easily.

8 Alia Hogben, one of the most vocal opponents of FBA, often gave my name after they interviewed her.

9 These terms are sometimes used interchangeably (Nesbitt-Larking 2001, 356–8).

10 See Korteweg, in this volume, Table 10.3: *Globe and Mail* Editorial Board, five editorials in favour; *National Post* Editorial Board, two; *Toronto Star* Editorial Board four.

11 Sharia in practice in Muslim countries at the present time is mostly about family law. Macfarlane's study (forthcoming) highlights the closeness of Islamic family law to Canadian family law. From my perspective, I believe some particular rulings of historical Islamic law (*fiqh*) are no longer applicable to current times, but I believe in the Sharia and its goal to bring justice. Islamic law is meant to be creative in its specificities to reflect local culture which in the twenty-first century ought to manifest concerns over women's equality and dignity. It is not meant to be a cut and paste code of law from seventh-century Arabia, even though some scholars allow patriarchal biases to cloud their legal rulings. I support legal reform in certain areas.

12 Alia Hogben had invited me to speak.

13 The same response of 'false consciousness' is applied to women who choose to wear hijab and niqab; these are oppressive, but even those who choose to wear them don't realize their own oppression. See Bullock (2002, Ch. 5).

14 See, e.g., Emon's policy recommendations in his chapter in this volume and MacFarlane's forthcoming work on Islamic divorce in North America.

15 See public statements delivered against the proposal by intellectuals June Callwood and Margaret Atwood (Urquhart 2005), and some of the statements made by members of the Liberal party's Women's Caucus. Harvey Simmons, a retired York University professor, who interviewed me for his study of the role of lobby groups in the decision, believes the Women's

Caucus played the pivotal role in McGuinty's final decision (personal communication, 19 June 2008).

16 Ms Arjomand stated explicitly that she is a secular-humanist not a Muslim on a CBC radio interview and was, in fact, opposed to the influence of any religion in the public sphere – her portrayal by the media as a 'progressive Muslim' against FBA was extremely disingenuous, and it served only to perpetuate negative stereotypes of 'fundamentalists.'

17 This perspective emerged in the United Kingdom, as well. Rahmanara Chowdhury, who started to wear a face veil in her final year of university after a year of spiritual searching, commented in a recent newspaper article: 'When Jack Straw made his comments on the veil it was an incredibly difficult time for us because there was so much pressure on niqab wearers to speak out but only from a self-defence point of view, rather than talking about the veil as something positive. That automatically colours any discussion of the veil in a negative light' (see Akbar and Taylor 2010).

REFERENCES

Akbar, Arifa, and Jerome Taylor. 2010. 'The Many Faces behind the Veil: A Symbol of Female Subjugation? These Women Believe Their Islamic Head-wear Is a Liberating Way of Expressing Their Identities' *The Independent UK*. 13 Jan. Accessed 8 March 2010. http://www.independent.co.uk/news/uk/this-britain/the-many-faces-behind-the-veil-1865772.html.

Bullock, Katherine. 2002. *Rethinking Muslim Women and the Veil: Challenging Historical and Modern Stereotypes.* Herndon, VA: The International Institute of Islamic Thought.

Bullock, Katherine, and Gul J. Jafri. 2000. 'Media (Mis)Representations: Muslim Women in the Canadian Nation.' *Canadian Woman Studies* 20 (Summer): 35–40.

Henry, Frances, and Carol Tator. 2002. *Discourses of Domination: Racial Bias in the Canadian English-Language Press.* Toronto: University of Toronto Press.

Karim, Karim H. 2003. *Islamic Peril: Media and Global Violence.* Montreal: Black Rose Books.

Leong, Melissa. 2005. 'Muslim Groups Promise Liberals a Fight on Sharia: Woman Concerned about Ignorance, "Level of Hatred."' *National Post*, 15 Sept., A12.

Macfarlane, Julie. (forthcoming). *Sustaining the Islamic Imagination: Islamic Marriage and Divorce in North America.* Oxford: Oxford University Press.

Mamdani, Mahmood. 2005. *Good Muslim, Bad Muslim: America, the Cold War and the Roots of Terror.* New York: Three Leaves Press, Doubleday.

Nesbitt-Larking, Paul. 2001. *Politics, Society and the Media.* Peterborough: Broadview Press.

Oakley, John. 2005. *The John Oakley Show.* AM 640, 12 Sept.

Poole, Elisabeth. 2002. *Reporting Islam: Media Representations and British Muslims.* London: I.B. Tauris.

Razack, Sherene. 2008. *Casting Out: The Eviction of Muslims from Western Law and Politics.* Toronto: University of Toronto Press.

Said, Edward W. 1979. *Orientalism.* New York: Vintage Books.

– 1981. *Covering Islam: How the Media and the Experts Determine How We See the Rest of the World.* New York: Pantheon Books.

– 1993. *Culture and Imperialism.* New York: Alfred Knopf.

Shaheen, Jack. 2007. *Reel Bad Arabs, How Hollywood Vilifies a People.* (DVD.) Northampton, MA: Media Education Foundation.

Sharify-Funk, Meena. 2009. 'Representing Canadian Muslims: Media, Muslim Advocacy Organizations, and Gender in the Ontario Shari'ah Debate.' *Global Media Journal* 2(2): 73–89.

Tannen, Deborah. 1999. *The Argument Culture: Stopping America's War of Words.* New York: Ballantine Books.

Urquhart, Ian. 2005. 'McGuinty Faced Rebellion in His Caucus; Why Premier Chose to Act.' *Toronto Star,* 12 Sept., A01

PART FIVE

Analysing Discourses of Race, Gender, and Religion

9 Sharia in Canada? Mapping Discourses of Race, Gender, and Religious Difference

JASMIN ZINE

Within the global dialectics of Islamophobia, religious extremism, and imperialism, Muslim women find themselves precariously positioned between these competing ideological campaigns. Converging within the political backdrop of the 9/11 tragedy and the ongoing imperialist 'war on terror,' the contradictory narratives of Islamophobia and neo-Orientalism on one hand and religiously based extremism on the other share an ironic similarity in the way they construct narrow views of Muslim womanhood and agency (Zine 2004). Both ideological camps limit Muslim women's rights and autonomy through invoking an irreconcilable civilizational discourse that constructs Muslim women as being in need of rescue from either the patriarchal religious zealotry of foreign mullahs (as the neo-Orientalist camp would have it) or from the moral decay of Western society (as some Islamists denounce). In either formulation, Muslim women's agency is diminished by the narrow and limiting discourses that render them as either politically immature captives of religious patriarchal designs or at risk of becoming fallen women trapped within the clutches of Western cultural degeneracy.

This context is important in situating the recent debates on faith-based arbitration in Ontario that were largely contested on the grounds that Muslim women needed to be rescued from the vulgarities and inequities of the proposed Sharia law being introduced and entrenched in the fabric of Canadian law. The intent of this chapter is to examine how the arguments for and against faith-based arbitration predicated on principles of Islamic law were socially and discursively constituted through the debates engaged in by various stakeholders in what was dubbed the 'Sharia tribunal affair.'[1] The debates took place in Ontario during the period of 2003–2005 (although they were echoed worldwide) and involved many sectors of the local Muslim community including faith-based and secular women's groups, religious leaders, and community organizations' legal advocates, as well as non-Muslim academics, journalists, and politicians. The public at large also weighed in on talk radio and in the opinions and letters sections of national newspapers. I approach the issues raised in the public discourse as both a Muslim and a feminist and do not regard these positions as contradictory. Rather, I have a stake in these debates by virtue of my spiritual commitment to Islam and my feminist ideals, which are informed by this spirituality.

My analysis of these debates is based on an anti-racist feminist perspective that is grounded in the principles of 'critical faith-centred feminism.' As I have argued elsewhere, this framework, 'develops an understanding of how religious and spiritual identities and identifications represent sites of oppression and are connected to broader sites/systems of discrimination based on race, class, gender, ethnicity, sexuality, and colonialism, while acknowledging that religion has at times been historically misused and become complicit in the perpetuation of these oppressions' (Zine 2004, 183–4).

This framework is relevant to the discussion of Sharia-based arbitration because it keeps in focus the way that religion can be a site of oppression or a source of oppression, as well as be used as a means to struggle against various oppressive arrangements. These understandings are central to the way this debate was framed and engaged with by various interlocutors. I will employ critical discourse analysis in order to unpack the competing narratives as they took shape in the community and media. In mapping the epistemological terrain of the Sharia debates I identified and analysed four primary discourses: (1) the religious/Islamic case, (2) liberal-democratic arguments, (3) the anti-racism perspective, and (4) feminist responses. These competing standpoints provided the ideological and political contestations that informed the dialogues, debates and ultimately the outcome of the government's position on faith-based arbitration. The pervasive climate of Islamophobia generated around this proposal that tied the implications of domesticating Islamic law in Canada to violent manifestations of Islamist geopolitics and 'Islamofascism' abroad will also be examined as the discursive backdrop that shaped the contours of public dialogue, fear, and dissent.

Before addressing these contestations, it is first necessary to map an understanding of the meaning of Sharia in the context of Islamic

philosophy and jurisprudence, in order to clarify the terms of engagement used within these highly politicized public debates and to elicit a
less sensationalized reaction to the term 'Sharia' itself, as well as to
work against rigid formations that cast it as immutably divine.

Demystifying Sharia

The word 'Sharia' can be understood as 'a path leading to the water'
and refers to a journey towards spiritual knowledge and more broadly
to a developing a way of living according to that knowledge. The more
precise term for the Islamic system of jurisprudence is *fiqh*. Reducing
the broad notion of Sharia to a narrow set of laws is a strategy employed
by Islamists and neo-Orientalists alike. Both benefit from narrow conceptions of Islamic law, whether it is to codify limited and dogmatic
systems of law that shore up patriarchal privilege with a divine seal of
authority or whether it is to generate Islamophobic fears of pre-modern
barbaric rites such as stoning. Both conceptions limit the ability for
Muslim intellectuals, scholars, and jurists interested in epistemological
reform based on alternative hermeneutics and more gender-positive
readings of the Qur'an and Islamic jurisprudence, to manoeuvre outside of the reductive polemics. Tariq Ramadan, an advocate of contemporary legal reform in Islam, reminds us of how Orientalist fears
continue to frame the way notions of Sharia are purveyed in the West,
creating distrust and suspicion against Islamic scholars and intellectuals: 'In the West, the idea of Sharia calls up all the darkest images of
Islam: repression of women, physical punishment, stoning and all other such things. It has reached the extent that many Muslim intellectuals
do not dare even refer to the concept for fear of frightening people or
arousing suspicion of all their work by the mere mention of the word'
(Ramadan 2004, 66).

The notion of Sharia therefore has become either immutably divine
or demonized. Both conceptions depend on on a kind of reification (another faulty construct) that on one hand conflates the humanly mediated process of deriving legal precepts from Qur'anic scripture with the
divine status of the Qur'an itself, and on the other concludes that these
human mediations when they violate human rights (and therefore the
Qur'anic ethos of justice) are irrefutable evidence of a barbaric faith
rather than contested codes. In these reductive, binary formulations
Sharia is presented as a static container for either cultural preservation
or cultural destruction, depending on which side of the coin (bearing

neo-Orientalist accusations or Islamist decrees) lands on the table. Neither speaks to the broad and complex terrain on which Islamic epistemology continues to grow in defiance of either set of static norms and assumptions that seek to contain it.

Given the miseducation around what Sharia is and is not and where feminist concerns (religious and secular) actually lie, it is important to understand the historical context through which Sharia has developed and become codified within Islamic canons. Islamic knowledge is derived from two primary sources: the Holy Qur'an, seen by Muslims as the unalloyed word of God or Allah and the *Sunnah* and *hadīth* literature (sets of practices and sayings related to the Prophet Muhammad). The collective corpus of these traditions forms the moral and ethical basis for the elaboration of Islamic laws.

The schools of jurisprudence or fiqh, developed as system in the mid-eighth century (over 100 years after the death of the prophet Muhammad) by male scholars who applied their understanding of the Qur'an and Sunnah to the development of a legal code. Rather than being divine ordinances, these scholars acknowledged that the judgments they made that formed this corpus of law were but interpretations. Nonetheless, many Muslims regard Sharia as divine law rather than a human attempt to apprehend divine intent and they see the precepts developed in these early schools of legal thought as inviolable and immutable. Therefore there is no consensus as to whether these laws were intended to be fixed and static or whether they were meant to be more fluid and adaptive to the changing historical and cultural conditions faced by Muslims. Historically, differences in Qur'anic interpretation developed regionally as local knowledges implicated the way the text came to be read, understood, and ultimately codified into law. For example, in early medieval Islamic society there were differences in marriage laws that prevented a woman living in Medina from contracting her own marriage, yet a woman living in Kufa – another region – was allowed the right to do so (Ahmad 1992, 89). Historically, then, Islamic law was characterized by a lack of uniformity in interpretation, and this unevenness and variability is evident also in the contemporary Muslim world. It is this lack of uniformity that underlies some of the key contentions with respect to implementing this system of law for the purposes of binding arbitration in Canada. Concerns have arisen with respect to which interpretations would be invoked and whether these would be in the best interests of women, who under many traditional interpretations have not fared well in the area of family law, including divorce, alimony, and child custody rights.

Underlying Contestations

While some interpretations of Islamic scripture that inform traditions of law have not always provided the Qur'anic principles of social justice to women and in fact have often severely compromised their rights, freedoms, and lived conditions, this does not mean that they are intrinsically unjust to women, only that the interpretive practices have historically been rooted in a largely patriarchal tradition. This is now being challenged and subject to epistemological reform based on feminist hermeneutics of religious texts through which more gender equitable reading have been derived (see, e.g., Wadud 1992; Abou El Fadl 2001; Barlas 2002). Those who are not in favour of faith-based arbitration based on Sharia codes express important and legitimate concerns about implementing a system that in practice has nowhere in the world achieved the ideals of justice on which it was meant to be predicated. Without epistemological reform, many traditional interpretations and applications of Muslim law continue to be detrimental to women, and therefore are not a just or truly Islamic rendering of these legal determinations.

Even though proponents argued that agreements made in the tribunals would be read and approved by a Canadian judge and could not contravene Canadian law, it is unlikely that a judge would truly question a 'mutual agreement' where a woman had given up custody of her children and agreed to a limited term of alimony. However, such concerns are not limited to Sharia-based arbitration but can also come into play in negotiations based on secular family law (see, e.g., MacFarlane, Cutting, and Macklin, in this volume). Nonetheless, media reports echoed these concerns: 'A Muslim woman in an abusive relationship might consent, out of fear, to submit to an arbitration tribunal rather than exercise her legal rights. A Muslim wife seeking a divorce might be persuaded that it is her religious duty to settle for less support than the courts would have awarded her. A Muslim mother who converts to Christianity might lose custody of her children. A Muslim cleric with limited knowledge of the complexities of Sharia might render a one-sided decision' (Goar 2004).

These scenarios raise another issue that was highlighted in the debates: the extent to which these tribunals were truly 'voluntary' in nature. Women's organizations raised serious concerns that many women would feel social pressure to take their disputes to their community tribunals as opposed to the Canadian secular courts (Bahkt 2004). This tacit coercion is evident in the publications put out by the Islamic Institute for Civil Justice (IICJ) that has spearheaded this proposal. Their publications state: 'a Muslim who would choose to opt out at this stage, for reasons of convenience would be guilty of a far greater crime than a mere breach of contract – this could be tantamount to blasphemy-apostasy' (Mills 1995).

Statements like this are coercive, especially for women who look to the religious authorities within the community for guidance on doing the 'right thing' and being a 'good Muslim.' They also inhibit women who might seek recourse outside the tribunal if they were not happy with the proceedings or outcome. This pressure would add additional social pressures on marginalized women who also might not have the political literacy to be aware of the rights accorded to them either in Islamic laws or in the Canadian legal system. Their ability to make informed decisions would be compromised. Based on anecdotal information from a Jewish studies scholar, I was informed that when women in the Jewish community go before the Rabbinical courts or Beit Din, an informal network of women 'advisers' well-versed in Jewish law often accompany them to the proceedings in order to provide them with the information they need to navigate the system and ensure that they negotiate the best possible outcome for themselves.

Proponents of faith-based arbitration have acknowledged and validated certain concerns such as the limits placed on women's autonomy as the result of social pressures, but have countered that formalizing the existing practices of informal arbitration within the Muslim community was an important means to ensure justice and equity:

> Critics contend that unfair decisions will come to light very rarely given that women will cave in to social pressure. The concern is valid given the insular nature of the community, but should not undermine the whole initiative. In fact, Islamic dispute resolution already exists and people are abiding by decisions that are often times crude or unfair. Formalizing the process will allow for greater transparency and accountability. As long as there are proper procedures and rules of conduct in place there is nothing preventing the community from instituting a dynamic and less disruptive alternative to the adversarial court system. (Kutty and Kutty 2004)

Muslim women's groups such as the Canadian Council for Muslim Women were not satisfied with such assurances, however, and argued that for women to give themselves over to the binding judgement of arbitrators, who themselves may not have an in-depth understanding of the complexities and variations of Islamic legal thought would be highly imprudent when so much is at stake in family disputes. Raising deeper concerns, a report by the Metropolitan Action Committee on Violence against Women and Children (METRAC), drew attention to the situation of women in abused relationships, stating that 'METRAC has taken the position for some years that mediation is not appropriate in cases where a power imbalance due to abuse and violence exists in a family relationship' (Cross 2005). The report goes on to acknowledge that it is not only faith-based arbitration that is of concern but rather the systemic inequality women in abused relationships face in secular courts and mediation, which they point out has often compromised the safety and well-being of these women. Therefore, in either secular or religious arbitration, women must engage within a system of unequal relations of power based on patriarchal authority, whether cloaked in the guise of a benevolent state or inscribed with a seal of religious authority. Many Muslim women and organizations representing them argued that they felt more secure with the rights and freedoms granted to them in the Canadian Charter of Rights and Freedoms and noted that the principles of gender-based equity contained therein are completely compatible with Islam (CCMW Statement 2004a).They advocated maintaining a singular, secular system for all Canadians so as to avoid the slippery slope towards the privatization of diversity and justice. Shachar outlines the idea of 'privatized diversity' in the context of the Sharia debate as one where 'respect for religious freedom or cultural integrity requires not inclusion in the public sphere but exclusion from it' (2008, 577). She goes on to argue that privatized diversity does not mandate greater inclusion within the institutions of the dominant society but rather involves creating alternatives to them, although she acknowledges how at the same time such moves serve to shore up the false division between the '*public* realm of citizenship and the *private* realm of group membership' (605, original emphasis).

Mapping the Discursive Terrain

The broader sociopolitical context of Sharia debates becomes an important backdrop for understanding the way public sentiments came to be shaped and conveyed. Framed by blatantly racist and xenophobic discourses based on racist fear-mongering, Islamophobic narratives circulated in the debate with increasing impunity. The new bogeyman of 'Islamofascism' being spread abroad became a common trope to purvey the neo-Orientalist fears and fantasies of the 'dangerous citizen' posing a subversive threat to liberal ideals and democratic freedoms. Media headlines bore witness to a national angst, warning 'Muslim invasion has begun' (Demers, 2004) and 'Canada allowing barbaric Sharia laws?' (Kutty & Kutty 2004) The narratives of cultural pollution and racial and religious degeneracy positioned Muslims as non-citizens unworthy of equal claims to the rights and freedoms enjoyed by others. Muslims were cast as pre-modern subjects (Razack 2007). In addition to the post-9/11 rhetoric and surveillance of Muslims as the 'enemy within,' we were now seen not just as physical threats to public safety but as bearers of civilizational danger poised to corrupt Western freedoms and civilized norms.

The move to introduce religious arbitration based on Islamic principles was seen as a subversion of Canadian, ideals and values and a threat to the nature of the country itself. The rhetoric purveyed from this standpoint argued that the nation was at risk of being corrupted by foreign ideologies that were regarded as illiberal, anti-democratic, and outside of the progressive turns of modernity and enlightened political values. For example, a representative of the Humanist Institute argued that these tribunals are 'the first step toward an Islamic state in Canada.' Elka Enola of the Humanist Association of Toronto, sketched a startling trajectory mapping the '"Worst Case (but probable) Scenario" of the effect of allowing Muslim faith-based arbitration, starting with "Stage One – Using the Arbitration Act, the Sharia courts appear to get legal sanction" and ending with "Stage Three – Muslims now outnumber Christians and the majority rule of democracy is turned on its head as the majority Muslims make Shari'a the law of the land."' It concludes, 'We must protect Canada from such a scenario' (cited in Fidler 2006). Commenting on the inflammatory nature of such rhetoric and the campaign of public miseducation, Sheema Khan (2005) writes: 'Undoubtedly, sharia-phobia has skewed the debate over Ontario faith-based arbitration to such a frenzied level that lies were perpetuated as facts, paranoia as patriotism.'

Secular Muslim groups and dissident organizations opposed to the tribunals also played into the fear mongering. In an open letter to the premier of Ontario, representatives of the Muslim Canadian Congress called the move 'Sharia by Stealth' and described it as a 'Christmas gift to the Mullahs of Iran and Saudi Arabia' (MCC Media Release, 20 Dec. 2004). The International Campaign against Shari'a Court in Canada, headed by Iranian activist and dissident Homa Arjomand – which claims a membership of eighty-seven organizations from fourteen countries with over a thousand activists – organized marches and protests across Canada and worldwide including Amsterdam, Dusseldorf, Stockholm, London, and Paris. In a letter to former Attorney General Marion Boyd, who Ontario Premier McGuinty charged with investigating the issues surrounding faith-based arbitration, Arjomand invokes a scenario where Sharia-based arbitration would inevitably lead to the subjugation and potential death of women: 'We strongly believe that sharia tribunals will crush women's civil liberties. It will enforce brutal laws and traditions on abused women who are living under the intensive influence of Islam. These tribunals will be applying Islamic sharia law which will compel abused women to stay in abusive relationships and will leave them no choice but to be obedient or attempt suicide'(Arjomand, 2004).

In Arjomand's etiological formulation, Islamic faith-based arbitration is tantamount to consigning women to a cycle of violence and subjugation. Whether or not such concerns are justified within the Canadian proposal (I am of course aware of how elsewhere the practice of Sharia law has indeed compromised women's safety), the tenor of these statements profoundly shapes public opinion. Concerns were also linked to how the Canadian example of integrating Sharia-based arbitration would 'give credibility to Sharia law around the world' (Arjomand 2004). The barbaric and irredeemable notion of Sharia law was a common trope employed to heighten fear and moral panic, which not only garnered sympathy and support for the opponents of the Sharia proposal but also played into the racist and xenophobic politics of the post-9/11 context.

In May 2005, the Quebec National Assembly unanimously adopted a resolution to oppose 'the establishment of so-called Islamic tribunals in Quebec and in Canada,' making the province the first to explicitly ban the use of Sharia law. Commenting on the developments in Ontario, Premier Jean Charest proclaimed: 'It's important to send a very clear message that there's one rule of law in Quebec. In our case, we are very much an inclusive society, but a society that will govern itself by one set of rules' (Dougherty 2005). Copies of the resolution were sent to all other legislatures across Canada. This move was spear-headed by Quebec Liberal Fatima Houda-Pepin, who proposed the private member's resolution. Pepin argued, 'The application of sharia in Canada is part of a strategy to isolate the Muslim community to impose an archaic vision of Islam' (ibid.). The president of the Muslim Council of Montreal (MCM), Salam Elmenyawi, condemned the Quebec government's decision as being 'disgraceful and tantamount to religious bigotry and discrimination against a Quebec minority' (MCM, Press Release 2004). In a public statement by the MCM, Elmenyawi argued that the government's view of Sharia was limited and did not take into account its goals to achieve social justice 'Instead, a negative and bigoted definition of Sharia is adopted to serve a political agenda which does nothing more than exclude Muslims and make them feel like second class citizens in their own country' (MCM, Press Release 2004). For Pepin the institution of Sharia tribunals was a move to isolate Muslims and open the door to political Islam, yet this was countered by the MCM, who claimed that the ban against them set the community apart as second class citizens. Marginality, then, was an attribute and reality that framed the Muslim experience in both scenarios.

Islamophobia was a clear by-product of the widespread attention surrounding this proposal, which as I mentioned at the outset made the terrain far more difficult for Muslim feminists and others to navigate. Any internal rejection of the tribunals, even on the legitimate faith-based grounds proposed, was seen as playing into the racism and Islamophobia already being perpetuated. I was involved in these debates as a faith-centred Muslim feminist and public intellectual, and in addressing these concerns I argued that despite the fact that Islamic law was not intrinsically unjust to women, the interpretive communities that determined these ordinances in the ninth century did privilege men. While more gender-just rulings are being developed by contemporary jurists (see, e.g., Abou El Fadl 2002), and encouraging family law reform is taking place in countries like Morocco, I was concerned that these moves had not gained legitimacy in the mainstream Muslim orthodoxy in Canada and so Sharia-based arbitration might be a risky proposition for upholding women's rights. At the same time I challenged Islamophobic narratives that were circulating, driven by neo-Orientalist fears of Muslim cultural degeneracy. It is a difficult challenge for Muslim feminists when we attempt to interrogate issues of sexism within our communities and find that our efforts become subject to the sensationalized racism outside of the community that feeds off such revelations (Zine 2004). Navigating between sexism and racism is a complicated manoeuvre because these are not discrete arenas of oppression but rather they are interlocking and mutually constitutive sites. Fuelling one provides strength for the other. In other words, arguing that Sharia-based arbitration may be detrimental for women can intentionally or unintentionally support racist and Islamophobic notions about dangerous and oppressive Muslim men, which in turn promotes further racist and sexist assumptions about passive and victimized Muslim women. In all of these formulations the specificities and diversity of Muslim women's and men's lives and their ability to exist outside of these negative and limiting narratives is sacrificed to this easy essentialism. It is therefore critical to consider the economies of difference and relations of power that are implicated within the high social cost of this debate.

To better understand the contextual landscape, I have outlined four primary discourses operating within the public debates and media coverage of this issue: (1) the religious/Islamic case, (2) liberal-democratic arguments; (3) the anti-racism perspective, and (4) feminist responses. While these are very much overlapping discourses given the varying positions within each area it is useful to address them with some analytical specificity. I will discuss these discourses and close with findings based on a report to the Ministry of the Attorney General and Minister Responsible for Women's Issues by Marion Boyd, who had been appointed to review the matter. I conclude by commenting on the subsequent decision of Ontario Premier Dalton McGuinty.

Religious/Islamic Case

Mahmoud Mamdani writes about the ways that since the 9/11 attacks neo-imperialist politics and the media that provide its ideological support have called for a weeding out of 'good Muslims' and 'bad Muslims' both abroad and in western nations (2004). According to Mamdani, in this binary conception, 'Good Muslims are modern, secular and westernized but bad Muslims are doctrinal, anti-modern and virulent' (24). In a different way, the same distinction of good Muslims versus bad Muslims is made by Muslims themselves. In these internal formulations 'good Muslims' are religiously conservative, mosque-going, hijab wearing, and do not question or challenge traditional religious edicts, thereby preserving a conservative ideological and theological hegemony and the concomitant status quo of gender relations (read: 'real' Muslims). In this view, 'bad Muslims' are those who challenge religious authority on grounds of equity; they are Westernized, feminists, and 'progressives' who are unsettling traditional norms and standards through heretical reinterpretations of religious texts and authority from these standpoints (read: wayward Muslims). These distinctions are made largely by authoritarian religious leaders and adherents of conservative dogmas. Transgressing the boundaries of the 'good Muslim' as dictated by these ascribed notions of pious behaviour and conduct becomes a sacrilegious violation of social norms and religious mandates. This is evident in the literature purveyed by the Islamic Institute of Civil Justice (IICJ) in their bid to promote Islamic arbitration (see also Reda, in this volume). Syed Mumtaz Ali, a lawyer and founder of Darul Qada writes: 'I have stated publicly, to the media, for instance, that to be a "good Muslim" one must get one's disputes settled by applying the Divine Muslim law. This is possible in Canada, if Muslims choose to seek recourse with Muslim Courts of Arbitration (Dar-ul-Qada) rather than secular courts' (2004a). Therefore the choice is made clear: 'good Muslims' will avail themselves of the Sharia court while 'bad Muslims' continue to flirt dangerously with the folly of secularism.

His point is heightened when the choice of Muslim women to seek out the Muslim court of arbitration or secular legal system is described. He imbues this choice with dire ontological implications for believing women:

> In response to the question: Why should women choose the Muslim court of arbitration over secular court? Is it not clear that that Muslim women will not only enjoy 1) more rights 2) but also the satisfaction that they will be good Muslims in the eyes of their creator as well as perhaps in the eyes of their fellow Muslims and non- Muslim counterparts for being true to their faith by following/obeying the Divine injunction/laws. *As Muslims who surrender to the Will of God (as expressed through Divine law) obeying the law is what makes them Muslim.* Thus by failing to be judged by the Divine laws they will be regarded as no better that 'unbelievers,' 'wrong doers' and 'evil livers' as the Qur'an would otherwise characterize them. (Syed Mumtaz Ali 2004b, emphasis added)

By stating that obeying Sharia law fundamentally determines one's Muslimness, Ali is not only positing the 'good Muslim' as an ontological category based on the acceptance of Sharia-based arbitration but is in fact asserting that to be a Muslim in essence and in scripture requires unquestioning fidelity to Sharia as divine law. Arguments equating dissent or disagreement are linked with apostasy. These statements re-entrench the perception that these laws mirror divine will rather than being the products of a humanly mediated process. Moreover this perspective roots the choice for or against the tribunals as being one of either compliance with divine will or the wholesale rejection of one's faith and status as a Muslim. By positioning acceptance or rejection of the Dar-ul-Qada as a fundamental choice between faith and apostasy, statements like these designed to elicit guilt and fear were perhaps the most coercive elements of this campaign. At the same time as these remarks were made public, assurances were made by the IICJ that the varying and competing interpretations of Islamic law do not pose a problem since they will practise a 'Canadianized Sharia.' According to Syed Mumtaz Ali, 'It will be a watered-down Sharia, not 100 per cent Sharia. Only those provisions that agree with Canadian laws will be used. If there is a conflict between the two, Canadian law will prevail' (in Hurst 2004). In what might be dubbed the 'Sharia lite' proposal there is an attempt to placate fears and sell the project to naysayers by asserting the supremacy of Canadian law in Sharia-based rulings, at the same time holding firm to the fact that these arbitration courts would be a litmus test for distinguishing good Muslims from bad Muslims.

Other pro-Sharia groups such as the CAIR–CAN and ISNA framed their position more positively as opening up possibilities for revitalizing a connection with prophetic tradition. For example, Kutty and Kutty, representatives of CAIR–CAN, write: 'Muslims would simply be reactivating their rich tradition of arbitration (*tahkim*); mediation (*wasatah*); and conciliation (*sulh*). The tradition, based on different assumptions from the Western model, has continued from the time of the prophet' (2004; see also the chapter by Kutty, in this volume). Dar-ul-Qada also noted that 'sharia inspired tribunals offer a greater inner "psychic satisfaction" and peace of mind to believers in a way secular courts could not' (Syed Mumtaz Ali 2004b).

Kutty and Kutty (2004) go further, to argue that contrary to public fears concerns over gender justice in Islamically based alternative dispute resolution (ADR) would actually be remedied by an open and transparent system that would allow for a contemporary re-examination of the culturally rooted patriarchal misinterpretations of Islamic jurisprudence:

> The status quo in Islamic law characterized far too often with abuse of women and minorities is the product of rigid interpretations shaped by tribal and cultural norms. The pure Islamic teachings of equality, justice and freedom must be brought to the fore again by using interpretations which are consistent with the spirit of Islam. Islamic dispute resolution if it is a simple exercise of grafting the western paradigm onto the existing Islamic rules will not be fair or just. This formal ADR initiative provides an

opportunity to shed the cultural baggage and revisit some of the patriarchally misinterpreted rulings by refocusing on the Qur'an's emphasis on gender equality.

The idea that 'gender friendly' tribunals could be a way to initiate epistemological reform was a seductive prospect. I previously noted that scholars such as Amina Wadud (1999), Asma Barlas (2002), and Khaled Abou El Fadl (2002) have formulated anti-patriarchal readings of religious texts and elaborated more gender friendly legal understandings derived from these alternative epistemologies. Incorporating these perspectives into the arbitration process was seen by some as having the potential to set new and important precedents. However, concerns were also raised regarding the lack of Canadian scholars with the discursive knowledge to take up these positions. Moreover, because Muslim women had yet to achieve full representation in the institutional structures of the community (such as the majority mosques, schools, and community centres) there was little confidence on the part of many women that Sharia-based tribunals would be any more responsive to their interests. The proposal was regarded by some women's groups such as the Canadian Council of Muslim Women (CCMW) as a social experiment being conducted at the expense of 'vulnerable women.' The CCMW recommended that Ontario follow the example of Quebec, where the Arbitration Act is not applied to family matters in order to neutralize and remove the 'gender question' (CCMW Submission to Marion Boyd 2004a) .

Religious discourses therefore ranged from faulty yet coercive theological and ontological claims regarding good and bad Muslims to more sober arguments regarding the way that religious tribunals can be incorporated into democratic practice without fracturing the foundations of secular society and how they might be opportunities to redress traditional patriarchal norms embedded in traditional formulations of Islamic jurisprudence. The hopefulness of the latter claim was tempered by concerns that given the present context of gender relations in the Muslim community making this the testing ground for epistemological reform might not be in the best interest of women.

Liberal Democratic/ Multiculturalism Arguments

Arguments both for and against Sharia-based arbitration relied on appeals to liberal democratic discourse and multicultural politics. The

Institute of Islamic Civil Justice used the rhetoric of liberalism and democracy to support their claims by speaking to notions of freedom of religion, freedom of conscience, and minority group rights. They argued that these rights and freedoms are enshrined in the Canadian Charter of Rights and Freedoms and therefore guaranteed protection. The IICJ calls for non-Muslim Canadians to 'carry out and act upon their fundamental principles and ideology which is put forward in the Canadian Charter of Rights and Freedoms.' From early on in their campaign the IICJ articulated the goal of pursuing a system of Muslim Personal Family Law (PFL) as a democratic imperative for Canadian Muslims: 'In the Canadian context, you cannot shirk from your civil responsibility to pitch in to bring your Canadian system a step closer to achieving that ideal of a perfect democracy. You must use democratic methods to seek democratic solutions to your problems, as suggested by the Canadian Society of Muslims. This is why the PFL is so important for you as Canadian Muslims – it is an opportunity to live your Islam to the best extent possible in the Canadian democratic context' (Syed Mumtaz Ali, cited in Mills 1995).

Therefore, Sharia-based arbitration was promoted by the IICJ as being not only compatible with democracy but also was seen as being contingent on the assertion of democratic ideals by Canadian Muslims.

The Canadian branch of the Islamic Society of North America (ISNA Canada) also supported the campaign and based their case on liberal democratic grounds. They challenged the notion that judicial autonomy in the form of 'sharia-inspired tribunals' would lead to a fracturing of the secular state. In their position statement submitted to Marion Boyd, ISNA Canada's argument drew on multicultural guarantees, precedents for religious courts, and political arguments regarding the possibilities for coexistence of religious law within a secular framework:

Canada has long led the world in formal multicultural policy. Hassidic Jews, Catholics and Ismailis have used their religious doctrine to settle disputes for a decade without a hue and cry about threats to the secular state. Secularism as practiced in Canada requires that the state remain neutral between religions and not promote a single faith at the expense of the other faith groups. Secular law can accommodate (and has been accommodating) law inspired by religious doctrine for decades. Secular and religious law aim for the same goals: justice. Hence the tribunals offer a way for these two bodies of law to work in tandem. (ISNA–Canada Statement on Muslim Tribunals, cited in Boyd, 2004, 87)

ISNA Canada also put forth that denying the claim of Sunni Muslim groups would be 'reckoned as discrimination and a singling out of a religious group in Ontario' and therefore in violation of Canada's Charter of Rights and Freedoms, which guarantees freedom to all religious groups.

Interestingly, those who were against the Sharia-based tribunals, such as Homa Arjomand's International Campaign against Sharia Court in Canada, also used the Canadian Charter as a means to argue against what they saw as the destructive impact of Sharia law that violated women's rights. Arjomand argued that religious tribunals would 'crush' women's freedom, human rights, civil liberties, and freedom of expression and fundamentally violates 'Canadian values and gender justice.' The rhetoric employed in their campaign raised concerns regarding the 'limits of multiculturalism' and tolerance for fundamentally 'illiberal' groups. Their interventions raised the issue of individual versus group rights with respect to women and question whether multiculturalism is 'bad for women' and being used to violate women's rights through various cultural practices (see Okin 1999). The question became two sided: Are we sacrificing women's rights on the altar of multiculturalism? Or are we sacrificing religious freedom on the altar of secularism? Okin uses extreme examples (child marriage, rape victims forced to marry their rapists, clitoridectomy, etc.) to make her case that multiculturalism and a privileging of cultural group rights over the individual rights of women has opened the door to misogynist cultures running amok (ibid.). This argument was echoed by Quebec MPP Fatima Houda-Pepin to justify the ban on Sharia in Quebec: 'Islamic fundamentalists have targeted Canada to introduce sharia law – a code of conduct based on the Koran that critics say discriminates against women – because of this country's rights guarantees and official multiculturalism' (Dougherty 2005). While there are legitimate concerns regarding the way women's rights and freedoms are compromised and abused in many patriarchal cultural traditions, this formulation of liberalism masks a paternal attitude to minoritized groups and upholds secular Eurocentric values and norms as superior to non-European religious ones. In this conception, group rights are only recognized for groups deemed 'liberal.' This model of multiculturalism posits fixed and static notions of culture that are referenced by the most extreme examples. Muslims do not fare well in these paradigms and are viewed as often irreconcilably illiberal and anti-democratic. The more progressive approaches within the Muslim tradition are therefore silenced. It is important to be attentive to the way these arguments reinscribe racism and fear of difference and cast cultures as fixed and static and in some cases anachronistic entities rather than socially negotiated sets of practices that are continually undergoing contestation and change from within.

Antiracism Perspective

The following statement highlights the ways both a 'clash of civilizations' paradigm and Islamophobic narratives were galvanized during the debates:

> The current debate in Canada is largely being framed in terms of a collision – dare I say 'clash'? – between two competing, immutable, centuries-old intellectual traditions: on the one hand, modern Islamic law-making and, and the other, the Enlightenment ideals dictating the separation of Church and state (or, in this case, Mosque and state). Within that framework, the worst elements of such disparate phenomena as racism, pluralism and multiculturalism are rendering toxic a discourse that either hides a regressive, thin-edge-of-the-wedge establishment of ghettoized religious courts behind a wall of banal pleasantries about diversity, or else appeals to the basest Islamophobia and prejudice in opposition to it. (Demers 2004)

In response to this framing, the campaign against Sharia-based arbitration was often fought on the grounds of anti-racism. I have already outlined the ways that racist and Islamophobic narratives were circulating with impunity during these debates and were challenged by pro-Sharia advocates as well as anti-racists. However, there was a different kind of anti-racism battle being waged by detractors of the proposal, who argued the implementation of these tribunals was evidence of differential treatment extended to an ethno-racial and religious group. Tarek Fatah, a spokesperson for the Muslim Canadian Congress (MCC), criticized Boyd's report for not rejecting the proposal: 'Marion Boyd today has given legitimacy and credibility to the right wing racists who fundamentally are against equal rights for men and women' (Mallan 2004). Supporting religious arbitration according to this view serves the interest of 'right wing racists' who are also anti-feminist. It is unlikely that right-wing racists would have campaigned to endorse Sharia-based arbitration, but the charge made by the MCC exemplifies the way that charges of racism were being deployed to support specific positions.

More sober and compelling arguments were put forward on anti-racist grounds by human rights·lawyer Amina Sherazee. She argued that instituting a separate system of religious arbitration was a way to avoid the current inequality and discrimination that exists within the legal system: 'For instance, if you look at the judiciary on the federal level you'll see that there isn't a single person of colour who is a judge – not one! In the provincial courts in Ontario it was not until 1989 (yes, 1989!) that we had the first black judge. By the year 2017 visible minorities are going to be the visible majority. But if that's the case then the composition of the judiciary should be reflecting that reality. Establishing sharia arbitration is a way for the government to avoid dealing with racism and exclusion in the legal system' (Braganza 2005).

Sherazee warns that because of the racist and classist nature of the Canadian judicial system, creating a separate system of arbitration for racially minoritized communities frees the legal system from working towards making the mainstream courts more inclusive and accountable to racial forms of justice. However, Sherazee's comments also bring an important reminder that racially minoritized women are not necessarily being well served by secular family law courts in the first place. She goes on to argue that the move for religious arbitration serves the interest of the government by allowing them to off-load responsibility for many of the services it should be providing to make the legal system 'more relevant, responsive and accessible to religious, cultural and racial communities' (Braganza 2005). She further outlines how this move reinforces the hegemony of the dominant society in the public realm by keeping the interests of racial and religiously minoritized groups relegated to the private sphere: 'Religious arbitration is a great way for the Ontario government to avoid these responsibilities by claiming that groups can just regulate themselves on their own and meet their own needs ... This frees the government to narrow its focus to the dominant cultures of society while claiming that special minority groups are both marginal to public interest and an unnecessary financial strain on the system' (ibid.).

While others characterize the move towards private faith-based arbitration as beneficial in reducing the burden on the strapped legal system, Sherazee warns that this actually absolves the government from instituting structural and systemic forms of change that would result in greater equity: 'To properly remedy the lack of legal services, the government would have to do a complete overhaul of the legal system: it would have to make the judiciary more representative, it would have to provide interpretation and cultural services, it would have to incorporate the values of litigants into both legal procedure and some of the law itself, and so on' (Braganza, 2005).

Religious arbitration in this view leads to the privatization of law and the privatization of legal services, which further economic and social imbalances on the lines of race, class, and gender (see also the chapter by Macklin, in this volume). The MCC characterizes this move as a commodification of the law and employed the adage of 'buyer beware.' Others also warned that this move heralded 'the dark side of multiculturalism' and that the creation of Islamic tribunals would 'lead to a two-tier and an apartheid-based legal system – one for the Muslims and one for everyone else. The result is a further ghettoization of Muslim communities' (Ahmed 2005). As Demers (2004) opined 'we ought to insist that the fundamental egalitarian principles of equality before the law and access to the courts of the land be upheld, and that no Jim Crow standards be allowed in our legal system.' It is significant to note that the use of terms like 'ghettoization,' 'apartheid,' and 'Jim Crow' were only used to characterize Sharia-based tribunals but have not been invoked in the case of Jewish Rabbinical courts (which had been operating since 1991). It seems to be the case that when racially and religiously minoritized groups advocate separate schools or in this case, separate systems of arbitration, terms like 'ghettoization' are summoned to characterize these moves. This in itself is the product of racist constructions, not racially conscious concerns.

Feminist Responses

In her essay 'Can the Subaltern Speak?' Gayatri Spivak reminds us that 'between patriarchy and imperialism, subject-constitution and object-formation, the figure of the woman disappears, not into a pristine nothingness but into a violent shuttling which is the displaced figuration of the "third world woman" caught between tradition and modernization' (1988, 304). Building on this point Kwok contends that 'the subaltern woman has been written, represented and argued about and even legislated for but she is allowed no discursive position from which to speak' (2002, 67). Throughout the debates on Sharia tribunals feminists raised concerns for 'vulnerable Muslim women,' yet the voices of these subaltern subjects were never heard (see Bullock and Korteweg chapters, in this volume). The state, politicians, feminist organizations, academics, and religious and community representatives all stood as vanguards for these women, who were not given the discursive space from which to speak or to even be present as subjects and actors in their own right.[2] The assumption that these were politically immature women unable to exercise agency or claim a voice was reinforced by their absence in the public dialogue and debate. According to Tarek Fatah from the MCC, immigrant Muslim women are unable to exercise agency and choice: 'To have choice you have to have the ability to make the choice. To suggest that Muslim immigrants, Muslim women, who are among the lowest income group in the country have the ability to make the choice is absolute nonsense' (cited in Dougherty 2005). In lamenting the image conjured in the media of a beaten abused, voiceless, victim Pakistani immigrant woman reiterated in countless Canadian news reports[3] Syed Mumtaz Ali rightly retorts: 'It should go without saying, but it clearly bears repeating, that not all Muslim women in Canada are immigrants, not all immigrant Muslim women are from Pakistan, not all Pakistani immigrant women are without fluency in English or French, and indeed not all are without agency, intelligence, or the capacity of resistance' (2006, 14).

The patronizing images purveyed in the media reassert the patriarchal impetus to appropriate the voice of women (that many feminists have also adopted) as well as play into Orientalist notions of backward downtrodden Muslim women who cannot represent themselves. This essentialist view deprives immigrant Muslim women of being regarded as agentic subjects who despite challenges of poverty and migration are capable of being rational and politically conscious beings (see also Kortweg, in this volume, for a discussion on Muslim women and agency). Such infantilizing narratives play into the imperialist need to 'rescue Muslim women,' from barbaric laws, as in Spivak's formulation of 'saving brown women from brown men' (1988). These paternalistic narratives not only serve to constitute the subjectivity of Canadian Muslim women as universally oppressed victims of cultural misogyny, but in turn reconfigure the construction of the state as the benevolent patron and vanguard of these women. The civilizing and recuperative power of the nation is seen to correct the problem of illiberal minorities misusing multiculturalism to promote their anti-democratic and anti-woman practices (Zine 2009).

Razack implicates the way feminist responses have reinscribed racialized colonial binaries that further entrench Muslims in subordinate positions vis-à-vis the West: 'In their concern to curtail conservative and patriarchal forces within the Muslim community, Canadian feminists (both Muslim and non-Muslim) utilized frameworks that installed a secular/religious divide that functions as a colour line, marking the difference between the white, modern, enlightened West, and people of colour, and in particular, Muslims' (2007, 6). By invoking the 'clash of civilizations' (Huntington 1993) narrative, feminist politics within this debate have not only recast negative epistemological and ontological (and civilizational) binaries but in doing so have reasserted their structural superiority over the women who are the objects of their concern and pity.

In taking up feminist claims within these debates, Razack reminds us that 'feminist responses helped to sustain a form of governmentality, one in which the productive power of the imperiled Muslim woman functions to keep in line Muslim communities at the same time that it defuses more radical feminist and anti-racist critique of conservative religious forces' (2007, 6). Therefore, this narrative not only maintains the Muslim woman as subaltern subject but also jeopardizes spaces of anti-racist feminist, and I would add Muslim feminist, critique and action (see, e.g., Zine 2004). Elsewhere I have argued that in this formulation Muslim women become 'imperiled Muslim women, imperilling the nation' (Zine 2009,13). The difference they embody is an imperilling difference; they are threatened by the barbaric misogyny of their culture and religion and at the same time they pose a threat to the sanctity of the nation as a space for dominant liberal, Christian, Eurocentric values to prevail. These paternalistic narratives not only serve to constitute the subjectivity of Canadian Muslim women as universally oppressed victims of cultural misogyny, but in turn reconfigure the construction of the state as the benevolent patron and vanguard of these women. The civilizing and recuperative power of the nation is seen to correct the problem of illiberal minorities misusing multiculturalism to promote their anti-democratic and anti-woman practices (Zine 2009).

Religious authorities also presumed to decide for Muslim women where their economy of rights would be best earned (in religious or secular courts) as described in this statement by Syed Mumtaz Ali (2004b):

I will let the readers decide for themselves whether Muslim women are going to be better off under the Muslim Arbitration system or under the secular Canadian regime. Using the Muslim Courts of Arbitration, Muslim women are guaranteed equity under the Canadian Charter of Rights & Freedoms, a bundle of, say, 100 rights (for the sake of illustration). Under the Muslim Arbitration system, Muslim women are likely to get, say, a bundle of 200 rights, i.e. MORE, NOT LESS, than the Canadian secular bundle of rights. Not exactly equal, but better than equal!

In these terms the proposal is cast as a pro-feminist move that accrues greater quantitative rights for Muslim women. Ali fails to account for the fact that while there are specific rights accorded to women within Islam that are beneficial, these have failed to provide a guarantee of their human rights in Muslim countries.

Conclusion

In her report Marion Boyd, the former Ontario attorney general who was appointed to review arbitration process and its impact on vulnerable people in Ontario, did not call for the end to faith-based arbitration in Ontario; a move that would have affected other religious groups such as the existing Rabbinical courts. Boyd argued that the use of arbitration may result in a ruling that is more acceptable to the individuals involved because they are more reflective of the individuals' religious and cultural values. Her report interprets the setting up of the tribunals as an incorporation of a religious minority into mainstream political processes and that 'by using mainstream legal instruments minority communities openly engage in institutional dialogue' (2004, 94).

Boyd also stressed in her report that religious arbitration is not a parallel legal system since it functions within Canadian law and is thus subordinate to the court system. Boyd noted: 'A policy of compelling people to submit to different legal regimes on the basis of religion or culture would be counter to Canada's Bill of Rights and the Charter of Rights and Freedoms (2004, 89).' She instead provided recommendations and 'safeguards' to the act in response to community concerns. Boyd's (2004) recommendations included the following:

- Mediators and arbitrators would screen clients in advance for indications of power imbalance and domestic violence (to ensure the process was voluntary and not the product of domestic violence or intimidation).
- Public education initiatives by the Government are needed to acquaint the public with the legal system, various dispute resolution options and family law provision. This was to mitigate against the possibility that 'ADR may provide a venue for continued abuse

after the breakdown of a relationship, and therefore safeguards must be in place. Many respondents to the Review recognized the need for the Muslim community to counter traditional attitudes that may condone violence against women.'

These recommendations did not satisfy detractors of the proposal, who remained sceptical that these safeguards would go the distance to ensuring that women would be 'protected.' All of this became moot on 11 September 2005, when Ontario Premier Dalton McGuinty announced to the press: 'There will be no Sharia law in Ontario. There will be no religious arbitration in Ontario. There will be one law for all Ontarians,' McGuinty argued that such courts 'threaten our common ground,' and promised that his Liberal government would introduce legislation as soon as possible to outlaw them in Ontario. 'Ontarians will always have the right to seek advice from anyone in matters of family law, including religious advice,' he said. 'But no longer will religious arbitration be deciding matters of family law (Leslie 2005).' This unilateralism not only silenced the public debate, but it reproduced the state as the civilizing arbiter. Muslim culture remained cast as a dangerous, static throwback in need of containment and disciplining. The assertion of group rights by recalcitrant minorities was quelled and rendered docile. The paternalism of the state was reinforced through this move in the name of rescuing 'imperilled' Muslim women (Razack 2007, Zine 2009). Shachar is also critical of this unilateralism and argues that this 'imposition by state fiat sends a strong symbolic message of unity; albeit a unity that is manufactured by ensuring compliance with a single monopolistic jurisdictional power-holder' (2008, 610).

The controversy over the possibility of Sharia-based religious arbitration being introduced in Ontario galvanized fears and racist fantasies. It also created more productive tensions that contribute to raising critical contestations regarding the interplay of race, gender, religion, and multiculturalism as well as the need for gender-based religious reform within Islam. I began this discussion with the explanation of how a critical faith-centred approach informs my analysis, by recognizing how religious and spiritual identities and identifications represent sites of oppression (based on race, class, gender, ethnicity, sexuality, and colonialism) but that religion can also be complicit in the construction and perpetuation of these oppressions. In this debate it was clear how Sharia-based arbitration was viewed as Shachar notes as a 'polarized oppositional dichotomy that allows *either* protecting women's rights *or*

promoting religious extremism' (2008, 585, original emphasis). This
equation constructs religion as being inherently extremist in nature
and compromising women's rights and therefore as a source of wom-
en's oppression. While there is no doubt that religious practices have
been complicit in denying women rights and liberties in many contexts, the easy essentialism of this binary makes religion, and in this
case Islam, irreconcilable with democracy and liberal values. In doing
so, Muslim identities and practices are demonized and vilified as disruptive to social harmony and destructive to human rights. Much of
the debate over Sharia-based arbitration existed within these extreme
parameters. Attending to the ways that the politics of race and gender
were implicated in these contestations allows for a more nuanced mapping of the narratives being purveyed by various interlocutors and
stakeholders. The debate also highlighted the ways in which multiculturalism in Canada is being unsettled by Muslim cultural politics in
which religious difference has lead to questions of how citizenship and
belonging are being defined and challenged by dominant and marginalized social actors. As a flashpoint then, the Sharia tribunal case is il-
lustrative of the need for a more engaged politics of equity that allows
for marginalized communities to craft spaces of ambivalence, affirmation, and dissent as part of a fluid process of cultural and discursive
formation that is free from the competing hegemonies that contain
these moves within racialized economies of difference.

NOTES

1 I have chosen to use the term 'Sharia' in this discussion since this was the
predominant way of defining and naming the proposal for Alternative
Dispute Resolution based on Islamic principles within the media and public discourse, despite the fact that the misappropriations of the term has
led to inflammatory rhetoric. At other times I have used the terms invoked
by various stakeholders in the debate such as 'Muslim Court of Arbitration,' 'Muslim Arbitration Board,' 'Muslim Tribunals,'or 'Faith-Based Arbitration'. I believe this shift in naming signalled an attempt to gain more
precise definition as well as distance the proposal from the negative stereotypes associated with Sharia law. Throughout this discussion the variances
of naming are reflected .The term 'Muslim Family Law' is used where it
has been traditionally employed.

2 The measures that would have made it possible to include the voices of marginalized Muslim women (i.e., a decentralized process of community-based outreach) was not employed as a part of Boyd's inquiry, therefore the structures of participation further limited the opportunity for women who did not possess the requisite cultural or political capital to be included.

3 Syed (2012), e.g., notes the following reference in the Montreal *Gazette:* 'Consider a hypothetical immigrant wife from Pakistan, who speaks little French or English. She has no money of her own; she has no idea that she has legal rights other than those her husband or imam choose to tell her about; she believes that her legal right to reside in Canada is entirely dependent on her husband … Taken to a Sharia court and divorced, she might be left with almost none of the family's assets. There is little or no chance that this woman would know how to complain, or to whom.'

REFERENCES

Abou El Fadl, Khalid. 2002. *Speaking in God's Name: Islamic Law, Authority and Women*. Oxford: Oneworld Press.

Ahmad, Leila.1992. *Women and Gender in Islam*. New Haven: Yale University Press.

Ahmed, Eman. 2005. 'Promoting Inclusivity; Protecting (Whose) Choice?' Accessed 1 Jan. 2011. http://www.awid.org/eng/Issues-and-Analysis/Library/Promoting-Inclusivity-Protecting-whose-Choice.

Ali, Syed, Mumtaz. 2004a. 'The Good Muslim/Bad Muslim Puzzle.' 14 June. Accessed 7 Feb. 2011. http://muslim-canada.org/goodbad.html.

– 2004b. 'Are Muslim Women's Rights Adversely Affected by *Shariah* Tribunals?' Accessed 7 Feb. 2011. http://muslim-canada.org/darulqadawomen.html.

– 2006. 'The Case for Judicial Autonomy through the Establishment and Operation of the Islamic Institute for Civil Justice.' Presented at Upper Canada College, Ontario Model Parliament, 8 April, Toronto. Accessed 7 Feb. 2011 http://muslim-canada.org/Islamic%20Civil%20Justice3.pdf.

Arjomand, Homa. 2004. Letter to Marion Boyd. 21 July 2004. Accessed 5 Jan. 2011. http://www.nosharia.com/let2boyd.htm#1.

Bakht, Natasha. 2004. 'Family Arbitration using Sharia Law: Examining Ontario's Arbitration Act and Its Impact on Women.' *Muslim World Journal of Human Rights* 1(1): Article 7. Accessed 7 Feb. 2011. http://www.bepress.com/mwjhr/vol1/iss1/art7/.

Barlas, Asma. 2002. *Believing Women in Islam: Unreading Patriarchal Interpretations of the Qur'an.* Austin: University of Texas Press.

Boyd, Marion. 2004. *'Dispute Resolution in Family Law: Protecting Choice, Promoting Inclusion.'* Accessed 5 March 2010. http://www.attorneygeneral. jus.gov.on.ca/english/about/pubs/boyd/.

Braganza, Neil. 2005. 'Sharia Law: Religious Arbitration and the Privatization of Law. An Interview with Amina Sherazee.' Accessed 7 Feb. 2010 New Socialist Issue no. 51 (May/June). http://www.newsocialist.org/

Canadian Council of Muslim Women. 2004a. 'Position Statement on the Proposed Implementation of Sections of Muslim Law [Sharia] in Canada.' Accessed 7 Feb. 2011. http://www.ccmw.com/activities/act_arb_ muslimlaw_sharia.html.

– 2004b. *'Review of the Ontario Arbitration Act and Arbitration Processes, Specifically in Matters of Family Law.'* Accessed 7 Feb. 2011. http://www.ccmw .com/activities/act_arb_Submission_Marion_Boyd.html.

Cross, Pamela. 2005. 'Should Different Kinds of People Living in the Same Province Be Governed by Different Kinds of Laws? Dossier 27. Women Living under Muslim Laws. Accessed 7 Oct 2011. http://www.wluml.org/ node/505

Demers, Charles. 2004. 'Framing the Sharia Debate.' *Seven Oaks Magazine.* 14 Sept. Accessed 7 Feb. 2011. http://sevenoaksmag.com/commentary/ 30_comm1.html.

Dougherty. Kevin. 2005. 'Québec Bans Sharia.' *Canwest News Service.* 25 May. Accessed 7 Feb. 2011. http://www.sikhtimes.com/news_052705b.html.

Fidler, Robert. 2006. 'Ontario's "Sharia Law" Controversy: How Muslims Were Hung Out to Dry.' *Monthly Review.* Accessed 7 Feb. 2011. http:// mrzine.monthlyreview.org/2006/fidler270506.html.

Goar, Carol. 2004. 'Testing the Limits of Tolerance.' *Toronto Star.* 16 Jan. Accessed 7 Feb. 2011. http://www.nosharia.com/ts.htm

Huntington, Samuel. 1993. 'The Clash of Civilizations.' *Foreign Affairs* 72(3): 22–8.

Hurst, Linda. 2004. 'Ontario Sharia Tribunals Assailed.' *Toronto Star.* 22 May. Accessed 7 Feb. 2011. http://www.religionnewsblog.com/7382.

Khan, Sheema. 2005. 'The Sharia Debate Deserves a Proper Hearing.' *Globe and Mail,* 15 Sept. Accessed Feb. 2011. http://www.caircan.ca/oped_more. php?id=1973_0_10_0_C.

Kutty, Faisal, and Ahmad Kutty. 2004. 'Sharia Courts in Canada: Myth and Reality.' Accessed Feb. 2011. www.faisalkutty.com.

Kwok, Pui Lan. 2002. 'Unbinding Our Feet: Saving Brown Women and Feminist Religious Discourse.' In Laura E. Donaldson and Kwok, Pui Lan, eds., *Postcolonialism, Feminism and Religious Discourse,* 62–81. London: Routledge.

Leslie, Keith. 2005. 'McGuinty Rejects Ontario's Use of Shariah Law and All Religious Arbitrations.' Canadian Press. 11 Sept.

Mallan, Caroline. 2004. 'Sharia Report Called "Betrayal" of Women: Proposal Backs Use of Islamic Principles in Settling Disputes; Ontario Heading in "Dangerous Direction," Opponents Say Sharia Report Called "Naïve."' *Toronto Star,* 21 Dec.

Mamdani, Mahmoud. 2004. *Good Muslim, Bad Muslim.* New York: Pantheon Press.

Mills, Rabia. 1995. 'Interview: A Review of the Muslim Personal/Family Law Campaign.' Canadian Society of Muslims. August. Accessed Feb. 2011. http://muslim-canada.org/pfl.htm#7.

Muslim Canadian Congress. 2004. 'Sharia-Based Arbitration Racist and Unconstitutional.' MCC Media Release. 20 Dec. Accessed Feb 2011. http://www.muslimcanadiancongress.org/20040826-2.pdf.

Muslim Council of Montreal. 2004. 'Muslim Council Of Montréal Condemns Québec's Decision to Ban the Use of Islamic Tribunals.' Press Release. 26 May. Accessed Feb. 2011. http://www.montrealmuslimnews.net/shariaquebec.htm.

Okin, Susan Moller. 1999. *Is Multiculturalism Bad for Women?* Princeton: Princeton University Press.

Shachar, Ayelet. 2008. 'Privatizing Diversity: A Cautionary Tale from Religious Arbitration in Family Law.' *Theoretical Inquiries in Law* 9(2): 573–607.

Sharify-Funk, Meena 2009. 'Representing Canadian Muslims: Media, Muslim Advocacy, Organizations and Gender in the Ontario Shari'ah Debate.' *Global Media Journal* 2(2): 73–89.

Spivak, Gayatri, C. 1988. 'Can the Subaltern Speak?' In Carl Nelson and Lawrence Grossberg, eds., *Marxism and the Interpretation of Culture,* 271–316. Urbana: University of Illinois Press.

Syed, Itrath. (forthcoming). 'The Great Canadian Shar'ia Debate.' In Jasmin Zine, ed., *Islam in the Hinterlands: Exploring Muslim Cultural Politics in Canada.* Vancouver: UBC Press.

Ramadan, Tariq. 2004. *Western Muslims and the Future of Islam.* London: Oxford University Press.

Razack, Sherene. 2007. 'The "Sharia Law Debate"in Ontario: The Modernity/Premodernity Distinction in Legal Efforts to Protect Women from Culture.' *Feminist Legal Studies* 15(1): 3–32.

Wadud, Amina. 1999. *Quran and Woman.* London: Oxford University Press.

Zine, Jasmin. 2004. 'Creating a Critical-Faith-Centred Space for Anti-Racist Feminism: Reflections of a Muslim Scholar-Activist.' *Journal of Feminist Studies in Religion* 20(2): 167–88.

– 2008. 'Honour and Identity: An Ethnographic Account of Muslim Girls in a Canadian Islamic school.' *Topia: Canadian Journal of Cultural Studies* 19(39): 39–67.

– 2009. 'Unsettling the Nation: Gender, Race and Muslim Cultural Politics in Canada.' *Studies in Ethnicity and Nationalism* 9(1): 146–63.

10 Agency and Representations: Voices and Silences in the Ontario Sharia Debate

ANNA C. KORTEWEG

This chapter analyses divergent perceptions of immigrant Muslim women's agency that were brought to light during the media debate on Islam and faith-based arbitration (FBA) in Ontario. Feminist critiques of Western understandings of women's agency focus on false universalisms and the damage their unthinking application can do to the political struggles of women in the global South (Bulbeck 1998, Mohanty 2003, Tripp 2006). Similar universalisms structure public debates on gender equality that occur in the context of large scale immigration from the global South to the global North, particularly in relation to Muslim immigrants (Abu-Lughod 2002, Korteweg 2006, Okin 1999). What are often conceptualized as geographically distinct cultural practices coincide as people from across the globe become neighbours in cities like Toronto, where in 2006, 45.7 per cent of the population was foreign born, most coming from Asia.[1] In such cities the north/south divide, conditioned by unequal global, capitalist development in a context of spatial separation, is transposed onto experientially far more intimate social-political contestations within what are now local communities of divergent origins, ethnicities, and migration statuses (Mohanty 2003). In these contexts, assumptions about agency rooted in Christian, but ostensibly secular, traditions (Mack 2003) are called into question.

The media debate on Sharia-based arbitration reflected two divergent representations of agency. Dominant discourses saw Muslim (immigrant) women's agency as contingent on their resistance to Islam. An alternate framing represented agency as embedded in religious (and other) contexts. As the theory of embedded agency would suggest, this latter framing facilitated more nuanced representations of Muslim women as both agentic and religious subjects. By contrast, seeing agency solely as resistance to gendered religious practices homogenized religious

Muslims as a group. This homogenization enabled the gendered racialization of the very diverse Canadian Muslim immigrant communities and discounted the idea that Muslim women's capacity to act could be informed by religion.[2]

Understanding Muslim Women's Agency

From a theoretical perspective, agency requires an underlying sense of self that can inform action, as well as an ability to assess the impact of one's actions on future outcomes and the impact that past actions have had on present conditions (Emirbayer and Mische 1998, McNay 2000). The media debates surrounding faith-based arbitration and Islamic jurisprudence did not address these facets of agency but rather questioned Muslim immigrant women's capacity to act in a self-interested way. The idea of self-interested action, however, can be based on two different understandings of agency: as a reaction against forces of domination, or as embedded in particular historic cultural, social, and economic contexts (Bulbeck 1998; see also, Ahearn 2000, Mahmood 2001, McNay 2000).

In my use of the concept of embedded agency, I draw on work by a number of feminist theorists from outside the field of sociology who argue that women's capacity to act is obscured when read only from their resistance to forces of domination (Ahearn 2000, Mack 2003, Mahmood 2001, McNay 2000, Mihelich and Storrs 2003, Ortner 1996 and 2001). Agency is, of course, always informed by social contexts. The distinction here is between seeing agency solely as resistance, which captures actions that explicitly aim to undermine hegemony, and embedded agency, which captures practices that do not have this explicit aim, yet still reflect active engagement in shaping one's life. The notion of embedded agency allows for a richer sense of how practices of domination and subordination, such as those associated with institutionalized religion, structure the subjectivity underlying the capacity to act (Mihelich and Storrs 2003). By seeing agency as potentially embedded in social forces like religion, which are typically construed as limiting agentic behavior, the capacity to act is not contingent on adopting liberal 'free will' and 'free choice' approaches to subjectivity (see also Ahearn 2000, Mihelich and Storrs 2003, Ortner 2001, and Macklin, in this volume).

Many of the debates on the integration of Muslim immigrants in the nation states of the global North have focused on the ability of Muslim women to resist forces of domination and avoid the gendered subordination often seen as inherent in Islam. For instance, the continuing debates on the hijab often construe the wearing of the veil as a sign of limited agency and of the incompatibility between Islamic and Western values (Ahmed 1992, Alvi et al. 2003, Atasoy 2006, Bartkowski and Read 2003, Bloul 1998, Fournier and Yurdakul 2006, Killian 2003, Macleod 1992). Discussions of forced marriage and honour killing similarly reinforce the impression that Muslim women's capacity to act is severely constrained by their religion (Kogacioglu 2004; Korteweg and Yurdakul 2009 and 2010; Razack 2004). Public debates often frame these issues as indications of the ways in which Islam coincides with a particular form of patriarchy that severely circumscribes Muslim women's capacity to act (Abu-Lughod 2002, Razack 2004). In this process, Muslims also become ethnically 'other,' and often actors both within and outside Muslim communities ethnicize religion through appeals to women's proper role in the family, their bodily comportment, and so on (Bloul 1998, Korteweg 2006). By positioning women as objects, this process of ethnicization also supports notions of Muslim women's limited agency.

Yet the agency of religious Muslim women can also be understood in dramatically different ways. In her work on the Egyptian Islamic revival movement, Saba Mahmood (2001, 2005) argues that liberal theories of freedom are the result of locally specific historic trajectories, rather than the universal set of norms and values they purport to be. Mahmood argues against feminist theories, such as those articulated by Judith Butler (1993), in which agency is understood as the capacity to resist dominant understandings of right action. Approaches like Butler's link agency to resistance and liberal subjectivity to freedom or autonomy (see also, Ahearn 2001, McNay 2000, Ortner 2001). Such a framework, Mahmood argues, can only understand women's active participation in an Islamic revival movement that seems to reinforce gender difference and attendant gender inequalities as either delusional or as somehow materially self-interested (Mahmood 2001; see also, Macleod 1992). Mahmood (2001) proposes a different reading in which women involved in this religious movement actively shape their desire through embodied practices linked to piety under Islam (such as veiling, modesty in clothing, the practice of shyness, etc.). She concludes that for these women agency does not flow from freedom (or those parts of our lives in which we are free from constraints by others) but rather is formed in direct relationship to structures of subordination.

These embedding contexts extend beyond religious ones. For example, Rachel Bloul (1998, 1) shows that the lives of Maghrebi immigrant women were informed by discourses of 'engendering ethnicity' practised by both French and Maghrebi men, in which the wearing of the veil became a way to draw ethnic boundaries between majority French and minority Maghrebi society. Yet these processes also had an impact on Muslim women's agency; the capacity of Muslim men to influence the local political economy of their neighborhoods increased women's participation in the labour force and extended the sphere in which (veiled) women could move (Bloul 1998). Similarly, North African women's responses to the French public debate regarding the headscarf shows that these women occupied a variety of subject positions regarding when to wear the veil and that they interpreted the veil differently depending on the strength of their connection to majority French society (Killian 2003). Such findings imply that Muslim women's agency is shaped by local and national social, cultural, and political struggles that intersect with but also move beyond religion (see also Fournier and Yurdakul 2006). Furthermore, this agency is not (solely) informed by resistance but directly shaped by these intersecting forces.

Misrecognition of the context within which women's agency is embedded can have profoundly negative consequences. For example, Tripp (2006) discusses the internet petitions that Western feminists circulated in the case of Amina Lawal, the Nigerian woman sentenced to stoning after being convicted of adultery by an Islamic religious court. Local women's organizations' capacity to act on behalf of Lawal was severely curtailed by the well-intentioned but misguided actions of some Western feminists, who had discounted local, Muslim activists' agency. In other words, conceptualizations of agency have real consequences that in and of themselves can shape women's capacity to act.

In sum, the literature implies the importance of identifying which conceptualizations of agency are mobilized in debates like the one considered here. As Audrey Macklin discusses in her chapter in this volume, the legal arbitration process presupposes a capacity to act in one's self-interest, and the concerns voiced by various community groups centered on whether Muslim women had the agentic capacity to resist forces of domination that many believed inhered in Islamic legal practice. In what follows, I analyse newspaper articles to see whether this conceptualization of agency dominated in the debate and to what extent a conceptualization of agency as embedded held sway. To see how these conceptualizations structure the contexts of women's agency, I pay attention to how divergent conceptualizations of agency fostered calls for different kinds of state intervention. Furthermore, I examine how conceptualizations of agency promoted visions of social groups as more or less different from majority society along ethnic and racial lines.

The 'Sharia Debate' in the Canadian Media

To analyse how Muslim women's agency was conceptualized in the context of Canadian press coverage, I looked at three newspapers: the *Globe and Mail*, *National Post*, and *Toronto Star*. The *Globe and Mail* and the *National Post* are Canada's two nationally distributed papers. The *Globe and Mail* generally reflects the political centre of Canadian politics, while the *National Post* is a more neo-conservative paper. The *Toronto Star* is Toronto's leading local paper. It has the largest distribution of any paper in Canada, the Greater Toronto Area having the greatest population density in the country. Reflecting the position of Toronto in Canadian politics, the *Star* tends to be politically to the left of the two national papers.

With the help of my research assistants, I created a database of articles by searching for the word 'Sharia' and filtering out the articles that concerned foreign countries. The three newspapers published between twenty-one and forty-five articles each in the period beginning in December 2003 with Syed Mumtaz Ali's announcement that he would introduce Islamic arbitration and ending with the cessation of religious arbitration altogether in February 2006, for a total of 108 articles. Roughly half of them are op-eds, editorials, comments, and opinion pieces. The remainder are national news or sometimes international news (see Table 10.1).

Newspapers construct social problems as they selectively report on certain issues and not others and as they highlight some aspects of these issues and not others (Best 2002, Critcher 2003. Ferree 2003, McCarthy et al. 1996, Smith et al. 2001, Spector and Kitsuse 1977). Recognizing this, I approached the data analysis in ways designed to uncover representations of agency reflected in arguments regarding the advisability of instituting Sharia-based arbitration. I quickly realized that a select group of people were treated as sources of authority on the topic in both news and opinion pieces. The debate was quite polarized and, as Katherine Bullock details in her chapter in this volume, members of the various Muslim communities were called on to comment on either the 'for' or 'against' side. I identified the actors who were quoted in more than one article or op-ed piece (see Table 10.2). I also focused on the op-eds and editorials as another place where the issue was strategically framed and again counted how many writers or editorial boards made arguments for and against (see Table 10.3).

I then conducted a qualitative discourse analysis of the portrayals of Muslim women's agency that drove these arguments. In my presentation

Table 10.1
Distribution of Articles Regarding Sharia-Based Arbitration by Newspaper

	Globe and Mail n (%)	National Post n (%)	Toronto Star n (%)	Total n (%)
News	25 (60)	9 (43)	22 (49)	56 (52)
Editorials	17 (40)	12 (57)	23 (51)	52 (48)
Total	42 (100)	21 (100)	45 (100)	108 (100)

Table 10.2
People Quoted Regarding Sharia-Based Arbitration in the *Globe and Mail*, *National Post*, and *Toronto Star*

Quoted in favour	Articles (n)	Quoted against	Articles (n)
1. Syed Mumtaz Ali	16	1. Homa Arjomand	22
2. Mohammed Elmasry	7	2. Tarek Fatah	14
3. Mubin Shaikh	6	3. Alia Hogben	14
4. Anver Emon	4	4. June Callwood	7
5. Katherine Bullock	3	5. Fatima Houda-Pepin	4
6. Riad Saloojee	2	6. Sally Armstrong	3
7. Ali Hindy	2	7. Marilou McPhedran	3
8. Wahida Valiante	2	8. Ayaan Hirsi Ali	3
		9. Soheib Bencheikh	2
Total	42		72

Table 10.3
Editorials and Opinion Pieces for and against Sharia-Based Arbitration in the *Globe and Mail*, *National Post*, and *Toronto Star*

Editorials for		(n)	Editorials against		(n)
GM	Editorial Board	5	*GM*	3 regular columnists	6
GM	3 guest columnists	3	*GM*	Open letter to McGuinty	1
TS	Editorial Board	4	*TS*	5 regular columnists	6
TS	1 regular columnists	5	*TS*	5 guest columnists	5
TS	2 guest columnists	2	*NP*	4 regular columnists	4
NP	Editorial Board	2	*NP*	3 guest columnists	2
NP	2 guest columnists	2			
Total		23			24

of these findings, I hone in on the voices of Muslim women and men who participated in the debate. Their assertions reflected the overall discursive representations of Muslim women's agency that structured the debate. Furthermore, the participation of Muslim women and men in the debate could itself be read as particular representations of agency, thus adding a layer of complexity to the analysis.

Representing Muslim Women's Agency

As in many debates about Islam and Western liberal values, gender (in) equality and presumptions of Muslim women's limited agency became a flashpoint for arguments against public recognition of Muslim religious practices (Abu-Lughod 2002; see also Okin 1999). While authors like Bloul (1998) show that both majority and minority men constitute ethnic difference by positioning Muslim women as objects, in the case of the Ontario Sharia debate, both self-identified secular and self-identified religious Muslim women, as well as men, actively participated in the debate. These participants both represented and articulated divergent understandings of agency.

The arguments against religiously informed family law arbitration put forth by Muslim women and men were widely shared among the participants in the debate. The tabulations of Table 10.2 and Table 10.3 show that largely secular Muslim voices arguing against Sharia-based tribunals were joined by those from members of majority society, most of whom were women, and that these voices, quoted in a total of seventy-two articles, dominated in the debate. The voices arguing for the institution (with state oversight) of Sharia-based arbitration were not as well represented, being quoted in forty-two articles and more narrowly confined to Canadian religious Muslim communities, although the editorial boards of all three newspapers shared their views.

Privileging Agency of Resistance

Secular Muslim women like Homa Arjomand, Fatima Houda-Pepin, and Ayaan Hirsi Ali occupied a prominent place in the debate (see Table 10.2). These three women contributed almost half of all quotations against the institutionalization of Sharia-based tribunals (as allowed within existing law). Their participation in the debate could be read as an example of agency through resistance – they were often portrayed in the newspapers as Muslim women who, through their own experience, came to understand Islam as inhibiting agency. Newspaper accounts juxtaposed their active engagement in the public sphere with quotations in which these women highlighted the detrimental effects of Islam on Muslim women's capacity to act.

Often the newspaper articles that quoted them started with a portrayal of Islamic law as riddled with injustice and (gendered) oppression. This line of argument took on multiple guises. For example, Fatima Houda-Pepin, a representative for the Liberal Party in Quebec's provincial parliament and a Muslim immigrant from Morocco, argued:

> We've seen the sharia at work in Iran ... We've seen it at work in Afghanistan, with the odious Taliban regime, we've seen it in Sudan where the hands of hundreds of innocent people were cut off. We've seen it in Nigeria with attempts of stoning ... The list is very long. Is that what we want to import to Canada? (*NP* 11 March 2005)

This equation of Sharia-based tribunals with the worst examples of justice enacted under the guise of Islam was widespread among the arguments against arbitration. Opponents framed immigrants from non-Western societies as bringing practices that contravene the dominant norms of majority society. In such quotations Houda-Pepin represented Muslim immigrants who rejected the importation of the norms and practices associated with Islam in non-Western countries. In so doing, Houda-Pepin exercised agency expressed through resistance to Islamic law and practice.

The link between gendered practices and Muslim women's agency came to the fore in discussions of how Sharia-based tribunals might work within Canada. Homa Arjomand, the most quoted person in the opposition, was one of the prime movers against the IICJ's proposal. The newspapers described Arjomand as a refugee from Iran who worked on women's rights issues there and saw her friends killed one by one. After a harrowing trip across the mountains from Iran into Turkey in the late 1980s, she ended up as a refugee in Canada. When the Islamic faith-based arbitration proposal hit the newspapers, she started the International Campaign against Sharia Courts in Canada. In one article, Arjomand described how:

> she has counseled many Muslim women whose rights were abused during informal arbitration by Muslim leaders. In the case of one family who turned to their Markham, Ont., mosque for resolution of a dispute, the results were not positive for the wife and adolescent daughter. The woman, of Pakistani origin, and her 15-year-old daughter were 'returned'

to Pakistan against their will, Ms. Arjomand said, and the daughter was placed in the custody of an uncle and preparations were made for an arranged marriage.

The father then married a 19-year-old woman and brought her to Canada.

'Was the mother forced to leave the country? We don't know what really happened here,' said Ms. Arjomand. (*GM*, 9 September 2004)

The Markham mother and daughter described above had their capacity to act taken away by Muslim leaders. Their story stands in sharp contrast to Arjomand's capacity to act (see also Selby's chapter, in this volume, on the response of Somali young women to Arjomand's centrality in the debate). Arjomand's agency was linked to her resistance, first to the Islamic regime in Iran, then to attempts to bring Islamic jurisprudence into the Canadian legal sphere. The juxtaposition between the descriptions of Arjomand and the Markham mother and daughter reinforced the link between Islam and limited agency, foreclosing any possible representations of embedded agency.

Descriptions of abuses of power in Canadian Muslim communities' interpretations of Islamic jurisprudence, as in the above quotation, became the bases for arguments that connected Islam directly to the oppression of women. In the resulting representation of women's relationship with Islam, the conceptualization of Muslim women's agency was implicitly or explicitly tied to secularism, privileging the modern, but deeply Western, subject, whose agency is expressed through resistance (Bulbeck 1997, Mack 2003, Mahmood 2001; see also the chapters by Bullock, Hogben, and Zine, in this volume). The most extreme version of the idea that agency depends on women's resistance to all expressions of religion appeared in a number of op-ed pieces by Margaret Wente, a regular columnist for the *Globe and Mail*. Wente often recounted arguments made by secular Muslim women. For example, when Ayaan Hirsi Ali (a Somali-born woman who at the time was a member of Dutch parliament and who now works for the American Enterprise Institute in the United States) visited Toronto in the summer of 2005 to help Arjomand's campaign, Wente wrote a full-page article based on this visit in which she interspersed her own analysis with quotations from Hirsi Ali:

'Canadian law,' [Ayaan Hirsi Ali] says, 'is now offering some Canadian men the opportunity to oppress us.' She believes in the strict separation of religion and state. She believes that the religious law of any faith – Muslim,

Christian, Jewish –invariably oppresses women. And she believes that the promised safeguards, such as the right to appeal any decision to a secular court, are a load of hooey for women who live, as many Muslim women do, in a closed society. 'What is freedom of choice when you depend on your family and clan for everything?' (*GM* August 20, 2005)

Again, such arguments predicated the agency of Muslim women on their resistance to religiously informed family and community practices. Secularization became the way to create the conditions within which Muslim women had the capacity to act; without secularization, family relationships structured by Islam could not be penetrated by the more liberal ways of the host society in which immigrants found themselves.

Representations of Embedded Agency

A conceptualization of agency as embedded takes seriously that women's subjectivity is informed by their religious practices in ways that directly shape their agentic behavior (Mahmood 2001). Marion Boyd's (2004) report to the McGuinty government on the advisability of Sharia-based tribunals recognized this link between subjectivity and agency and argued for continuing to allow arbitration based on Islamic principles, contingent on institutionalizing oversight measures. The participation of self-identified religious Muslim women and men in the debate further showed that agency could be embedded in religion.

Religiously observant Muslim participants in the debate constructed the link between agency and Islam in three ways that reflected concep-tualizations of embedded agency. First, proponents of Sharia-based arbitration made claims against the state from a perspective in which Muslim women's agency was embedded in religious and other con-texts. After Ontario Premier McGuinty's announcement that he was going to end all religiously based arbitration, they emphasized that religious immigrant Muslim women needed state protection, claiming that religious arbitration would continue but now without the over-sight of Canadian legal institutions. For example, in one of her editori-als for the *Globe and Mail*, regular columnist Sheema Khan argued that women suffered under informal Islamic jurisprudential practices and she claimed that women could be protected only through institutional-ized state oversight:

... too many unqualified, ignorant imams [make] back-alley pronounce-ments on the lives of women, men and children. The practice will continue,

without any regulation, oversight or accountability. [...] [W]e have missed
a golden opportunity to shine light on abuses masquerading as faith, and
to ensure that rulings don't contradict the Charter of Rights and Freedoms.
(*GM*, 15 September 2005)

Khan, in her participation in Canadian society as a self-identified
religious woman, illustrated the possibility of embedded agency, or a
capacity to act informed by religiosity. In her columns on Sharia-based
arbitration, she extended this capacity to all religious Muslim women.
However, given the possibility of abuse in unmonitored, informal arbitration processes, this agency could not solely be embedded in religious
contexts but also needed to be safeguarded by the Canadian state. Thus,
Khan and others who argued for the institution of Sharia-based tribunals nuanced the negative link between Islam and agency put forth by
secular Muslim women (and others) by pointing the finger at poorly
trained imams and a lack of transparency in decision making rather
than at Islam in general. In claiming that Sharia-based arbitration needed to be institutionalized, proponents argued that Islamic jurisprudence does not necessarily contradict Canadian standards of gender
equality, and, by extension, does not solely curtail women's agency.
Rather than making agency contingent on resistance, these women and
men promoted the intersection of religion with state oversight, or a
strengthening of some of the social forces in which agency was embedded to increase the possibility of gender equality in Sharia-based decision making. As Faisal Kutty argues, in this volume, such an approach
also enables the ongoing production of Islamic jurisprudence tailored
to the contemporary, Canadian context.

A second line of argument put forth by religiously identified Muslim
women also nuanced the dominant understanding of Islam as always
limiting women's agency. Alia Hogben, the president of the Canadian
Council for Muslim Women, was, like Khan, a self-described religious
woman. In an op-ed piece written for the *Toronto Star*, Hogben, the second most cited person against Sharia-based arbitration, argued that it
was impossible for Muslims to be against Sharia as the term 'metaphor-
ically describes the way Muslims are to live' (*TS*, 1 June 2004; see also,
Raza, *TS*, 24 Dec. 2004). Yet, she was against Sharia-based tribunals because she believed that allowing them would negatively affect (a group
of) religious Muslim women within Canadian society.

One of Hogben's primary concerns, also articulated by Nevin Reda
in her critique of the IICJ, in this volume, was that the use of the term
'Sharia' would lead religious Muslim women to believe they were

mandated to go to Sharia-based tribunals rather than the secular court system to negotiate issues surrounding family dissolution and inheritance. According to Hogben, Canadian law was already 'congruent with the principles of Islam,' and Sharia-based tribunals were simply unnecessary except to make rulings that are detrimental to women (*TS*, 1 June 2004). In other words, even though their agency was embedded in religious contexts, religious Muslim women might act in ways that were detrimental to their self-interest. Thus, Hogben differed from Khan in arguing that institutionalized recognition of Islamic jurisprudential practice would amount to public recognition of those aspects of Islam that would always curtail women's agency. For Hogben, women's agency could be informed by Islam as private practice but also needed to be embedded in a secular public sphere. Taken jointly, Khan and Hogben's participation in the debate showed that being embedded in a religious context created more nuanced representations of the ways in which religion could inform agency than the outright rejection of such a possibility that dominated in approaches that construed Muslim women's agency as resistance to religion.

A third link between agency and religiosity was articulated by the person who started the debate, Syed Mumtaz Ali. He was the most quoted proponent of Sharia-based arbitration and the only interlocutor to voice a perspective in which the agency associated with using Sharia-based tribunals was unproblematically embedded in religion; for Mumtaz Ali there was no tension between the strictures of religion and religious Muslim women's agency. Early on in the debate, the *Globe and Mail* stated that Mumtaz Ali 'hopes some of the arbitrators will be women' (13 Dec. 2003). However, from his religious perspective, women's attendant capacity for agency was based on a particular understanding of the relationship between women and men within Islam:

> [Mr Mumtaz Ali] also acknowledged that inheritance and divorce rulings under Islamic law tend to favour men, for historical reasons. 'Brothers and sons always get more. But it is because under the Islamic system, the man has the duty and responsibility to look after the woman,' he said.
>
> Women may use the tribunal to negotiate prenuptial agreements that allow them to initiate divorce proceedings without the permission of their husbands: 'They are in the driver's seat before they marry,' Mr Mumtaz Ali said. (*GM*, 11 Dec. 2003)

This argument represented devout Muslim women's agency as embedded. They had the capacity to act as religious women; they could be arbitrators and negotiate an equal right to divorce prior to their marriage. In Mumtaz Ali's interpretation, Islam renders women and men unequal but this inequality, in Mumtaz Ali's perception at least, is erased by differences in obligation. Yet, conceptualizations of embedded agency are about recognizing that agency can be differently informed by historically, culturally, and socially specific interacting social forces. Mumtaz Ali's assertions were clearly problematic in that, unlike the arguments put forth by religious Muslim women like Khan and Hogben, his did not recognize how these contexts contained complex forces of resistance and domination (see also Reda's analysis of Mumtaz Ali's proposal, in this volume).

Mumtaz Ali, notwithstanding, the vast majority of media arguments, whether for or against the institution of Sharia-based tribunals, reflected widespread agreement across the Muslim communities in Canada that Sharia-based tribunals risked constraining devout Muslim women's agency, either by definition or because of abusive practices by imams in a context of limited state oversight. Religious Muslim women, particularly recent immigrants, according to the arguments, would not be able to act in their own self-interest given the pressures of their family and community and given existing experiences with the treatment of women within informal Islamic jurisprudential practices.

These possibilities were assessed differently depending on whether agency was (implicitly) recognized as embedded or as solely expressed through resistance. The dominant representations of agency as resistance to religious strictures led to arguments against state recognition of Sharia-based tribunals. These arguments rooted agency in secularism and positioned the state as the guardian of the secular public sphere. The less dominant representations of agency as embedded in religion more often led to calls for state oversight of Sharia-based tribunals in order to reduce the potential for abuse and strengthen the aspects of Islamic jurisprudence that support women's capacity to act in their own interest (see also Kutty's arguments to this effect, in this volume). In these representations, the state facilitated the agency of devout Muslim women.

Implications: The Problem of Racialization

A failure to recognize that Muslim women's agency can be embedded in religion is problematic, not only because it narrows public debate, but also because it risks a narrowing of possible policy responses to concerns of immigrants from the global South to the North. An expanding literature explores the ways portrayals of gender inequality within the Muslim world, whether that world is situated in the global South or in immigrant communities within the global North, are rooted in Orientalist discourses that strategically justify Western actors' interventions in these communities (Abu-Lughod 2002, Falah 2005, Kogacioglu 2004, Razack 2004 and 2007). These discourses reify monolithic portrayals of the impact of religion on Muslim women. A similar reification occurred in representations of Muslim women's agency as resistance that dominated in the Canadian Sharia debate.

Some participants in the debate, mostly proponents, but also opponents of Sharia-based arbitration, highlighted the potential racialization of Muslim immigrants in the dominant portrayals of Muslim women's agency. Racialization refers to the process of imputing innate group differences that distinguish subordinate groups from majority society. Where Bloul (1998) discusses the engendering of ethnicity in French discourses on the veil, participants in the Canadian Sharia debate saw a process of racialization that was clearly gendered. For example, Tarek Fatah, communications director for the Muslim Canadian Congress, an organization that advocates against bringing religion into the public sphere, saw such racialization intersecting with Muslims' immigrant status. In an editorial, Fatah wrote:

> If implemented, this law will also cut along class and race lines: a publicly funded, accountable legal system run by experienced judges for mainstream Canadian society, and cheap, private-sector, part-time arbitrators for the already marginalized and recently arrived Muslim community.
>
> For groups like the Muslim Canadian Congress, there is no such thing as a monolithic 'Muslim family/personal law,' which is just a euphemistic, racist way of saying we will apply the equivalent of 'Christian law' or 'Asian law' or 'African law.' (*TS*, 22 June 2005)

The first part of the quotation above echoed arguments that recent immigrants should have the same rights and privileges as long-time Canadians, which informed discourses that saw agency solely in resistance. However, the second part indicated how the dominant discursive portrayals of Islam fostering this understanding of Muslim women's agency could also be read as a form of racialization. This racialization occurred through the homogenization of 'the' Muslim community and the drawing of stark boundaries between that community and the rest of Canadian society facilitated by discourses that linked Muslim women's agency to resistance to Islam.

Faisal Kutty, writing as general counsel for the Canadian-Muslim Civil Liberties Association, which supported the institutionalization of Sharia-based tribunals, implicitly argued that the racialization of Muslims within the debate prevented (state) recognition of the ways all women's agency was embedded:

> I can appreciate that many are concerned about the exploitation of Muslim women. However, the discourse is now bordering on being racist. For instance, critics contend that true consent cannot be ascertained, as Muslim women will be forced to cave in to social pressure and accept unfair decisions. The concern is valid but is not restricted to Muslims and can be partly addressed by imposing duties on arbitrators. (*NP*, 4 Jan. 2005)

Kutty accepted that women's agency was embedded in social contexts, and that such social contexts could lead to curtailing women's agency (like Khan, he advocated institutional oversight of Sharia-based arbitration). However, he also asserted that in the public debate gender inequality was recognized when it was situated within the Muslim community but not in majority society. As Kutty argued, the debate singled out Islam, rather than addressing systemic expressions of gender domination that, according to some, structured all overtly gender-neutral arbitration processes (see also Macklin, in this volume; Bakht 2004). By associating gender inequality with Muslim communities, gender equality was discursively linked to majority society. In doing so, the debate positioned Canadian Muslims as racialized others. This racialization became gendered through the associations between gender inequality and Islam that flowed from linking agency solely to resistance.

Conclusion

The concept of embedded agency draws our attention to the way forces like religion have multiple effects on women's agency. By approaching agency as embedded in such forces, public debates can move away from associating liberty and freedom with pulling women out of the contexts that shape agency and ultimately subjectivity. In the case of the debate on Sharia-based arbitration, the relative absence of such an approach to agency led to the homogenization of Islam and diverse Canadian Muslim communities to the point of 'being racist,' in the words of one of the participants in the media debate. Furthermore, the privileging of agency as resistance to religion and its concomitant emphasis on secularism as that which can safeguard women's capacity to act seems to have informed the Ontario government's decision to halt all religious arbitration in the province. This decision not only constituted a failure to recognize the possibility that religious women might want to be able to enact certain religious practices, but also that they might need government assistance in securing a fair interpretation of Islamic jurisprudence.

Many of the tensions surrounding the integration of immigrants in Western Europe and, to a lesser degree, in Canada, centre on the presumed incompatibility between Western and Muslim religious values. As the Sharia debate exemplified, these debates often focus on issues of gender inequality and the treatment of women within Islam. These debates could unfold differently if they were guided by a conceptualization of Muslim women's agency as embedded. This would enable an analysis that does not predicate women's capacity to act on liberal freedom, but rather carefully situates agency in the contexts that inform it. As Tripp (2006) illustrates in her analysis of Western feminists' interventions in the case of Amina Lawal, the Nigerian woman sentenced to death by stoning for adultery, misrecognizing the forces that inform women's agency can hinder, rather than facilitate, their capacity to act.

To investigate the broader implications of the findings reported in this article, two further avenues of research should be pursued. First, the newspaper debates discussed here tell us little of what happens in the daily lives of Muslim women who do not actively participate in public debate. Further research needs to examine the ways devout Muslim women negotiate their lives in the intersections of Canadian (and other states') legal practices and their (communities') interpretations of religious dictates. This research should seek out such women in order to understand their perspectives and desires with respect to living a life in accordance with religious practice within multidimensional social and political contexts. Here, understanding religion and other social forces as intersecting in dynamic ways will help us move towards a fuller understanding of how agency is embedded in religious and other contexts. Such research can and should occur in any immigrant-receiving nation states that grapple with religious and other culturally informed differences.

The chapters by Julie MacFarlane and Christopher Cutting, in this volume, show that such research reveals a far more complex picture than the media allowed for. In particular, it turns out that the media debate was largely misguided: arbitration is not used by divorcing Muslim couples, but mediation, which continues to be allowed, is. In addition, it is largely *women* who turn to imams and Islamic legal counsel, to obtain the religious divorce decrees that let them move on with their lives after relationship breakdown. In other words, contemporary

Muslim religious leaders more often than not work to ameliorate gender inequalities in their interpretations of Islamic law.

Second, we need to see how policy (mis)recognition of women's agency, as reflected for example in policy approaches to wearing the veil, arranged marriages, and honour-related violence, affects women's capacity to act. These issues all come up repeatedly in debates on Muslim women's integration in the global North. Knowing the various ways Muslim women relate to these practices and how their religiosity intersects with gender, class, migration status, ethnicity, and race can provide the basis for an analysis that assesses whether (proposed) policies impede or facilitate women's agency. Such assessments require us to understand agency as embedded in multiple social forces, rather than flowing solely from liberal, secular practices. This research would further our understanding of how various state institutions can work to support rather than undermine women's varied expressions of agency. As Macklin points out, all women would benefit from understanding agency as embedded, because the assumption of Western women's liberal subjectivity renders the forces that shape their agency invisible.

Ultimately, the concept of embedded agency is applicable to any inquiry into what shapes women's (and men's) capacity to act. Representations of agency rooted in the Western, liberal tradition do not produce socially untethered free-floating subjects. As the portrayals of the secular Muslim women's arguments in the Sharia debate show, they produce an agentic subject embedded in her own particular political-philosophical tradition. In our globalizing world, these traditions increasingly stand in tension with other conceptualizations of the forces that shape agency.

ACKNOWLEDGMENT

An earlier version of this chapter appeared under the title 'The Sharia Debate in Ontario: Gender, Islam, and Representations of Muslim Women's Agency, in *Gender and Society,* 2008, 22(4): 434–54.

NOTES

1 See 2006 Census: Immigration in Canada: A Portrait the Foreign-born Population, 2006 Census: Findings http://www12.statcan.ca/english/census06/analysis/immcit/toronto.cfm, accessed 4 Oct. 2011.

2 A caveat about terminology – in 2006, an estimated 700,000 Muslims
   resided in Canada, the majority in the Greater Toronto Area and the
   province of Ontario. Taken together, Muslim communities constitute the
   largest religious minority in Canada. However, the Muslim world stretches
   across the globe, and Canadian Muslims reflect the resulting cultural, ethnic, and linguistic diversity, as well as diverse interpretations of Islam. I
   use the terms 'Muslim women' and 'Muslim men' throughout this chapter
   to identify people who are situated as Muslims within public debate,
   sometimes adding the modifiers 'secular' and 'religious' or 'devout.' By
   secular Muslim women, I mean those who in their self-descriptions, as
   published in the newspapers, adhere to the ideal of a secular public
   sphere, but who might (or might not) practise their religion in private.
   When I discuss women who self-identify or who were presented as religious, I use the modifiers 'devout' or 'religious.'

REFERENCES

Abu-Lughod, Lila. 2002. 'Do Muslim Women Really Need Saving?
   Anthropological Reflections on Cultural Relativism and Its Others.'
   American Anthropologist 104(3): 783–90.
Ahearn, Laura M. 2000. 'Language and Agency.' *Annual Review of Anthropology*
   30: 109–37.
Ahmed, Leila. 1992. *Women and Gender in Islam: Historical Roots of a Modern
   Debate.* New Haven: Yale University Press.
Alvi, Sajida Sultana, Homa Hoodfar, and Sheila McDonough. 2003. *The Muslim
   Veil in North America: Issues and Debates.* Toronto: Women's Press.
Atasoy, Yildiz. 2006. 'Governing Women's Morality: A Study of Islamic Veiling
   in Canada.' *European Journal of Cultural Studies* 9(2): 203–21.
Bakht, Natasha. 2004. 'Family Arbitration Using Sharia Law: Examining
   Ontario's Arbitration Act and Its Impact on Women.' *Muslim World Journal
   of Human Rights* 1(1): 1–24.
Bartkowski, John P., and Jen'nan Ghazal Read. 2003. 'Veiled Submission:
   Gender, Power, and Identity among Evangelical and Muslim Women in the
   United States.' *Qualitative Sociology* 26(1): 71–92.
Best, Joel. 2002. 'Review. Constructing the Sociology of Social Problems – Spector
   and Kitsuse Twenty-Five Years Later. Reviewed Work(s): *Constructing Social
   Problems* by Malcolm Spector, John I. Kitsuse.' *Sociological Forum* 17(4): 699–706.
Bloul, Rachel. 1998. 'Engendering Muslim Identities: Deterritorializaiton and
   the Ethnicization Process in France.' Published by Women Living Under
   Muslim Law. Accessed 4 Oct. 2011. http://www.wluml.org/node/378.

Boyd, Marion. 2004. *Dispute Resolution in Family Law: Protecting Choice, Promoting Inclusion*. Accessed 12 Sept. 2005. http://www.attorneygeneral. jus.gov.on.ca/english/about/pubs/boyd/.

Bulbeck, Chilla. 1998. *Re-Orienting Western Feminism: Women's Diversity in a Postcolonial World*. Cambridge: Cambridge University Press.

Butler, Judith. 1993. *Bodies that Matter: On the Discursive Limits of 'Sex.'* New York: Routledge.

Critcher, Chas. 2003. *Moral Panics and the Media*. Buckingham: Open University Press.

Emirbayer, Mustafa, and Ann Mische. 1998. 'What Is Agency?' *American Journal of Sociology* 103(4): 962–1023.

Falah, Ghazi-Walid. 2005. 'The Visual Representation of Muslim/Arab Women in Daily Newspapers in the United States.' In Ghazi-Walid Falah and Caroline Nagel, eds., *Geographies of Muslim Women: Gender, Religion, and Space*, 300–20. New York: Guildford Press.

Ferree, Myra Marx. 2003. 'Resonance and Radicalism: Feminist Framing in the Abortion Debates of the United States and Germany.' *American Journal of Sociology* 109(2): 301–44.

Fournier, Pascale, and Gökçe Yurdakul. 2006. 'Unveiling Distribution: Muslim Women with Headscarves in France and Germany.' In Y. Michal Bodemann and Gökçe Yurdakul, eds., *Migration, Citizenship, Ethnos*,167–84. New York: Palgrave Macmillan.

Killian, Caitlin. 2003. 'The Other Side of the Veil: North African Women in France Respond to the Headscarf Affair.' *Gender and Society* 17(4): 567–90.

Kogacioglu, Dicle. 2004. 'The Tradition Effect: Framing Honor Crimes in Turkey.' *Differences: A Journal of Feminist Cultural Studies* 15(2): 118–52.

Korteweg, Anna C. 2006. 'The Murder of Theo Van Gogh: Gender, Religion and the Struggle over Immigrant Integration in the Netherlands.' In Y. Michal Bodemann and Gökçe Yurdakul, eds., *Migration, Citizenship, Ethnos*,147–66. New York: Palgrave Macmillan.

Korteweg, Anna, and Gökçe Yurdakul. 2009. 'Islam, Gender, and Immigrant Integration: Boundary Drawing in Discourses on Honour Killing in the Netherlands and Germany.' *Ethnic and Racial Studies* 32(2): 218–38.

– 2010. 'Religion, Culture and the Politicization of Honour-Related Violence: A Critical Analysis of Media and Policy Debate in Western Europe and North America.' United Nations Research Institute for Social Development project on *Religion, Politics and Gender Equality*. Acessed 24 Jan. 2011. www.unrisd.org.

Mack, Phyllis. 2003. 'Religion, Feminism, and the Problem of Agency: Reflections on Eighteenth-Century Quakerism.' *Signs* 29(1): 149–77.

MacLeod, Arlene Elowe. 1992. 'Hegemonic Relations and Gender Resistance: The New Veiling as Accommodating Protest in Cairo.' *Signs* 17(3): 533–57.

McCarthy, John D., Clark McPhail, and Jackie Smith. 1996. 'Images of Protest: Dimensions of Selection Bias in Media Coverage of Washington Demonstrations, 1982 and 1991.' *American Sociological Review* 61(June): 478–99.

McNay, Lois. 2000. *Gender and Agency: Reconfiguring the Subject in Feminist and Social Theory.* Cambridge: Polity Press.

Mahmood, Saba. 2001. 'Feminist Theory, Embodiment, and the Docile Agent: Some Reflections on the Egyptian Islamic Revival.' *Cultural Anthropology* 16(2): 202–36.

– 2005. *Politics of Piety: The Islamic Revival and the Feminist Subject.* Princeton: Princeton University Press.

Mihelich, John, and Debbie Storrs. 2003. 'Higher Education and the Negotiated Process of Hegemony: Embedded Resistance among Mormon Women.' *Gender and Society* 17(3): 404–22.

Mohanty, Chandra Talpade. 2003. '"Under Western Eyes" Revisited: Feminist Solidarity through Anticapitalist Struggles.' In *Feminism without Borders: Decolonizing Theory, Practicing Solidarity.* Durham: Duke University Press.

Okin, Susan Moller. 1999. 'Is Multiculturalism Bad for Women?' In Joshua Cohen, Matthew Howard, and Martha C. Nussbaum, eds., *Is Multiculturalism Bad for Women?*, 9–24. Princeton: Princeton University Press.

Ortner, Sherri. 1996. *Making Gender: The Politics and Erotics of Culture.* Boston: Beacon Press.

– 2001. 'Specifying Agency: The Comaroffs and their Critics.' *Interventions* 3(1): 76–84.

Razack, Sherene. 2004. 'Imperilled Muslim Women, Dangerous Muslim Men, and Civilized Europeans: Legal and Social Responses to Forced Marriages.' *Feminist Legal Studies* 12: 129–74.

– 2007. 'The "Sharia Law Debate" in Ontario: The Modernity/Premodernity Distinction in Legal Efforts to Protect Women from Culture.' *Feminist Legal Studies* 15: 3–32.

Smith, Jackie, John. D. McCarthy, Clark McPhail, B. Augustyn. 2001. 'From Protest to Agenda Building: Description Bias in Media Coverage of Protest Events in Washington, D.C.' *Social Forces* 79(4): 1397–1423.

Spector, Malcom, and John I. Kitsuse. 1977. *Constructing Social Problems.* Menlo Park: Cummings.

Tripp, Aili Mari. 2006. 'Challenges in Transnational Feminist Mobilization.' In Myra Marx Ferree and Aili Mari Tripp, eds., *Global Feminism: Transnational Women's Activism, Organizing, and Human Rights,* 51–75. New York: New York University Press.

PART SIX

Managing Religion in the Canadian State

11 Managing the Mosaic: The Work of Form in 'Dispute Resolution in Family Law: Protecting Choice, Promoting Inclusion'

ALEXANDRA BROWN

Responding to intense public debate sweeping the province in the summer of 2004, Premier Dalton McGuinty requested an investigation into the issue of private dispute arbitration in Ontario. The resulting report, assembled by former Attorney General Marion Boyd and entitled *Dispute Resolution in Family Law: Protecting Choice, Promoting Inclusion* (the Boyd Report) recommended the continued allowance of private arbitration. This chapter analyses Boyd's report in its guise as the government's balanced response to the inevitable conflicts between the fragments of the Canadian mosaic, and asks what the document 'is' and what it 'does' as a product of a state-commissioned review.[1] Textual analysis suggests that the report functions to make and maintain the legitimizing claims of the Canadian state.

Focusing on this report, I interpret the document's formal and visual properties with respect to its social context. Employing cultural analysis to pay sustained attention to the object itself, I look 'to issues of cultural relevance ... to articulate how the object contributes to social debates' (Bal 2002, 9). I interpret the report as a participant in the debate and in the broader context of the Canadian state and its policy of official multiculturalism.[2]

My analysis suggests that the report, as a product of a government commission, 'does' the work of a Canadian state legitimized through official multiculturalism. I draw on Himani Bannerji's (2000) assertion that the Canadian state claims legitimacy to rule by casting itself as a transcendent agent managing contrasting and varied multicultures.[3] I identify three features through which the report reveals and participates in state legitimation: the report's shifting target audience, which obscures its work instructing the public on behalf of the state; its origin narrative, which conveys an image of the state as a transcendent agent and denies any complicity initiating the conflict; and its stylistic and visual structure as a mosaic, which creates an authoritative role for the state arranging and managing a series of contrasting fragments. I conclude with consideration of the provincial government's eventual rejection of the Boyd Report and suggest that the decision both enabled the report's work instructing the public and asserted government authority over the review, replicating the mosaic form and subverting the document to another fragment in the multicultural mosaic.

Textual Analysis and Social Context: A Note on Method

An approach privileging cultural objects, including reports, seeks 'to keep together what only scholars would separate: "form" (whatever that may mean), "content," and "context;" issues that go by the names of cultural, social, or political' (Bal 2002, 289). As sites for the production and communication of meaning, texts both indicate and execute the relations of power in which they are formed.[4] As demonstrated by the likes of Michel Foucault (1972) and Edward Said (1978), literary analysis of the form and style of texts can reveal the power dynamics at play in the context of their production. In affirming the inseparability of form and content, a cultural analysis approach demands interpretation of an object through close reading. To this end, this chapter provides textual analysis of the Boyd Report, addressing the document's formal features. This approach brings tools of literary analysis to bear on the report, addressing the need for a 'qualified return to the practice of "close reading"' (Bal 2002, 10). Comprehensive textual analysis, in addition to attending to the report's style, also addresses its materiality and visual appearance as an object, including its page layout and composition.

Employing textual analysis as a 'form of attention' to this cultural object does not suggest that the report is independent from the context of its production and reception (Bal 2002, 289). Objects are 'always-already engaged, as interlocutors, within the larger culture from which they have emerged' (9) and coming to terms with the report as a cultural object involves addressing the 'inseparability of ideology, politics, and aesthetics' (269). In addressing the report as the product of a government-commissioned review, I frame it as a participant within a Canadian state, therein combining textual analysis of the report's formal and visual features with a consideration of its work in the context of the state and its multiculturalist ideology.

The Report: Defining 'Dispute Resolution in Family Law'

Approaching the report as a cultural object first involves paying close attention to what it is and where it comes from. In the most straightforward terms, the Boyd Report is the product of a review conducted by former Attorney General Marion Boyd in the summer of 2004. Commissioned by the Ontario premier, the review was to 'provide advice and recommendations to the Attorney General and the Minister Responsible for Women's Issues about the use of private arbitration to resolve family and inheritance cases ... [including] consideration of religious based arbitrations' (Boyd 2004, 144). Marion Boyd was asked to consult with 'concerned Ontarians' and to provide a recommendation regarding private arbitration based on these consultations (5).

Nearly fifty organizations participated in the review, including women's organizations representing the interests of immigrants and domestic violence, religious representatives from the Muslim, Jewish, and Christian communities, lawyers and legal organizations, and private individuals (Boyd 2004, 5). These consultations, as well as 'countless' letters and submissions from both organizations and individuals provide the material from which the review (re)presents the opinions of concerned Ontarians regarding private arbitration.

'Dispute Resolution in Family Law' is the product of this review. The document is most widely accessible as a .pdf image, which maintains the appearance of the report as a series of numbered pages adhering to the conventions of margin and layout of a paper document. Prefaced with the covering letter that accompanied its submission to the government, the report (and its digital representation) is 191 pages in length and includes detailed appendices, a list of abbreviations, and a bibliography. In the first seven of its eight sections, the report summarizes the review's findings alongside an overview of government legislation and policy including the Arbitration Act, the Family Law Act, and the Canadian Charter of Rights and Freedoms in its reference to religious freedom and multiculturalism. In its final chapter the report presents the review's conclusion that private dispute resolution should be permitted to continue in Ontario, although adjusted on the basis of forty-six recommended safeguards.

Boyd presented the report to the provincial ministers in December 2004. Its recommendation for continued use of private arbitration met an escalation of the public debate. The report did not quell fears. In the midst of continued provincial, national, and international commotion over alternative dispute resolution, Premier Dalton McGuinty announced in September 2005 that private arbitration would no longer be permitted in the province, thus acting against the recommendations of the review he had commissioned.

Context: The Boyd Report in the State

Any cultural object or articulation may carry multiple meanings and be subject to various interpretations depending on its context. This analysis is contextualized within the Canadian state responsible for its production.[5] Although dismissed by the provincial government, I identify the report as a product of the Canadian 'state.' For the purposes of this analysis, I consider the state in its most multifaceted and flexible form, as that apparatus claiming political authority over the imagined community of the nation (Anderson 1991) as a ruling institution, a system of power seeking to maintain its own domination, through ideology or otherwise. As Bannerji (2000) elucidates, the Canadian state in this widest sense might be understood to perpetuate itself through the creation of difference in the form of multiculturalism. Inspired by the insights of Louis Althusser (1971) into the mechanics of state ideology, in Bannerji's formulation multiculturalism functions to uphold the ideological apparatus of the state by constructing and ascribing particular political subjectivities on its citizens (2000, 6). In its narrow sense the government, here the province of Ontario and its constituent representatives, parties, and organizations, constitutes the tangible, superficial dimension of the more abstract generalized state.

The Boyd Report provides a particularly fruitful site in which to discern the workings of ideology at the broadest level of the state. The report participates in a genre that selects, interprets, and apparently objectively presents a body of data in authoritative form.[6] The report is not the statement of an official government representative such as Premier McGuinty or Minister Pupatello and Attorney General Bryant, who were most closely involved in commissioning it, nor is it an act of official legislation or policy. Nonetheless, in the sense that the review process and report were the primary means through which the Ontario government sought to engage and address the public with respect to the issue of private arbitration, they can be understood to be both produced by and acting for the state. As my analysis demonstrates, it is the claims of this abstract authority to legitimate political rule which are shored up by the images of the state contained in the report.[7]

The report itself illustrates (and exploits) this complicated relationship between state and government, explicitly addressing itself to the premier and ministers in an advisory capacity and therein positioning itself outside of the official government and its representatives. Yet, while the report appears to speak on behalf of members of the public, the opinions of affected communities must be considered in light of their solicitation, reception, selection, and transmission through the state's review (Boyd 2004, 5). As textual analysis of the resulting report demonstrates, it is precisely from this ambiguous position that the report disguises its work on behalf of the state.

My theorization of the Canadian state in this respect is undergirded by Bannerji (2000) and Sunera Thobani's (2007) critiques of multiculturalism. They suggest that the Canadian state claims and maintains legitimacy by presenting itself to the public as the agent creating 'unity in diversity' from a fragmented population, carefully balancing a series of reified multicultures under the skilful management of a transcendent and neutral state institution. In this sense, the Canadian state relies on discourses of pluralism and diversity for its legitimation (Bannerji 2000, 97). By displaying difference in this allegedly balanced and managed form, Canada's diversity discourse acknowledges and actively constructs difference within the public, positioning itself as the necessary agent for its resolution. An official policy of multiculturalism promotes this 'communalizing power' of the state (Thobani 2007, 149), and both depoliticizes differences of class and gender as the problems of essentialized and discrete multicultures (Bannerji 2000, 34). This policy also positions the state as the agent resolving but never causing conflicts among them (74).

In Canada 'multiculturalism' maintains multiple meanings extending far beyond a simple description of an ethnically diverse population. Here I identify three. First, at a popular level, multiculturalism is a social value that signals a national tradition of respect for pluralism and diversity. This version is often juxtaposed to an American model of assimilation as a key aspect of imagined Canadian identity (Mackey 1995, 408; Li 2003, 149; Bramadat and Seljak 2005, 10). Second, what Bramadat and Seljak identify as a 'philosophical tradition' of multiculturalism provides a means for resisting systems of power and a basis for formulating innovative new models of citizenship and belonging (2005, 10). It is in this capacity that Canada has gained international recognition for theorizing multiculturalism as the solution to the global problem of how to live together with differences.[8]

Finally, Canada is somewhat unusual in that its multiculturalism also manifests in the official policy of the federal government, formulated by Pierre Trudeau's Liberal government in 1971 and passed into law with the Canadian Multiculturalism Act of 1988. This official variant of multiculturalism 'from above,' on which this analysis focuses, can be distinguished from forms of popular multiculturalism observable in other countries (Bannerji 2000, 5). As more than the rhetoric espoused by an intellectual elite, multiculturalism as a state-initiated enterprise in Canada contains a 'legal and a governing apparatus consisting of legislation and official policies with appropriate administrative bureaus' (16).

Official multiculturalism can become the means through which the state claims as its foundational metaphor a harmonious mosaic of diverse immigrant and cultural groups whose interests and differences it manages (Thobani 2007, 144, 150).[9] The language of diversity and image of a cultural mosaic characterizing official multiculturalism play a crucial role in its legitimation because of its apparently neutral, descriptive quality. The neutral appearance of the language of diversity and multiculturalism masks its legitimizing role and its complicity in exercises of power and subject formation enacted in multiculturalism 'from above.'

Bannerji (2000) locates the emergence of Canadian multicultural ideology in the substantial immigration from the third world beginning in the 1960s and the subsequent heterogenization of the population. At the same moment, the state faced claims from aboriginal communities for self-determination and the challenge of negotiating a bicultural and bilingual nation. A discourse of diversity emerged as an 'ideological coping mechanism' through which the state could contain and manage heterogeneity (43).[10] Eventually, the state came to legitimate itself through an official discourse of multiculturalism. While such a negotiation of heterogeneity avoided the pitfalls of a purely assimilative program, multiculturalist ideology is, as Bannerji's analysis demonstrates, far from neutral. Distinguishing this form of elite multiculturalism which emerges as a mechanism for coping with heterogeneity, Bannerji targets her critique at a multiculturalism that is not the product of demands from a diverse ethnic population but the outcome of a state aiming to placate discontented white Canadians (44).

Each of these manifestations of multiculturalism played a role in the 2003–2005 debate over private dispute arbitration, and although the debate concerned the claims of religious communities to private arbitration, actors on both sides of the issue, as well as the media and the government, framed the issue in terms of multiculturalism. Proponents of arbitration drew on multiculturalism to support its lobby for faith-based arbitration (Boyd 2004, 72), while opponents of arbitration emphasized the dangers of an excessive multiculturalism overshadowing individual rights, particularly those of women (91). Media coverage and public discourse returned repeatedly to analysis of the debate as a multicultural issue, and the report notes both the importance of multiculturalism to its participants and analyses the validity of private arbitration in light of official government policy (89–94). Audrey Macklin's chapter in this volume further suggests that multiculturalism functioned as the debate's 'normative driver,' providing the primary language for the negotiation and representation of the private arbitration debate (see Macklin, in this volume).

Multiculturalism, then, emerged as a key category in the private dispute resolution debate. Bannerji's formulation of the Canadian state as legitimated through multicultural ideology is a particularly appropriate formulation for contextualizing the Boyd Report. In official multiculturalism, the state (re)presents itself as the objective and transcendent agent which creates unity from a series of reified fragments. It claims legitimacy to manage these conflicting differences, resolving (and never instigating) conflicts among them. I now turn to a consideration of the ways that the report's formal properties both reveal and enable its work.

Legitimizing the State

Having defined the report and its context, the remainder of this chapter explores the relationship between them, considering the ways that the report's form both reveals and enables its work on behalf of the state. Textual analysis identifies three features through which the report instructs the public on multicultural ideology: (1) In shifting its tone and language, the report obscures its intended audience, appearing to address the state while functioning to instruct and inform the public; (2) the narrative structure and content of the report's opening 'origin account' provide a normative vision of the state in which the state appears as the ultimate agent of resolution in questions of cultural difference and obscures its complicity in their production; (3) the report's visual and stylistic structure as a mosaic composed of diverse voices articulates a vision of the Canadian nation as a series of mutually exclusive components harmoniously arranged and managed by the state. In this feature the connection between the report's formal (re)presentation of the Canadian state and its legitimation in multicultural ideology is made explicit. The cumulative effect of these three formal features is to create and instruct the public in an image of the state as the objective agent resolving differences among a series of reified multicultural fragments.

Audience

By explicitly recognizing the government as its stated audience, the report appears to address the state and to (re)present the views of the public participating in the review. But the report's stylistic features – including its marked inconsistency in tone and language – belie its state origins and its work to instruct a public audience. In fact, through its representation of the arbitration debate, review submissions, Canadian law and policy, and government recommendations, the report instructs the Canadian public in an authoritative and normative vision of the state. This masked didactic function of the report is apparent when contrasting the letter of introduction and official recommendations (Boyd 2004, 133–42), and the chapters summarizing the report's findings (29–68).

The report's opening letter and concluding recommendations explicitly address a state audience and employ official, formal language and tone (Boyd 2004, 133–42). Here the report presents itself as an external mediator conveying public opinion to the Canadian government, emphasizing its mandate to 'transmit' the opinions of Ontarians regarding faith-based arbitration to the government. The report opens with a formal covering letter and the salutation, 'Dear Attorney General and Minister Responsible for Women's Issues.' This explicit statement of the report's audience identifies the recipients using their government titles and omits their personal names and identities, a device that emphasizes their capacity as representatives of the government.

The report's final recommendations also appear directed towards the government audience, as signalled in its style associated with official state or legal communication, and opposed to informal discourse. Structured as a list of forty-six recommendations in numbered sequence, these pages parallel official government and policy documents (Boyd 2004, 133–42). The language in this section is considerably more formal, employing elevated vocabulary, legal terms, and complex sentence structure. The recommendations frequently make reference to particular sections of the Family Law Act and Arbitration Act, assuming the reader's familiarity with the sections at issue. Finally, the report employs third-person exposition in referring to the practices of the review in summarizing its findings, avoiding a more familiar first-person narrative voice. A representative point within recommendation 12 reads: 'An explicit statement that s.56 of the Family Law Act applies to the agreement and cannot be waived and therefore a party can apply to set the agreement aside for additional reasons including if it is not in the best interest of any children affected by the agreement, there was not full and frank financial disclosure, or a party did not understand the nature or consequences of the agreement' (Boyd 2004, 135).

In sum, the introductory letter and recommendations, which frame the body of the report, appear to fulfil its mandate to (re)present the opinions of review participants to the commissioning provincial government.

While these framing pages appear to address the government, the tone and language in the remainder of the report indicate a different intended audience. The stylistic inconsistency between the report's framing pages and its primary content suggest that rather than communicating the voices of review participants to the government, the document in fact addresses (and indeed, instructs) the public on behalf of the state. This function is particularly evident in the sections that review legislative and legal procedures, and outline provincial legislation, including the Arbitration Act (in Section 1) and the Family Law Act (in Section 2), the national Charter of Rights and Freedoms (Section 5), and international models for citizenship from France, Germany, and the United Kingdom (Boyd 2004, 80–4).

While Boyd's mandate requests that the report take a form suitable for public release (2004, 144), the language and tone of the document do more than simply ensure accessibility for a public audience. The informal, personal, and pedagogical tone is underscored by the use of colloquial language and the repetitive first-person narrative form, which positions Boyd as the narrator of the document. The report's friendly but didactic tone enables it to educate the (presumed mis- or uninformed) audience regarding complex government policies and esoteric legal codes, not to mention unfamiliar religious practices. For instance, the overview of arbitration practices opens by positioning Boyd in an instructive narrative role: 'The following section of my report provides an overview of the Arbitration Act' (9), and proceeds to provide an outline of the legal practice of arbitration in the simplest of terms: 'People who live together in any kind of society inevitably find themselves in disputes with other people: with family, friends, neighbours, employers, businesses or governments. They also find a wide range of methods of dealing with these disputes ... They may resolve them directly between parties, by informal discussion or by formal negotiation or by arbitrary measures, like flipping a coin' (9). Thus, the language and tone comprising the majority of the report suggest that the intended audience is in fact the general public whose voices it appears to represent.

The audience in these portions of the report remains unspecified as the report surreptitiously instructs the public in normative understandings of state law, policy, and authority. In a telling passage Boyd explains that, 'because it was clear ... that the general public know less about Muslim religious laws than about Jewish or Christian religious laws, I am going to try to provide a bit more information about Muslim religious laws than I did for the other forms'(2004, 41). This statement gives way to a summary of 'Islamic law' that reads as objective description but, as Anver Emon details, conveys a particular and normative view of the tradition as inflexible and of Sharia as an immutable code of religious rules (2006, 3; see also Emon's chapter in this volume). The report implies that it is compelled by a dearth of understanding among the public to provide an account of Islamic law. Yet, the intended audience for such instruction remains obscure: while the mandate and explicit address of the report would direct the explanation to the state, the friendly, informal tone of address suggests that it is intended for the public. The inconsistency illustrated by this example is notable throughout the document.

This variation in tone and address within the report, then, achieves a style that allows the report to address the public while simultaneously masking its purpose as an instructional instrument. Bannerji considers how multicultural ideology functions to uphold the state as an ideological apparatus that constructs and ascribes particular political subjectivities (Bannjerji 2000, 6).[11] The ideology not only produces differences within the Canadian nation but masks this creation as a relation of power, obscuring the means through which differences are produced and denying complicity in the state's ideologies of ruling (102). The report similarly masks its function in representing and upholding the state even while instructing the public. Further textual analysis considers the 'content' of this surreptitious instruction, a (re)presentation of the state as the agent resolving and managing (yet, never complicit in) the struggles of a multicultural nation.

Origin Story

The state presents itself to the public as the primary protagonist that resolves, but is not responsible for causing, clashes among constituent multicultural elements. This image of the state is contained in an origin narrative at the beginning of the report, which traces the emergence of the debate over faith-based arbitration, the review, and the report itself. The image of the state as resolution but never cause of the controversy emerges in the stylistic devices of the origin account, including its use of narrative, plot, and characterization. Placed at the outset of the report (Boyd 2004, 3–6), this account provides background information, contextualizes the emergence of the report, and introduces the reader to the debate. It frames the report as the culmination of a chain of events resulting from an initial conflict. This series of events reads in the report as a plot, initiated by a single action, advanced by a tension between several characters, and ultimately resolved by the commission and the document's publication. As this section demonstrates, through this origin narrative the report forecloses alternate readings of the arbitration debate and maintains the legitimizing discourses of the state.

The plot commences with an account of the initial incident triggering the arbitration debate: the IICJ's announcement in 2003 that it would begin conducting arbitrations in Ontario according to Islamic personal law (Boyd 2004, 3). Rather than considering the debate in terms of a longer history of negotiation over private arbitration, the report frames the IICJ's announcements as the cause of action and commencement of the plot. In this respect, although subsequent paragraphs provide a description of the use of the Arbitration Act prior to the IICJ's announcement, this narrative addresses it only as a matter of secondary background and thus forecloses a possible reading of the debate as the eventual but inevitable outcome of government policy in the form of the Arbitration Act.

The plot moves forward with IICJ President Syed Mumtaz Ali's suggestion 'that the government had given some form of special permission to the IICJ to undertake its project' (Boyd 2004, 3). These 'persistent myths' were disseminated through the public press and electronic media into the 'public consciousness,' raising 'acute alarm' and 'intense fear' 'throughout Ontario and Canada' (3–4). Here, the conflict escalates and the plot progresses due to action by the IICJ, in the form of inaccurate claims made in the public sphere and their subsequent misrepresentation by the media. The IICJ is the driving factor in this progression, juxtaposed with the passive figure of the government. In these initial phases the state appears as the subject of debate but does not actively participate in the emergence of the controversy. In addition to releasing the government from responsibility in the emergence of the arbitration debate, identifying the IICJ's announcements as the initial cause absolves it from blame in the escalation of public controversy.[12]

The origin story continues as civil society organizations, alarmed and misinformed by inaccurate media reports, bring the issue to the attention of the provincial government. Again, the report stresses the innocence of the state (here in its tangible form as the provincial government) in the events immediately surrounding the initiation of the conflict, noting that provincial officials initially felt that there was 'no clear role for government to intervene' (Boyd 2004, 4). However, increasingly strong concerns amongst the public 'about the implications of using the Arbitration Act for family law and inheritance matters at all, and in particular, allowing the principles of religious laws to prevail in these arbitrations' spurred government action (5). In this origin story it is only once the conflict emerges into full-blown international public controversy that the government moves from the subject of controversy to a key character negotiating its resolution. According to the narrative, the government (re)acts to the demands of a concerned Ontarian public with a formal request from the premier to the attorney general and minister responsible for Women's Issues for advice. 'Soon afterward,' Boyd writes, now introducing herself into the narrative in first person form, 'the Ministers sought my assistance in speaking to affected communities' (5). The resulting report, she explains, represents her 'best efforts' to address the arbitration issue and do justice to the concerns and suggestions of respondents (6). The origin story concludes with this comment on the creation of the report, in which the central conflict is presumed to have been resolved through the process of the review and its recommendations in the report, to be presented in the pages that follow.

Two key characters figure in this origin story. The Boyd Report immediately establishes the first, the IICJ, through the figure of President Mumtaz Ali, 'a retired Ontario lawyer determined to ensure that Islamic principles of family and inheritance law could be used to resolve disputes within the Muslim community in Canada' (2004, 3). Personalizing the IICJ in Mumtaz Ali reinforces the importance of the organization as a central character in the origin narrative. Although other characters act throughout the story (e.g., lawyer Phil Epstein, organizations such as the National Association of Women and the Law, and the nebulous figure of 'the media'), they are not assigned the same function as a synecdoche linking the desires and actions of a representative individual with the policy and action of a social movement or organization.

The second personalized character addressed in the narrative is Boyd, reflecting the review and the commissioning government. Of note, the government is introduced relatively late in the plot's timeline. In this narrative, the conflict and key players have already developed when the government, in the form of the premier, the ministers to whom he turns for advice, and by extension Boyd and her review, enter the scene. The review and the government are cast as agents functioning to resolve an escalating, progressing conflict. The narrative thus occludes alternate characterizations that hold the government, given its role creating the Arbitration Act and official multicultural discourse, responsible for that conflict. In this sense the report illustrates what Bannerji identifies as the Canadian state's claim to 'rise above all partisan interests and [function] as an arbitrator between different cultural groups. This is the moral high ground, the political instrument with which the state maintains the hegemony of an anglo-Canada' (2000, 74). Through this claim the state positions itself as the transcendent agent which resolves but does not participate in conflicts within the multicultural nation (74).

In sum, the report places the beginning of the controversy squarely with the announcements of the IICJ as opposed to the creation of the Arbitration Act in 1991 or even the establishment of official multicultural policy in 1971, and describes the debate as a conflict between the IICJ and the Ontarian public. This characterization distances the state from involvement in the conflict by directly removing the government and its agents from participation in the events leading up to and the initial stages of the debate, and represents the state as transcendent over the skirmishes between the constituent groups of a multicultural nation. The state then appears to act from this transcendent 'moral high ground' above participating characters. Furthermore, according to the narrative, once pressed by the public, and after the plot has advanced to a state of crisis, the state acts to manage and ultimately resolve the conflict, a (re)presentation that casts the intervention of the state as necessary and legitimate act of management as opposed to a hegemonic exercise. The state is thus excused from its complicity in the conflict in a manner that makes its role in its resolution appear admirable, emphasizing how unity is crafted from diversity in the Canadian state (Bannerji

2000, 74). In its origin narrative, then, the report (re)presents the state in a manner that denies its complicity in creating and maintaining conflict while also presenting it as the most appropriate agent for the management and resolution of such conflict. This image of the multicultural managing state also underlies the report's most evident formal property: its structure as a mosaic.

Mosaic Structure

Through its form as a visual and textual mosaic the report appears as a model of diversity, reflecting the popular metaphor for Canadian multiculturalism as a 'mosaic.' In artistic terms, within a mosaic each fragment maintains its own boundary, form, and content without necessarily resembling or referring to other constituent elements. In the composition of these elements a pattern emerges that is both greater than and dependent on the individual fragments. The report displays two key features that render the mosaic metaphor visually effective: difference and balance. The image created by a mosaic is dependent on variations in colour, shape, and texture between the constituent elements; without such contrast, no image could be produced. Furthermore, the constituent elements of a mosaic must balance one another, arranged in a manner which suggests harmony between these elements so that each contributes to the whole.

These elements of an effective mosaic emerge in the report's form both visually and stylistically. The report portrays a variety of public opinions on the issue of private arbitration in a manner that both depends on their differences and presents them as balanced with one another and with the existing legislation and policy of the state. The stylistic reference to a mosaic applies not only to the report document but also to the structure of the wider review, whose creation, activity, and ultimate rejection by the official government can be understood as a performative mosaic in which it received, arranged, and (re)presented public opinions into a comprehensive whole.

The mosaic appearance of the report document is most prevalent and relevant in its lengthy summary of review findings (Boyd 2004, 29–69). The section is both a fragment in the larger report that balances the public opinion against existing legal standards and government legislation, and is itself a mosaic constituted by a series of fragmented public views on arbitration. Claiming to summarize diverse opinions and concerns expressed during the review and organize them into a set of common themes and concerns (7), this section is primarily comprised of quotations from submissions to the review interspersed with commentary from Boyd. The commentary between and the framing of these quotations introduces the contributors, provides a context for their comments, and summarizes their viewpoints. The pages in this section present indented quotations of various lengths interspersed with one or two lines of commentary, a layout producing the visual effect of a mosaic (for a representative example, see Boyd 2004, 45). The quotations occupy less page width but more space, given their comparative length, and form the individual fragments of the mosaic. The commentary between the various excerpts appears to frame them and links each indented quotation to what precedes and follows it, as well as distinguishing one from another within the frame of the page. The layout and appearance of the section resemble a mosaic.

The differing and juxtaposed styles of the quoted excerpts from review contributions also work to portray the constituent fragments of the report's mosaic in terms of contrast and difference. Each excerpt maintains its distinctive tone and style, a function of printing responses to the review as they were submitted, without stylistic standardization or error correction. Boyd states in the introduction that she has done so to give respondents a recognizable voice (2004, 8). Thus, there is a juxtaposition emphasizing differences between the various fragments and drawing attention to the mosaic structure.

Yet, while employing contrast to emphasize the differences between its constituent fragments, the report's mosaic structure creates an overall impression of balance. Thus, rather than suggesting disjunction and disorganization, stylistic differences among the constituent elements in the report are ultimately presented as a cohesive montage, achieved through their balanced arrangement. The balance among constitutive elements is visually apparent in the spaces allotted to excerpts from contributors. While excerpts range in length, none exceeds a page, and most are from five to fifteen lines in length. This produces a visual effect in which no single quotation overtakes another.

The report furthers its display of balance by presenting the submissions of the wide array of contributors in the same format. Even though the contributions were carefully selected and edited for display, they appear as a presentation of equal, and equally authoritative, positions. The editing and commentary do not address factors such as the political prominence or influence one group may have compared to another, the number of individuals represented by a particular organization, or the relative authority with which they make factual claims. Outlining and analysing aspects of religious law, the report is as likely to cite the opinion contributed by an individual, a report conducted by a civil society organization, or a secondary scholarly source. Such visual balance suggests an analogous equality, as when a letter submitted by an individual citizen merits equal page space and legitimacy relative to full-length reports by civil society organizations. The balance recalls a (multicultural) mosaic in which each constituent element is equally significant in contributing to an overall meaning or image.

In stylistically emphasizing the difference and contrast between public contributions to the review, the report models Bannerji's (2000) assertion that the state displays (and even creates) forms of difference in multicultural ideology in order to depoliticize challenges to its legitimacy. Reifying the nation's constituent elements as inherently different and fragmented cultures, the state creates a display of diversity that 'distracts us from what actually happens to us in our raced and gendered class existence and culturalizes our politics. In other words, it depoliticizes us' (34). In recognizing difference the state simultaneously creates it and casts it as a straightforward issue of a plurality of cultures. Difference here is 'ideologically evoked ... [and] neutralized' (96). The report's mosaic structure, which emphasizes the contrasts between its constituent excerpts, can be understood to participate in this display of difference.

At the same time, in displaying these reified and diverse fragments in a balanced format, the report oppositionally positions the state as the agent responsible for arranging them into a comprehensive and meaningful form.[13] The state claims legitimacy as the 'artist' through which meaning and order are created from a disorienting array of irresolvable differences. Thus, despite the stylistic differences among the excerpts, they are all represented as meaningful contributors to a balanced whole, thanks to their skilful management by the state. The effect of this formal feature in legitimizing the state is thus similar to that of the origin story; it casts the state as the rightful arbiter of a series of component elements, justifying its right to rule as necessary for the arrangement of a multicultural nation into a cohesive and meaningful whole. The report's form as a mosaic arranging a fragmented public therefore participates in the galvanization of a state that crafts its own transcendence through emphasizing difference.

This textual analysis of 'Dispute Resolution in Family Law' charts the ways that this report's formal features reveal and enable its work within the context of the state. The report's inconsistencies in terms of address and audience serve to mask its work, didactically instructing the public in a particular understanding of the state. This understanding, as contained in the origin story, (re)presents the state as the legitimate power resolving the controversy over private arbitration while absolving it from any blame in its emergence. Further, the report engages the familiar metaphor of the Canadian mosaic, in this case stylistically and visually portraying a series of contrasting national fragments, skilfully arranged by the state to achieve an overall effect of balance. Through these features the report presents to the public an image of the state as the agent crafting meaningful unity from dizzying diversity. In transcending its constituent multicultural fragments, the state is depicted as responsible for the resolution but never the instigation of conflicts such as the private arbitration debate, ultimately claiming legitimacy as the agent responsible for arranging the fragments into a meaningful and balanced whole.

Epilogue: The Rejection of the Boyd Report

This chapter has considered the work that *Dispute Resolution in Family Law,* and specifically its form, 'does' within its state context. To close my analysis, I follow the report through its public release and its subsequent rejection by the Ontario government. I argue that despite its failure to have its recommendations met, the report ultimately succeeded in its legitimation of the multicultural state.

Following the December 2004 release of the review's findings in the form of a report, public controversy around the issue of private arbitration escalated both in Canada and abroad, increasing to the point of what Natasha Bakht identifies as 'moral panic' (2006, 67). Despite the recommendations contained in the report, which suggested that arbitration be allowed to continue with some qualifications, as depicted elsewhere in this volume, Premier Dalton McGuinty ultimately struck down the Arbitration Act and announced a new policy of 'one law for all Ontarians' (Ministry of the Attorney General 2005).

This announcement had two implications with respect to the report and its legitimating function. First, it served paradoxically to reinforce the work of the report in its public instruction. By dismissing the report's recommendation the government distanced itself from the state origins of the review, reinforcing the report's appearance as external to the state. In this sense the dismissal reinforces the report's work to obscure its origin and function by casting itself as external to the state, and enables the report's continued operation to (re)present the state, regardless of the acceptance or rejection of its recommendations.

Second, and more significantly, in rejecting the report the provincial government replicated the mosaic form of the report, recasting *Dispute Resolution and Family Law* as one of the contrasting fragments to be balanced by a legitimate and authoritative state (now also 'government') apparatus. Commentators have stressed that the premier's decision functioned primarily on an optical level, and that while it appeared to emphatically eradicate all forms of religious arbitration, the practical reality may be quite different (see Bakht 2006; Emon 2006; Farrow 2006; Cutting, MacFarlane, and Macklin, in this volume). While the government described the bill as proscribing legally enforceable religious decision making, the actual amendments are limited (Bakht 2006), thus creating few practical changes with respect to those individuals it claims to protect (Emon 2006, 24: Farrow 2006, 81; Kutty, in this volume). This gap between the amendment's appearance and its practical outcome suggests that it may have functioned more as a performance, portraying the government's rejection of religious arbitration, than a substantive alteration of provincial legal practice.

Understood as a performance, the government's rejection of the recommendations repeats the mosaic that characterizes the review and the report. Just as the report appeared to skilfully arrange a series of contrasting fragments into a meaningful whole, as the controversy escalated the provincial government had to acknowledge and assert authority over contrasting claims from numerous sites, including national and international media, civil society organizations, and private individuals. In rejecting the report's recommendations the government publicly asserted its authority over the review. The report, in this performative repetition of the mosaic form, became one more contrasting fragment to be balanced and managed by the provincial government. Following the Boyd Report through its public life (and death) then suggests that despite its failure to guarantee the continued practice of religiously based arbitration, its rejection by the provincial government reconfirms and recapitulates its work on behalf of the multicultural state.

NOTES

1 The imagination of Canada as a mosaic incorporating numerous distinct cultural groups coexisting alongside one another and maintaining indi-

vidual identity, yet contributing to a larger framework of national unity, was instantiated by John Gibbons in *The Canadian Mosaic* (1938). The metaphor has since remained an important and prominent aspect of Canadian national identity (see Porter 1965).

2 This interpretation brackets the question of authorial intent, emphasizing that 'it is not the artist or the author but the objects they make and "give" to the public domain that are the "speakers" in analytic discussion' (Bal 2002, 9). Thus, while recognizing Boyd's role as the report's author, my analysis is not to be taken as an attempt to determine, let alone to evaluate, her intent. I am concerned rather with the ways that the formal aspects of the report, irrespective of the intentions of its author, articulate and shape its work within the Canadian context.

3 As elaborated below, this understanding of the Canadian state draws the formulation of multiculturalism 'from above' as an ideological state apparatus that erases and occludes social relations of power and ruling while maintaining a status quo of domination (Bannerji 2000, 50).

4 Drawing from Stuart Hall's (1997) understanding of texts as material systems of representation through which cultural meanings are produced and circulated. Further, an approach to texts that considers their work as ideology is found in the work of discourse analysts such as Norman Fairclough (2003).

5 My interpretation joins considerable commentary exploring the report's role in both obscuring and negotiating salient tensions in the Canadian public, including the tension between individual and 'cultural' rights (Emon 2006), the maintenance of social cohesion alongside recognition of difference (Soroka, Johnson, and Banting 2005), and the privatization of justice (Farrow 2006) as 'boutique law' (Morris 2004). My purpose is not to suggest that one of these functions takes precedence – the report and commission operate at many levels simultaneously and many factors may be at play in a given context.

6 In this respect the report shares generic similarities to ethnography which interprets, translates, or reports the voices of 'informants.' These politics of anthropological (re)presentation in ethnographic writing have provided the impetus for considerable self-reflection in the discipline since the publication of Clifford and Marcus (1986).

7 While this analysis considers the work of the report on behalf of the Canadian state, it is important to keep in mind that this state does not exist in independence from the public over which it claims authority. Neither the state nor the government can be completely distinguished from the public and civil societies over which they rule; the civil servants, bureaucrats, and politicians whose daily work shapes and executes the work of

the state are equally members of the public. While I explore in detail
here one function of the report in its support for the state, this does not
occlude a recognition of the fuzzy boundaries of the state and the complexity of the processes through which it acts upon its citizens, nor an
acknowledgment of the considerable presence of resisting agents, as
Bannerji (2000) outlines in some detail for the case of multiculturalism
from below.

8 Focusing on the object itself, this analysis does not seek to interpret the
report as an example of the various models of multicultural citizenship
currently debated in the Canadian public sphere, or to evaluate its success
or failure in promoting such models. Rather, official multiculturalism
becomes an important factor in an analysis of the report as a cultural object
and in questioning what it does within the context of its production, that
is, in relation to the state. For examples of internationally renowned
Canadian intellectuals formulating models of multiculturalism, see
Kymlicka (1995) and Taylor (1994).

9 Scholarship in this line further draws on an anti-racist and/or feminist
perspective to critique elite multiculturalist discourse as a mask for systemic inequalities that structure society (and, indeed, often occur beyond
the bounds of the state). In an international context, see Gordon and
Newfield (1996) and Hage (2002). For a critique of Canadian multiculturalism as it manifests itself at the popular national level, see
Mackey (2002).

10 The Canadian state required this 'coping mechanism' to deal with several
challenges, including the implementation of a labour importation policy
meant to create a working class; the subsequent resistance of white
Canadians to such policy, and the need to contain the mobility drive of the
immigrants constituting that class (Bannerji 2000, 44). For detailed consideration of internal and external factors promoting the emergence of state
multiculturalism, see Bannerji (2000) and Thobani (2007).

11 Bannerji is concerned with the ways that multicultural ideology works to
produce political subjects, drawing from Althusser (1971). While influenced by Bannerji's understanding of the Canadian state and its legitimation through multicultural ideology, my interest in this chapter is with its
work (re)presenting a certain image of the state as opposed to the
construction of its political subjects.

12 As much can be said about the image of the IICJ contained in the report as
about the image of the Canadian state. This origin narrative presents the
IICJ as the instigator of public controversy regarding private arbitration
and characterizes it as the epitome of a reified multiculture. In doing so,

the report positions the IICJ as responsible for the controversy and also as the quintessential national fragment that can, and must, be managed by the ruling state. This chapter is concerned only with how this characterization shapes a particular image of the state.

13 At least one analysis of the arbitration debate makes an analogous claim that a continual emphasis on the religious and cultural aspects of the debate serves to present the state as secular and therefore neutral in its management of the conflict (Razack 2007).

REFERENCES

Althusser, Louis. 1971. *Lenin and Philosophy and Other Essays*. Translated by Ben Brewster. London: Verso.

Anderson, Benedict. 1991. *Imagined Communities: Reflections on the Origin and Spread of Nationalism*. London: Verso.

Bakht, Natasha. 2006. 'Were Muslim Barbarians Really Knocking on the Gates of Ontario? The Religious Arbitration Controversy – Another Perspective.' *Ottawa Law Review, 40th Anniversary Edition* 35 (Summer): 67–82.

Bal, Mieke. 2002. *Travelling Concepts in the Humanities: A Rough Guide*. Toronto: University of Toronto Press.

Bannerji, Himani. 2000. *The Dark Side of the Nation: Essays on Multiculturalism, Nationalism, and Gender*. Toronto: Canadian Scholars' Press.

Boyd, Marion. 2004. *Dispute Resolution in Family Law: Protecting Choice, Promoting Inclusion*. Ministry of the Attorney General. Accessed 20 Jan. 2011. http://www.attorneygeneral.jus.gov.on.ca/english/about/pubs/boyd/fullreport.pdf.

Bramadat, Paul, and David Seljak, eds. 2005. *Religion and Ethnicity in Canada*. Toronto: Pearson Longman.

Clifford, James, and George E. Marcus, eds. 1986. *Writing Culture: The Politics and Poetics of Ethnography*. Berkeley: University of California Press.

Emon, Anver. 2006. 'Islamic Law and the Canadian Mosaic.' *University of Toronto Legal Studies Series Research Paper No. 947149*. Toronto: University of Toronto Faculty of Law.

Fairclough, Norman. 2003. *Analysing Discourse: Textual Analysis for Social Research*. New York: Routledge.

Farrow, Trevor. 2006. 'Reframing the Sharia Arbitration Debate.' *Constitutional Forum* 15 (2): 79–86.

Foucault, Michel. 1972. *The Archaeology of Knowledge and the Discoures on Language*. New York: Pantheon.

Gibbons, John Murray. 1938. *The Canadian Mosaic: The Making of a Northern Nation*. Toronto: McClelland and Stewart.

Gordon, Avery, and Christopher Newfield, eds. 1996. *Mapping Multiculturalism*. Minneapolis: University of Minnesota Press.

Hage, Ghassan. 2002. *White Nation: Fantasies of White Supremacy in a Multicultural Society*. New York: Routledge.

Hall, Stuart, ed. 1997. *Representation: Cultural Representations and Signifying Practices*. London: Sage.

Kymlicka, Will. 1995. *Multicultural Citizenship: A Liberal Theory of Minority Rights*. Oxford: Clarendon Press.

Li, Peter. 2003. *Destination Canada: Immigration Debates and Issues*. Oxford: Oxford University Press.

Mackey, Eva. 2002. *The House of Difference*. Toronto: University of Toronto Press.

Ministry of the Attorney General. 2005. 'McGuinty Government Declares One Law for All Canadians – News Release.' Ontario: Ministry of the Attorney General. 15 Nov. Accessed 25 Nov. 2011. http://news.ontario.ca/archive/en/2005/11/15/McGuinty-Government-Declares-One-Law-For-All-Ontarians.html

Morris, Catherine. 2004. 'Religion, Law, Alternative Dispute Resolution and the Media: The Case of *Shari'a* in Canada.' Panel Presentation ADR Subsection, Canadian Bar Association, 17 Nov., Victoria, BC.

Porter, John. 1965. *The Vertical Mosaic: An Analysis of Social Class and Power in Canada*. Toronto: University of Toronto Press.

Razack, Sherene H. 2007. 'The "Sharia Law Debate" in Ontario: The Modernity/ Premodernity Distinction in Legal Efforts to Protect Women from Culture.' *Feminist Legal Studies* 15: 3–32.

Said, Edward. 1978. *Orientalism*. New York: Pantheon.

Soroka, Stewart, Richard Johnson, and Keith Banting. 2005. 'Ties that Bind? Social Cohesion and Diversity in Canada.' Paper Presented at The Art of the State III: Diversity and Canada's Future, 13–15 Oct., Montebello, Quebec.

Taylor, Charles. 1994. 'The Politics of Recognition.' In Amy Gutman, ed., *Multiculturalism and the Politics of Recognition*, 25–74. Princeton: Princeton University Press.

Thobani, Sunera. 2007. 'Multiculturalism and the Liberalizing Nation.' In *Exalted Subjects: Studies on the Making of Race and Nation in Canada*, 143–75. Toronto: University of Toronto Press.

12 Construing the Secular: Implications of the Ontario Sharia Debate

JENNIFER A. SELBY

This volume has examined the Ontario Sharia debate through a number of vantage points. Among others, contributors have considered the meanings and colonial histories of Sharia, how Sharia was positioned vis-à-vis Canadian multiculturalism and gender politics, and the way popular media negatively portrayed Islam and religiously observant Muslim women. In this chapter, I suggest that the debate also offers a useful lens through which to examine the parameters of contemporary Canadian secularism. Recall how in September 2005, in an effort to quell fears and restore 'normalcy,' provincial Premier Dalton McGuinty announced that faith-based arbitration in alternative dispute resolution would be outlawed in favour of 'one law for all Ontarians.' This 'one law' referred to rejecting the option of binding faith-based arbitration and substituting existing law with a secular-only model. This chapter examines the implications of this statement with reference to the debate that preceded the announcement and to a debate on private school funding that followed it.

As we have seen, from 2003 to 2005 the appropriateness of legally binding religiously based family law arbitration was called into question within the province of Ontario, within Canada, and around the world. Advocates on different sides watched and waited to see how the provincial government would manage religion (in particular, Islam) within public policy and the law[1] in the context of international pressures, a still-powerful ethic of multiculturalism, and rising costs and backlogs within the provincial court system. As a testing ground for questions of religion, tolerance, and secularism, the outcome was of interest to many outside of Ontario, particularly in Western Europe, where 'Sharia' is increasingly heard in discussions of Islamic-compliant banking and in concerns about the presence of so-called political Islam.

Canada, like a number of other nation states such as Britain and Norway, and unlike France or the United States, has no official legal separation of church and state. Historically, Ontario's (and Canada's) public policy has privileged its majority-Christian population, but its contemporary urban population is among the most religiously and ethnically diverse in the world, which leads to questions about the place of religious pluralism in public life.[2] McGuinty's concluding announcement put the Liberal government squarely on the side of a seemingly secularized understanding of a separation of church and state. My analysis of the debate, its outcomes, and a separate debate on religious school funding two years later highlights three undercurrents within expressions of secularity in Ontario: first, the partiality and Christian biases of so-called neutral secularism; second, the blurred distinctions between the private and public spheres; and third, a privileging of anti-institutional religion feminist politics. Separating these undercurrents enables a clearer articulation of the often-assumed meanings and positions of secularism. I suggest that such an approach will permit a more thoughtful treatment of religion, public policy, and their implications in the lives of ordinary Canadians.[3]

In the first section of this chapter, I argue that secularism in Ontario at the beginning of the twenty-first century is far from religiously neutral. Two instances exemplify this point and highlight a prevailing 'Christosecular' paradigm: first, the international outrage at the legal possibility of 'Sharia courts' when Orthodox Jews and other Christian groups had used the arbitration system without fanfare since 1991; and second, a later 2007 provincial debate on the public funding of private religious schools.[4] The term Christo-secular parallels French historian Jean Baubérot's characterization of *laïcité* (French secularism) in contemporary France as *catholaïcité* or catho-secularism (Baubérot 2003).[5] This compound word suggests that the separation of church and state is modeled on Christian theological notions of religion and, in the case of France, works best for French Catholics. Recent public discourse and governmental decisions in Ontario similarly privilege Christian versions of religion in the public sphere (for examples in Canada more generally, see Bramadat and Seljak 2008, Weinrib 2008, and Beaman 2008a and 2008b).[6]

In the second section, I point to how the debate reveals cleavages between conceptions of the private and public spheres in the Canadian secular imagination. While Canadian formulations of secularism are formally predicated on this separation, which holds that religious beliefs and practices should be private matters, the debate made clear their interconnectedness and the renewed emergence of religious claims in public politics. Here, with reference to José Casanova's (1994) claim for the 'de-privatization' of religious traditions in Western contexts, I argue that the debate's nebulous characterization of 'private' and 'public' signals a notable 'de-privatization' of religion. In an arguably 'post-secular' public political sphere (see Habermas 2008), the debate made evident that religious claims are manifest in the public sphere. Jürgen Habermas posits that a religion-free public sphere has never existed and that, despite privatization and individualization, in contemporary globalized Western contexts, religion remains relevant in the political arena. Habermas argues that religious groups, in particular churches and religious organizations, are 'increasingly assuming the role of "communities of interpretation" in the public arena of secular societies' (2008, 20). In my view, this nebulousness does not necessarily reflect an opening to religious discourse, but highlights a not yet fully articulated possibility of religion's legitimacy in the public sphere. There are limits, however, as depicted in the fear-laden characterizations of 'Sharia courts.'

In section three, I suggest that the Sharia debate also reveals the significance of women's rights in reinforcing secularism in the public sphere. As I have argued elsewhere (Selby 2012), notions of secularity are increasingly mobilized in the West as a way to secure liberal notions of women's rights. Implicit in this conception is that the protection of institutionalized religious traditions in the public sphere necessarily erodes the equal status of women. Recent affirmations of secularism in North America and Western Europe have emerged against the *hijab* and other forms of Muslim dress and female comportment perceived as reducing women's full civic participation (see MacMaster and Lewis 1998; Abu-Lughod 2002; Bowen 2007; Cesari 2010). The affirmation of secularity as the absence of religiosity in the public sphere therefore has a considerable negative impact on visibly Muslim women and their access to political lobby, particularly for women seeking to promote religiously informed positions. Following discussion of these three points – the lack of religious neutrality, the redefinition of private/public distinctions, and the relative silencing of Muslim women supporting faith-based arbitration – I conclude by considering the implications of these elements and formulating new ways to think critically about Canadian secularism 'on the ground' in Ontario.

Secularism's Partiality

The Sharia debate posed several questions concerning how secularism is defined and practised. In both theory and practice, secularism is tied to notions of religion. Significant historical factors have conditioned how secularism is expressed in relation to normative Christianity in particular.[7] To consider this suggestion, I begin with a theoretical and theological discussion of the term 'secularism,' seeking to highlight its multiple linkages to Christianity. I then briefly consider the family law arbitration debate before charting the post–'one law for all' period by analysing a religion and public policy issue that emerged in the province two years later. Despite McGuinty's claim for religious neutrality in 2005, secularism in Ontario following the Sharia debate maintains a Christo-secular bias in its application as evident in the 2007 'One School' debate.

More broadly, how has secularism been contemporarily configured in the framework of Western nation states? As several studies of modern-day secularism reveal, its meaning and application are far from uniform (see Bhargava 1998a and 1998b, Jakobsen and Pellegrini 2008, Levy and Modood 2009). These versions of secularism emerge in varying sociohistorical contexts. The term generally indicates the separation and removal of 'the religious' or the private spaces of morality from domains considered public or political (Walzer 1984, Casanova 1994, Weintraub 1997, Taylor 1998, Asad 2003). It can also refer to an official state political position of neutrality vis-à-vis religious beliefs and practices, or as an 'exit from religion,' which keeps religion as referent while situating it outside the shared political sphere (Gauchet 1985, 1998). The term is used to frame and coincide with other concepts, such as modernization, democratization (Walzer 1984, Baubérot 1998, Taylor 1998 and 2007) and nationhood (Rousseau 1994, Bellah 1970, Anderson 1991). In these associations, secularism is often trumpeted as 'modernity's fundamental identity' (Greenfeld 1996, 10–11). Deeming a person and/or space as 'secular' and another as 'religious' are thus not neutral ascriptions. There may be negative elements implicit in the designation of religiosity. For instance, Talal Asad points to a common assumption of theorists of secularism, that there is always an *unconscious* motive in religious acts (2003, 11).

Beyond this often negative reading of the religious, the category of secular remains imbued with Christian references. Etymological investigation reveals how the Latin term *saeculum* ('age' or 'period') was employed to delineate the era of profane human activity on earth between the Fall and the *Parousia* (the Second Coming of Christ; see Taylor 1998). The term thus served to distinguish between secular this-worldly time and sacred moments directly sanctioned by a Christian God.[8] The secular/religious separation was, arguably, most important for the vocation of the Christian Church, which held stakes in interpreting ultimate salvation. This intertwining of secularism and religion appears within Christian theological texts and Western philosophical political theory, as well. The two concepts – secularism and Christianity – are thus necessarily intertwined; one determines and mirrors the other. This link between secularism and Christianity explains why public manifestations of Islam are not so easily compartmentalized into private religiosity, in so far as the secularization of Christianity is privileged by this association in ways that other religious traditions are not.

Returning to contemporary Ontario, despite the province's claim for religiously neutral public policies, the characterization of Islam in the debate on family law arbitration provides a good example of the biased orientation of secularism in Canada. Jewish legally binding family law arbitration flew under the radar in Ontario for twelve years without notable public debate locally or internationally. In contrast, the announcement by the Islamic Institute of Civil Justice (IICJ) that they would set up arbitration services in 2003, as was their legal right, to conduct similar alternate dispute resolution (ADR) caused an international outcry. This bias could be termed 'Judeo-Christian.'[9] Of note in the debate, Islam was emphatically not associated with Christianity, and the implications of this dissimilarity are clear in the discrepancy between the way Jewish Beit Din could use faith-based ADR while the IICJ's announcement initiated such debate. This discrepancy offers evidence of the existence of a bias against expressions of Islam in law and in the public sphere (see also Zine, in this volume, and Zine 2001). Of course, the 2001 Census confirms that most Canadians are Christian, and Christianity has played an integral role in the development of Canadian society and culture (Bramadat 2005, 3). The social power and influence of the tradition in Ontario cannot be denied. Nevertheless, Christian-favouring factors within Canadian secularism – some as banal as days of rest and clothing-related restrictions – need dislodging if the state is to become neutral towards all peoples.

One might have the impression from this volume that the outcome of the Sharia debate ensured a newfound separation of religion and politics in public policy in the province. The 2007 'One School' controversy that followed the Sharia debate suggests a continuing lack of uniformity with regards to religious neutrality in Ontario. At issue in this later case was the continued public funding of private Catholic schools in Ontario; other private religious denominational schools do not receive public money. The province debated this question in October 2007 in the midst of provincial elections. Then-Conservative Party of Ontario leader John Tory focused his election platform on the public funding of private religious schools, suggesting that the province should extend its financial support of private Catholic schools to all other religious denominations, to include Muslims, Jews, and Hindus among others.[10] Public funding for private Catholic schools in Ontario was defended by the provincial Liberal party with reference to the Constitutional Act of 1867, in which Section 93 enshrined Catholic schools' rights before Confederation as both historic and exceptional (Sweet 1997, McLaren 2006, Jaimet 2007). Separate Roman Catholic publicly funded schools have thus existed since the nineteenth century. Catholic Quebec legislators insisted on their creation as a condition for their cooperation, first in the Union Parliament before Confederation and again before Quebec joined Canada.

This continued privileging of Catholic schools in the province has received sanction and has been ruled as contrary to international legal standards. In 1999 and 2005, the United Nations Human Rights Committee officially censured Ontario for violating equality rights by virtue of religious discrimination in the province's school system (One School System 2006). The current system may also contravene Charter provisions (Weinrib n.d.). However, unlike the debate on religiously based family law arbitration two years earlier, discussions on extending funding to non-Christian schools did not garner interest in the international press. No one appeared outside of Canadian embassies in London and Paris to protest that non-Christian children were not accorded the same rights as their Catholic counterparts.

The incumbent Premier Dalton McGuinty and his majority Liberal party, who were against the proposed change to publicly fund all religious schools, responded to John Tory's proposal noting that the province was a relatively cohesive society, primarily due to its publicly funded education system 'where we invite children of all backgrounds and faiths, economic circumstances to ... learn together' (in Greenberg

2007). In short, McGuinty relied on arguments which suggested that publicly funding Muslim, Sikh, or Hindu schools might challenge agreed-on democratic ideals and disintegrate (Christo-) 'secular' society. More generally, the Liberals responded with two arguments to counter full funding of all private religious schooling: the 'let sleeping dogs lie' approach, and that the proposal would be extremely costly. In addition, the issue did not resonate with many Ontario voters, who felt that the question of school funding was not an election issue and was best left alone. For instance, in a conversation about the 2007 debate, one of McGuinty's advisers conceded that while the premier acknowledged that the current system may be unfair, he knew he would not have won the election with such a contested issue. The adviser explained, 'McGuinty knew he couldn't touch that whole issue. It's like political suicide' (telephone interview, 6 July 2008). John Tory ultimately lost his seat, and subsequently, the leadership of the party; many suggest these losses were the result of his raising this issue.

Moreover, extending the current single-faith funding to multiple religions was not considered an option by the majority of politicians, given the projected cost for taxpayers. McGuinty claimed it would cost $400 million to use public funds to pay for religious schools for the 53,000 students attending Muslim, Jewish, Hindu, Sikh, and other faith-based schools. Of this total, there are approximately 6,000 Muslim students in twenty-five privately funded schools (Seljak 2005, 64). Parents who send their children to non-Catholic faith-based schools pay taxes to support the public system while paying additional fees for their faith-based education. While 53,000 students may not have been too costly, other politicians pointed to how, in 1984 when the Catholic school system went from partial funding to full-funding, enrolment went up threefold (Greenberg 2007). Should the same trend occur with other religious denominations, the plan to publicly fund all private religious schools would have cost upward of $1.5 billion. Again, the Liberal Leader added that John Tory's proposal would take much-needed funds out of public education and could jeopardize the social cohesion in multicultural and multi-faith Ontario. There was no discussion of the possible savings of moving to a public-only system. Indeed, such a change to the Constitution Act of 1867 (the British North America Act) would necessitate a constitutional amendment, which would need consensus to move forward. When the province of Quebec began questioning its confessional school boards in the 1960s, it took until 1997 to make the change and required the support of the province's Catholic bishops (Jaimet 2007).

The Ontario government has thus continued with the status quo and funds only public and Catholic schools. Although the current system has been censured by the United Nations, opinion polls suggest that there was not sustained popular public concern about the inequality of the current funding model; for example, Howlett (2007) notes that only 26 per cent of Ontarians supported Tory's proposal. Unlike in the conclusion of the Sharia debate, there was no declaration from the provincial government championing 'publicly funded private religious schools for all Ontarians' at any point during the elections. The continuing Christo-secular bias evident in the status quo funding structure can be explained in part by the majority-Christian population and by the theological underpinnings of secularism itself. In sum, the preservation of religious neutrality or equality within public policy in Ontario is clearly selective, calling into question the current secular status quo's impartiality. A 'one law' approach could have either proposed to abolish funding Catholic schools – politically disadvantageous for the Liberals and perhaps difficult given that it would require consensus to amend the constitution[11] (see Jaimet 2007) – or, like John Tory's proposal, might have extended support to all religious schools. Neither emerged as a viable option. Unlike the Sharia debate where McGuinty announced that 'one law' ensured 'our common ground,' dismantling Christian privilege in the current system is not on the political agenda.

Confused Private/Public Distinctions

Religious neutrality is not the only secularist ideal called into question by the Sharia debate. The controversy also underscored the blurred separation of the 'private' spaces of morality and belief from 'public' political spaces. This commonly held ideal of secularism is based on the presupposition that the political sphere works best when religion is kept outside. In this case, a pushing of private religiosity into the public realm resulted from concerns surrounding women's rights in Islam and in Islamic law. As contributors of this volume highlight, a great deal of the provincial and international public debate centred on accommodating ethnic and religio-cultural diversity in the context of a commitment to women's equality. In particular, critics of the IICJ, such as the Canadian Council of Muslim Women (CCMW), headed by Alia Hogben, expressed concern for the agency of newly settled Muslim women and power dynamics within religiously based alternative dispute resolution agreements (see Hogben 2004). In this section, I suggest that part of the unease with religious law-based arbitration and women's rights is related to a category confusion regarding the way in which public and private realms are commonly configured in understandings of secularism. This point is further complicated by the way that women's rights have often sought the assurance of rights within the private sphere. Following a brief discussion of how these public and private categories are typically organized in Western societies, I return to the Sharia debate and argue that public commentators conflated the legal rights of women and the family (often understood as interests within the public sphere) with the legitimacy of religious practice and belief (focused on the private sphere). The blurring of the distinctions between these two spheres is an example of how religious beliefs and practices inevitably emerge in the public sphere. Following Asad (2003), this religiously informed lobby is not unconscious. In short, the Sharia debate characterizes a tension between how secularism is often theorized and how it unfolds in practice.

Theorists have charted how religion in the West progressively and forcibly withdrew from the modern secular state and economy, creating two protean spheres (see Luhmann 1982, Weintraub 1997). This public/private separation parallels what Charles Taylor terms the 'independent ethic' model of secularism (Taylor 1988, 35). In this liberal model, citizens can do whatever they please in the private sphere so long as they respect publicly established forms, ceremonies, and laws; in other words, religion is completely removed from the public domain. Recent scholarship has acknowledged that public and private spheres are 'never mutually reducible nor wholly unrelated' (Weintraub 1997, 2; see also Asad 2003, 182). As mentioned, much unease emerged surrounding the public and legal implications of private religious agreements and beliefs. As argued by Audrey Macklin (in this volume), concern for what is shadowed from public scrutiny in ADR captures a primary issue in the debate. From a feminist perspective, this privatization of happenings from the domestic sphere is problematic because it has also 'shielded [domestic] abuse and domination from political scrutiny and legal redress' (Weintraub 1997, 29; see also Cohen 1997, 134, 141). This concern led many to argue, as outlined by Faisal Kutty, that women would be treated more fairly if agreements were given attention in the Charter-driven light of day (see Kutty, in this volume; Kutty and Kutty 2004).

As a result, the debate led to the following conundrum: On the one hand, to grant legal status to decisions made about the family by religious leaders within traditions which have often rationalized secondary status for women could potentially doubly marginalize religiously practising women. There are also clear disadvantages for a newly immigrant woman in any legal system – she may be unaware of her rights in her country of arrival; she may have been sponsored by her husband, creating a potentially unequal power relationship; she may have linguistic disadvantages or little support from outside her community of arrival (see Bakht 2004 and 2006). Private arbitration can replicate already-present social inequities. Yet, on the other hand, religiously practising women are thus positioned as disenfranchised members within civic society and within their religious traditions, which is a far too simplistic characterization. Ultimately a tripartite conceptualization of reality emerged: either (a) Islam is patriarchal and the so-called Sharia courts would entrench this, or (b) Islam is patriarchal and faith-based ADR would force arbiters to live within a Charter-driven legal context, or (c) Islam is patriarchal and rejecting Sharia-based ADR would mean women would continue to be victimized and would continue to live on the margins of the Canadian legal terrain. No matter which side stepped up to the microphone, religiously -practising women were presented as or assumed to be disenfranchised and in need of intervention by the public because of fear that their religiosity (assumed as patriarchal) precludes the protection of their rights.

I turn to the gender dynamics of this blurring of categories in the next section. Here I focus on how appreciating the way that these private religious concerns entered public debate can signal a transformative move of perceptions of religion in the public sphere. The blurring distinction of private/public in this particular debate makes clear that the boundaries between the private and the public, or in this case, between religion and the state, are not so discrete, nor is the public sphere ever devoid of all religious sensibilities. José Casanova's claim for the continued evidence of the 'de-privatization' of religious traditions in Western contexts sheds light on this point. Casanova argues that while secularization in the West has entailed three elements – differentiation of tasks historically taken on by the church (which are now taken up by the state, the family, and ngos), the decline of religious belief and practices, and the marginalization and privatization of religion – it nevertheless can also be described by what he calls 'de-privatization' (1994, 212–13). De-privatization refers to religion's return from the private sphere to the public arena – both through demands for the recognition of religion, as in the case of FBA and public funding for religious education, and through religiously informed political lobbying. Despite its outcome, the Sharia debate makes evident that religiously based claims are increasingly considered as legitimate topics for discussion in the public political sphere. That is, following a period wherein institutional religion was disentangled or differentiated from various state and other institutions, religion-based claims have become increasingly salient in debates regarding public institutions.

Although for secularists this 'return' might be viewed with suspicion, Casanova lists three circumstances wherein the de-privatization of religion can be justified: first, when religion contributes to public debates to improve modern freedoms, rights, and democracy against an authoritarian state; second, when there is a struggle against the pretension of the secular spheres to be independent from external ethical considerations or principles; and third, when religion acts to protect the 'traditional life-world from administrative or juridical state penetration' (Casanova 1994, 57–8). In re-emerging in the public sphere, religiously based lobbying arguably allows for a differing perspective, creating a more dynamic and more versatile public debate. Indeed, a number of authors of this volume have noted democratic benefits related to the Sharia debate that were not evident in its immediate aftermath.

These potential benefits become evident when we look to how the 'de-privatization' of religion played out in the debates over the now-abolished faith-based Alternate Dispute Resolution system in Ontario. As Wahida Valiente, then-vice president, now president of the Canadian Islamic Congress (CIC) noted in a personal interview in February 2008, there was a missed opportunity to recast Sharia in the Canadian sphere and create greater general knowledge of Islam and Islamic law. Moreover, according to the half dozen imams and religious leaders I interviewed in the Greater Toronto Area (GTA) between January and July 2008, many Muslims in the GTA became politically mobilized in the 'One School' debate. There was a sense of urgency in this lobby that had not emerged initially in the Sharia debate that signals how mosques are public gathering places where these political questions are increasingly discussed and debated.

Even if, as L. Clarke noted in her chapter, public education on Islam and Islamic law were not tremendously successful, the 2003–2005 debate can be considered the beginning of a period of 'de-privatization' or a movement towards post-secularism when Muslims in the GTA began engaging in provincial public policy debates emphasizing their religiousness. For instance, a member of the Islamic Institute of Toronto mosque in Scarborough, 'Mounir,' a Canadian of Pakistani-origin working in the provincial legislature, was inspired by the 2007 discussions in the mosque to begin teaching public policy and government courses one evening a week. Mounir's aim was to help members – first-generation Canadian Muslims in particular – navigate the provincial political system to teach them advocacy skills. One of the two-hour courses I attended in May 2008 described the breakdown of municipal politics and offered useful insider-perspective advice about the best moments to affect policy change. Mounir stressed to the six male students in the evening class that advocating change at town hall meetings was too late. An informed citizen must lobby his or her council member prior to the conception of a bill. From a theoretical perspective, this political emphasis on Muslim-focused citizenship is significant because it implies a qualified rejection of the modern idea of secularism: to place religion or religiously informed lobby outside of public, political debates (Taylor 1998; Casanova 1994). In an extremely religiously diverse city like Toronto, a pluralistic position of returning to religious identities in public political lobby signals a decided shift in how the secular state operates (see also Khan 2007, 478). The blurring of these spheres evident in the Sharia and One School debates masks the gender dynamics within their separation however, a point to which I now turn.

Privileging a Specific Feminist Politics

Thus far I have highlighted the privileging of Christian perspectives within Ontarian secularism and the private/public category complications highlighted by the Sharia debate, but it is important to keep in mind that much of the family law arbitration discussion was centred on the perceived harm done to women within the Islamic legal system (see the chapters by Bullock, Korteweg, Macklin, and Zine, in this volume). In September of 2005 when protests were organized throughout North America and Europe (in Montreal, Amsterdam, Paris, and Rome) against legally binding religious rulings in family law arbitration in Ontario, I was living outside of Paris undertaking doctoral ethnographic research on Islam, public policy, and gender politics among women of North African origin. I also conducted research with a French feminist organization, Femmes Solidaires ('Women in Solidarity'), which is very active in promoting secularism. Members of this organization recognize laïcité as integral to the feminist movement and to the assurance of women's rights. In their publicly available documentation and literature, the organization openly places visibly headscarf-wearing Muslim women outside the accepted boundaries of women's rights. One of this group's most important public actions in 2005 involved a public demonstration against the possible installation of what they understood as Sharia tribunals in Ontario. In a petition letter written by Sabine Salmon, the national president of this organization, and circulated by members at a demonstration of about five hundred people in front of the Canadian Embassy in Paris on 8 September 2005, the threat of Islam to secularism and women's rights was made clear: 'Our experience as an Association has shown us the importance of secularism for the respect of women, their rights, and their citizenship ... The Canadian Sharia court must be outlawed' (my translation of the Petition Letter from 7 September 2005). Over the course of this demonstration, several women spoke in support of the work of Homa Arjomand of the International Campaign against Shar'iah Court in Canada and the other 80 groups and organizations organized under the umbrella of the 'No Religious Arbitration' coalition. While formulations of secularism in France and Canada certainly differ,[12] current debates in both contexts highlight to what extent secularism has become an essential principle in modern feminist endeavours and activism.

In the Ontario context, the emphasis on secularism as a guarantor of women's rights gave little space for practising Muslim women in support of religiously based family law arbitration. In her chapter, Katherine Bullock describes how practising Muslim women voicing their support for arbitration were largely absent from the mediatized debate and not granted nuance in the coverage (i.e., it was not considered that a Muslim women could be both religiously conservative and a feminist). Indeed, certain Muslim women received a great deal more attention from the media than others. On this point, I compare the position and experiences of two women among the thirty that I interviewed concerning their engagement in the debate: Homa Arjomand, leader of the International Campaign against Shari'ah Court in Canada group who calls herself a 'secular Muslim' and 'Amina,' a first-generation Somali young female university student who is a practising Muslim. I interviewed Arjomand at a busy food court in Markham and Amina with a group of six young Somali women following *jumu'ah* (congregational) prayers on a Friday evening at a mosque in Scarborough. Both Markham and Scarborough are suburbs of Toronto.

Arjomand, an Iranian-born women's rights activist who migrated to a Toronto suburb in the 1990s, is an outspoken advocate of secularism in Canada. On her website, in media interviews and in a personal interview, she claims that she seeks to preserve democracy by demonstrating that all religiously based law is inappropriate because it renders women vulnerable. As one of the most vocal critics of the IICJ's proposal, she advocates a 'human rights' culture. She fears that multiculturalist perspectives and ethnocultural group rights give too much power to cultural difference in the public domain. In an interview in January 2008, Arjomand remained pleased with the outcome of the debate, but fearful for the safety of Muslim women under non-legally binding religious mediation and for the advancement of 'political Islam' in Canada. With reference to her experiences in Iran, she feels that all versions of Islam in the public sphere are dangerous. Echoing a position made famous by Susan Okin (1999; see also Bakht 2004) about the perils of multicultural politics for women, Arjomand claims:

> To me they [women supporting Sharia] are trying to save political Islam. They don't know the damage they are causing in their own country, with their own people [...] I'm seeing Canada as the most vulnerable country. Because of this multiculturalism. This policy of multiculturalism and government help everyone ignore what's happening around them. (Interview, 22 Jan. 2008)[13]

Arjomand garnered much attention as *the* voice for Muslim women in the GTA. However, she had critics. A group of six first-generation Somalian young women who arrived to Scarborough as refugees in the 1990s were upset by the attention given to Arjomand as 'the' Muslim woman when she has said elsewhere she is an atheist. In a round table interview with the young women in the women's section of their mosque, one of these first-generation women, Amina, 23 years old, claimed:

> When the whole debate erupted we had never heard of it [binding arbitration] before and then suddenly people were wondering what we thought about the whole thing. When we saw her [Arjomand] on tv saying things about how Muslim women are repressed by their husbands and don't have their own perspectives, it was really insulting [other young women nod in agreement]. Ok, maybe that's true in Iran, but she can't just take her personal experience and say it's true for all of us. I'm a first-generation immigrant too, and it's an insult. Ok yeah, get rid of religious law because Canada is secular, but don't say it's to protect me from myself. (Interview, 18 Jan. 2008)

Amina and her friends do not disagree with the outcome of the debate, but find Arjomand's rationale paternalistic and her vision of secularism as a guarantor of gender equality inappropriate – their experience of Islam is quite different, both because of their generation and because of their different socioreligious experiences.

What were the positions of pro-Sharia, practising Muslim women in this debate? As mentioned, Bullock for one described her sense of frustration in her chapter. Similarly, several women in the Greater Toronto Area noted to me in interviews and in a discussion group at a Mississauga mosque that they felt that the debated unfolded too quickly and they did not have occasion to participate. Indeed, a sense of frustration characterized the experience of the debate for most of these Sunni women of Pakistani origin. Others claimed that as non-specialists in Sharia they felt unqualified to answer questions in the media. Others argued that raising children and caring for their families in the private sphere left little time for political engagement. These practical concerns were likely compounded by the demographic reality of the tremendous ethno-cultural diversity in the Muslim community in Ontario. While reduced to a single category (that of 'Muslims') by the way in which the debate was articulated in the press and by political leaders, 'Canadian Muslim-ness' differs from Muslim diasporas in Western Europe, reflecting more than sixty ethno-cultural groups and Islamic organizations (and more under construction), ranging from Somali to Pakistani to Saudi to Bosnian, and varying from groups self-defined as secular Muslims through to more conservative religious groups. This diversity was made clear in *where* activism on this question took place. While many Muslim advocates for the public funding of private Muslim schools met in local mosques in the GTA, others pointedly did not. Moreover, as several authors in this volume have pointed out (see also Sharify-Funk 2009), Muslim organizations were split on the question of faith-based arbitration.

These silencing factors must be examined by looking to why some women were privileged in the mediatization of the debate (see also Korteweg in this volume). If secular norms are undergirded by certain feminist positions and understandings of agency, these norms must be made more evident so as to address the concerns of visibly religious women in the domestic and private sphere who felt they were ignored throughout the Sharia debate. Moreover, we must tread carefully: policing Muslim women in the name of gender equality is not a new phenomenon (see, e.g., Ahmed 1992, MacMaster and Lewis 1998,

Hirschkind and Mahmood 2002). Ironically, Western secularism coincides with liberalism's privileging of the individual political agent, which is denied to the Muslim woman when she is policed and silenced. In sum, secularism was also articulated in the debate as integral to ensuring women's rights. This equation meant that certain women gained a privileged space in the debate.

Conclusion

In this chapter I have considered the Sharia debate to examine how elements of secularism emerged on the ground. I have sought to shed light on the changing definitions and construals of secularism and religion in the public sphere by asking: in the wake of the Sharia debate, why does Christianity maintain a privileged position in the current 'neutral' system? In what ways might religion have been 'deprivatized' during this debate, and what might be the impact of this shift for Muslims in Ontario and for non-Muslim Ontarians? And, why are decisions affecting some Muslim women and their welfare often made without a proper consultative process? Responses to the IICJ made clear the partiality of a Christo-secularism. At the same time, as evidenced in the One-School debate about publicly funding private Catholic schools in 2007 following this debate, even if not dismantling biases, non-Christian religiously based lobbying has gained ground in the public sphere, like Mounir's courses on public policy at the IIT in Scarborough attest. I have also suggested that while secular lobby groups might legitimately seek to ensure the separation of religion and the state as a measure to protect women's rights, this positioning may unintentionally silence the political participation of some religiously practising Muslim women.

Demography is also shifting these notions of secularity. Religious diversity in the province's urban spaces like the Greater Toronto Area has increased tremendously since the nineteenth century. Since 1967 non-Christian religious traditions have increased in Canada's urban centres. Although they account for fewer than 2 per cent of the national population, Muslims in Canada constitute its fastest growing religious population; a 130 per cent increase from 1991 to 2001, and by 2017, estimates suggest the population will increase by approximately 160 per cent from 2001 (Jedwab 2005). This increase signals the growing presence of Muslims in the Canadian landscape, specifically in the suburban regions of Toronto, such as Mississauga and Scarborough. John Tory's 2007 election platform on publicly funding private religious schools captures a significant shift in the way in which Muslims are politically perceived in the province: the 'Muslim' vote did not especially interest politicians in the 2003 election, but was part of how the Tories imagined the suburban vote for victory in 2007.[14] Tories platform is certainly not the only example of the increasing political importance of the Muslim community. The growing number of visits to mosques by Canadian representatives of different institutions reflects the recent solicitation of Muslims for political and nationally related issues.[15]

We can look at the lobbying within mosques and outside them during the 2007 Ontario provincial elections and to the heated and extended Ontario Sharia debate to see how in a broader sense Canadian secularism is shifting. As the Muslim population in Canada grows and rightfully requests equal rights for their own religious expressions, debates like these require analysis. Secular tensions and construals elucidate how these theoretically rich debates create occasions to take stock of the order of things, the power implications within the status quo, and the legitimacy of religion in the public sphere.

ACKNOWLEDGMENT

Thank you to Paul Bramadat and Richard Moon for their helpful comments and suggestions.

NOTES

1 Following Paul Bramadat (2008, 122), I consider public policy as both the official policies and laws by the provincial government and the discourses that surround these.
2 According to 2006 census data, 46.9% of Torontonians are members of visible minorities, making the city among the most ethnically diverse in the world (Statistics Canada 2006). Almost half of new immigrants to Canada settle in the Greater Toronto Area (Becklumb 2008).
3 On this point I appreciate that I am optimistic about the law's ability to resolve or construct neutrality among cultural claims. Benjamin Berger (2006, 1) succinctly states that we must be wary 'that the goal of accommodation and appropriate balancing can be achieved.' While the law can be a mechanism for maintaining social stability and implementing governmental aims, it is clearly not intrinsically committed to particular goods or social aims (16).

4   Education in Canada falls under provincial jurisdiction, and varies as to whether governments support private religious education or not. Denominational schools were abolished in New Brunswick in 1871 and in Manitoba in 1890. The early twentieth century saw controversies emerge on this point in the Canadian prairies by pacifist communal Christians like the Hutterites, Strict Order Mennonites, and the Doukhobors (McLaren 2006; see Sweet 1997, 131, regarding full funding for religious schools in the Netherlands).

5   I use 'Christo-' rather than 'catho-' because even if 2001 Census data demonstrate that most Ontarians are Catholic, there are also important numbers of Protestants and 'Other Christians' (Statistics Canada 2001). In Ontario, Protestantism is historically far more dominant than Catholicism. Catholicism is historically Ontario's minority religion, hence, its protection in the 1867 Constitution.

6   While the proportion of Canadians who are Protestant or Catholic dropped significantly through the twenieth century (from about 98% in 1901 to approximately 72% in 2001), Canada remains influenced by its Christian heritage (Ontario Consultants on Religious Tolerance 2005).

7   Lori G. Beaman (2008a; 2008b, 195) has done extensive work examining the exclusion of some Christian groups from this normativity, like the Jehovah's Witnesses.

8   Indian secularism presents an important counter-case. Political theorist Rajeev Bhargava (1998b, 498) suggests in his analysis of contemporary India that secularism is not necessarily a Christian by-product, but this argument falls outside the bounds of this chapter.

9   While the Orthodox Jews in question are not Christians nor do they fall within the rubric of 'Christo-secularism,' rethinking the relationship between Christians and Jews after the Second World War led to the common positioning of Judaism as the foundation of Christianity and the use of the term 'Judeo-Christian' to exemplify a shared morality and religious heritage.

10 A similar funding program is run in the province of Alberta.

11 The example of a constitutional amendment in the province of Quebec in 1997 suggests that the change to a public-only system may be more politically than constitutionally difficult (see Jaimet 2007).

12 Beyond the important legal differences in the way religion is conceptualized in both countries, for *Femmes Solidaires* and other French commentators, the possibility of this allowance of religion in the public sphere in Ontario also promotes multiculturalism, undesirable in normative French discourse because of the threat of communitarianism (*communautarisme*) and, that when the central state is no longer in control of the law, the

individual ceases to exist, and his or her subject-ness is lost in favour of an ethnic community. On the question of religion in public schools, the two countries also differ: In France, conspicuous religious signs were banned in 2004, whereas in 1980 the Toronto District School board made it clear that the Lord's Prayer was not to be read exclusively during opening exercises in schools. Instead of banning the prayer, the board assembled a 40-member interfaith panel to compile a multi-faith prayer brochure.

13 Susan Okin (1999) assumes these 'ethnic' minority immigrant women are unable to speak for themselves and want to remain members of patriarchal communities. Okin's perspective on how multiculturalism is 'bad' for women is a dangerously misrepresentative place to begin discussion, however, as it excludes other issues that these women may be facing, unrelated to multiculturalism: issues like material inequality, exploitation, and economic marginalization.

14 Dalton McGuinty, who has since banned Christian prayers in the legislature without touching the schooling question, won a majority government in the 2007 provincial election (71 of the 107 seats; CBC 2007).

15 In an effort to generate interest among Muslims in careers in the Canadian military, the Canadian Forces have begun making appearances in mosques. Reception is mixed. At the Al-Salaam mosque in Burnaby, British Columbia, for instance, some members claim religious institutions should not be used to showcase the military, while others warn of an organization involved in a combat mission in Afghanistan where fellow Muslims are being killed. The sessions seek to disseminate information directly to minority groups. They also highlight the army's 'Muslim-friendly' accommodations, including the availability of *halal* foods and Muslim chaplains (*Globe and Mail* 2008). Politicians are also making this effort. Similarly, the May 2008 ISNA (Islamic Society of North America) Canada Conference in Mississauga concluded with four local politicians (and the mayor) speaking about the value and importance of Islam in the Greater Toronto Area.

REFERENCES

Abu-Lughod, Lila. 2002. 'Do Muslim Women Really Need Saving? Anthropological Reflections on Cultural Relativism and Its Others.' *American Anthropologist* 104 (Sept.): 783–90.
Ahmed, Leila. 1992. *Women and Gender in Islam: Historical Roots of a Modern Debate.* New Haven and London: Yale University Press.

Anderson, Benedict. 1991. *Imagined Communities: Reflections on the Origin and Spread of Nationalism.* 2nd ed. London: Verso.

Asad, Talal. 2003. *Formations of the Secular: Christianity, Islam, and Modernity.* Stanford: Stanford University Press.

Bakht, Natasha. 2004. 'Family Arbitration Using Shariah Law: Examining Ontario's Arbitration Act and Its Impact on Women.' *Muslim World Journal of Human Rights* 1(1): 1–24.

– 2006. 'Were Muslim Barbarians Really Knocking on the Gates of Ontario? The Religious Arbitration Controversy – Another Perspective.' *Ottawa Law Review, 40th Anniversary Edition* 35 (Summer): 67–82.

Baubérot, Jean. 1998. 'La laïcité française et ses mutations.' *Social Compass* 45(1): 175–87.

– 2003. 'Editorial.' *Libération* 15 (Dec.): 39.

Beaman, Lori G. 2008a. *Defining Harm: Religious Freedom and the Limits of the Law.* Vancouver: UBC Press.

– 2008b. 'Defining Religion: The Promise and the Peril of Legal Interpretation.' In Richard Moon, ed., *Law and Religious Pluralism in Canada,* 192–216. Vancouver: UBC Press.

Becklumb, Penny. 2008. *Canada's Immigration Program.* Accessed 21 Jan. 2011. http://www2.parl.gc.ca/content/lop/researchpublications/bp190-e.htm.

Bellah, Robert N. 1970 [1967]. 'Civil Religion in America.' In *Beyond Belief: Essays on Religion in a Post-Traditional World,* 168–92. New York: Harper and Row.

Berger, Benjamin L. 2006. 'Understanding Law And Religion As Culture: Making Room For Meaning In The Public Sphere.' *Forum Constitutionnel* 15(1) 15–22.

Beyer, Peter. 2005. 'Appendix: Demographics of Religious Identification in Canada.' In Paul Bramadat and David Seljak, eds., *Religion and Ethnicity in Canada,* 240. Toronto: Pearson Longman.

Bhargava, Rajeev. 1998a. 'Introduction.' In Rajeev Bhargava, ed., *Secularism and Its Critics,* 1–28. Delhi: Oxford University Press.

– 1998b. 'What Is Secularism For?' In Rajeev Bhargava, ed., *Secularism and Its Critics,* 486–542. Delhi: Oxford University Press.

Bowen, John R. 2007. *Why the French Don't Like Headscarves: Islam, the State, and Public Space.* Princeton: Princeton University Press.

Bramadat, Paul. 2005. 'Toward a New Politics of Authenticity: Ethno-Cultural Representation in Theory and Practice.' *Canadian Ethnic Studies* 37(1): 1–20.

– 2008. 'Religion and Public Policy in Canada: An Itinerary.' *Studies in Religion* 37: 121–43.

Bramadat, Paul, and David Seljak, eds. 2005. *Religion and Ethnicity in Canada.* Toronto: Pearson Longman.

– 2008. *Christianity and Ethnicity in Canada*. Toronto: University of Toronto Press.

Canadian Broadcasting Corporation (CBC). 2007. 'McGuinty Wins Massive Majority, Tory Loses Seat.' 11 Oct. Accessed 21 Jan. 2011. http://www.cbc.ca/canada/ontariovotes2007/story/2007/10/10/leaders.html.

Casanova, José. 1994. *Public Religions in the Modern World*. Chicago: University of Chicago Press.

Cesari, Jocelyne, ed. 2010. *Muslims in the West after 9/11: Religion, Law and Politics*. New York: Routledge.

Cohen, Jean L. 1997. 'Rethinking Privacy: Autonomy, Identity, and the Abortion Controversy.' In Jeff Weintraub and Krishan Kumar, eds., *Public and Private in Thought and Practice: Perspectives on a Grand Dichotomy*, 133–65. Chicago: University of Chicago Press.

Gauchet, Marcel. 1985. *Le désenchantement du monde: Une histoire politique de la religion*. Paris: Éditions Gallimard.

–1998. *La Religion dans la Démocratie: Parcours de la Laïcité*. Paris: Éditions Gallimard.

Globe and Mail. 2008. 'Canadian Forces to Recruit at Mosque.' 8 Oct. Accessed 21 Jan. 2011. http://www.theglobeandmail.com/servlet/story/LAC.20081008.BCFORCES08/TPStory/National.

Greenberg, Lee. 2007. 'Faith-Based Schools Idea Backward – McGuinty; Tory's Pledge Seized as an Election Issue.' *National Post*, 23 Aug.

Greenfeld, Liah. 1996. 'Nationalism and Modernity.' *Social Research* 63 (Spring): 3–40.

Habermas, Jürgen. 2008. 'Notes on a Post-Secular Society.' *Signandsight.com*. 18 June. Accessed 15 Aug. 2010. http://signandsight.com-slash-features-slash-1714.html.

Hirschkind, Charles, and Saba Mahmood. 2002. 'Feminism, the Taliban, and the Politics of Counter-Insurgency.' *Anthropological Quarterly* 75(2): 337–54.

Hogben, Alia. 2004. 'Should Ontario Allow Shariah Law?' *Toronto Star*, 1 June, A19.

Howlett, Karen. 2007. 'Ontario Voters Pan Faith-based Education: Poll.' *Globe and Mail*, 18 Sept. Accessed 15 Aug. 2010. http://www.theglobeandmail.com/archives/article782722.ece.

Jaimet, Kate. 2007. 'Experts Split on School Reforms: Quebec Experience Leads to Different Conclusions on How Simple Secularization Would Be.' *Ottawa Citizen*, 11 Sept. A9.

Jakobsen, Janet R., and Ann Pellegrini, eds. 2008. *Secularisms*. Durham: Duke University Press.

Jedwab, Jack. 2005. 'Canada's Demo-Religious Revolution: 2017 Will Bring Considerable Change to the Profile of the Mosaic.' *Association for Canadian*

Studies. Accessed 21 Jan. 2011. http://www.acs-aec.ca/oldsite/Polls/
30-03-2005.pdf.

Khan, Sheema. 2007. 'The Ontario Sharia Debate: Transformational Accommo-
dation, Multiculturalism and Muslim Identity.' In Keith Bantin, Thomas J.
Courchene, and F. Lesie Seidle, *Belonging?: Diversity, Recognition and Shared
Citizenship in Canada*, 475–85. Montreal: Institute for Research on Public
Policy.

Kutty, Faisal, and Ahmad Kutty. 2004. 'Shariah Courts in Canada: Myth and
Reality.' *Law Times*, 31 May.

Levy, Geoffrey Brahm, and Tariq Modood, eds. 2009. *Secularism, Religion and
Multicultural Citizenship*. Cambridge: Cambridge University Press.

Luhmann, Niklas. 1982. *The Differentiation of Society*. New York: Columbia
University Press.

MacMaster, Neil, and Toni Lewis. 1998. 'Orientalism: From Unveiling to
Hyperveiling.' *European Studies Journal* 28: 121–35.

McLaren, John. 2006. 'Protecting Confessions of Faith and Securing Equality
of Treatment for Religious Minorities in Education.' In Avigail Eisenberg,
ed., *Diversity and Equality: The Changing Framework of Freedom in Canada*,
164–76. Vancouver: UBC Press.

Okin, Susan Moller. 1999. 'Is Multiculturalism Bad for Women?' In Joshua
Cohen, Matthew Howard, and Martha C. Nussbaum, eds., *Is Multiculturalism Bad for Women?* 9–24. Princeton: Princeton University Press.

One School System. 2006. 'Point by Point: "The One Public School System for
Ontario" Petition.' 25 Sept. Accessed 21 Jan. 2011. http://www.oneschool-
system.org/documents/PointByPointOneSchoolSystemPetition.pdf.

Ontario Consultants on Religious Tolerance. 2005. 'Religion Data from the
2001 Canadian Census.' 15 Dec. Accessed 21 Jan. 2011. http://www
.religioustolerance.org/can_rel0.htm.

Rousseau, Jean Jacques. 1994 [1762]. *Discourse on Political Economy and The Social
Contract*. Translated by Christopher Betts. Oxford: Oxford University Press.

Selby, Jennifer. 2012. *Questioning French Secularism: Gender Politics and Islam in
a Parisian Banlieue*. New York: Palgrave Macmillan.

Seljak, David. 2005. 'Multiculturalism and Funding for Ontario's Islamic
Schools.' *Canadian Diversity* (Autumn): 63–6.

Sharify-Funk, Meena. 2009. 'Representing Canadian Muslims: Media, Muslim
Advocacy Organizations, and Gender in the Ontario Shari'ah Debate.'
Global Media Journal 2(2): 73–89.

Statistics Canada. 2001. 'Population by Religion, by Province and Territory:
2001 Census: Quebec, Ontario, Manitoba, Saskatchewan.' Accessed 21 Jan.
2011. http://www40.statcan.ca/l01/cst01/demo30b-eng.htm.

- 2005. '2001 Census Data: Religion (95) and Visible Minority Groups (15) for Population, for Canada, Provinces, Territories, Census Metropolitan Areas and Census Agglomerations, 2001 Census – 20% Sample Data.' Accessed 21 Jan. 2011. http://www12.statcan.ca/english/census01/products/standard/themes/RetrieveProductTable.cfm?Temporal=2001&PID=55825&APATH=3&GID=431515&METH=1&PTYPE=55440&THEME=56&FOCUS=0&AID=0&PLACENAME=0&PROVINCE=0&SEARCH=0&GC=0&GK=0&VID=0&VNAMEE=&VNAMEF=&FL=0&RL=0&FREE=0.
- 2006. '2006 Community Profiles: Toronto.' Accessed 21 Jan. 2011. http://www12.statcan.ca/census-recensement/2006/dp-pd/prof/92-591/details/page.cfm?Lang=E&Geo1=CSD&Code1=3520005&Geo2=PR&Code2=35&-Data=Count&SearchText=Toronto&SearchType=Begins&SearchPR=01&B1=Visible%20minority&Custom.

Sweet, Lois. 1997. *God in the Classroom: The Controversial Issue of Religion in Canada's Schools.* Toronto: McClelland and Stewart.

Taylor, Charles. 2007. *A Secular Age.* Cambridge, MA and London, England: The Belknap Press of Harvard University Press.

- 1998. 'Modes of Secularism.' In Rajeev Bhargava, ed., *Secularism and Its Critics,* 31–53. Delhi: Oxford University Press.

Walzer, Michael. 1984. 'Liberalism and the Art of Separation.' *Political Theory* 12: 315–30.

Weinrib, Lorraine. 2008. 'Ontario's Sharia Law Debate: Law and Politics under the *Charter.*' In Richard Moon, ed., *Law and Religious Pluralism in Canada,* 239–63. Vancouver: UBC Press.

- n.d. 'Ontario Tories Tout Direct Funding for Faith-Based Schools.' *Law Times.* Accessed 2 Sept. 2010. http://www.lawtimesnews.com/200708272829/Headline-News/Ontario-Tories-tout-direct-funding-for-faith-based-schools.

Weintraub, Jeff. 1997. 'The Theory and Politics of the Public/Private Distinction.' In Jeff Weintraub and Krishan Kumar, eds., *Public and Private in Thought and Practice: Perspectives on a Grand Dichotomy,* 1–42. Chicago: University of Chicago Press.

Zine, Jasmin. 2001. '"Negotiating Equity": The Dynamics of Minority Community Engagement in Constructing Inclusive Educational Policy.' *Cambridge Journal of Education* 31(2): 239–69.

Concluding Thoughts

Conclusion: Debating Sharia in the West

ANNA C. KORTEWEG AND JENNIFER A. SELBY

What came to be known as the 'Sharia debate' might appear to be distinctly Canadian. The debate revolved around the possibility of Sharia-based binding arbitration derived from particular openings in the legal system and the Canadian Charter of Rights and Freedoms. In theory, these elements seek to protect religious freedom and promote gender equality, as well as the pluralism in governance rooted in Canadian multiculturalism. The debate reflected a very Canadian, intensely diverse immigration context. In many of the municipalities that make up the Greater Toronto Area (where 5.5 million of Canada's 33 million inhabitants live), half of the residents are first-generation immigrants. Muslims cut across the settled and immigrant populations: they have both deep historical roots in Canada and, given the wide variety in their countries of origin, exemplify the diversity of the current Canadian urban immigrant population. In addition, Muslims are one of the fastest growing religious groups in Canada.

In fact, Sharia debates are not unique to Canada. As discussed by Jocelyne Cesari in her foreword, many Western immigrant-receiving countries include a religiously and ethnically diverse Muslim population and are negotiating the legal and social implications of Sharia. One high-profile discussion took place in 2008 when the Archbishop of Canterbury claimed that Sharia could, and perhaps should, be accommodated in British law making. His comments, as well as subsequent reports by a conservative British think tank that eighty-five Sharia Councils were deciding various legal matters in Britain (MacEoin 2009), resulted in an uproar with clear parallels to the Canadian debate. Ongoing headscarf debates (and more recently, anti-niqab and burqa legislation) in a number of Western European countries including

France, Switzerland, Belgium, Spain, and the Netherlands can similarly be interpreted as conflicts over religious accommodation in the context of particular ideas about secularism and gender equality, again with important resemblances to the Ontario Sharia debate. The mediatization of these debates has had effects analogous to the silencing of some practising Muslim women's voices, racialization, and stigmatization, as outlined in the chapters in this volume by Bullock, Zine, and Korteweg (see also, Parvez, 2011; Bowen 2007; Saharso and Lettinga 2007; Sauer 2009).

Taken as a whole, this volume suggests that such debates can be more fruitful if participants realize that Sharia, which informs the meaning of being Muslim and practising Islam, is not a uniform dogma that structures people's lives in deterministic ways. Rather, as shown in the ethnography-based chapters by Macfarlane and Cutting, individual Muslims have fluid, often ad hoc, relationships with Sharia and Islamic jurisprudence (fiqh). Clarke suggests that individual Muslims have only a partial understanding of fiqh (for related qualitative studies on Sharia in Quebec, see Saris and Potvin 2008; for the United States, see Quraishi and Syeed-Miller n.d.; for Britain, see Menski 2000; Yilmaz 2003; and Bano 2007; for Denmark, Waerstads 2011; for Australia, Kreyam 2010). Similarly, as Emon and Kutty illustrate in the area of jurisprudence and as Clarke and Reda note with respect to religiosity and religious practice, jurisprudence and religion as understood and propagated by many Islamic scholars are historically fluid, contingent, and open to interpretation.

For those raised in the Western Christian tradition, this fluidity in knowledge and interpretation should be familiar. How many Christians have a deep understanding of the underpinnings of their religion and the theologically mandated ways of aligning everyday living with religious doctrine? The same can be asked of Jews, who share with Muslims a strong sense of God-given legal imperative in the ethical conduct of everyday practices. Do Christian and Jewish religious authorities agree in their interpretations of these religious doctrines? Few lay people have a deep understanding of religious law, and scholars rarely agree fully in their interpretations of religious doctrine. In all articulations of these religious traditions, everyday, ad hoc, partial understandings, and even the learned opinions of scholars and professional practitioners can differ considerably. These differences have implications for the integration of Islamic legal precepts and practice into the legal structures of European and North American immigrant-receiving societies. Many European states instituted structures for resolving conflict between Christian doctrines (through various forms of church/state separation) about four hundred years ago. Islam has not been similarly integrated into legal (and political) frameworks of accommodation and negotiation in Western nation states. In addition, while Muslim-majority countries tend to have limited religious diversity, Muslim communities in European and North American immigrant-receiving countries are marked by internal religious diversity, creating both opportunities and frictions in negotiating the place of Islam within these societies (see Esposito 1999; Al-Azmeh 1993; Tibi 2002; Crone 2004).

The issue of gender inequality raised in the Canadian Sharia debate appears to influence all these debates about the role of Islam in the West.[1] On the one hand, the portrayal of Islam as a backward, anti- or pre-modern religion informing patriarchal cultural practices has deep roots in colonial and Orientalist portrayals (see Ahmed 1992; Clancy-Smith 1998; Mamdani 2004; Razack 2008). Many public debates about the place of Islam in the West involve arguments regarding the gender inequality purportedly inherent in Islamic practice and doctrine; these arguments are at times deployed strategically and even cynically to further assimilationist political agendas (Abu-Lughod 2002; Mahmood 2008; Korteweg and Yurdakul 2009, 2010; Selby, in this volume). On the other hand, this kind of manipulation does not minimize the fact that the Sharia debate identified a number of problematic gender issues related to Islam: namely, the power disparities in *talaq* and the insufficient response by some imams to domestic violence. In addition, the Sharia debate underscored insufficiencies in the legal practice of private arbitration by showing how gendered power inequalities can inform private ordering in ways that go unchecked. Therefore, addressing gendered and other issues while fostering a constructive dialogue around religious pluralism in public spaces will require circumventing the stereotyping and stigmatizing of entire communities, which often coincides with the very necessary discussions of gender inequality in the context of Islam (see Bunting and Mokhtari 2009). These considerations will require adequately identifying the roots of gender inequality in all aspects of the practices under debate: those related to Islam as well as those that are not.

In this Conclusion, we summarize how the Ontario Sharia debate can inform this kind of constructive dialogue, which may contribute to the full integration of highly diverse Muslim communities in immigrant-receiving societies. The following subsections discuss four themes we believe undergird how the debate emerged and how conversations might move in future debates: first, the everyday reality of living a Muslim life in a Western country; second, legal issues related to both Western legal practice and Islamic jurisprudence; third, the symbolic politics of the debate; and finally, formal politics and law making in the context of secularism.

Everyday Muslim Life in the West

Muslim life in Western countries is complex and multifaceted. Individuals use various and fluid ways to express (and not express) their religiosity in everyday life. While Muslims vary in the degree to which they engage with religious practice and belief,[2] Macfarlane and Cutting both note that Muslim women and men are likely to turn to religious frameworks and norms in times of personal need or crisis, such as divorce. They also argue that religious authorities can play a constructive role in everyday religious practice, facilitating the connection between an individual's religiosity and other aspects of their life within a religiously plural, immigrant-receiving society. In particular, these authorities can become conduits to connect Islamic legal practice and Western civil law in the case of divorce.

Much of the debate about Sharia (in Ontario and elsewhere) is focused on the fear that Islam is oppressive to women and will undermine Western achievements towards gender equality. This fear masks a far more complex reality. Macfarlane and Cutting demonstrate that many imams and other Islamic authorities interpret Islamic jurisprudence in ways that are beneficial to women. However, these authorities may do so without addressing the foundational gender issues that give rise to these inequalities. Public debates, like the one that took place in Ontario, can both facilitate and impede such discussions or processes for gender-related or theological change. In the Ontario case, as suggested by Zine, Kutty, and others in this volume, the larger public's failure to understand the intricacies of everyday life led to misplaced concern about violations of women's rights. While such violations may exist, Cutting suggests these are not linked to arbitration processes, in large part because most Muslims do not appear to use faith-based arbitration, even when it was available.[3] As a result, even if the provincial government claimed it was safeguarding women by impeding faith-based arbitration in 2006, women might be subject to abuses of power from sources other than arbitration. Zine suggests in her chapter that the tenor of public debate made it more rather than less difficult to debate issues associated with some imams' lack of understanding of domestic violence or the fundamental inequalities related to fiqh regarding religious divorce within Muslim communities. Miscommunication also impeded sustained dialogue between Muslim and non-Muslim communities, as well as various aspects of the state with regard to improving gender equality while acknowledging allegiance to religious beliefs and practice.

Macfarlane and Cutting's work, as well as Kutty's experience melding Canadian and Islamic law, suggests a need to support the ongoing processes of developing religious practice in immigrant-receiving countries in accordance with Western legal principles. Many studies of Islam in the West have suggested that this process is necessary not only to support majority societies, but also to support many of the Muslims living within those societies (Ramadan 2004; Cesari 2004 and 2010; Shah 2007; Fournier 2010; Nielsen and Christoffersen 2010). Ethnographic research about how Muslim women and men have varying and complex everyday attachments to religiosity and religious practice needs to be accompanied by research into how Islamic jurisprudence is similarly varied, multiple, and historically contextual.[4] This symbiosis does not mean that Islam is easily 'liberalized' – or can be subsumed into a liberal democratic understanding of subjectivity and political participation – but rather that it is not a monolithic, or by definition a politically dangerous influence. This point leads us to our second observation.

Legal Contexts: Congruencies between Western and Islamic Lawmaking

The Sharia debate in Ontario, ostensibly about gender equality and unmonitored contract making in private family affairs, was less about Sharia-based arbitration (something no one used or truly desired to begin with) and more about the privatization of law. Audrey Macklin's chapter provocatively suggests that the problems associated with Sharia (gendered power inequalities in personal, intimate relationships) actually result from this privatization. She argues that these issues are better addressed by ensuring gender equality in *all* legal proceedings pertaining to private ordering, not by buttressing a Muslim 'encultured' subject in tandem with a (non-Muslim) Western, liberal subject. Creating law and conducting legal practice based on these two distinct subject positions creates a two-fold problem: it underestimates the degree to which Western law can reinforce structural gender inequality, and it overestimates the degree to which it can protect Muslim women (from Muslim men and even from themselves) by treating them as singularly non-agentic subjects (see also Abu-Lughod 2002).

This volume also points out the problematic nature of monolithic understandings of Islamic jurisprudence and its purported incompatibility with Western legal principles. On the one hand, as Emon suggests, Muslims have historically negotiated the codification of Islamic legal principles through Western colonial interventions. Emon demonstrates how the history of the Indian legal system, used as a point of orientation by Syed Mumtaz Ali, the founder of the IICJ, is to some degree the result of the fossilization of dynamic legal practices. In contrast, Kutty illustrates that the Canadian legal context already makes it possible to insert Islamic principles in Western private contracts, as many schools of Islamic jurisprudence allow for adjustment to the laws of the land in which Muslims live as minorities, as long as these adjustments do not conflict with interpretable tenets of Sharia. This integration of Islamic law is already taking place in several realms. For instance, business contracts related to finance and banking are being made congruent with Islamic principles (as is the case in Britain) and increasing numbers of law schools are offering courses in Islamic finance and banking. However, these are, in a sense, 'easy' issues because they do not raise concerns about power and inequality, which are explicit within private family arbitration. For example, marriage contracts conducted abroad are reciprocally recognized by some Western countries; at certain times and in certain places this response has led to the recognition of polygamous marriage and the regulation of polygamous divorce (Christoffersen 2010, 62), although the legal recognition of polygamy has become highly contested in countries such as France and Denmark (Selby forthcoming; Rohe 2006). These contestations reveal, as Cesari argues in her foreword, how lawyers and judges are already integrating Sharia-based legal contracts into Western jurisprudential practice.

In terms of the development of Islamic jurisprudence itself, the Sharia debate also revealed that within the globalizing immigration context, interpretations of Islam are diverse. Many Islamic schools of jurisprudence are territorially based, with different countries traditionally adhering to different schools of fiqh. In the immigration context, cross-school referencing increases, resulting in a new vibrancy in legal interpretations. This phenomenon is encouraged by practices such as 'imam shopping' as documented by Macfarlane (see also Bunting and Mokhtari 2009, 234), in which Muslim women may approach multiple imams until they find one who grants them a religious divorce in keeping with their beliefs and interests. Emon hypothesizes that the imams with the best 'deal' can attract the most 'customers.' Cutting avoids the marketplace metaphor, suggesting that imams respond to a real need to solve women's divorce problems by borrowing from various schools of jurisprudence they might otherwise approach reluctantly, in order to abide by the larger ethical principles of Sharia.

Taken together, these chapters suggest that public debate should focus on how the privatization of law through contracting reinforces certain power hierarchies and undermines others. Focusing solely on the particularities of Sharia-based contract making fosters the kind of ineffective policy making exemplified by the McGuinty government in the wake of the Ontario Sharia debate: on the one hand it paid lip service to an idea of 'one law for all,' while on the other it continued to allow couples to 'opt out' of the default legal system by enabling private contracts in the context of intimate relationships. The authors in this volume suggest that McGuinty's response neglected the fact that Islamic legal developments have the potential to be fluid and flexible. Many Muslims actively seek ways to make their (often very personally experienced) need to live in accordance with Islamic legal principles and Sharia more broadly congruent with the legal context of the country in which they live. Governments might instead seek to facilitate these dialogues by addressing the issues associated with creating contracts in the context of unequal intimate relationships (pertaining to gender and other power differences) without quashing the right to adhere to religious tenets and principles of individual freedoms that underlie Western legal systems.

Symbolic Politics

This volume suggests that the symbolic politics of the Ontario Sharia debate acted as obstacles, rather than facilitators. The Sharia debate can be understood as 'symbolic politics,' in both the colloquial and the academic sense. Colloquially, symbolic politics refers to political gestures without material impact. Indeed, this debate was not about real practices and real changes in law. Evidence suggests that Muslims actually had very limited interest in engaging in faith-based arbitration, while McGuinty's decision did relatively little to address the shortcomings of the arbitration process. Rather, the debate symbolically demarcated the ways in which a majority 'Western' society should relate to 'its' Muslim populations, with the changes to the Ontario Arbitration Act symbolizing a general rejection of allowing Islamic legal principles to become part of discourse and practice in the public sphere. Academically, symbolic politics refers to how the signs deployed to articulate various positions about a social issue actually shape what kinds of actions can be imagined and practised. As both Macklin and Kutty show, the terms of the debate limited much-needed discussion of two issues: (1) how the existing arbitration processes reinforced gender inequalities, and (2) how including Islamic jurisprudential practices more explicitly in the Canadian legal system might generate innovative interpretations of Islamic law that at least some religiously observant Muslims appear to desire.

When Macfarlane and Cutting's findings are compared with the media portrayals of Sharia-based arbitration, the disparities suggest that the public debate in Ontario largely failed to take into account the everyday realities of Muslim lives. Rather, the public debate superimposed understandings of Sharia gleaned from other contexts or countries where stoning, beheading, and the amputation of hands are sensationalized. These images allowed quick and easy colonial understandings of Islam in the West, in which Islam becomes discursively linked to barbarism and an absence of civilization (Ramadan 2004; Razack 2008; Zine, in this volume). The resulting symbolic politics facilitated stigmatization and racialization of entire Muslim communities.

Furthermore, Islam has been portrayed as a system of thought antithetical to Western liberal values, including those of gender equality. As Anna Korteweg shows, this equation meant that in public debate Muslim women were rarely depicted as simultaneously religious and agentic. One such agentic and religious interpretation comes from Nevin Reda, who opposed Sharia-based arbitration in private family matters. In a textually based, theological reading, Reda underlines the complications of arbitrating within the context of disputed Islamic jurisprudential practices. She offers an alternative, dialogical framework, based on an understanding of the word Islam, which she interprets, not as submission, the most common translation, but as wholeness-making, peace-making, and well-being-making. Reda suggests that given these constraints, mediation and not arbitration is preferable to resolve contracts and disagreements. Standing on the side of supporting faith-based arbitration, Katherine Bullock narrates her personal account of how this conceptualization inhibited her ability to be heard in the press, as an academic aware of Orientalist portrayals and as a hijab-wearing feminist who holds to 'mostly traditional' interpretations of Islamic law.

Research about other countries has demonstrated similar symbolic politics, with France possibly taking to an extreme the absence of agency among religious women (see Freedman and Tarr 2000; Guénif-Souilamas and Macé 2004; Scott 2007; Bowen 2007). When discussing debates and commissions about headscarves and full-face veils, French media and government commissions typically portray Muslim women as fundamentally incapable of choosing to wear hijabs, burqas, and niqabs (Scott 2007; Bowen 2007). When it comes to face-covering, many European countries are following the French example. Symbolic politics governing the headscarf, however, are slightly more nuanced in other European countries, with debates in Britain, the Netherlands, and Germany allowing for the possibility that women might freely choose to wear the headscarf in public spaces, even if they are sometimes denied that right if they work in government offices and/or public schools (each of these countries differs in its exact rules and regulations) (Saharso and Lettinga 2007; Sauer 2009; Buckley 2010). Yet, even this conceptualization of diversity inscribes a particularly Western, liberal understanding of subjectivity and agency (see Mahmood 2001, 2005).

In all of these countries, symbolic politics not only structure majority society debates but also less-publicized debates within Muslim communities. Close analysis of the Ontario Sharia debate, as conducted by Zine and confirmed by Kutty and Reda, illustrates how the debate occurred between two bifurcated positions: one that dominated largely outside the Muslim community, and another that set the tone for debate within. Zine labels the two opposing figures inhabiting these positions: 'the neo-colonialist' (who demonizes Islam in part through repeated appeals to save Muslim women from Muslim men), and 'the Islamist' (who deifies the process of interpreting Sharia), respectively (see also Abu-Lughod 2002; Spivak 1988; Shryock 2010). The relative dominance of these figures vis-à-vis their respective audiences impeded discussion of the flexibility of Islamic jurisprudential practice in conjunction with the history of patriarchal practices justified through appeals to Sharia and fiqh. Zine carefully traces the need for an altered understanding of gender relations within Muslim communities (this issue is also flagged by both Kutty and Reda), and the risk of furthering the stigmatization of all Muslims when this point is used to bolster the purported backwardness of Islam and its adherents. One approach that moves away from these stereotypes is exemplified by the work of Moira Dustin and Anne Phillips (2008) on British policy formation. They argue for a mature multicultural approach that takes into account multiple practices and rights, rather than privileging religion over gender or vice versa (see also Phillips 2007; Meetoo and Mirza 2007). For instance, they warn against positioning orthodox, rather than liberal clerics as experts on religious practice in policy debates, in a misguided attempt to be inclusive with respect to religion.

Unfortunately, evidence from Canada and other Western countries suggests that many public discussions continue to be infused with fear of Islamists, while scholarly analyses sometimes career between neo-colonial and relativistic understandings of women's rights and desires. It is difficult to argue simultaneously for recognition of religious practice in the public sphere while holding that religious practice is both always changing and in need of change. In their respective chapters, Zine, Bullock, and Reda show, in different ways, what analyses of Sharia and debates of Sharia by practising Muslim women might look like. The differences in their voices and positions demonstrate the potential for a symbolic politics that differs from that currently practised in media and to some extent in academic debate across Western Europe and North America.

Formal Politics: Lawmaking in the Context of Secularism

Symbolic politics not only informs public discourse, but also structures legal and policy debates. The accommodation of religion in the public sphere was one of the central issues in the Ontario Sharia debate. Government commissions and consequent reports, such as the Boyd Report, are an increasingly common way to map out solutions to the purported problems associated with secularism in our arguably post-secular age (see Côté 2008; Habermas 2008; Casanova 1994; Phillips 2007 and 2009).[5] In her chapter, Alexandra Brown shows how such reports can bolster the legitimacy of state rule, while being ineffective in directing policy. An alternate outcome has appeared in France: the 2003 and 2010 reports of the Stasi and Gerin committees guided the 2004 ban on conspicuous religious symbols in schools and the 2011 law banning the burqa and niqab in the public sphere. Yet, regardless of these divergent outcomes, Brown suggests the need for careful deconstruction of such reports if we are to understand how the state is building itself (or how politicians and other political actors engage in state building) vis-à-vis Muslim minority populations.

Jennifer Selby's chapter illustrates how discussions of religious accommodation are often far less neutral about religion than they

appear at first sight. Acknowledging the inherently Christian underpinnings of most Western conceptions of secularism offers a different
starting point to think about: (1) whether neutrality should be the desired response to religiosity in Western democratic states; (2) how private religious matters emerge in the public sphere; and (3) how some of
the most salient and persuasive arguments pushing for 'secularity'
against the public visibility of religiosity (particularly of Muslim wom-
en's social comportment and dress) are couched in Western feminist
terms that have their own historic legacies and problematics.

This last point can also be charted by examining burqa and niqab
debates in Western Europe. Scott (2007) argues that France's decision
to ban conspicuous religious symbols (read headscarves) in 2004 resulted in part from the desire to safeguard the dominant French highly
gendered performance of embodiment and sexuality. One often cited
argument for banning headscarves in particular was that girls without
them were being sexually harassed and assaulted and that the French
state had an obligation to end such violations. In the 2010 Gerin commission on the full-face veil, feminists were privileged interlocutors in
determining the submissiveness of burqa- and niqab-wearing women.
Interlocutors cited in the report upheld that certain versions of femi-
ninity and agency through seduction were worthy of protection (see
Wesselhoeft 2010).

In other countries, debates about different forms of veiling are framed
in the terms of choice and coercion that structured Western liberal feminism, rather than the French arguments of safeguarding the expression
of gender difference. When analysing how this discourse informs policy making, it is important to remember that the feminist critique of
organized religion in Canada and elsewhere emerged alongside the
relatively recent twentieth century accordance of women's rights.
Therefore, critiques of Muslim women's rights and visibility and concern for the patriarchal elements in Sharia-based interpretations of family law must be contextualized within legitimate concerns for a seeming
denial and loss of rights and agency that are not yet firmly secured in
countries like Canada.

Conclusion

By focusing on these four issues (Muslim everyday life, the integration
of Islamic and Western legal principles, symbolic politics, and formal
politics), we can develop an approach to discussion that does not

immediately put all of Islam up for debate. Although the Ontario Sharia debate was arguably about faith-based family law arbitration, the concerns regarding agency, consent, and gender equality it raised derived more from the privatization of law than from religious practice. At the same time, ethnographic research into Muslims' divorce practices revealed gender-related issues that need addressing, although as the authors in this volume suggest, the tenor of the Ontario Sharia debate made these conversations more difficult rather than less.

The collapse of complex public political debates about 'Islam' in the Ontario Sharia debate echoes other recent debates. By discursively linking concerns of gender equality to Islam, public debate becomes focused on the advisability of 'allowing' religion into the public sphere, rather than on the specific inequalities at stake. Instead of asking the unanswerable question 'how shall we accommodate Islam?' it is more useful to identify the specific issues of power and agency that are at issue in these debates. The Ontario Sharia debate, in all its failures, suggests that the ensuing discussions will be most fruitful if they engage a wide variety of stakeholders, both from religious and other communities. In this way, debates can focus on addressing issues, rather than stigmatizing one minority group of people.

NOTES

1 We use the West here to draw the contrast with the Orient in order to critique it. The monoliths of 'Islam' and 'the West' must be used with care so not to replicate Huntingtonian dichotomies; for critiques of Huntington, see Mottahedeh (1995), Said (2001), Mustafa (2002), and Shryock (2010).

2 According to the Canadian Muslim Profile Survey conducted in 2008 by the Canadian Institute of Policy Studies, 37% of respondents went to the mosque more than twice a week, and 31% once a week. Some 15% of respondents attend the mosque only for special programs, and 2% of respondents never go to the mosque; see http://www.c-ips.ca/docs/CIPS_Survey_Report.pdf.

3 A number of instances exemplify assumptions of misogyny. For example, in one newspaper report Homa Arjomand, leader of the International Campaign against Sharia in Ontario, discusses a case of a woman who was sent back to Pakistan and whose daughter was forced to marry an older relative (Jiménez 2004). While the story is evocative, it does not pertain to a process of binding arbitration but rather suggests abuse of power within

a larger family, sanctioned by an imam. This situation is not the same as drawing up an exploitative contract.

4 Some of these issues have been addressed from within the Muslim community. The Canadian Council of Muslim Women (CCMW) has responded to 'chaotic' divorce situations with a sample Muslim marriage contract in keeping with Canadian and Islamic law and has conducted workshops and presentations in community centres related to family law and women's rights in Islam (see: http://www.ccmw.com/documents/ MuslimMarraigeKit/contract_english.pdf). As Christopher Cutting describes (in this volume), the CCWM has also lobbied for the training of 'cultural interpreters' who could act as intermediaries and who could potentially make the Canadian legal system more accessible for all new Canadians, no matter their religious or cultural background. This proposal addresses the legitimate concerns of more recent immigrants (women especially) who may initially struggle with English- or French-language services or have limited access to interact with the Canadian justice system. In short, even if the CCMW does not represent the positions of all Canadian Muslims, they are part of the movements afoot to address the current needs around making Canadian law and Sharia compliant.

5 Post-secularity reflects on the previous popularity of secularization theories, which called for the demise of organized religion in the public sphere. Several contemporary thinkers have convincingly argued for the continued prevalence and importance of religiosity.

REFERENCES

Abu-Lughod, Lila. 2002. 'Do Muslim Women Really Need Saving? Anthropological Reflections on Cultural Relativism and Its Others.' *American Anthropologist* 104(3): 783–90.

Ahmed, Leila. 1992. *Women and Gender in Islam: Historical Roots of a Modern Debate.* New Haven: Yale University Press.

Al-Azmeh, Aziz. 1993. *Islams and Modernities.* New York: Verso.

Bano, Samia. 2007. 'Islamic Family Arbitration, Justice and Human Rights in Britain.' *Law, Social Justice and Global Development Journal.* http://www2 .warwick.ac.uk/fac/soc/law/elj/lgd/2007_1/bano/, Accessed 14 Jan. 2011.

Bowen, John R. 2007. *Why the French Don't Like Headscarves: Islam, the State, and Public Space.* Princeton: Princeton University Press.

Buckley, Anisa. 2010. 'Shari'ah, State Law and the "Divorce Dilemma": Challenges Facing Muslim Women in Western Countries.' In Shahram

Akbarzadeh, ed., *Challenging Identities: Muslim Women in Australia*, 76–104. Carlton, Victoria: Melbourne University Press.

Bunting, Annie, and Shadi Mokhtari. 2009. 'Migrant Muslim Women's Interests and the Case of "Shari'a" Tribunals in Ontario.' In Vijay Agnew, ed., *Racialized Migrant Women in Canada: Essays on Health, Violence and Equity*, 232–64. Toronto: University of Toronto Press.

Casanova, José. 1994. *Public Religions in the Modern World*. Chicago: University of Chicago Press.

Cesari, Jocelyne. 2004. *When Islam and democracy meet: Muslims in Europe and in the United States*. New York: Palgrave Macmillan.

–, ed. 2010. *Muslims in the West after 9/11: Religion, Law and Politics*. New York: Routledge.

Christoffersen, Lisbet. 2010. 'Is Shari'a Law, Religion or a Combination? European Legal Discourses on Shari'a.' In Jørgen S. Nielsen and Lisbet Christoffersen, eds., *Shari'a as Discourse: Legal Traditions and the Encounter with Europe*, 57–76. Farham: Ashgate.

Clancy-Smith, Julia. 1998. 'Islam, Gender, and Identities in the Making of French Algeria, 1830–1962.' In Julia Clancy-Smith and Frances Gouda, eds., *Domesticating the Empire: Race, Gender, and Family Life in French and Dutch Colonialism*, 154–74. Charlottesville: University of Virginia Press.

Côté, Pauline. 2008. 'Québec and Reasonable Accommodation: Uses and Misuses of Public Consultation.' In Lori G. Beaman and Peter Beyer, eds., *Religion and Diversity in Canada*, 41–66. Leiden: Brill.

Crone, Patricia. 2004. *God's Rule: Government and Islam*. New York: Columbia University Press.

Dustin, Moira, and Anne Phillips. 2008. 'Whose Agenda Is It? Abuses of Women and Abuses of "Culture" in Britain.' *Ethnicities* 8(3): 405–24.

Esposito, John L. 1999. '"Clash of Civilizations"? Contemporary Images of Islam in the West.' In Gema Martín Muñoz, ed., *Islam, Modernism and the West: Cultural and Political Relations at the End of the Millennium*, 94–108. London: I.B. Tauris.

Fournier, Pascale. 2010. *Muslim Marriage in Western Courts: Lost in Transplantation*. Farnham: Ashgate.

Freedman, Jane, and Carrie Tarr, eds. 2000. *Women Immigration and Identities in France*. Oxford: Berg.

Guénif- Souilamas, Nacira, and Eric Macé. 2004: *Les féministes et le garçon arabe*. Paris: Éditions de l'Aube.

Habermas, Jürgen. 2008. 'Notes on a Post-Secular Society.' *Signandsight.com*. 18 June. Accessed 15 Aug. 2010. http://signandsight.com-slash-features-slash-1714.html.

Jiménez, Marina. 2004. 'B'nai Brith Recommend Sharia-Based Tribunals.' *Globe and Mail*, 9 Sept., A8.

Korteweg, Anna, and Gökçe Yurdakul. 2009. 'Islam, Gender, and Immigrant Integration: Boundary Drawing in Discourses on Honour Killing in the Netherlands and Germany.' *Ethnic and Racial Studies* 32(2): 218–38.

– 2010. 'Religion, Culture and the Politicization of Honour-Related Violence: A Critical Analysis of Media and Policy Debate in Western Europe and North America.' United Nations Research Institute for Social Development, project on Religion, Politics and Gender Equality. Accessed 24 Jan. 2011. www.unrisd.org.

Krayem, Ghena. 2010. 'Multiculturalism and Its Challenges for Muslim Women.' In Shahram Akbarzadeh, ed., *Challenging Identities: Muslim Women in Australia*, 105–29. Carlton, Victoria: Melbourne University Press.

MacEoin, Denis. 2009. 'Sharia Law or 'One Law for All?' *Civitas*. Accessed 24 Jan. 2011. http://www.civitas.org.uk/pdf/ShariaLawOrOneLawForAll.pdf.

Mahmood, Saba. 2001. 'Feminist Theory, Embodiment, and the Docile Agent: Some Reflections on the Egyptian Islamic Revival.' *Cultural Anthropology* 16(2): 202–36.

– 2005. *Politics of Piety: The Islamic Revival and the Feminist Subject*. Princeton: Princeton University Press.

– 2008. 'Feminism, Democracy, and Empire: Islam and the War of Terror.' In Joan Wallach Scott, ed., *Women's Studies on the Edge*, 81–114. Durham: Duke University Press.

Mamdani, Mahmood. 2004. *Good Muslim, Bad Muslim: America, the Cold War, and the Roots of Terror*. New York: Doubleday.

Meetoo, Veena, and Heidi Safia Mirza. 2007. 'There Is Nothing "Honourable" about Honour Killings: Gender, Violence and the Limits of Multiculturalism.' *Women's Studies International Forum* 30: 187–200.

Menski, Werner. 2000. 'Muslim Law in Britain.' In M. Koga, M. Naito and T. Hamaguchi, eds., *From Migrant to Citizen: South Asian Communities Overseas*, 294–318. Tokyo: Institute for the Study of Languages and Cultures of Asia and Africa.

Mottahedeh, Roy. 1995. 'Clash of Civilizations: An Islamicist's Critique.' *Harvard Middle Eastern and Islamic Review* 2(1): 1–26.

Mustafa, Hala. 2002. 'Islam and the West in an Era of Globalization: Clash of Civilization or Coexistence?' In Nezar AlSayyad and Manuel Castells, eds., *Muslim Europe or Euro-Islam: Politics, Culture, and Citizenship in the Age of Globalization*, 91–112. Lanham: Lexington Books.

Nielsen, Jørgen S., and Lisbet Christoffersen, eds. 2010. *Shari'a as Discourse: Legal Traditions and the Encounter with Europe*. Farham: Ashgate.

Parvez, Z. Fareen. 2011. 'Debating the Burqa in France: The Antipolitics of
    Islamic Revival.' *Qualitative Sociology*, 34:287–312.
Phillips, Anne. 2007. *Multiculturalism without Culture*. Princeton: Princeton
    University Press.
– 2009. 'Religion: Ally, Threat, or Just Religion?' In *A Debate on the Public Role of
    Religion and Its Social and Gender Implications*. United Nations Research Insti-
    tution on Social Development. Accessed 24 Jan. 2011. www.unrisd.org.
Quraishi, Asifa, and Najeeba Syeed-Miller. n.d. 'No Altars: A Survey of Islamic
    Family Law in the United States. Accessed 14 Jan. 2011. http://www.law
    .emory.edu/ifl/cases/USA.htm.
Ramadan, Tariq. 2004. *Western Muslims and the Future of Islam*. New York:
    Oxford University Press.
Razack, Sherene. 2008. 'Modern Women as Imperialists: Geopolitics, Culture
    Clash, and Gender after 9/11.' In *Casting Out: The Eviction of Muslims from
    Western Law and Politics*, 83–106. Toronto: University of Toronto Press.
Rohe, Mathias. 2006. 'The Migration and Settlement of Muslims: The
    Challenges for European Legal Systems. ' In Prakash Shah and Werner
    Menski, eds., *Migration, Diasporas and Legal Systems in Europe*, 57–72.
    London: Routledge.
Saharso, Sawitri, and Doutje Lettinga. 2007. 'Contentious Citizenship: Policies
    and Debates on the Veil in the Netherlands.' *Social Politics* (Winter): 455–80.
Said, Edward. 2001. 'A Clash of Ignorance.' *The Nation* 273: 1–13.
Saris, Anne and Jean-Mathieu Potvin. 2008. 'Shari'a in Canada Family Dispute
    Resolution among Muslim Minorities in the West: Analysis of a Case Study
    of Muslim Women, Religious Counselors and Civil Actors in Montreal.'
    Accessed 14 Jan. 2011. http://canada.metropolis.net/pdfs/annesaris_
    jmpotvin_e.pdf.
Sauer, Birgit. 2009. 'Headscarf Regimes in Europe: Diversity Policies at the
    Intersection of Gender, Culture, and Religion.' *Comparative European Politics*
    7(1): 75–94.
Scott, Joan Wallach. 2007. *The Politics of the Veil*. Princeton: Princeton
    UniversityPress.
Selby, Jennifer A.(Forthcoming). 'Polygamy in the Parisian *Banlieues*:
    Discourse and Debate on the 2005 French Urban Riots.' In Gillian Calder
    and Lori Beaman, eds., *Polygamy's Wrongs? The Social Family in the Culture of
    Rights*. Vancouver: UBC Press.
Shah, Prakash, 2007. 'Introduction: Socio-Legal Perspectives on Ethnic
    Diversity.' In Prakash Shah, ed., *Law and Ethnic Plurality: Socio-Legal
    Perspectives*, 1–8. Leiden: Brill.

Shryock, Andrew. 2010. 'Introduction: Islam as an Object of Fear and Affection.' In *Islamophobia/Islamophilia: Beyond the Politics of Enemy and Friend*, 1–28. Bloomington: Indiana University Press.

Spivak, Gayatri Chakravorty. 1988. 'Can the Subaltern Speak?' In Cary Nelson and Lawrence Grossberg, eds., *Marxism and the Interpretation of Culture*, 271–313. Urbana: University of Illinois Press.

Tibi, Bassam. 2002. 'Muslim Migrants in Europe: Between Euro-Islam and Ghettoization.' In Nezar AlSayyad and Manuel Castells, eds., *Muslim Europe or Euro-Islam: Politics, Culture, and Citizenship in the Age of Globalization*, 31–52. Lanham: Lexington Books.

Waerstads, Tone Linn. 2011. 'Minority Women's Equality Rights at the Dissolution of Marriage.' Doctoral dissertation (Danish). http://www.jus .uio.no/ior/forskning/arrangementer/midtveisevalueringer/2011/ 20110112-warstad.html.

Wesselhoeft, Kirsten. 2010. 'Sex and Secularity: The Feminine Individual in the Gerin Report.' Paper presented at the American Anthropological Association, 21 Nov. 2010, New Orleans.

Yilmaz, Ihsan. 2003. 'Muslim Alternative Dispute Resolution and Neo-Ijtihad in England.' *Turkish Journal of International Relations* 2(1). Accessed 14 Jan. 2011. http://www.alternativesjournal.net/volume2/number1/yilmaz.html.

Contributors

Alexandra Brown is a PhD candidate in anthropology at McMaster University and guest researcher at the Amsterdam School for Cultural Analysis. Her work explores the visual and material form of debates over Islam in Europe and North America. This research is supported by the Social Science and Humanities Research Council.

Katherine Bullock is a lecturer in political science at the University of Toronto, Mississauga campus. Her research interests include representation of Muslims in Western media; the civic activism and political participation of Muslims in Western societies, with a focus on Canada; and debates over Muslim women and the veil.

Jocelyne Cesari is a scholar of religion and international relations; the 2011–12 MINERVA Chair at the National Defense University in Washington, DC; director of the Islam in the West Program at Harvard University; and a senior research fellow at CNRS-Paris. Her most recent book is the edited volume *Muslims in the West After 9/11: Religion, Law and Politics* (Routledge 2010).

L. Clarke is a professor of religious studies and Islam at Concordia University in Montreal. Her research interests include Shiism, gender, and law, and she is currently working on popular discourses about Shariah in the West.

Christopher Cutting is a PhD candidate in religious studies at the University of Waterloo in the Religious Diversity in North America Program. He received his MA in religion and culture from Wilfrid

Laurier University. He is a sociologist of religion, researching religious immigrant communities in North America regarding issues of religion and multiculturalism and religion in public life, mainly among Muslim communities in North America.

Anver M. Emon is an associate professor at the Faculty of Law, University of Toronto. He specializes in premodern and modern Islamic law and history, premodern modes of governance and adjudication, and the role of Sharia both inside and outside the Muslim world. The author of *Islamic Natural Law Theories* (Oxford University Press, 2010), Professor Emon is the founding editor of *Middle East Law and Governance: An Interdisciplinary Journal*.

Anna C. Korteweg is an associate professor of sociology at the University of Toronto. Her research focuses on the integration of Muslim immigrants in Western Europe and Canada. She looks at citizenship, constructions of national belonging in public and parliamentary debates on immigrant integration, and the ways in which the problems of immigrant integration are defined in the intersections of gender, religion, ethnicity, and national origin.

Faisal Kutty is an assistant professor of law at Valparaiso University School of Law. His areas of interest are comparative law, religion and law, international law, Islamic law, and human rights.

Julie Macfarlane is a professor in the Faculty of Law at the University of Windsor and at the Kroc Institute for International Peace Studies at the University of Notre Dame. She writes and conducts empirical research and evaluation on conflict resolution. She is also an active mediator.

Audrey Macklin is a professor of law at the University of Toronto. Her areas of research and teaching include migration and citizenship law, multiculturalism, and business and human rights. She has published in the field of gender and migration, securitization of migration and citizenship post- 9/11, and Canadian migration policy. She was a member of Canada's Immigration and Refugee Board (1994–96).

Nevin Reda is Program Coordinator, Emmanuel College of Victoria University, University of Toronto, and an Executive Member of the Canadian Council of Muslim Women.

Jennifer A. Selby is an assistant professor of religious studies at Memorial University of Newfoundland. Her research examines expressions of gender and secularism among Muslim societies in the West, with ethnographic work focusing on France and Canada.

Jasmin Zine is an associate professor in the Department of Sociology and the Muslim Studies Option at Wilfrid Laurier University. Her areas of research include Muslim cultural politics in Canada, Muslim women's studies, and the politics of race, empire, and imperialism.